Fodor's

BARCELONA

T0049677

Welcome to Barcelona

Strolling along La Rambla or through Barceloneta on the sun-drenched Mediterranean, exploring art museums or such unique Gaudí creations as the majestic Sagrada Família, and browsing in boutiques or markets are all part of a visit to Catalonia's beguiling capital. Barcelona is equally lively at night, when you can linger over regional wine and cuisine at buzzing tapas bars. Note that this book was updated during the pandemic. When planning, please confirm that places are still open, and let us know when we need to make updates at editors@fodors.com.

TOP REASONS TO GO

★ **Gaudí:** The iconic Sagrada Família, undulating Casa Batlló, and playful Park Güell.

★ **Food:** From the Boqueria market's bounty to tapas bars to avant-garde restaurants.

★ **Museums:** Museu Picasso and the Museu Nacional d'Art de Catalunya lead the list.

★ **Architecture:** Roman and medieval in the Barri Gòtic, Moderniste in the Eixample.

★ **Shopping:** Stylish fashion boutiques and innovative design emporia tempt buyers.

★ **Beautiful Beaches:** Sandy havens and surfing hubs delight urban sun worshippers.

Contents

MAPS

Chapter 1

EXPERIENCE
BARCELONA

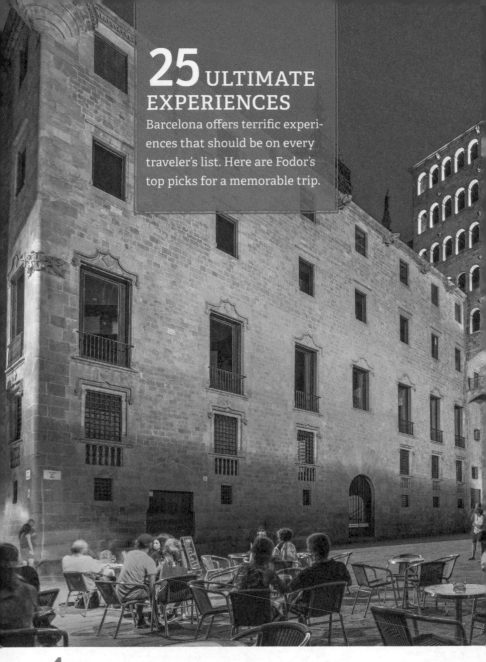

25 ULTIMATE EXPERIENCES

Barcelona offers terrific experiences that should be on every traveler's list. Here are Fodor's top picks for a memorable trip.

1 People Watch at Plaça del Rei

Located in the heart of Barri Gòtic, Plaça del Rei was once the center of all noble activity in Barcelona. In fact, when Christopher Columbus returned from the New World, it was here that the Catalan-Aragonese monarchs received him. *(Ch. 4)*

2 Find Hidden Tapas Bars

What better way to get to know a city than by sampling its most delectable dishes in miniature? The grazing is particularly good in smaller bars outside the city center.

3 Hit the Beach at La Barceloneta

What Barcelona's famed seaside district lacks in natural beauty, it makes up for in liveliness. Think: kites, vendors, music, people-watching, and seaside dining. *(Ch. 7)*

4 Wander La Rambla

No visit to Barcelona would be complete without a stroll along La Rambla, the wide, shady boulevard that runs through the heart of the city from Plaça de Catalunya down to Port Vell. *(Ch. 3)*

5 Explore MACBA

With a collection spanning from the mid-20th century to today, the Museu d'Art Contemporani de Barcelona showcases Catalonia's most celebrated contemporary artists and emerging talent. *(Ch.5)*

6 Hang out in Park Güell

With the Collserola foothills as his canvas, Gaudí's architectural park features columns that shoot up like tree trunks and fountains guarded by giant lizards with scales fashioned out of mosaic tiles. *(Ch. 9)*

7 Feast in Gràcia

Forgo English-menu-touting restaurants and chain stores for the mom-and-pop joints, trendy restaurants, and hip little bars and cafés tucked away in the jumble of Gràcia's streets. *(Ch. 9)*

8 Visit Fundació Joan Miró

A gift from the artist Joan Miró to his native city, this airy museum perched on Montjuïc contains more than 10,000 of Miro's playful and colorful masterpieces. *(Ch. 11)*

9 Marvel at La Sagrada Família

If/when it's completed in 2026, after 150 years of construction, Gaudí's basilica will be the tallest religious building in Europe. Skip the crowds and visit for Sunday Mass. *(Ch. 8)*

10 Shop in Barri Gòtic

The Barri Gòtic, home to a namesake market, was built around craft industries, and artisans still work along its stone streets. Look for handmade espadrilles and leather goods. *(Ch. 4)*

11 Say Salud to Cava

Prosecco and other budget sparklers rely on industrial carbonization to make their wines bubble. But Catalan cava, like fine Champagne, gets its effervescence and complexity from bottle fermentation.

12 Cheer for Barça!

Join local soccer fans by rooting for the home team, Futbol Club Barcelona ("Barça" for short), at either Camp Nou or the Olympic Stadium while Camp Nou undergoes renovations. *(Chs. 10, 11)*

13 Revel in Upper Barcelona Vistas

Routes like the Carretera de les Aigües, an ancient road that passes just below Vallvidrera, overlook the city and Serra de Collserola Natural Park. *(Ch. 10)*

14 Enjoy El Palau de la Música Catalana

If you can't catch a performance, be sure to at least take a tour of this incredible auditorium, which is also a UNESCO World Heritage Site. *(Ch. 6)*

15 Chill in Parc de la Ciutadella

After a promenade under the trees in this lush 19th-century park, take a moment to admire the handiwork of the central fountain, a neoclassical work designed by Josep Fontserè. *(Ch. 7)*

16 Taste Everything at La Boqueria

This glass-and-steel market hall welcomes more than 45,000 visitors a day with its artful displays of the region's finest cheeses, charcuterie, seafood, and produce. *(Ch. 3)*

17 The Santa María del Mar

The boulders used to construct this soaring Gothic temple were hauled, one by one, from the surrounding mountainsides by ordinary civilians. *(Ch. 6)*

18 Take a Day Trip

Popular day trip destinations include Girona for its Gothic architecture, Figueres for its theater-museum designed by Salvador Dalí, and Sitges, a beach (and nightlife) paradise. *(Ch. 12)*

19 Explore Casa Milà

Better known as La Pedrera, Casa Milà features wavy interior patios, curved walls, slanting columns, and a rooftop with plunging stairways and sculptural chimneys. *(Ch. 8)*

20 Wander the Museu Nacional D'Art de Catalunya

MNAC's Romanesque collection is one of the most exhaustive in the world and chronicles the pre-Gothic beginnings of religious art in Catalonia. *(Ch. 11)*

21 Visit the Museu Picasso

Picasso's early works in sculpture, paint, and engraving are not the only draw here; the five adjoining 13th- and 14th-century residences that comprise the museum are impressive in their own right. (Ch. 6)

22 Climb Tibidabo

Towering above Barcelona's northern rim, the 1,700-foot peak of Tibidabo is the best vantage point to take in panoramic views of the cityscape against the cobalt-blue backdrop of the Mediterranean. (Ch. 10)

23 Barhop Along Passeig del Born

Less touristed than La Rambla, this leafy promenade is lined with bars offering zippy Menorca-style pomadas (ice-cold gin and lemonade cocktails) and tapas. (Ch. 6)

24 Find Solace in La Catedral de Barcelona

Gargoyles, flying buttresses, barrel vaults, and a shadowy interior accent this Gothic structure, which predates La Sagrada Família by six centuries. *(Ch. 4)*

25 Pick Your Modernisme Favorite in Manzana de la Discòrdia

This block along Passeig de Gràcia is known for its four different interpretations of Modernisme architecture, including Gaudí's Casa Batlló. *(Ch. 8)*

WHAT'S WHERE

1 La Rambla. This emblematic promenade was once a seasonal watercourse that flowed along the outside of the 13th-century city walls. A stroll on La Rambla—where tourists mix with pickpockets, buskers, street performers, and locals—passes the Boqueria market, the Liceu opera house, and, at the port end, Drassanes, the medieval shipyards. Just off La Rambla is Plaça Reial, a stately neoclassical square; off the other side is Gaudí's masterly Palau Güell.

2 Barri Gòtic. The medieval Gothic Quarter surrounds La Catedral de Barcelona on high ground settled by 1st century BC Romans. The Jewish quarter, antiquers' row, and Plaça Sant Jaume are quintessential Barcelona.

3 El Raval. Once a slum, this area has brightened considerably, thanks partly to the Barcelona Museum of Contemporary Art, designed by Richard Meier. Behind the Boqueria market is the stunning Antic Hospital de la Santa Creu, with its high-vaulted Gothic Biblioteca de

Catalunya reading room; just steps away is Sant Pau del Camp, Barcelona's earliest church.

4 Sant Pere and La Ribera. Sant Pere is the city's old textile neighborhood. La Ribera, whose narrow cobblestone streets are lined with interesting shops and restaurants, is known for the palaces of Barcelona's medieval nobles and merchant princes—five of which are now part of the Picasso Museum.

5 La Ciutedella and Barceloneta. La Ciutedella was created in the mid-18th century, when some of the water was filled in to accommodate housing for those displaced by the construction of its namesake fortress—a symbol of the hated Bourbon regime. Stellar seafood restaurants make Barceloneta a favorite for Sunday-afternoon paella gatherings.

6 The Eixample. The Eixample (Expansion), the post-1860 grid of city blocks uphill from Ciutat Vella, contains most of Barcelona's Moderniste (Art Nouveau) architecture, including Gaudí's unfinished work, the Sagrada Família church. Passeig de Gràcia, the city's premier shopping street, is lined with still more Gaudí masterpieces.

WHAT'S WHERE

7 Gràcia. This former outlying village begins at Gaudí's playful Park Güell and continues past his first commissioned house, Casa Vicens, through two markets and various pretty squares, such as Plaça de la Vila de Gràcia and Plaça del Sol. Carrer Gran de Gràcia, though narrow and noisy, is lined with buildings designed by Gaudí's assistant, Francesc Berenguer i Mestres.

8 Upper Barcelona. Sarrià was incorporated into the burgeoning metropolis in 1927, but it still feels like an independent village— one with a gratifying number of gourmet shops and fine restaurants. Nearby are the Monestir de Pedralbes, a 14th-century architectural gem with a rare triple-tiered cloister, and Gaudí's Col·legi de les Teresianes and Torre Bellesguard. Although the amusement park atop Tibidabo, Barcelona's perch, is a bit kitschy, do take the Tramvia Blau (Blue Tram) to the lower end of the funicular that goes up to the park: the square in front of the terminus has restaurants, bars, and city views. Even

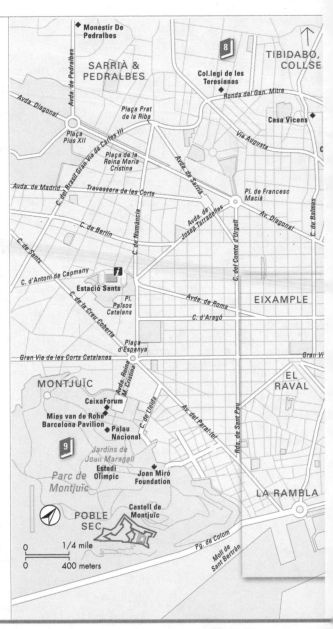

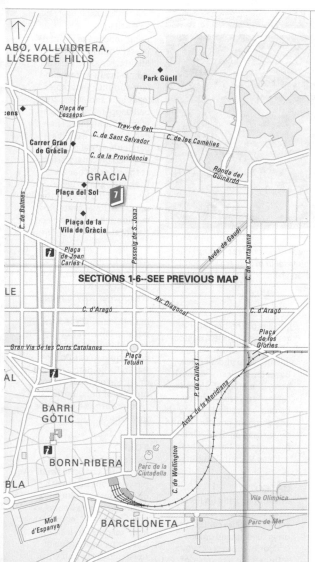

ABO, VALLVIDRERA,
LLSEROLE HILLS

Park Güell

Plaça de
Lesseps

Trav. de Dalt

C. de Sant Salvador

C. de les Camèlies

Carrer Gran
de Gràcia

C. de la Providència

Ronda del
Guinardó

GRÀCIA

Plaça del Sol   **7**

Plaça de la
Vila de Gràcia

Passeig de S. Joan

Avda. de Gaudí

C. de Cartagena

C. de Balmes

Plaça
de Joan
Carles I

SECTIONS 1-6--SEE PREVIOUS MAP

Av. Diagonal

C. d'Aragó

C. d'Aragó

Plaça
de les
Glòries

Gran Via de les Corts Catalanes

Plaça
Tetuán

BARRI
GÒTIC

P. de Carles I

Avda. de la Meridiana

BORN-RIBERA

Parc de la
Ciutadella

C. de Wellington

BLA

Vila Olímpica

Moll
d'Espanya

BARCELONETA

Parc de Mar

Mediterranean Sea

better is the Collserola forest and park on the far side of the hill, accessible by the FGC train to Vallvidrera, a sleepy village with a good restaurant (Can Trampa), a Moderniste funicular station, and views west to the Montserrat massif.

9 Montjuïc and Poble Sec. Barcelona's playground, Montjuïc is a sprawling complex of parks and gardens, sports facilities, open-air theater spaces, and museums. Among the latter are the Museu Nacional d'Art de Catalunya (MNAC) in the Palau Nacional, repository of a thousand years of Catalonia's artistic treasures, and the Joan Miró Foundation collection of contemporary art and sculpture. Poble Sec, one of Barcelona's oldest neighborhoods, has an up-and-coming food scene.

What to Eat and Drink in Barcelona

BOMBAS

Mashed-potato fritters stuffed with succulent ground beef and drenched in *allioli* and spicy *salsa brava* are the bomb. Try a nongreasy, juicy rendition at La Cova Fumada, the bar that created the dish in 1955.

CAVA

Catalan sparkling wine, called cava, gets its effervescence and complexity from bottle fermentation. Taste some of the region's best bubblies at La Vinya del Senyor, a cozy, understated restaurant with several by-the-glass boutique cavas to choose from. If you're lucky enough to snag a table on the plaça, you'll be rewarded with views of Santa María del Mar's 14th-century facade.

VERMUT

On sunny weekend afternoons, neighborhood bars fill up with locals out to *fer el vermut*, the Catalan ritual of catching up with friends over a few dainty glasses of the herbaceous, garnet-red aperitif, customarily garnished with an orange slice and an olive. Barcelona's best vermouth bars, like Morro Fi, blend their own vermouths by infusing fortified wine with any range of botanicals, and pour them on draft. Or look for a quality Catalan brand such as Vermut Yzaguirre.

CALÇOTS

Short of scoring an invite to a *calçotada*, a Catalan-style barbecue centering on grilled spring onions (calçots), you can get your allium fix at a number of Barcelona *braserías* such as El Quatre de Londres and Taverna El Glop. From November to April, calçot season, these grill-centric restaurants cook the slender onions over open flame until blackened on the outside and tender and sweet within.

ESCALIVADA

Escalivada is the ultimate poster child of the Mediterranean diet: it's a simple medley of roasted late-summer vegetables (eggplant, tomatoes, and bell peppers) rounded out with nothing more than garlic and olive oil. It's particularly delectable spooned on crusty bread at the no-frills bar En Diagonal; goat-cheese lovers shouldn't miss the nontraditional gratinéed version served at Cervecería Catalana.

ALLIOLI

Barcelona takes its allioli seriously—after all, the creamy, garlicky spread is said to have been invented in Catalonia. Try it over *patatas bravas* at Elsa y Fred, alongside black rice with squid ink at Paella Bar in La Boqueria market, or spread on toast at any number of neighborhood restaurants as a requisite first course.

TORRÓ

Come Christmastime, Barcelona's bakeries and pastry shops brim with one of southern Europe's most addictive sweets, *torró* (" turrón " in Spanish and " torrone " in Italian), a crunchy confection of toasted nuts bound with egg whites and honey. Turrones Sirvent, founded in 1920, is a one-stop shop for all your torró needs.

Ibérico ham

IBÉRICO HAM

Though most *jamón ibérico*—the world-famous dry-cured ham made from indigenous black-footed pigs—hails from western and southern Spain, the delicacy is relished in restaurants across Barcelona. Sample the best of the best at Cinco Jotas Rambla, a ham lover's paradise operated by the eponymous brand known for using only purebred ibérico hogs fattened on acorns.

TORTILLA ESPAÑOLA

If there's one thing almost all Spaniards can get behind, it's the country's most popular dish, *tortilla española*. A hubcap-size omelet filled with melty olive oil–poached potatoes and caramelized onions, it can be eaten hot or cold and at breakfast, lunch, or dinner. Choose from 140 different tortilla types at Les Truites in Sant Gervasi.

PA AMB TOMÀQUET

Anyone can make *pa amb tomàquet* (literally "bread with tomato"), but it's elevated to an art form at La Bodegueta, whose thick-crusted *payés* bread gives the dish an extra crunch.

CROQUETAS

The best *croquetas* have a shatteringly crisp exterior and a molten béchamel center flavored with whatever's handy: chopped ham ends, flaked *bacalao*, leftover roast chicken—you name it. Find classic croqueta nirvana at Bodega Sepúlveda, whose meticulous cooks change the breading type depending on the croqueta add-in, or have your mind blown at Catacroquet, with fillings like monkfish and sherry-braised pork jowl.

PAELLA

You can't leave Spain's Mediterranean coast without trying one of the region's most famous dishes: paella. Catalans love arguing about what constitutes an *"autèntica"* paella, but you can't go wrong at rice-focused restaurants like El Nou Cafetí, a hidden gem in the Raval neighborhood famous for its seafood preparations, or Can Solé, a white-tablecloth Barceloneta institution that's been packed since 1903.

FIDEUÁ

Imagine paella made with pasta instead of rice and you have *fideuá*, a Catalan specialty that's typical Sunday lunch fare. It's worth shelling out the euros for the impeccable, seafood-packed version at La Mar Salada, which gets its comfort-food deliciousness from homemade fish stock.

What to Buy in Barcelona

ESPARDENYES

You'll see *espardenyes*, the rope-soled sandals also called espadrilles or *alpargatas*, all over the world. But, for a pair of the originals, you must visit Catalonia, where locals have been donning them since the 14th century. Find a perfect pair at La Manual Alpargatera in the Barri Gòtic.

VERMOUTH

L'hora del vermut is sacred in Barcelona—that hour-long window just before lunch when locals flood the bodegas (wine bars) to catch up over icy glasses of vermouth and heaping plates of olives. Emulate that signature Mediterranean *alegria* at home by throwing your own tapas and vermut party; when in Barcelona, scoop up a bottle or two of the local stuff, like Morro Fi (rich with chocolate and coffee notes) or Casa Mariol (heady with rosemary and thyme plucked from the surrounding mountains), available for purchase at their namesake bars.

DESIGNER DECORATIONS

Support local artisans and impress your friends by investing in one-of-a-kind design pieces made in Barcelona. If home entertaining is your thing, make the journey to the Luesma & Vega showroom in Molins de Rei, for the latest nature-inspired dinnerware. Art enthusiasts should seek out handmade works by Catalan design studio Apparatu; the studio itself is a bit far afield, in Rubí, but you can find a solid selection of Apparatu ceramic sculptures and furniture at Domésticoshop in the Eixample neighborhood—and while you're up there, stop by Matèria

to purchase butter-soft blankets and shawls by Teixidors, a family-run company that trains developmentally disabled people to weave on traditional wooden looms.

CAVA

Prosecco and other budget sparklers rely on industrial carbonization to make their wines fizz, but cava, bottled in the Penedès region just south of Barcelona, gets its effervescence from a long and leisurely fermentation—the same process used in fine Champagne. You can probably find cava on the shelves of your local wine shop, but chances are, it pales in comparison to the complex *Gran Reserva* gems on offer at Barcelona wine purveyors like Cellarer and Vila Viniteca, whose staff will lovingly pack your purchases so they don't explode in transit.

CAGANER FIGURINE

A peasant in a red Catalan cap, squatting to take a dump, is perhaps the world's most improbable symbol of Christmas, but come holiday season, families across Catalonia adorn their household nativity scenes with *caganer* (literally "crapper" or "pooper") figurines. The origins and meaning of the tradition are unknown (something to do, it's asserted, with fertility), but that doesn't stop barcelonins from keeping it alive. Elicit a few laughs next December by setting out your own caganer, purchased at Tienda Caganer, opposite the church of Santa Maria del Mar. Even better, browse the caganer stalls at the

Fira de Santa Llúcia, from the end of November to December 26; the tradition has long been updated to include squatting figures from entertainment, sports, and politics—from Groucho Marks to Donald Trump—and you'll find a wide selection here.

PAINTED CERAMICS

The Moors brought exquisite ceramic craftsmanship to the Iberian Peninsula in the 8th century with their florid mosaics and *azulejos* (painted tiles) and the tradition further blossomed in Renaissance Spain with Barcelona as Catalonia's leading hub of production. Though you won't find specimens from the city's glory days of pottery outside museums, the modern reproductions at Art Escudellers in the Gothic Quarter, or at Gemma, near the church of Santa Maria del Mar, are a close approximation and make excellent souvenirs. Choose from playfully decorated pitchers, ancient-looking wine jugs, ornately patterned bowls, and more.

FC BARCELONA T-SHIRT

Millions of soccer fans make the pilgrimage to Barcelona each year to cheer on Barcelona's home team, Futbol Club Barcelona. But even if you don't make it to the bleachers at Camp Nou stadium, you can flaunt your Barça pride by sporting a jersey with your favorite *futbolista's* name on the back. Avoid counterfeit swag by shopping in an official store, of which there are several in the city center.

L'ESCALA ANCHOVIES

These plump, umami-packed fillets from the Catalan coast will make you question everything you ever thought you knew about anchovies. With just the right amount of salt and funk, they're as satisfying eaten straight from the can over the kitchen sink—we won't snitch—as they are draped over toasted, garlic-rubbed slices of baguette (as you'll find them in Barcelona tapas bars). Find them at any of the gourmet *conserves* stalls in neighborhood markets like Mercat de Santa Caterina or Mercat de Sants.

OLD-SCHOOL MORTAR AND PESTLE

A fixture in home kitchens the city over, the mortar and pestle is an essential tool for making Catalonia's favorite mother sauces such as allioli (the garlicky mayonnaise invented by the Catalans) and *romescu* (roasted peppers pounded with garlic and almonds). Spanish-style *morteros*, which you can find in any neighborhood hardware store in Barcelona, are canary-yellow with bright green splotches—making them as aesthetically pleasing as they are practical.

A PIECE OF GAUDÍ

If Gaudí's physics-defying constructions bursting with colors, patterns, and textures leave you inspired—and how could they not!—consider taking home a memento that will get your creative juices flowing. At the well-appointed gift shops inside La Pedrera and Casa Batlló, take your pick

Mortar and pestle

from Moderniste-style jewelry, kitchenware, posters, and decorations made by local artisans. The coffee mugs with gilded handles modeled after the doorknobs at La Pedrera are particularly eye-catching. Also, look for Gaudí tiles: the decorative hexagonal tiles now lining Passeig de Gràcia were originally designed by Gaudí to pave the floors of Casa Milà and they represent the two constants in his work—geometry and symbolism. You can purchase Gaudí tiles at most Gaudí property gift shops as well as tile-inspired handbags and purses. If you need even more Gaudí gifts, there's an excellent gift shop in La Sagrada Família with a wide selection of Gaudí-related items.

The Best Museums in Barcelona

MUSEU MARITIM

Spain's reputation as a seafaring nation is legendary and—for better or worse—Spanish explorers crossed the globe and established a powerful empire. Inside this museum's enormous vaulted chambers, you'll find navigational tools, nautical maps, paintings, and even entire ships.

POBLE ESPANYOL

Created for the 1929 Barcelona International Exhibition, this collection of buildings showcasing architectural styles from across Spain was so popular that the government kept it intact. Today, you can stroll its stone streets and buy traditional textiles, painted glass, jewelry, and other crafts from artisans.

MUSEU PICASSO

As Barcelona was so important to Picasso during his formative years as an artist, he gifted some 4,000 of his early works to this eponymous museum, which is now a complex that incorporates five contiguous, 13th- and 14th-century *palacios* (stately homes of medieval merchant princes and nobles).

MOCO MUSEUM BARCELONA

In the 16th-century Palacio Cervelló, this collection of contemporary art has all the familiar names, including Banksy, Basquiat, Haring, Kusama, Warhol, and more.

MUSEU NACIONAL D'ART DE CATALUNYA

The palatial MNAC was built as part of the 1929 Barcelona International Exposition. Today the classical-style building—whose enormous pillared cupola was modeled after St. Peter's Basilica—houses a massive and diverse collection of Catalan and Spanish art from multiple styles and centuries, including medieval, Renaissance, and Moderniste. The curatorial skill alone, at rescuing and remounting fragile medieval frescoes from abandoned chapels and monasteries from all over Catalunya, is remarkable. At more than 50,000 square feet, there's a lot of ground to cover here.

FUNDACIÓ ANTONI TÀPIES

Atop the building which houses Antoni Tàpies's museum and foundation sits "Cloud and Chair," an interwoven sculpture of steel and aluminum designed to represent, as the title tells us, a chair emerging from a large cloud. The museum collections—both permanent and rotating—reflect the abstract and avant-garde sensibilities of the artist, said to have emerged during two teenage years spent recuperating from a tuberculosis-related heart

Museu Nacional d'Art de Catalunya

attack. This is an important center of art in Barcelona and a must-stop for those interested in Catalan Modernisme.

MUSEU D'ART CONTEMPORANI DE BARCELONA (MACBA)

The MACBA houses a rotating collection of approximately 5,000 pieces of art representing three eras beginning in the mid-20th century. Noteworthy as well is the building itself, with its top-to-bottom glass facade designed to allow the maximum natural light. Looking for a broad exposure to Catalan and Spanish Modernisme? Give yourself plenty of time for the MACBA.

PALAU DE LA MÚSICA CATALANA

This Catalan Art Nouveau concert hall, designed and built by the Modernist architect Lluís Domènech i Montaner in the first years of the 1900s, is so spectacular that it's been designated a UNESCO World Heritage site. While open for tours, it also remains an active music venue.

MUSEU D'HISTÒRIA DE CATALUNYA

Dedicated to the history of Catalonia, this museum's exhibits examine the cultural, social, and political evolution of the region, from the Paleolithic era all the way to contemporary society. Housed inside a former warehouse, the photographs, artifacts, and historical re-creations make it an interesting departure from other museums in Barcelona.

FUNDACIÓ JOAN MIRÓ

Located on Montjuïc hill (with a lovely city view from its terrace), and designed by Miró's longtime collaborator architect Josep Lluis Sert, this minimalist building houses hundreds of paintings, sculptures, ceramics, and tapestries from one of the world's most celebrated modern artists.

Best Day Trips from Barcelona

Zaragoza

THE BEACHES OF SITGES

A pleasant coastal town right on the Mediterranean, Sitges is about an hour south of Barcelona and easily accessible by car, bus, and train. Apart from its clean, beautiful beaches, Sitges is perhaps best known for its substantial gay community, its Carnival in February, and its International Fantasy Film Festival.

SEASIDE AT CAMBRILS

Located about an hour and a half by either car or train from Barcelona, Cambrils is a peaceful and demure setting known for its Michelin-starred restaurants and clean beaches with calm, cerulean-colored waters. All nine of the town's beaches are Blue Flag certified, meaning that they're clean, ecologically maintained, and well posted.

GIRONA

An hour and a half north of Barcelona by car or train, Girona is a vision from the Middle Ages with its brooding castle, soaring cathedral, its labyrinth of climbing cobblestone streets and connecting staircases, and dreamy riverside setting. No wonder it was one of the filming locations for the sixth season of *Game of Thrones*.

Girona

ZARAGOZA

The capital of the Spanish region of Aragon is about 90 minutes from Barcelona by car or train and has everything you could want from a day-trip destination: multiple museums, fabulous fountains, wonderful tapas restaurants with outdoor seating, gorgeous avenues, and meandering side streets.

MONTSERRAT

With its shrine to La Moreneta (the Black Virgin), this Benedictine monastery, a short day trip from Barcelona and surrounded by jagged peaks, is regarded as the spiritual home of Catalunya. Time your visit to coincide with a recital by Montserrat's world-famous boys' choir. From the monastery, take the funicular to the peak above for views that stretch over the mountains to the Pyrenees.

COLÒNIA GÜELL

Colònia Güell is a remnant from a time when the villages (called colonies) were built around rural industrial centers and factories. This particular colony remains intact in part because it features the spectacular Güell Crypt, one of Gaudí's least known works. The crypt—a UNESCO World Heritage Site—is both architecturally unique and incredibly beautiful, making it a great option for an afternoon trip. It's easily accessible via public transportation.

SALVADOR DALÍ MUSEUMS

Salvador Dalí was a native son of Catalonia who spent a good portion of his life north of Barcelona. Appropriately, several museums related to his work exist close to his hometown of Figueres: the Castell Gala Dalí, in Púbol, a medieval estate dedicated to his wife Gala; the Teatre-Museo Dalí (where his body is entombed beneath the theater's stage); and the Salvador Dalí House in Portlligat. You may want to rent a car to visit all of them.

PARC NATURAL DE LA ZONA VOLCÀNICA DE LA GARROTXA

Although its landscape is varied, the most remarkable features of the Garrotxa Volcanic Zone Natural Park are its 40 dormant volcanic cones. Incredibly vast, this park offers a plethora of outdoor activities that include trekking its scenic trails either on foot or via horse, cycling and mountain biking, and carriage rides.

Free Things to Do in Barcelona

FREE HOURS AT MUSEUMS

Many museums in Barcelona offer free admission on the first Sunday of the month including, MNAC (also free Saturday after 3), Palau Güell, Museu Frederic Marès (also free other Sundays after 5:00), and Museu Picasso (also free Thursday evening).

CATEDRAL DE BARCELONA

Entry to the city's Gothic cathedral is free between 8 am and 12:45 and after 3:15. If you visit between-times, a modest donation is expected. A €9 admission ticket gets you access to the choir, the roof, the cloister and the museum. Call ahead if you'd like to arrange for a guided tour. Although

MONTJUÏC MAGIC FOUNTAIN

Built in the 1920s, this fountain features a music-and-light show choreo-graphed with undulating jets of water. Dormant from January 7 through February, it comes to life at 8:00, 9:00, or 9:30 at night, depending on the month. It's a lively spot and a beautiful setting.

PARK GÜELL

Park Güell is another of Catalan architect Antoni Gaudí's beautiful creations. Admission to the "monumental core" of the park—the pavilions, the fountain stairs with their iconic lizard guardian, the terrace and its *trencadis* (polychromatic tile) undulating banquette—requires a €10 ticket, but there are sections you can enter free of charge.

WALKING TOUR

Barcelona is a beautiful city perfect for walking and there are multiple compa-nies offering free walking tours. Sandemans New Europe and Runner Bean are both solid operations with knowledgeable tour guides and nice itineraries. Another is Donkey Tours, and yet one more—appro-priately named—is Free Walking Tours Barcelona. (While these tours are free there is an expectation you'll tip your guide at the end.)

PARC DE LA CIUTADELLA

While this leafy park is home to several institutions which require tickets (such as the Museu d'Art Modern, the zoo, Museum of Natural Sciences, and the Museu de Geologia) one could argue that the main attraction is the park itself. It's also a popular place for runners and walkers alike, who are drawn in by its fountains, beautiful staircases, and towering palm trees.

FOOD MARKETS

Barcelona is justifiably known for its markets filled with vendors selling

Park Güell

high-quality food, drink, and merchandise, and even if you don't buy anything they're a great way to experience the city's culture. The most famous by far is La Boqueria, but other, less elbow-to-elbow options include Mercat de la Llibertat, Mercat de Santa Caterina, and Mercat de Sant Antoni.

EXPLORE POBLENOU
Once a neighborhood of commercial warehouses and factories, Poblenou is now Barcelona's cutting-edge creative space, home to art galleries and artist's lofts, design studios, dance clubs, hip cafés, wine bars, and micro-breweries. If your visit falls on the first Sunday of the month, head for the Rotonda del Casino

and join the outdoor dance party, from 12:00 to 2:30 (weather permitting).

CONCERT IN A PARK
Barcelona's Music in the Parks Festival is a yearly summer series of free concerts hosted in green spaces across the city. The performances, which provide a platform for young up-and-coming musicians, feature a variety of musical styles and act as a way of drawing people into the parks on summer evenings. It's a lovely way to listen to some free music, and to experience Barcelona's many parks.

THE BEACH
One of Barcelona's many charms is its free municipal beaches, such as Barceloneta and Sant Miguel. The weather is good year round; the beaches are centrally located and mostly populated with locals; and there are lots of amenities.

Barcelona Today

Capital of the autonomous Community of Catalonia, bilingual Barcelona (Catalan and Spanish) is the unrivaled visitor destination in Spain, and with good reason: dazzling art and architecture, creative cuisine, great weather, and warm hospitality are just part of what the city offers. Barcelona is proud of its cultural past and confident about its future.

A TALE OF TWO CITIES

Restive for centuries in the shadow of Madrid, where Spain ruled from the center—more often than not, with an iron hand—Barcelona has a drive to innovate and excel that stems largely from a determination to eclipse its longtime rival. A powerful sense of national identity (Catalans consider themselves a "nation" and decidedly not a province of Spain) motivates designers, architects, merchants, and industrialists to ever-higher levels of originality and achievement.

Especially since the success of the 1992 Olympic Games, national pride and confidence have grown stronger and stronger. Today, a substantial portion of the Catalan population believes the nation would be better served—whatever implications that might have for membership in the European Union—by complete independence.

CUISINE: HAUTE AND HOT

Since Ferran Adrià's northern Catalonian phenomenon El Bulli closed, *chef d'auteur* successes in Barcelona have proliferated. Among them Disfrutar (under three former El Bulli chefs, Oriol Castro, Eduard Xatruch, and Mateu Casañas), Moments, in the Mandarin Oriental hotel, Lasarte, in the Monument Hotel, and Jordi Cruz's ÀBaC, bear ample evidence of what a gastronomic haven Barcelona has become.

DESIGN AND ARCHITECTURE

Barcelona's cutting-edge achievements in interior design and couture continue to threaten the traditional dominance of Paris and Milan, while "starchitect" landmarks like Jean Nouvel's Torre Agbar, Norman Foster's communications tower on the Collserola skyline, and Ricardo Bofill's W Barcelona hotel (nicknamed Vela: the Sail) on the waterfront transform the city into a showcase of postmodern visual surprises.

Visitors can now marvel at some recently reopened Catalan Modernisme masterworks: Puig i Cadafalch's landmark Casa de les Punxes and Gaudí's Casa Vicens are open to the public and the restoration of Domènech i Montaner's Hospital de Sant Pau (now Europe's largest Art Nouveau architectural complex, rechristened the Sant Pau Recinte Modernista) is complete and a must-visit.

The Sagrada Família, Gaudí's masterpiece that's been in the works since 1882, is finally nearing completion, expected to be finished by the centenary of Gaudí's death in 2026. The basilica was consecrated by Pope Benedict XVI in 2010, and today portions of the interior are open to visitors. Drawing some 3 million visitors a year, it is Barcelona's most iconic structure.

BREAKING NEW GROUND

With a new airport terminal, a behemoth new convention center complex, and a new AVE high-speed train connection to Madrid, Barcelona is again on the move. City planners predict that the recent redesign of Plaça de les Glòries will someday shift the city center eastward, and that the new Barcelona hub will surround the Torre Agbar and the Fòrum at the Mediterranean end of the Diagonal.

POLITICAL PROGRESS

The approval of Catalonia's controversial Autonomy Statute in 2008 ushered in a wave of change in Catalonia. Bitterly opposed by the right-wing Partido Popular, the autonomy agreement gives Catalonia a larger slice of local taxes and more control of its own infrastructure. The statute formally establishes Catalonia as one of the most progressive societies in Europe, with special provisions safeguarding human rights, same-sex marriage, euthanasia, and abortion that would win scant support in other more traditional regions of Spain.

The Partido Popular, coming into power in 2011, rolled back many of the progressive laws passed in the previous eight years of Socialist government; support grew steadily through 2017 for a referendum which eventually took place in October of the same year. Of those who voted, 90% supported independence; however, only 43% of all voters turned out, as many who opposed the split refused to vote in a referendum that is illegal under the present Spanish Constitution. A subsequent declaration of independence from Spain resulted in the Catalan leader, Carles Puigdemont, being exiled and several other members of the Catalan Parliament arrested and imprisoned.

While protests are commonplace—particularly over recent right-wing efforts to modify the public school curriculum, where Catalan is the language of instruction (nothing drives the Catalans postal like a threat to what they regard as the cornerstone of their national identity)—none of this is likely to impact your visit.

What to Watch and Read Before Your Trip

HOMAGE TO CATALONIA BY GEORGE ORWELL

George Orwell's life was strongly influenced by his time in Spain fighting against the Nationalist army led by Francisco Franco, whose victory led to a dark time in the history of Spain and Catalonia. This narrative provides a first-person account of war-torn Barcelona.

BARCELONA BY ROBERT HUGHES

This magisterial, 573-page book is a gracefully written introduction to the city's history, culture, and political twists and turns.

THE SHADOW OF THE WIND BY CARLOS RUIZ ZAFÓN

Daniel Sempere is 10 years old when his father, a bookseller in post–civil war Barcelona, takes him to a mysterious labyrinth filled with treasured but forgotten tomes and tells him to pick one that he will then dedicate his life to preserving. What follows is a tale of a young man who discovers that a mysterious person—or perhaps creature—is destroying all remaining works of Julián Carax, the author whose book he now protects. Zafón followed on this success of this book with two more novels that follow Daniel into his adulthood, *The Angel's Game* and *The Prisoner of Heaven*.

THE BEST THING THAT CAN HAPPEN TO A CROISSANT BY PABLO TUSSET

Pablo "Baloo" Miralles is the lazy, debaucherous scion of a well-to-do Spanish family. When his elder (and more accomplished) brother inexplicably disappears, Baloo suddenly finds himself pulled into the dealings of the family's powerful financial firm, a turn of events which inspires him to try to locate his missing sibling. Within this satirical quasi-detective story, *The Best Thing That Can Happen to a Croissant*, is a modern-day tale about the city of Barcelona.

THE CITY OF MARVELS BY EDUARDO MENDOZA

The City of Marvels is Mendoza's tale of a boy who rises from abject poverty to great wealth and power and a city—Barcelona—that expands from a small provincial capital to a metropolitan city. The action spans the years between Barcelona's two economically disastrous World's Fairs of 1888 and 1929.

HOMAGE TO BARCELONA BY COLM TÓIBÍN

Irish author Colm Tóibín moved to Barcelona in 1975 when he was 20. In this book, written with deep affection and knowledge, he celebrates one of Europe's greatest cities and explores its history, moving from its foundations through to nationalism, civil war, and the transition from dictatorship to democracy. Tóibín is the perfect guide to Barcelona, and this is a sensuous and beguiling portrait of a unique Mediterranean port and an adopted home.

MARKS OF IDENTITY BY JUAN GOYTISOLO

A searing masterpiece from Spain's greatest living novelist describes the return of an exile to Barcelona. Goytisolo comes to the conclusion that every man carries his own exile about with him, wherever he lives. The narrator (Goytisolo) rejects Spain itself and searches instead for poetry. This is a shocking and influential work, and an affirmation of the ability of the individual to survive the political tyrannies of the last century and the current one. *Marks of Identity* was banned in Spain until after Franco's death.

THE TIME OF THE DOVES BY MERCÈ RODOREDA

Written by exiled Catalan writer Mercè Rodoreda, this novel, a masterpiece of Catalan literature, was published in 1962 as *La plaça del Diamant* (translated as

The Time of the Doves by David Rosenthal in 1981) and is now required reading in Catalan secondary schools. We learn about life during the Spanish Civil War not from battles but rather from the perspective of a shopkeeper named Natalia whose controlling husband is fighting with the Republicans while she works hard to feed herself and her two children. Gabriel García Márquez learned Catalan just to read this book and declared it "the most beautiful novel that's been published in Spain after the Civil War." The author, who died in 1983, is also known for her first novel, *Aloma*.

NADA BY CARMEN LAFORET

In the aftermath of the Spanish Civil War a young woman named Andrea moves to Barcelona so that she can attend university on a government scholarship. Once there she finds herself living in the home of her grandmother, a decrepit building haunted by the emotionally and physically violent confrontations and betrayals of the array of family members who reside there. *Nada* is considered to be a Catalan Existentialist classic, a rare volume from a time when Franco's censors suppressed novels from Catalan writers and tamped down on anything which showed how desperate life could be.

ALL ABOUT MY MOTHER DIRECTED BY PEDRO ALMODÓVAR

After Manuela's 17-year-old son Esteban is killed before her eyes she decides to move to Barcelona in order to find his father, a transvestite named Lola who doesn't know that Esteban exists. *All About My Mother* is a brilliantly directed tale which sensitively examines a variety of complex topics such as bereavement, addiction, gender identity, and the impacts of HIV. It also earned director Pedro Almodóvar the Best Director award at the 1999 Cannes Film Festival and

the Academy Award for Best Foreign Language Film in 2000.

BIUTIFUL DIRECTED BY ALEJANDRO GONZÁLEZ IÑÁRRITU

Iñárritu's *Biutiful*, his first feature since *Babel*, is the moving story of a single father of two (Javier Bardem) in Barcelona who finds out he has terminal cancer and tries to find someone to care for his children before his death. While melancholy, this is also a story of redemption as a father seeks a better life for his children.

A GUN IN EACH HAND DIRECTED BY CESC GAY

Catalan director Cesc Gay recruited some top-notch Spanish actors and actresses for this comedy. Told through a series of vignettes, *A Gun in Each Hand* explores how changing gender roles in Spain affect modern relationships—typically by having the central male characters either embarrass themselves directly, or suffer some form of emasculation at the hands of their much more clever female counterparts. It speaks to how Spanish ideas about masculinity and relationships are changing, and how the an evolution can benefit women in Spain.

SUMMER 1993 DIRECTED BY CARLA SIMÓN

Director Carla Simón was only six years old when she went to live with her aunt and uncle after her parents died of AIDS. In her debut film, *Summer 1993*, the character of Frida shares the same fate and goes to live in the Catalan countryside outside of Barcelona. In the mid-'90s, Spain had the highest number of AIDS cases in Europe, and this film is a courageous and personal exploration of the tragedy of Spain's AIDS crisis.

GAUDÍ

ARCHITECTURE
THROUGH
THE LOOKING
GLASS

(left) The undulating rooftop of Casa Batlló. (top) Right angles are notably absent in the Casa Milà façade.

Before his 75th birthday in 1926, Antoni Gaudí was hit by a trolley car while on his way to Mass. The great architect—initially unidentified—was taken to the medieval Hospital de la Santa Creu in Barcelona's Raval and left in a pauper's ward, where he died two days later without regaining consciousness. It was a dramatic and tragic end for a man whose entire life seemed to court the extraordinary and the exceptional.

Gaudí's singularity made him hard to define. Indeed, eulogists at the time, and decades later, wondered how history would treat him. Was he a religious mystic, a rebel, a bohemian artist, a Moderniste genius? Was he, perhaps, all of these? He certainly had a rebellious streak, as his architecture stridently broke with tradition. Yet the same sensibility that created the avant-garde benchmarks Park Güell and La Pedrera also created one of Spain's greatest shrines to Catholicism, the Temple Expiatori de la Sagrada Família (Expiatory Temple of the Holy Family), which

architects agree is one of the world's most enigmatic structures; work on the cathedral continues to this day. And while Gaudí's works suggest a futurist aesthetic, he also reveled in the use of ornamentation, which 20th century architecture largely eschewed.

What is no longer in doubt is Gaudí's place among the great architects in history. Eyed with suspicion by traditionalists in the 1920s and '30s, vilified during the Franco regime, and ultimately redeemed as a Barcelona icon after Spain's democratic transition in the late '70s, Gaudí has finally gained universal admiration.

THE MAKING OF A GENIUS

Gaudí was born in 1852 the son of a boilermaker and coppersmith in Reus, an hour south of Barcelona. As a child, he helped his father forge boilers and cauldrons in the family foundry, which is where Gaudí's fascination with three-dimensional and organic forms began. Afflicted from an early age with reoccuring rheumatic fever, the young architect devoted his energies to studying and drawing flora and fauna in the natural world. In school Gaudí was erratic: brilliant in the subjects that interested him, absent and disinterested in the others. As a 17-year-old architecture student in Barcelona, his academic results were mediocre. Still, his mentors agreed that he was brilliant.

Unfortunately being brilliant didn't mean instant success. By the late 1870s, when Gaudí was well into his twenties, he'd only completed a handful of projects, including the Plaça Reial lampposts, a flower stall, and the factory and part of a planned workers' community in Mataró. Gaudí's career got the boost it needed when, in 1878, he met Eusebi Güell, heir to a textiles fortune and a man who, like Gaudí, had a refined sensibility. (The two bonded over a mutual admiration for the visionary Catalan poet Jacint Verdaguer.) In 1883, Gaudí became Güell's architect and for the next three decades, until Güell's death in 1918, the two collaborated on Gaudí's most important architectural achievements, from high-profile endeavors like Palau Güell, Park Güell, and Pabellones Güell to smaller projects for the Güell family.

(top) Interior of Casa Batlló. (bottom) Chimneys on rooftop of Casa Milà recall helmeted warriors or veiled women.

GAUDÍ TIMELINE

1883–84

Gaudí builds a summer palace, El Capricho in Comillas, Santander for the brother-in-law of his benefactor, Eusebi Güell. Another gig comes his way during this same period when Barcelona ceramics tile mogul Manuel Vicens hires him to build his town house, Casa Vicens, in the Gràcia neighborhood.

El Capricho

1884–1900

Gaudí whips up the Pabellones Güell, Palau Güell, the Palacio Episcopal of Astorga, Barcelona's Teresianas school, the Casa de los Botines in León, Casa Calvet, and Bellesguard. These have his classic look of this time, featuring interpretation of Mudéjar (Moorish motifs), Gothic, and Baroque styles.

Palacio Episcopal

BREAKING OUT OF THE T-SQUARE PRISON

If Eusebi Güell had not believed in Gaudí's unusual approach to Modernisme, his creations might not have seen the light of day. Güell recognized that Gaudí was imbued with a vision that separated him from the crowd. That vision was his fascination with the organic. Gaudí had observed early in his career that buildings were being composed of shapes that could only be drawn by the compass and the T-square: circles, triangles, squares, and rectangles—shapes that in three dimensions became prisms, pyramids, cylinders and spheres. He saw that in nature these shapes are unknown. Admiring the structural efficiency of trees, mammals, and the human form, Gaudí noted ". . . neither are trees prismatic, nor bones cylindrical, nor leaves triangular." The study of natural forms revealed that bones, branches, muscles, and tendons are all supported by internal fibers. Thus, though a surface curves, it is supported from within by a fibrous network that Gaudí translated into what he called "ruled geometry," a system of inner reinforcement he used to make hyperboloids, conoids, helicoids, or parabolic hyperboloids.

These tongue-tying words are simple forms and familiar shapes: the femur is hyperboloid; the way shoots grow

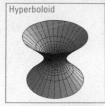

Hyperboloid

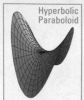

Hyperbolic Paraboloid

The top of the gatehouse in Park Güell at the main entrance; note the mushroom-like form.

off a branch is helicoidal; the web between your fingers is a hyperbolic paraboloid. To varying degrees, these ideas find expression in all of Gaudí's work, but nowhere are they more clearly stated than in the two masterpieces La Pedrera and Park Güell.

1900–17

Gaudí's Golden Years—his most creative and innovative period. Topping each success with another, he tackles Park Güell, the reform of Casa Batlló, the Güell Colony church, Casa Milà (La Pedrera), and the Sagrada Família school.

Casa Batlló's complex chimneys

1918–26

A crushing blow: Gaudí suffers the death of his assistant, Francesc Berenguer. Grieving and rudderless, he devotes himself fully to his great unfinished opus, La Sagrada Família—to the point of obsession. On June 10th, 1926, he's hit by a trolley car. He dies two days later.

La Sagrada Família

HOW TO SEE GAUDÍ IN BARCELONA

Few architects have left their stamp on a major city as thoroughly as Gaudí did in Barcelona. Paris may have the Eiffel Tower, but Barcelona has Gaudí's still unfinished master-piece, the **Temple Expiatori de la Sagrada Família,** the city's most emblematic structure. Dozens of other build-ings, parks, gateways and even pav-ing stones around town bear Gaudí's personal Art Nouveau signature, but the continuing progress on his last and most ambitious project makes his creative energy an ongoing part of everyday Barcelona life in a unique and almost spectral fashion.

In Barcelona, nearly all of Gaudí's work can be visited on foot or, at most, with a couple of metro or taxi rides. A walk from **Palau Güell** near the Mediterranean end of La Rambla, up past **Casa Calvet** just above Plaça Catalunya, and on to **Casa Batlló** and **Casa Milà** is an hour's stroll, which, of course, could take a full day with thor-ough visits to the sites. **Casa Vicens** is a half hour's walk up into Gràcia from

(top) The serpentine ceramic bench at Park Güell, designed by Gaudí collaborator Josep Maria Jujol, curves sinuously around the edge of the open square. (bottom) Sculptures by Josep María Subi-rachs grace the temple of La Sagrada Família.

Casa Milà. Park Güell is another thirty-to forty-minute walk up from that. **La Sagrada Família,** on the other hand, is a good hour's hike from the next near-est Gaudí point and is best reached by taxi or metro. The **Teresianas** school, the **Bellesguard Tower,** and **Pabellones Güell** are within an hour's walk of each other, but to get out to Sarrià you will need to take the comfortable Gener-alitat (FGC) train.

Chapter 2

TRAVEL SMART

Updated by
Jared Lubarsky

CATALUNYA

★ **CAPITAL**
Barcelona

POPULATION
7.5 million
(Barcelona 1.6 million)

LANGUAGES
Catalan, Spanish

$ CURRENCY
Euro

COUNTRY CODE
34

⚠ EMERGENCIES
112

DRIVING
On the right side

⚡ ELECTRICITY
220 volts/50 cycles; electrical
plugs have two round prongs

⏱ TIME
Six hours ahead of New York

⊕ WEB RESOURCES
www.spain.info
www.barcelona.cat/en

Know Before You Go

Should you tip? When can you eat? Should you skip the touristy bits? We've got answers and a few tips to help you make the most of your visit to this vibrant city.

CATALAN CULTURE IS STRONG

Before the rise of modern-day Spain there was Aragon, a kingdom on the Iberian Peninsula whose territories included the regions we know as Catalonia and Aragon, as well as Roussillon, a part of southern France. The Catalan people and their culture are tenacious and Barcelona—the capital of Catalonia—remains strongly Catalan. This means that you'll see signage printed in both Spanish and Catalan and will also hear Catalan being spoken. While you won't be expected to learn the language, it's a sign of respect to learn at least a few Catalan words. As a visitor you should also keep in mind that the Catalan bid for independence remains an unresolved and politically sensitive issue for a number of people, and the polite thing to do is avoid talking about Spanish politics in public.

YOU DON'T NEED TO TIP (BUT ROUNDING UP IS NICE)

Service industry jobs in Europe tend to pay better than they do in the United States, and in Spain tipping is neither expected nor required. Rounding up a euro or two in a restaurant where you had good service is a nice and appreciated gesture though, and the same goes for throwing in an extra euro for a cab ride, or even just letting your driver keep the change.

MEALS ARE LATE AND LONG

The Spanish internal clock is set about three hours behind that of America, which means late lunches and even later dinners. Brunch starts at noon, lunch starts at 2 or 3, and dinner starts at 10 or 11. Keep in mind that meals, and particularly dinners, can be multi-hour affairs as well, with the potential for more than one round of food and certainly multiple drink orders. If you're not up for adopting the Spanish meal schedule you can of course eat whenever you want, but you won't always have the same restaurant options available off-hours, especially for lunch.

WATCH OUT FOR PICKPOCKETS

For all of its charms Barcelona is also a place where petty theft is common. Pickpocketing, mugging, and bag snatching remain a chronic, daily problem in Barcelona, and this is particularly true in any place where you'll find crowds of distracted people, such as train platforms and on La Rambla. Leave original documents—especially plane tickets, your ID, and your passport—in your place of lodging and instead carry photocopies if you think you'll need to show ID. As with any major city, keep bags and purses closed at all times and wear them on your front. If you are the victim of theft, dial "112" (which offers services in English) or contact the Help Centre for Tourists in the Ciutat Vella (Old City) offices of the Guardia Urbana—the municipal police—at La Rambla 43: It's open 24 hours a day; the phone number is ☎ 93-256-2430.

GO AHEAD AND ORDER THE BOTTLE

You already know that Spanish wine is world famous, but you might be surprised—and delighted—to hear that in Spain it's also wildly inexpensive. Spain offers some of the best wine values in all of Europe, and ordering a bottle of wine in a tapas bar could easily mean spending less than 10 euros, with that same bottle costing half of that in a shop. Catalonia has its share of quality appellations (areas producing distinct wines), among them Penedes, Priorat and Montsant.

FC BARCELONA IS EVERYTHING

Despite recent setbacks that have shaken its reputation as one of the single best *futbol* teams on the planet, look for la Barça to make a comeback. It does, after all, have an incredibly successful youth soccer program designed to groom the next generation of sports idols. Fandom is a religion here, so if you want to worship alongside locals, buy advance tickets online, at kiosks throughout the city, or at Caixa de Catalunya ATMs. Note, too, that while the home stadium, Camp Nou, is undergoing a multiyear renovation, the team will play at the Olympic Stadium in Montjuïc. Regardless, if you can't get tickets, find a bar with a big-screen TV during a match and enjoy the experience of watching—and *feeling*—a game with locals.

THE BEACHES ARE FREE, BUT BUSY

Barcelona is a seaside city and that means easy access to the beach—and everyone goes. For that reason, the most central beaches—Barceloneta and Sant Miguel—are also the most crowded and chaotic. If you're looking for a stretch of sand that isn't completely crammed with people, leave the city entirely: there are beautiful, clean beaches just outside of the city that are perfect for a day trip.

THE RESTAURANTS ARE GREAT, BUT YOU'LL ALSO WANT TO EAT AT THE MARKET

While it might be hard to turn yourself away from one of Barcelona's countless restaurants, at least one of your meals should be a picnic made up of ingredients like jamón ibérico, olives, cheese, olive oil, bread, and tomatoes—or whatever strikes your fancy at one of the city's many incredible markets. Barcelona's most famous food market is La Boqueria, but other top options include Mercat Santa Caterina in La Ribera, and the open-air artisanal food fair in the Plaça del Pi in Barri Gòtic; the latter takes place the first and third Friday to Sunday of the month, from 10 am to 9 pm.

LA RAMBLA IS SUPER CROWDED

Once upon a time the wide avenue called La Rambla was considered one of Barcelona's essential tourism destinations, and then everyone went there, all at once! La Rambla now has something of a reputation for pushy street vendors, overpriced sidewalk cafés, and pickpockets. It's not exactly an unsafe area, but neither is it much fun in peak tourist season; think of it as your default access to the Barri Gòtic and the port promenade. In summer especially, do yourself a favor and visit early in the day.

SUNDAY IS A DAY OF REST

Spain is a Catholic-majority country and while Barcelona doesn't completely shut down on Sundays it is a day when a significant number of businesses close. This doesn't mean that you can't still have fun or find a place to eat, but your options will definitely be limited and stores (including supermarkets) will likely not be open.

EAT PAELLA ON SUNDAY

Paella is Valencian, not Catalan, but Sunday paella in La Barceloneta, usually with seafront views, is a local family tradition. Popular tourist options include Pez Vela Chiringuito (☎ 932/216–317), Xiringuito Escriba (☎ 932/210–729), La Barraca (☎ 932/241–253), and Restaurante la Barca del Salamanca (☎ 932/211–837); calling ahead to book a table is a wise move. Note that paella marinera is a dish of rice boiled in fish stock, with clams, mussels, prawns, and jumbo shrimp; paella valenciana omits seafood and includes chicken, rice, and snails. An order of paella is normally for two diners, but is usually enough for three people to share.

Getting Here and Around

With some planning, finding your way around in Barcelona can be simple. All of Barcelona's Ciutat Vella (Old City), including the Barri Gòtic (Gothic Quarter), can be explored on foot. Your transport needs will be mainly to get to Sarrià, Gràcia, Park Güell, Gaudí's Sagrada Família, Montjuïc, and the Auditori near Plaça de les Glòries. The metro system will normally get you wherever you need to go. The commuter trains on the Catalan regional government's FGC system are also handy. The municipal metro lines are useful, air-conditioned, and safe. Buses are practical for certain runs, and taxis are rarely much more than €15 for a complete crosstown ride.

The Eixample, the modern part of Barcelona above Plaça de Catalunya, was designed and built on a grid. The Barri Gòtic (Old City), however, from Plaça de Catalunya to the port, is a labyrinth of narrow streets, so you'll need a good street map (or GPS) and a good pair of shoes to explore it. Whenever possible, it's best to avoid driving in the city. *(For information about driving, see Car.)*

Maps of the bus and metro routes are available free from the main tourist information office on Plaça de Catalunya.

 Air

Transatlantic flying time to Barcelona's El Prat Airport averages about 7 hours and 30 minutes from New York's JFK Airport. Other U.S. cities with direct flights to Barcelona are Atlanta, Chicago, Miami, Newark, and Philadelphia. Low-cost carrier Norwegian Airlines also has direct routes from Fort Lauderdale, Oakland, Newark, and Los Angeles. Flying from other cities in North America usually requires a connection.

Nonstop flights from London to Barcelona average 2 hours and 30 minutes. Flights from the United Kingdom to a number of destinations in Spain are frequent and offered at competitive fares, particularly on low-cost carriers such as Ryanair or easyJet.

Iberia operates a shuttle, the *puente aereo*, between Barcelona and Madrid, ten times a day from 8 am to 9:05 pm; planes depart from Terminal T1, most frequently in the morning and afternoon commuter hours. Flying time is about an hour and a half; given the time you need for airport transfers (and the hefty cost of the flight), many commuters now prefer the high-speed rail connection between Estació de Sants in Barcelona and Atocha Station in Madrid. You don't need to reserve ahead for the shuttle flight; you can buy your tickets at the counter when you get to the airport.

Charter flights of varying prices routinely fly in and out of El Prat Airport. Top charter companies include NetJets, Global Jet Concept, and Luxaviation.

AIRPORTS

Most connecting flights arriving in Spain from the United States and Canada pass through Madrid's Barajas Airport (MAD), but the major gateway to Catalonia and other regions in this book is Spain's second-largest airport, Barcelona's spectacular glass, steel, and marble El Prat del Llobregat (BCN). The second of two terminals, the T1 terminal, which opened in 2009, is a sleek ultramodern facility that uses solar panels for sustainable energy and offers a spa, a fitness center, restaurants and cafés, and VIP lounges. This airport is about 12 km (7½ miles) southwest from the center of Barcelona and is served by numerous international carriers, but Catalonia also has two other airports that handle passenger traffic, including charter flights. One is Girona-Costa Brava Airport (GRO) 12½ km (8 miles) southwest of Girona, 90 km (56 miles) north of Barcelona and convenient to the resort towns of the Costa Brava. Bus and train connections from Girona to Barcelona are convenient and affordable, provided you have the time. The other Catalonia airport is the tiny Reus Airport (REU), 110 km (68 miles) south of Barcelona and a gateway to neighboring Tarragona, Port Adventura theme park, and the beaches of the Costa Daurada. Both airports are considerably smaller than El Prat and offer the bare essentials: a limited number of duty-free shops, restaurants, and car rental services. For information about airports in Spain, consult Aena, the company that operates them all, on their website (⊕ *aena.es*) or call ☎ *91/321–1000*.

FLIGHTS

If you are flying to Barcelona from North America, consider booking on a British or other European carrier, though you may have to change planes in London, Paris, Amsterdam, or elsewhere in Europe. Savings can be significant.

The least expensive airfares to Barcelona are priced for round-trip travel and must usually be purchased in advance. Airlines generally allow you to change your return date for a fee; most low-fare tickets, however, are nonrefundable.

On certain days of the week, Iberia offers minifares (*minitarifas*), which can save you 40% on domestic flights. Tickets must be purchased at least two days in advance, and you must stay over at your destination on a Saturday night.

American, United/Continental, Delta, and Iberia fly to Madrid and Barcelona; Norwegian Air Shuttle flies to Barcelona from San Francisco, Los Angeles, New York, Miami, and Orlando; US Airways

and Air Europa fly to Madrid. Within Spain, Iberia is the main domestic airline; two independent airlines, Air Europa and Vueling, fly a number of domestic routes at somewhat lower prices.

GROUND TRANSPORTATION

Check first to see if your hotel in Barcelona is one of the very few that provides airport-shuttle service. If not, visitors typically get into town by train, bus, taxi, or rental car.

Cab fare from the airport into town is €30–€35, depending on traffic, the part of town you're heading to, and the amount of baggage you have (there's a €3.10 surcharge for airport pickups/drop-offs, and a €1 surcharge for each suitcase that goes in the trunk). If you're driving your own car, follow signs to the Centre Ciutat, from which you can enter the city along Gran Vía. For the port area, follow signs for the Ronda Litoral. The journey to the center of town can take 25–45 minutes, depending on traffic.

The Aerobus leaves Terminal 1 at the airport for Plaça de Catalunya every 10 minutes 5:35 am–7:20 am and 10:25 pm–1:05 am, and every 5 minutes 7:30 am–10:20 pm. From Plaça de Catalunya the bus leaves for the airport every 5 or 10 minutes between 5 am and 12:10 am. The fare is €5.90 one way and €10.20 round trip. Aerobuses for Terminals 1 and 2 pick up and drop off passengers at the same stops en route, so if you're outward bound make sure that you board the right one. The A1 Aerobus for Terminal 1 is two-tone light and dark blue; the A2 Aerobus for Terminal 2 is dark blue and yellow.

The train's only drawback is that it's a 10- to 15-minute walk from your gate through Terminal 2 over the bridge. From Terminal 1 a shuttle bus drops you at the train. Trains leave the airport every 30

Getting Here and Around

minutes between 5:42 am and 11:38 pm, stopping at Estació de Sants, for transfer to the Arc de Triomf, then at Passeig de Gràcia and finally at El Clot–Aragó. Trains going to the airport begin at 5:21 am from El Clot, stopping at Passeig de Gràcia at 5:27 am, and Sants at 5:32 am. The trip to Sants takes about 20 minutes, and the fare is €4.10. For getting around the city, the best bargain is the T10 (aka T-Casual) metro card; with it, you have ten rides on any of the subways, buses or FGC trains (Ferrocarils de la Generalitat to Catalunya, a separate system), with free transfers between them, all for €11.35. Take note: you can't share the card.

If you plan to make extensive use of public transportation, consider buying a "Hola Barcelona" card at the Tourist Information Center in Plaça Catalunya; the card gives you unlimited rides for anywhere from two to five days, at €14.76 to €34.38.

TRANSFERS BETWEEN AIRPORTS

To get to Girona Airport from Barcelona Airport by train you have to first take the RENFE train that leaves from the airport and then change at Barcelona Sants station. From Barcelona Sants you need to catch the train for Figueres, and get off at Girona, two stops before. Travel times vary between 38 minutes and 2 hours 10 minutes depending on the train line. From there you will have to take a 30-minute bus ride, or a 17-minute taxi ride to the airport for around €25–€30.

Sagales runs the Barcelona Bus shuttle buses between Girona airport and El Prat. The trip takes about 1 hour and 15 minutes. The schedules, set up to coincide with RyanAir arrivals and departures at Girona, are a bit tortuous; consult the Sagales website or call ☎ *902/130014* for bus information.

Boat

There are regular ferry services between the United Kingdom and northwestern Spain. Brittany Ferries sails from Portsmouth to Bilbao and Santander. The trip is more than 24 hours, so not practical unless you love the ocean and have some extra time on your hands. Spain's major ferry line, Trasmediterránea, links mainland Spain (including Barcelona) with the Balearics and the Canary Islands. This ferry's fast catamaran service takes half the time of the standard ferry, but catamarans are often canceled because they can navigate only in very calm waters. Trasmediterránea and Balearia operate overnight ferries from Barcelona, Valencia, and Dénia to the islands of Mallorca, Menorca, and Ibiza. Formentera can be reached from Ibiza via Balearia and Transmapi, a local ferry company. At 7 hours, 30 minutes from Barcelona via ferry crossing, Mallorca is the closest island. Long-stretch ferries are equipped with a choice of seating options including sleepers, a restaurant, several bars, and small shopping area.

You can pick up schedules and buy tickets at the ferry ticket office in the port.

Bus

Barcelona's main bus station for intra-Spain routes is Estació del Nord, a few blocks east of the Arc de Triomf. Buses also depart from the Estació de Sants for long-distance and international routes, as well as from the depots of Barcelona's various private bus companies. Spain's major national long-haul company is ALSA. Grup Sarbus serves Catalonia; aka Moventis Sarfa, it connects the numerous small towns along the Costa Brava. Bus timetables are complicated and confusing; trying to get information by phone will probably get you put on interminable hold. Better to plan your bus trip online or through a local travel agent, who can quickly book you the best way to your destination.

Within Spain, private companies provide comfortable and efficient bus services between major cities. Fares are lower than the corresponding train fares, and service is more extensive: if you want to get somewhere not served by rail, you can be sure a bus will go there.

See the planner section in the Catalonia, Valencia, and the Costa Blanca chapter for companies serving Catalonia.

Most larger bus companies have buses with comfortable seats and adequate legroom; on longer journeys (two to three hours or more) a movie is shown on board, and earphones are provided. Except for smaller, regional buses that travel short hops, buses have bathrooms on board. Smoking is prohibited. Most long-haul buses stop at least once every two to three hours for a snack and bathroom break. Although buses are subject to road and traffic conditions, highways in Catalonia, particularly along major routes, are well maintained. That may not be the case in more rural areas, where you could be in for a bumpy ride.

You can get to Spain by bus from London, Paris, Rome, Frankfurt, Prague, and other major European cities. It is a long journey, but the buses are modern and inexpensive. Eurolines, the main carrier, connects many European cities with Barcelona.

ALSA, Spain's largest national bus company, has two luxury classes in addition to its regular coach services. The top of the line is Supra Clase, with roomy leather seats, free Wi-Fi Internet connection,

and onboard meals; in this class you also have the option of asientos individuales, single-file seats along one side of the bus. The next class is the Eurobus, with comfy seats and plenty of legroom, but no asientos individuales or onboard meals. The Supra Clase and Eurobus cost up to one-third and one-quarter more, respectively, than the regular coaches.

Some smaller, regional bus lines (Sarfa, for example) offer multitrip bus passes, which are worthwhile if you plan on making multiple trips between two destinations. Generally, these tickets offer a savings of 20% per journey; you can buy them only in the bus station (not on the bus).

In Barcelona you can pick up schedule and fare information at the tourist information offices in Plaça de Catalunya, Plaça Sant Jaume, or at the Sants train station. For local bus information, check online at ⊕ tmb.cat/en/home, the website of the Transports Metropolitans de Barcelona.

At bus-station ticket counters, major credit cards (except for American Express) are universally accepted. You must pay in cash for tickets purchased on the bus. Traveler's checks are almost never accepted.

During peak travel times (Easter, August, and Christmas), it's always a good idea to make a reservation at least three to four days in advance.

City buses run daily 5:30 am–11:30 pm. Route maps are displayed at bus stops. Note that those with a red band always stop at a central square—Catalunya, Universitat, or Urquinaona—and blue, with an N prefix on the bus number, indicates a night bus. Barcelona's 17 night buses generally run until about 5 am.

Getting Here and Around

🚡 Cable Car and Funicular

The Montjuïc Funicular is a cog railway that runs from the junction of Avinguda Paral·lel and Nou de la Rambla (Metro L2/L3, *Paral·lel*) to Montjuïc Castle, with stops en route at Parc de Monjuïc and Miramar. It operates weekdays 7:30 am–8 pm and weekends 9 am–9 pm; the fare is €2.15, or one ride on a T10 card.

A Transbordador Aeri del Port (Harbor Cable Car) runs between Miramar and Montjuïc across the harbor to Torre de Jaume I, on Barcelona's *moll* (quay), and on to Torre de Sant Sebastià, at the end of Passeig Joan de Borbó in Barceloneta. You can board at either stage. One-way fare is €11; round-trip fare is €16.50. The car runs every eight minutes, November through February 11 am–5:30 pm, March through May and September and October 11 am–7 pm, and June–August 11 am–8 pm.

To reach the summit of Tibidabo, take the metro to Avinguda de Tibidabo, then the Tramvía Blau (€5.50 one way) to Peu del Funicular, and finally the Tibidabo Funicular (€7.70 round-trip; €4.10 with purchase of admission to the Tibidabo Amusement Park) from there to the top. The Tramvia runs daily March through December, and weekends only in February. Generally it runs every 15–30 minutes, beginning at 10 am and finishing at dusk (around 6 pm in winter and 8 pm in summer).

🚗 Car

Major routes throughout Spain bear heavy traffic, especially in peak holiday periods, so be extremely cautious; Spain has one of the highest traffic accident rates in Europe, and the roads are shared by a mixture of local drivers, immigrants en route elsewhere from Eastern Europe and North Africa, and non-Spanish travelers on vacation, some of whom are more accustomed to driving on the left-hand side of the road. Watch out for heavy truck traffic on national routes. Expect the near-impossibility of on-street parking in the major cities. Parking garages are common and affordable, and provide added safety to your vehicle and possessions.

The country's main cities are well connected by a network of four-lane *autovías* (freeways). The letter N stands for a national route (*carretera nacional*), either four- or two-lane. An *autopista* (AP) is a toll road. At the tollbooth plazas (the term in Castilian is *peaje*; in Catalan, *peatge*), there are three systems to choose from—*automàtic*, with machines for credit cards or coins; *manual*, with an attendant; or *telepago*, an automatic chip-driven system mostly used by Spanish drivers.

GETTING AROUND AND OUT OF BARCELONA

Arriving in Barcelona by car from the north along the AP7 autopista or from the west along the AP2, follow signs for the Ronda Litoral (the coastal ring road—but beware: it's most prominently marked "Aeroport," which can be misleading) to lower and central Barcelona along the waterfront, or the Ronda de Dalt (the upper-ring road) along the edge of upper Barcelona to Horta, the Bonanova, Sarrià, and Pedralbes. For the center of town, take the Ronda Litoral and look for Exit 21 ("Paral·lel–Les Ramblas") or 22 ("Barceloneta–Via Laietana–Hospital de Mar"). If you are arriving from the Pyrenees on the C1411/E9 through the Tunel del Cadí, the Tunels de Vallvidrera will put you on the upper end of Via Augusta with off-ramps to Sarrià, Pedralbes, and La

Bonanova. The Eixample and Ciutat Vella are 10–15 minutes farther if traffic is fluid. Watch out for the new variable speed limits on the approaches to Barcelona. While 80 kph (48 mph) is the maximum speed on the *rondas,* flashing signs over the motorway sometimes cut the speed limit down to 40 kph (24 mph) during peak hours.

Barcelona's main crosstown traffic arteries are Diagonal (running diagonally through the city) and the midtown avenues, Carrer d'Aragó, and Gran Via de les Corts Catalanes, both cutting northeast–southwest through the heart of the city. Passeig de Gràcia, which becomes Gran de Gràcia above Diagonal, runs all the way from Plaça de Catalunya up to Plaça Lesseps, but the main up-and-down streets, for motorists, are Balmes, Muntaner, Aribau, and Comtes d'Urgell. The general urban speed limit is 50 kph (30 mph).

Getting around Barcelona by car is generally more trouble than it's worth. It's better to walk or travel via subway, taxi, or bus.

Leaving Barcelona is not difficult. Follow signs for the rondas, do some advance mapping, and you're off. Follow signs for Girona and França for the Costa Brava, Girona, Figueres, and France. Follow Via Augusta and signs for Tunels de Vallvidrera or E9 and Manresa for the Tunel del Cadí and the Pyrenean Cerdanya valley. Follow Diagonal west and then the freeway AP7 signs for Lleida, Zaragoza, Tarragona, and Valencia to leave the city headed west. Look for airport, Castelldefells, and Sitges signs to head southwest down the coast for these beach points on the Costa Daurada. The C32 freeway to Sitges joins the AP7 to Tarragona and Valencia.

For travel outside Barcelona, the freeways to Girona, Figueres, Sitges, Tarragona, and Lleida are surprisingly fast. The distance to Girona, 97 km (58 miles), is a 45-minute shot. The French border is an hour away. Perpignan, at 188 km (113 miles) away, is an hour and 20 minutes.

 ## Cruise

Barcelona is Europe's busiest cruise port, and the fourth largest in the world. Vessels dock at the Port Vell facility, which has seven terminals catering to cruiseship traffic. All terminals are equipped with duty-free shops, telephones, bar/restaurants, information desks, and currency-exchange booths. The ships docking closest to the terminal entrance are a 10-minute walk from the southern end of La Rambla, but those docked at the farthest end require passengers to catch a shuttle bus (the Autobús Azul, a distinctive blue bus) to the port entrance. The shuttle, which runs every 20 minutes, links all terminals with the public square at the bottom of La Rambla. Some five minutes' walk up La Rambla is the Drassanes metro station (L3) for onward public transport around the city. The shuttle runs about every 30 minutes.

 ## Metro

In Barcelona the underground metro, or subway, is the fastest, cheapest, and easiest way to get around. Metro lines run Monday through Thursday and Sunday 5 am–midnight, Friday to 2 am, Saturday and holiday evenings all night. The FGC trains run 5 am to just after midnight on weekdays and to 1:52 am on weekends and the eves of holidays. Sunday trains run on weekday schedules.

Getting Here and Around

Ticket/Pass	Price
Single Fare	€2.20
10-Ride Pass	€11.35

Transfers from a metro line to the FGC (or vice versa), or to a local bus, are free within an hour and 15 minutes. Note that in many stations, you need to validate your ticket at both ends of your journey. Maps showing bus and metro routes are available free from the tourist information office in Plaça de Catalunya.

Taxi

In Barcelona taxis are black and yellow and show a green rooftop sign on the front right corner when available for hire. The meter currently starts at €2.10 and rises in increments of €1.07 every kilometer. These rates apply 6 am–10 pm weekdays. At hours outside of these, the rates rise 20%. There are official supplements of €1 per bag for luggage.

Trips to or from a train station entail a supplemental charge of €2.10; a cab to or from the airport, or the Barcelona Cruise Terminal, adds a supplemental charge of €4.20, as do trips to or from a football match. The minimum price for taxi service to or from the Barcelona airport is €20 for terminals T1, T2, and T3, and €39 from T4. There are cabstands (*parades,* in Catalan) all over town, and you can also hail cabs on the street, though if you are too close to an official stand they may not stop. You can call for a cab by phone 24 hours a day. Drivers do not expect a tip, but rounding up the fare is standard.

Train

International overnight trains to Barcelona arrive from many European cities, including Paris, Grenoble, Geneva, Zurich, and Milan; high-speed trains to and from Paris take about 5½ hours, and advance-purchase tickets online are competitive with flight prices. Almost all long-distance trains arrive at and depart from Estació de Sants, though many make a stop at Passeig de Gràcia that comes in handy for hotels in the Eixample or in the Ciutat Vella. Estació de França, near the port, handles primarily regional trains within Catalonia. Train service connects Barcelona with most other major cities in Spain; in addition a high-speed Euromed route connects Barcelona to Tarragona and Valencia.

Spain's intercity services (along with some of Barcelona's local train routes) are the province of the government-run railroad system—RENFE (Red Nacional de Ferrocarriles Españoles). The high-speed AVE train now connects Barcelona and Madrid (via Lleida and Zaragoza) in less than three hours. (Spain has more high-speed tracks in service than any other country in Europe.) The fast TALGO and ALTARIA trains are efficient, though local trains remain slow and tedious. The Catalan government's FGC (Ferrocarril de la Generalitat de Catalunya) also provide train service, notably to Barcelona's commuter suburbs of Sant Cugat, Terrassa, and Sabadell.

Information on the local/commuter lines (*rodalies* in Catalan, *cercanías* in Castilian) can be found on the RENFE website, ⊕ *www.renfe.com.* Rodalies go, for example, to Sitges from Barcelona, whereas you would take a regular RENFE train to, say, Tarragona. It's important to know whether you are traveling on REN-FE or on rodalies (the latter distinguished by a stylized C), so you don't end up in the wrong line.

Both Catalonia and the Basque Country offer scenic railroad excursions. The day train from Barcelona to Madrid runs through bougainvillea-choked towns before leaping out across Spain's central *meseta* (plateau) via Zaragoza, most trains arriving at Atocha Station in Madrid in about 2½ hours. The train from Barcelona's Plaça de Catalunya north to Sant Pol de Mar and Blanes runs along the edge of the beach.

First-class train service in Spain, with the exception of the *coche-cama* (Pullman) overnight service, barely differs from second class or *turista*. The TALGO or the AVE trains, however, are much faster than second-class carriers like the slowpoke Estrella overnight from Barcelona to Madrid, both with limited legroom and general comforts. The AVE is the exception: these sleek, comfortable bullet trains travel between Barcelona and Madrid or between Madrid and Seville. Some 30 AVE trains a day connect Barcelona and Madrid, with departures from 5:50 am to 9:15 pm. Trips take from 2 hours 30 minutes to 3 hours 10 minutes.

During peak travel times (Easter, August, and Christmas), it's important to make a reservation weeks or even months in advance; on routes between major cities (Barcelona to Bilbao or Madrid, for example), it's a good idea to reserve well in advance, especially for overnight trips.

Essentials

🧭 Addresses

Abbreviations used in the book for street names are Av. for *avinguda* in Catalan; *avenida* in Spanish, and Ctra. for *carreter* (or *carretera* in Spanish). The letters *s/n* following an address mean *sin número* (without a street number). *Carrer* (*calle* in Spanish) is often dropped entirely or not abbreviated at all. *Camí* (*camino* in Spanish) is abbreviated to *C.* *Passeig* (*paseo* in Spanish) is sometimes abbreviated as P., but is usually written out in full. Plaça/plaza is usually not abbreviated (in this book it is abbreviated as Pl.).

Addresses in Barcelona may include the street name, building number, floor level, and apartment number. For example, Carrer Balmes 155, 3°, 1ª indicates that the apartment is on the *tercero* (third) floor, *primera* (first) door. In older buildings, the first floor is often called the *entresuelo*; one floor above it is *principal* (sometimes called the *planta baja*), and above this, the first floor (*primera*). The top floor of a building is the *ático*; occasionally there is a floor above that, called the *sobreàtico*. In more modern buildings there is often no *entresuelo* or *principal*.

🍴 Dining

Catalans are legendary lovers of fish, vegetables, rabbit, duck, lamb, game, and natural ingredients from the Pyrenees or the Mediterranean. The *mar i muntanya* (literally, "sea and mountain"—that is, surf and turf) is a standard. Combining salty and sweet tastes—a Moorish legacy—is another common theme. The Mediterranean diet—based on olive oil, seafood, fibrous vegetables, onions, garlic, and red wine—is at home in Barcelona, embellished by Catalonia's four basic sauces: *allioli* (whipped garlic and olive oil), *romesco* (almonds, nyora peppers, hazelnuts, tomato, garlic, and olive oil), *sofregit* (fried onion, tomato, and garlic), and *samfaina* (a ratatouille-like vegetable mixture). Typical entrées include *faves a la catalana* (a broad-bean stew), *arròs caldós* (a rice dish more typical of Catalonia than paella, often made with lobster), and *espinacas a la catalana* (spinach cooked with oil, garlic, pine nuts, raisins, and cured ham). Toasted bread is often doused with olive oil and rubbed with squeezed tomato to make *pa amb tomaquet*—delicious on its own or as a side order. Beware of the advice of hotel concierges and taxi drivers, who have been known to falsely warn that the place you are going is either closed or no good anymore, and to instead recommend places where they get kickbacks. Aside from restaurants, Barcelona is brimming with bars and cafés, the latter of which can serve as an outdoor meeting spot or a place to socialize and enjoy a cocktail. However, the sidewalk cafés along La Rambla are noisy, dusty, overpriced, and exposed to pickpockets.

HOURS

Barcelona dines late. Lunch is served from 2 to 4 pm and dinner from 9 to 11 pm. Arrive a half-hour early if you want to secure a table, but the liveliness of each place picks up later in the evening. The city is slowly adapting to the eating timetables of tourists, and a number of restaurants now offer all-day and late-night hours. Satiate cravings between meals in the city's numerous cafés and tapas bars.

PRICES

Barcelona is no longer a bargain. Though low-end fixed-price lunch menus can be found for as little as €10, most good restaurants cost closer to €40 or €50 for a full meal when ordering à la carte. For serious evening dining, plan on spending €55–€80 (or more) per person.
■ TIP→ **Barcelona restaurants, even many of the pricey establishments, offer a daily lunchtime menu (menú del dia) consisting of two courses plus wine, coffee, or dessert.**

Restaurant reviews have been shortened. For full information, visit Fodors. com. Restaurant prices are for a main course at dinner or if dinner is not served, at lunch.

What It Costs

$	$$	$$$	$$$$
AT DINNER			
under €15	€15–€22	€23–€29	over €29

RESERVATIONS

Nearly all of Barcelona's best restaurants require reservations. As the city has grown in popularity, more and more receptionists are able to take your reservations in English. Your hotel concierge will also be happy to call and reserve you a table.

TIPPING AND TAXES

Tipping, though common (and appreciated), is not required; the gratuity is included in the check. If you do tip as an extra courtesy, anywhere from 5% to 10% is perfectly acceptable.

The 10% Value-Added Tax (IVA) will not appear on the menu, but is tacked on to the final tally on your check.

◉ Language

After the dictator Franco's death in 1975, a renaissance of Catalan language and literature began in Catalonia, and similar movements have gathered momentum in other regions. Catalans are proud of their language, which is heard and used everywhere in the country.

Although Barcelona, for the most part, is bilingual, Catalans prefer to speak Catalan amongst themselves. This being said, things are slowly changing. The city's top two newspapers, *El Periódico* and *La Vanguardia* feature both Catalan and Spanish editions—the former even offering a limited edition in English. Radio stations and regional TV channels are also varied, though several of the most popular are still broadcasting exclusively in Catalan. In general, road and street signs are in Catalan as well. Spanish, which is referred to as Castellano (Castilian Spanish) in Spain, will likely never be Catalonia's main language, though it's more accepted here than ever before.

Fortunately, Catalans speak Spanish, which is comparatively much easier to get a grip on. If your Spanish fails you, you should have no trouble finding people who speak English in major cities and coastal resorts, but you won't necessarily be able to count on the bus driver or the passerby on the street. Most guided tours offered at museums and historic sites in Barcelona are in Catalan and/or Castellano, but there are very often at least one or two scheduled in English during the week; ask about the language that will be spoken before signing up. Any effort at all to speak the local language will be ecstatically received and applauded as a sign that you know where you are and what culture you are visiting.

Essentials

A phrase book and language-tape set can help get you started. *Fodor's Spanish for Travelers* (available at bookstores everywhere) is excellent.

A number of private schools offer Spanish courses for foreigners. Don Quijote is one network with schools in several locations around Spain. The international network Inlingua has 30 schools in Spain. Some Spanish universities, including University of Barcelona, have Spanish study programs, but these are over longer periods, usually two months or more. The state-run Cervantes Institute, devoted to promoting the Spanish language, organizes courses at its centers worldwide and can provide information on courses in Spain.

Lodging

Barcelona's hotel trade may be centuries removed from Miguel de Cervantes's 17th-century description of it as a fountain of courtesy and a shelter for strangers, but in the 400 years or so since *Don Quixote* was written, the city continues to pamper and impress visitors.

Barcelona's pre-Olympics hotel surge in the early 1990s was matched only by its post-Olympics hotel surge in the early 2000s. The city is the premier tourist destination in Spain, and the major cruise port in the Mediterranean. "Starchitects" like Ricardo Bofill and Rafael Moneo have changed the skyline with skyscraper hotels of eye-popping luxury; the real heroes of this story, however, are the architect-designer teams that take one after another of the city's historic properties and restore them with an astonishing tour de force of taste. Hotel restaurants, too—from the Arts' Enoteca to the Mandarin's Moments—are among the superstar attractions in the city's gastronomic scene.

Hotels in the Barri Gòtic and along La Rambla now compete with the newer lodgings in the Eixample, or west along Diagonal; waterfront monoliths like the W Barcelona, removed from the bustle of midtown, set the standard for upscale hospitality. Many Eixample hotels occupy restored late 19th- or early 20th-century town houses.

Small hotels in the Ciutat Vella are considerably less expensive and—in the accommodations you'll find listed here—at no substantial sacrifice of comfort and convenience. Wherever you choose to stay, you'll never be far from anything you'll want to see and do in this hospitable city.

FACILITIES

Hotel entrances are marked with a plaque bearing the letter H and the number of stars. The letter R (standing for *residencia*) after the letter H indicates an establishment with no meal service. The designations *fonda* (F), *pensión* (P), and *hostal* (Hs) indicate budget accommodations—although a Spanish *hostal* (hostel) can often be just as well-appointed and comfortable as a hotel.

Hotel ratings used by the Turisme de Barcelona are expressed in stars, with five stars as the highest category. The rating system, however, is essentially based on a checklist of facilities (pool, restaurant, concierge, etc.) more than an evaluation of quality; a hotel can lack one or more of the amenities on the list and still be a better choice than one in the next highest category.

PRICES

Barcelona's finer hotels are as expensive as those of any other major city—but rates can vary as widely (and mysteriously) as airline tickets. Prices are generally lower from November through March, when hotels have more availability, except when there are huge conventions in town or other special events.

Hotel reviews have been shortened. For full information, see Fodors.com. Prices in the hotel reviews are the lowest cost of a standard double room in high season.

What It Costs

$	$$	$$$	$$$$
FOR TWO PEOPLE			
under €125	€125–€175	€176–€225	over €225

RESERVATIONS

Because of the annual summer onslaught of millions of tourists, you'll want to reserve well in advance from early April to late October. Note that high-season rates (May and June for most hotels, rather than July and August) prevail also during the week before Easter, during local fiestas, and for events like the Mobile World Congress in February, the Formula 1 Grand Prix races in May, and for the at-home classic confrontation between FC Barcelona and Real Madrid. When reserving, specify whether you prefer two beds or one double bed. Although single rooms (*habitacións sencillas*) are usually available, they are often on the small side, and you might prefer to pay a bit extra for single occupancy in a double room (*habitación doble uso individual*).

 # Nightlife

Barcelona nights are long and as wild as you want. Most of the best clubs don't even open until after midnight, but cafés and music bars serve as recruiting venues for the night's mission. The typical progression begins with drinks, tapas and dinner, a jazz or flamenco concert around 11 pm, then a pub or a music bar or two, and then—if the body can keep up with the spirit—dancing. Late-night bars and early-morning cafés provide an all-important break to refresh and refuel.

New wine bars, cafés, music bars, and tiny live-music clubs are constantly scraping plaster from 500-year-old brick walls to expose medieval structural elements that offer striking backdrops for postmodern people and conversations. The most common closing time for Barcelona's nocturnal bars is 3 am, while clubs are open until 5 am.

 # Passports

Visitors from the United States, Australia, Canada, New Zealand, and the United Kingdom need a valid passport to enter Spain. No visa is required for U.S. passport holders for a stay of up to three months; for stays exceeding three months, contact the Consulate of Spain nearest you. Australians require a visa for stays longer than one month; you should obtain it from the Spanish Embassy before you leave.

Essentials

Where to Stay?

	NEIGHBORHOOD VIBE	PROS	CONS
Barri Gòtic and Born-Ribera	With lamps glowing in the Roman and Gothic corners, this is a romantic part of town. The Picasso Museum and Santa Maria del Mar are nearby.	Plaça Sant Jaume, the cathedral, Plaça del Rei, and the Born-Ribera district are among the main reasons to visit the city.	It's easy to lose yourself in this labyrinth of narrow cobblestone streets. It can also be noisy, with echoes reverberating around this ancient sound chamber.
El Raval	A rough-and-tumble part of town, but the nightlife is exciting and the diversity of the neighborhood is exemplary. It's just steps from the Boqueria market.	El Raval has a buzz all its own. A contemporary art museum, the medieval hospital, and the Mercat de Sant Antoni offer plenty to explore.	El Raval can seem dangerous, and demands street-sense, especially at night.
La Rambla	Constantly bustling, La Rambla is a virtual anthology of Barcelona street life.	The Boqueria market, flower stalls, the Liceu opera house, and Plaça Reial are all quintessential Barcelona sites.	The crowds can be overwhelming, especially if FC Barcelona wins a championship match.
Barceloneta and Port Olímpic	At one time the fishermen's quarter, Barceloneta retains its informal and working-class ambience.	Near the beach, this part of town has a laid-back feel. It's where to go for casual seafood restaurants.	Barceloneta offers few accommodations beyond the W Hotel; Port Olímpic is a bit isolated.
Eixample	Casa Milà and Casa Battló are here, on the Passeig de Gràcia along with great restaurants and shopping.	Art Nouveau architecture is everywhere. La Sagrada Família is within walking distance.	Too few buildings here have street numbers; the grid is easy to understand, but it can be difficult to find a specific address.
Upper Barcelona	Leafy and residential, Pedralbes is Barcelona's wealthiest residential quarter; Sarrià is the rustic little village next door.	A 15-minute train ride connects Sarrià with the middle of the Eixample and La Rambla.	Staying in upper Barcelona involves a 15-minute trip, at least, to the most important attractions. After midnight on weeknights will require a taxi.

🎭 Performing Arts

Countless concerts and performances can be found in Barcelona any night of the week. To find out what's on (in Spanish or Catalan), check "Ocio y Cultura" listings in Barcelona's leading daily newspapers online versions: La Vanguardia (⊕ www.lavanguardia.com) and El Periódico (⊕ www.elperiodico.com) or the weekly English-language edition of TimeOut (⊕ www.timeout.com/barcelona).

Le Cool (⊕ barcelona.lecool.com) offers a curated list of events and activities online (available in English). Barcelona Metropolitan magazine updates its online "what's on" section regularly and features a monthly print version, available for free in English-language bookstores and hotel lobbies (⊕ www.barcelona-metropolitan.com).

Local websites like Guia del Ocio (⊕ www.guiadelocio.com) and Barcelona Cultura (⊕ lameva.barcelona.cat/barcelonacultura) have more comprehensive lists. And, while exploring, keep your eyes peeled for flyers and posters in shops, bars, and cafés.

TICKETS

Tickets for performances are available either at the theater (ticket offices generally open only in the evenings) or online: Ticketmaster (⊕ www.ticketmaster.es) has an English-language options. After ordering your seats and giving credit-card information, pick up tickets at the door of the venue or print them out in advance. Ticketmaster uses the ATMs of local bank La Caixa, which print the tickets for you. If you want to do things the old-fashioned way, FNAC on Plaça de Catalunya has an office on the ground floor that sells tickets to many pop and rock performances.

WHAT TO WEAR

The dress code in Barcelona is eclectic but casual but typically a bit more formal for performances. Although there are rarely hard-and-fast rules at elegant restaurants or concert venues, tourists in shorts, tank tops, and baseball caps will feel out of place. The Liceu Opera House often has black-tie evening galas; the Palau de la Música Catalana and the Auditori are less formal than the Liceu, but upscale dress is still expected.

➕ Safety

Petty crime is a perennial problem in Barcelona. Pickpocketing and thefts from parked cars are the most common offenses. The lower Raval and parts of Poblenou are particularly prone to these problems. Be especially cautious in train and bus stations, getting on and off the metro, and on La Rambla, where masses of people sometimes offer opportunities for petty thieves.

🛍 Shopping

Characterized by originality and relative affordability, the shopping scene in Barcelona has become a jubilant fair of fashion, design, craft, and gourmet food. Different parts of town specialize in different goods, and you can explore parts of the city through shopping and browsing boutiques.

The Ciutat Vella, especially the Born-Ribera area, is rich in small-crafts shops, young designers, and an endless potpourri of artisans and merchants operating in restored medieval spaces that are often as dazzling as the wares on sale. Even the pharmacies and grocery stores of Barcelona are often sumptuous

Essentials

aesthetic feasts filled with charming details. Although the end of rent protection has seen many heritage establishments close, a new law will at least ensure that their unique architectural and decorative details will remain intact.

Shopping for design objects and chic fashion in the Eixample is like buying art supplies at the Louvre: it's an Art Nouveau architecture theme park spinning off into dozens of sideshows—textiles, furnishings, curios, and knickknacks of every kind. Any specific shop or boutique will inevitably lead you past a dozen emporiums that you hadn't known were there. Original and surprising yet wearable clothing items are Barcelona's signature contribution to fashion. Rather than copying the runways, Barcelona designers are relentlessly daring and innovative, combining fine materials with masterful workmanship.

Browsing through shops in this unique metropolis feels more like museum-hopping than it does a shopping spree. The city's many design shops delight the eye and stimulate the imagination, while the area around the Passeig del Born beckons young designers from across the globe. Passeig de Gràcia has joined the ranks of the Champs Elysées in Paris and Rome's Via Condotti as one of the great shopping avenues in the world, with the planet's fashion houses well represented, from Armani to Zara. Exploring Barcelona's antiques district along Carrer Banys Nous and Carrer de la Palla is always an adventure. The shops open daily around Santa Maria del Mar in the Born-Ribera district range from Catalan and international design retailers to shoe and leather handbag designers, to T-shirt decorators and coffee emporiums. The megastores in Plaça de Catalunya, along Diagonal,

and in L'Illa Diagonal farther west sell clothing, furniture, furs, books, music, and more. The village-like Sarrià and Gràcia are filled with intimate antique and clothing shops, with friendly boutique owners who add a personal touch.

HOURS

Outside of the tourist areas, stores are generally open Monday–Saturday 9 am–2 pm, and 4:30–8 pm. Most stores are closed on Sundays except during the Christmas shopping period, and in July and August in the city center. Many stores in the Eixample, Barri Gòtic, and in the malls, such as L'Illa Diagonal, stay open through the lunch hour. Big department stores like El Corte Inglés and FNAC are open all day 9:30 am–9:30 pm. Designated pharmacies are open all night.

🅢 Tipping

While tipping isn't expected in Spain, it is always welcome, and if you feel so inclined you can be sure that your contribution will be appreciated. On the other hand, if you experience bad or surly service, don't feel obligated to leave a tip.

Restaurant checks always include service. The bill may not tell you that the service is included, but it is. An extra tip of 5% to 10% of the bill is icing on the cake. Leave tips in cash, even if paying by credit card. If you eat tapas or sandwiches at a bar, just round up the bill to the nearest euro. Tip cocktail servers €0.50 a drink, depending on the bar. In a fancy establishment, leave no more than a 10% tip even though service is included—likewise if you had a great time.

Barcelona's Discount Cards

Museum Discounts

The **Articket BCN** (AKA the Art Passport, ⊕ *www.articketbcn.org*, €28.50), valid for a year, gives you half-price admission to the Museu Picasso, Fundació Antoni Tapies, CCCB Barcelona Centre de Cultura Contemporànea, MACBA Museum of Contemporary Art, Fundació Joan Miró, and MNAC Museu Nacional d'Art de Catalunya. It also lets you skip long lines. The **Arqueoticket** (€14.50), valid for a year, grants free entry to the Museu d'Arqueologia de Catalunya, Museu Egipci de Barcelona, Museum of the History of the City and historical buildings of the Plaça del Rei, and Born Centre de Cultura i Memòria. It's available at any of the four museums.

Transportation Discounts

The **Barcelona Card** (⊕ *www.barce-lonaturisme.com;*valid three days €45, four days €55) gets you access to all public transportation and free or discounted admissions to various museums, sites, and tours. The *Modernisme Route Guidebook* (€12), available at bookstores and at the Centro del Modernismo in the Güell Pavillions, features 120 Catalan Art Nouveau architectural sites and includes a book of discount vouchers. The **T-10 Metro Card** (€9.95), from the ticket dispensers at all subway stations, is good for 10 rides on the city's metro, bus, and tram systems as well as the FGC lines. You can transfer from any one to another for free (within 75 minutes), and the card can be shared. Fares on the hop-on, hop-off double-decker **Barcelona Bus Turistic** (€29 for one day, €39 for two consecutive days), which has color-coded (blue, red, and green) tour routes, include a voucher booklet of discounts to cultural sites, attractions, shows, and restaurants. Purchase tickets at any tourist information office, kiosks in the city center, or on the bus.

Taxi drivers expect no tip and are happy if you round up in their favor. A tip of 5% of the total fare is considered generous. Long rides or extra help with luggage may merit a tip, but if you're short of change, you'll never hear a complaint. On the contrary, your driver may sometimes round down in *your* favor instead of ransacking his pockets for exact change.

Tip hotel porters €1 a bag, and the bearer of room service €1. A doorman who calls a taxi for you gets €1. If you stay in a hotel for more than two nights, tip the maid about €1 per night. A concierge should receive a tip for service, from €1 for basic help to €5 or more for special assistance such as getting reservations at a popular restaurant.

Tour guides should be tipped about €2, barbers €1, and women's hairdressers at least €2 for a wash and style. Restroom attendants (though you won't see many of them today) are tipped €1 or whatever loose change is at hand.

Essentials

What to Pack

Summer will be hot nearly everywhere; winter, fall, and spring call for warm clothing and, in winter, sturdy walking shoes or boots. It makes sense to wear casual, comfortable clothing and shoes for sightseeing, but you'll want to dress up a bit in Barcelona and Bilbao, especially in the evening.

Good walking shoes make all the difference for exploring Barcelona. In summer, sturdy sandals that you might even wear hiking are best for city trekking. On the beach, anything goes; it's common to see females of all ages wearing only bikini bottoms, and many of the more remote beaches allow nude sunbathing. Regardless of your style, bring a cover-up for when you leave the beach. Shorts are acceptable, though light skirts and summery dresses are the norm.

If you're coming before the COVID pandemic has run its course, be sure you have your QR-coded proof of vaccination in your mobile phone; some venues—especially bars and restaurants—might refuse you entry without it.

If you get to Barcelona and realize you need sportswear for a trek through the Pyrenees, or a yoga mat, check out the Decathlon sporting goods store (⊕ *www. decathlon.es*).

When to Go

For optimal weather and fewer tourists, visit Barcelona and Catalonia from April through June and mid-September through mid-December. Expect traffic at the start and end of August when locals leave for vacation. Many shops and even restaurants close for at least part of the month, though Gràcia's Festa Major in Barcelona and an extensive slate of music festivals and cultural events keeps city alive during summer, and museums remain open.

Barcelona summers can be very hot, but temperatures rarely surpass 100°F (38°C), and air-conditioning is becoming more widespread. Dining alfresco on a warm summer night is one of Spain's finest pleasures. Spring and fall offer the best temperatures at both ends of the Pyrenees. Barcelona winters—chilly, but never freezing—are ideal for fireside dining and hearty cuisine.

On the Calendar

There's something going on all year long in Barcelona, including events associated with religious feast days. Carnaval (Carnestoltes), which rivals its more flamboyant counterpart in Sitges, arrives just before Lent in February or March and travels down the coast. Semana Santa (the week before Easter), however, is Spain's most important celebration everywhere but Barcelona, as the locals depart in droves for vacations elsewhere.

La Diada de Sant Jordi (April 23) is Barcelona's Valentine's Day, celebrated with gifts of flowers and books in observance of International Book Day and to honor the deaths of Miguel de Cervantes and William Shakespeare. La Fira de Sant Ponç brings farmers to town for an open-air market in the Raval on May 11.

La Verbena de Sant Joan celebrates the summer solstice and Midsummer's Eve with fireworks and all-night beach parties on June 23. La Festa Major de Gràcia honors Santa Maria with street dances and concerts in Barcelona's village-turned-neighborhood, Gràcia, in mid-August. Festes de La Mercé celebrates Barcelona's patron saint, Nostra Senyora de la Mercé, for a week in late September.

The calendar is also dotted with arts and cultural festivals, many of which are devoted to music.

Winter–Summer

Between mid-February and late July, the annual **Guitar Bcn** (⊕ www.guitarbcn.com/es) festival features concerts in the Palau de la Música Catalana and other venues by master guitarists of all musical genres and styles. Folk, jazz, classical, and flamenco are all well represented.

Summer–Fall

Every Sunday from June to September local and international DJs play at the family-friendly **Brunch in the Park** (⊕ barcelona.brunch-in.com/park) in the Jardins de Joan Brossa on Montjuïc, with its beautiful view over the city. Bring your own brunch, or partake of what the assembled food trucks and stalls have to offer.

Fall–Winter

One of Europe's oldest jazz festivals, **Barcelona International Jazz Festival** (⊕ www.jazz.barcelona) takes place from late September to early December, with concerts all around the city in illustrious venues like the Palau de la Música, L'Auditori, and smoky side-street bars. Highlights include vocal and instrumental jazz renditions from around the globe.

May

Held annually in May, the lively **Ciutat Flamenco Festival** (⊕ ciutatflamenco.com), co-organized by the Taller de Músics (Musicians' Workshop) and the Center for Contemporary Culture of Barcelona (CCCB) in the Mercat de les Flors, offers visitors a chance to experience authentic flamenco instrumental, song, and dance performances by both local and international artists.

At **Primavera Sound** (⊕ www.primavera-sound.com), which has evolved into one of the biggest and most exciting music festivals in Europe, attracts more than 200,000 visitors each year. Concerts are organized in small venues around the city during the weeks leading up to the event, but the main stint takes place over four days in late May or early June

On the Calendar

at the Parc del Fòrum. Everybody who's anybody in rave music has played here, and you can rest assured that whoever is doing the big summer festival circuit will pass through Primavera. Festival tickets can be bought online—and are quickly sold out, so buy early.

June

One of Spain's most popular gay festivals, **Pride Barcelona** brings together the local LGBTQIA community, friends, and allies to the Gay Village on the last weekend in June, for a full calendar of cultural activities and celebrations. The highlight is the parade on Saturday afternoon, followed by a massive party.

For more than 15 years, **Sónar** (⊕ *www. sonar.es*) has grown from a niche festival for electronic and dance music fans to one of Barcelona's largest and most celebrated happenings. Over three days in summer (sometimes mid-June, sometimes mid-July), thousands descend upon the city, turning Plaça Espanya—the site of the festival's principal venues—into a huge rave. The celebration is divided into "Day" and "Night" activities. Sónar by Day sees sets by international DJs, record fairs, and digital art exhibits at the Fira Montjuïc. Sónar by Night takes place in the Fira Gran Via Hospitalet for acts on the forefront of the dance-music scene. It's best to purchase tickets early via the festival website.

Bringing together labels and artists at the cutting edge of dance music for Europe's biggest party week, **OFFSónar** (⊕ *offsonar. co*) presents nine parties over four days in a variety of locations throughout the city, including rooftops, bars, night-clubs—and especially the beautiful open-air spaces of Poble Espanyol.

July

Barcelona's monthlong summer arts festival in July, **Festival del Grec** (⊕ *www. barcelona.cat/grec/en/grec-festival*) features acts from the world of dance, performance art, music, and theater. Performances take place in such historic venues as Mercat de les Flors and the Teatre Grec on Montjuïc—an open-air theater built for the 1929 Barcelona International Exposition, which gives the festival its name and serves as the main venue.

September

Held over a week toward late September, the **Barcelona Acció Musical** (BAM ⊕ *www.barcelona.cat/bam*) musical celebration is part of the lively La Mercè festival, an annual event honoring Our Lady of Mercy, Barcelona's patron saint. BAM showcases emerging talent (both national and international) in dance, rock, pop, and electronic genres; acts perform in parks, squares, and venues around the city.

Best Tours

Aula Gastronómica. Tapas workshops at this cooking school include visits to the nearby Boqueria or Santa Caterina markets. ✉ *Carrer Sagristans 5, Entresuelo, Barri Gòtic* ☎ *93/301–1944, 628–30–1502 mobile* ⊕ *www.aulagastronomica.com/ cooking-classes* ✆ *From €42* ⊘ *Closed Sun.* Ⓜ *Jaume I (Metro L4).*

Epicurean Ways. Jane Gregg, founder of Epicurean Ways, offers gourmet and wine tours of Barcelona and Catalonia, ranging from the architecture, cuisine and culture of the Catalan capital itself, to the dramatic cliffs and secluded towns of the Costa Brava and idyllic nearby Girona, to the Catalan wine country, with Penedès, Priorat, Montsant, and many more quality areas making some of Spain's best wine. A three-day trip around Barcelona and the surrounding areas runs around $400 per person, not including accommodation. ☎ *4434/738–2293 in U.S., 636–102–46 in Spain* ⊕ *www.epicureanways.com* ✆ *From €400.*

Julia Travel. One of the largest tour operators in Spain offers a good selection of excursions from Barcelona, including the Port Aventura amusement park complex, Girona and Figueres, Monserrat—and in the city, a guided walking tour of Park Güell. ✉ *Carrer d'Alí Bei 80* ☎ *934/317–6454* ⊕ *www.juliatravel.com* ✆ *From €27 to €81, depending on the tour* ⊘ *Closed Sun.*

Las Golondrinas. Golondrina harbor boats make short trips from the Portal de la Pau, near the Columbus monument. There's a 45-minute "Barcelona Port" tour of the harbor, and a one-hour "Barcelona Sea" ride out past the beaches and up the coast to the Fòrum at the eastern end of Diagonal. Departure times and schedules are updated constantly on the website, where you can also make reservations. ✉ *Pl. Portal de la Pau s/n, Moll de les Drassanes, La Rambla* ☎ *93/442–3106* ⊕ *lasgolondrinas.com/en* ✆ *From €7.70* Ⓜ *Drassanes (Metro L3).*

Turisme de Barcelona. In addition to being a useful resource for information, tickets, and bookings, Turisme de Barcelona offers daily walking tours of the Barri Gòtic, Picasso's Barcelona, Modernisme, and more. There is also an Easy Walking Tour of the Barri Gòtic, which has been adapted for people with reduced mobility: Departure times for tours in English depend on which of the tours you choose. Book online for a 10% discount. The Picasso tour, which includes the entry fee for the Museu Picasso, is a great bargain. All tours depart from the Plaça de Catalunya tourist office, except for the Easy Walking Tour, which starts at The Tourist Office in Plaça Sant Jaume. ✉ *Passatge de la Concepció 7–9, Eixample* ☎ *93/368–9700* ⊕ *barcelonaturisme. com* ⊘ *Closed Sat. and Sun.* Ⓜ *Pl. de Catalunya.*

Helpful Phrases in Spanish

BASICS

Hello	Hola	**oh**-lah
Yes/no	Sí/no	see/no
Please	Por favor	pore fah-**vore**
May I?	¿Me permite?	may pair-**mee**-tay
Thank you	Gracias	**Grah**-see-as
You're welcome	De nada	day **nah**-dah
I'm sorry	Lo siento	lo see-**en**-toh
Good morning!	¡Buenos días!	**bway**-nohs **dee**-ahs
Good evening!	¡Buenas tardes! (after 2pm)	**bway**-nahs-**tar**-dess
	¡Buenas noches! (after 8pm)	**bway**-nahs **no**-chess
Good-bye!	¡Adiós!/¡Hasta luego!	ah-dee-**ohss/ah**-stah **lwe**-go
Mr./Mrs.	Señor/Señora	sen-**yor/** sen-**yohr**-ah
Miss	Señorita	sen-yo-**ree**-tah
Pleased to meet you	Mucho gusto	**moo**-cho **goose**-toh
How are you?	¿Que tal?	keh-tal

NUMBERS

one	un, uno	oon, **oo**-no
two	dos	dos
three	tres	tress
four	cuatro	**kwah**-tro
five	cinco	**sink**-oh
six	seis	saice
seven	siete	see-**et**-eh
eight	ocho	**o**-cho
nine	nueve	new-**eh**-vey
ten	diez	dee-**es**
eleven	once	**ohn**-seh
twelve	doce	**doh**-seh
thirteen	trece	**treh**-seh
fourteen	catorce	ka-**tohr**-seh
fifteen	quince	**keen**-seh
sixteen	dieciséis	dee-**es**-ee-**saice**
seventeen	diecisiete	dee-**es**-ee-see-**et**-eh
eighteen	dieciocho	dee-**es**-ee-**o**-cho
nineteen	diecinueve	dee-**es**-ee-new-**ev**-ey
twenty	veinte	**vain**-teh
twenty-one	veintiuno	**vain**-te-**oo**-noh
thirty	treinta	**train**-tah
forty	cuarenta	kwah-**ren**-tah
fifty	cincuenta	seen-**kwen**-tah
sixty	sesenta	sess-**en**-tah
seventy	setenta	set-**en**-tah
eighty	ochenta	oh-**chen**-tah
ninety	noventa	no-**ven**-tah
one hundred	cien	see-**en**
one thousand	mil	meel
one million	un millón	oon meel-**yohn**

COLORS

black	negro	**neh**-groh
blue	azul	ah-**sool**
brown	marrón	mah-**ron**
green	verde	**ver**-deh
orange	naranja	na-**rahn**-hah
red	rojo	**roh**-hoh
white	blanco	**blahn**-koh
yellow	amarillo	ah-mah-**ree**-yoh

DAYS OF THE WEEK

Sunday	domingo	doe-**meen**-goh
Monday	lunes	**loo**-ness
Tuesday	martes	**mahr**-tess
Wednesday	miércoles	me-**air**-koh-less
Thursday	jueves	hoo-**ev**-ess
Friday	viernes	vee-**air**-ness
Saturday	sábado	**sah**-bah-doh

MONTHS

January	enero	eh-**neh**-roh
February	febrero	feh-**breh**-roh
March	marzo	**mahr**-soh
April	abril	ah-**breel**
May	mayo	**my**-oh
June	junio	**hoo**-nee-oh
July	julio	**hoo**-lee-yoh
August	agosto	ah-**ghost**-toh
September	septiembre	sep-tee-**em**-breh
October	octubre	oak-**too**-breh
November	noviembre	no-vee-**em**-breh
December	diciembre	dee-see-**em**-breh

USEFUL WORDS AND PHRASES

Do you speak English?	¿Habla usted inglés?	ah-blah oos-**ted** in-**glehs**
I don't speak Spanish.	No hablo español	no **ah**-bloh es-pahn-**yol**
I don't understand.	No entiendo	no en-tee-en-en-doh
I understand.	Entiendo	en-tee-**en**-doh
I don't know.	No sé	no **seh**
I'm American.	Soy americano (americana)	soy ah-meh-ree-**kah**-no (ah-meh-ree-**kah**-nah)
What's your name?	¿Cómo se llama ?	koh-mo seh **yah**-mah
My name is . . .	Me llamo . . .	may **yah**-moh
What time is it?	¿Qué hora es?	keh o-rah-es
How?	¿Cómo?	**koh**-mo
When?	¿Cuándo?	**kwahn**-doh
Yesterday	Ayer	ah-**yehr**
Today	hoy	oy
Tomorrow	mañana	mahn-**yah**-nah
Tonight	Esta noche	es-tah **no**-cheh
What?	¿Qué?	keh
What is it?	¿Qué es esto?	keh es **es**-toh

English	Spanish	Pronunciation
Why?	¿Por qué?	pore **keh**
Who?	¿Quién?	kee-**yen**
Where is . . .	¿Dónde está . . .	**dohn**-deh es-**tah**
. . . the train station?	la estación del tren?	la es-tah-see-**on** del trehn
. . . the subway station?	estación de metro	la es-ta-see-**on** del **meh**-tro
. . . the bus stop?	la parada del autobus?	la pah-**rah**-dah del ow-toh-**boos**
. . . the terminal? (airport)	el aeropuerto	el air-oh-**pwar**-toh
. . . the post office?	la oficina de correos?	la oh-fee-**see**- nah deh koh-**rreh**-os
. . . the bank?	el banco?	el **bahn**-koh
. . . the hotel?	el hotel?	el oh-**tel**
. . . the museum?	el museo?	el moo-**seh**-oh
. . . the hospital?	el hospital?	el ohss-pee-**tal**
. . . the elevator?	el ascensor?	el ah-sen-**sohr**
Where are the restrooms?	el baño?	el **bahn**-yoh
Here/there	Aquí/allí	ah-**key**/ah-**yee**
Open/closed	Abierto/cerrado	ah-bee-**er**-toh/ ser-**ah**-doh
Left/right	Izquierda/derecha	iss-key-**eh**-dah/ dare-**eh**-chah
Is it near?	¿Está cerca?	es-**tah** sehr-kah
Is it far?	¿Está lejos?	es-**tah** leh-hoss
I'd like . . .	Quisiera . . .	kee-see-**ehr**-ah
. . . a room	un cuarto/una habitación	oon **kwahr**-toh/**oo**-nah ah-bee-tah-see-**on**
. . . the key	la llave	lah **yah**-veh
. . . a newspaper	un periódico	oon pehr-ee-oh-**oh**-dee-koh
. . . a stamp	un sello de correo	oon **seh**-yo deh korr-**eh**-oh
I'd like to buy . . .	Quisiera comprar . . .	kee-see-**ehr**-ah kohm-**prahr**
. . . soap	jabón	hah-**bohn**
. . . suntan lotion	crema solar	**kreh**-mah soh-**lar**
. . . envelopes	sobres	**so**-brehs
. . . writing paper	papel	pah-**pel**
. . . a postcard	una tarjeta postal	**oon**-ah tar-**het**-ah post-**ahl**
. . . a ticket	un billete (travel)	oon bee-**yee**-teh
	una entrada (concert etc.)	**oona** en-**trah**-dah
How much is it?	¿Cuánto cuesta?	**kwahn**-toh **kwes**-tah
It's expensive/ cheap	Es caro/barato	es **kah**-roh/ bah-**rah**-toh
A little/a lot	Un poquito/mucho	oon poh-**kee**-toh/ **moo**-choh
More/less	Más/menos	mahss/**men**-ohss
Enough/too (much)	Suficiente/	soo-fee-see-**en**-teh/
I am ill/sick	Estoy enfermo(a)	es-**toy** en-**fehr**-moh(mah)
Call a doctor	Llame a un medico	**ya**-meh ah oon **med**-ee-koh

English	Spanish	Pronunciation
Help!	Socorro	soh-**koh**-roh
Stop!	Pare	**pah**-reh

DINING OUT

English	Spanish	Pronunciation
I'd like to reserve a table . . .	Quisiera reservar una mesa . . .	kee-**syeh**-rah rreh-sehr-**bahr** oo-nah **meh**-sah . . .
. . . for two people.	para dos personas.	pah-rah dohs pehr-**soh**-nahs
. . . for this evening.	para esta noche.	pah-rah **ehs**-tah **noh**-cheh
. . . for 8 PM	para las ocho de la noche.	pah-rah lahs **oh**-choh deh lah **noh**-cheh
A bottle of . . .	Una botella de . . .	oo-nah bo-**teh**-yah deh
A cup of . . .	Una taza de . . .	oo-nah **tah**-sah deh
A glass of . . .	Un vaso (water, soda, etc.) de...	oon **vah**-so deh
	Una copa (wine, spirits, etc.) de...	oona **coh**-pah deh
Bill/check	La cuenta	lah **kwen**-tah
Bread	El pan	el pahn
Breakfast	El desayuno	el deh-sah-**yoon**-oh
Butter	La mantequilla	lah man-teh-**kee**-yah
Coffee	Café	kah-**feh**
Dinner	La cena	lah **seh**-nah
Fork	El tenedor	el ten-eh-**dor**
I don't eat meat	No como carne	noh koh-moh **kahr**-neh
I cannot eat . . .	No puedo comer . . .	noh **pweh**-doh koh-**mehr**
I'd like to order . . .	Quiero pedir . . .	**kee**-yehr-oh peh-**deer**
I'd like . . .	Me gustaría . . .	Meh goo-stah-**ee**-ah
I'm hungry/thirsty	Tengo hambre/sed	**Tehn**-goh **hahm**-breh/seth
Is service/the tip included?	¿Está incluida la propina?	es-**tah** in-cloo-**ee**-dah lah pro-**pee**-nah
Knife	El cuchillo	el koo-**chee**-yo
Lunch	La comida	lah koh-**mee**-dah
Menu	La carta, el menú	lah **cart**-ah, el meh-**noo**
Napkin	La servilleta	lah sehr-vee-**yet**-ah
Pepper	La pimienta	lah pee-mee-**en**-tah
Plate	plato	**plato**
Please give me . . .	Por favor déme . . .	pore fah-**vor** **deh**-meh
Salt	La sal	lah sahl
Spoon	Una cuchara	oo-nah koo-**chah**-rah
Sugar	El azucar	el ah-**su**-kar
Tea	té	teh
Water	agua	**ah**-gwah
Wine	vino	**vee**-noh

Contacts

Air

Aeroport de Girona–Costa Brava. (*GRO*). ✉ *17185 Vilobi de Onyar*, ☎ *9102/321–1000 general info on Spanish airports* ⊕ *www.aena.es*. **Aeropuerto de Madrid (Adolfo Suárez Madrid-Barajas).** (*MAD*). ✉ *Av. de la Hispanidad s/n*, ☎ *91/321–1000 general info on Spanish airports* ⊕ *www.aeropuertomadrid-barajas.com/eng*. **Aeropuerto de Reus.** (*REU*). ✉ *Autovía Tarragona–Reus*, ☎ *9/321–1000 general info on Spanish airports* ⊕ *www.aena.es/en/reus-airport/reus.html*. **Aeropuerto Internacional de Bilbao.** (*BIO*). ✉ *Loiu 48180*, ☎ *902/404704 general info on Spanish airports* ⊕ *www.aeropuertodebilbao.net/en*. **Barcelona El Prat de Llobregat.** (*BCN*). ✉ *C–32B s/n* ☎ *902/404704 general info on Spanish airports* ⊕ *www.aena.es/en/barcelona-airport/index.html*.

Bus

ALSA. ✉ *Carrer de Virat s/n*, ☎ *902/2422242* ⊕ *www.alsa.es*. **Estació de Sants.** ✉ *Pl. dels Països Catalans s/n, Les Corts* ☎ *912/243–2343* Ⓜ *L3/L5 Sants Estació*. **Estació del Nord.** ✉ *Carrer d'Ali Bei 80,*

Eixample ☎ *902/706–5366* ⊕ *www.barcelonanord.com*. **Grup Sarbus.** ✉ *Estació d'Autobusos Barcelona-Nord, Carrer d' Alí Bei 80, Eixample* ☎ *902/02302025 Sarfa, 9/35806700 Sarbus* ⊕ *www.moventis.es* Ⓜ *L1 Arc de Triomf*. **Julià Travel.** ✉ *Carrer Balmes 5, Eixample* ☎ *93/3317–6454* ⊕ *www.juliatravel.com*.

Metro

Transports Metropolitans de Barcelona. (*TMB*). ✉ *Carrer 60, 21–23* ☎ *93/298–7000* ⊕ *www.tmb.cat/en/home*.

Taxi

Barna Taxi. ✉ *Calle Marina 82* ☎ *93/357–7755, 93/322–2222* ⊕ *www.barnataxi.com*. **Radio Taxi.** ✉ *Carrer del Cánem 71* ☎ *93/303–3033* ⊕ *radiotaxi033.com*. **Taxi Class Rent.** ✉ *Calle Espronceda 43, bajos* ☎ *93/307–0707* ⊕ *www.taxiclassrent.com/en*.

🚆 Train

Estació de França. ✉ *Av. Marquès de l'Argentera 1, Born-Ribera* Ⓜ *Barceloneta (Metro L4)*. **Estació de Passeig de Gràcia.** ✉ *Passeig de Gràcia/Carrer Aragó,*

Eixample ☎ *912/343–2343 station info* ⊕ *www.adif.es/en* Ⓜ *L2/L3/L4 Passeig de Gràcia*. **Estació de Sants.** ✉ *Pl. dels Països Catalans s/n, Les Corts* ☎ *912/243–2343* Ⓜ *L3/L5 Sants Estació*. **Ferrocarrils de la Generalitat de Catalunya (FGC).** ✉ *Carrer Vergos 44, Sarrià* ☎ *93/3366–3000* ⊕ *www.fgc.cat/en* Ⓜ *Sarrià (FGC)*. **RENFE.** ✉ *Av. de la Ciudad de Barcelona 8, Madrid* ☎ *9/210–9420 for tickets, 912/232–0320 general information* ⊕ *www.renfe.com*.

📍 Visitor Information

Plaça Sant Jaume. ✉ *Carrer de la Ciutat 2, Ajuntament de Barcelona, Barri Gòtic* ☎ *93/285–3834* ⊕ *www.barcelonaturisme.com* Ⓜ *L3 Liceu, L4 Jaume I*. **Sants Estació.** ✉ *Pl. dels Països Catalans s/n, Eixample* ☎ *93/285–3823* ⊕ *www.barcelonaturisme.com* Ⓜ *Sants Estació (Metro L3/L5)*. **Servei d'Informació Cultural–Palau de la Virreina.** (*Tiquet Rambles*). ✉ *Rambla 99, La Rambla* ☎ *93/316–1000, 93/316–1111* ⊕ *lameva.barcelona.cat/tiquetrambles* Ⓜ *Pl. Catalunya, Liceu (Metro L3)*.

Chapter 3

LA RAMBLA

3

Updated by
Megan Eileen McDonough

👁 **Sights**
★★★★★

🍴 **Restaurants**
★★★☆☆

🛏 **Hotels**
★★★★☆

🛍 **Shopping**
★★★☆☆

🍸 **Nightlife**
★★★★☆

NEIGHBORHOOD SNAPSHOT

TOP EXPERIENCES

■ **La Boqueria:** Wander and graze the stalls of this glass-and-steel market hall, packed with culinary riches.

■ **Gran Teatre del Liceu:** Plan to take in an opera at one of Europe's leading opera houses or at least take a tour of its spectacular rooms and halls.

■ **Palau Güell:** This extraordinary Gothic mansion, built for Gaudí's wealthy patron, is a magnificent example of the architect's imagination.

■ **Strolling La Rambla:** A stroll here, with thousands of visitors from around the world, is sensory overload, and should be experienced both in the early morning and late at night.

■ **Carrer Petitxol:** Enjoy a hot chocolate and pastry on one of Barcelona's most charming streets.

GETTING HERE

The Plaça de Catalunya metro stop will put you at the head of La Rambla in front of the Café Zurich, Barcelona's most famous rendezvous point. From here it's just a few steps down to the fountain on the right side of La Rambla de Canaletes.

PLANNING YOUR TIME

Allow three to four hours, including stops, for exploring La Rambla. The best times to find things open are between 9 am and 2 pm and 4 pm and 8 pm, although this popular promenade has a life of its own 24 hours a day. Not all museums remain open through the lunch hour—go online or ask at your nearest tourist information office to check. Most church hours are 9 am to 1:30 pm and 4:30 pm to 8 pm.

FUN FACTS: MOORISH INFLUENCES

Hundreds of years ago, the Moors—the Arab and Berber Muslims of the time—conquered present-day Spain. As a result, the two cultures share many common elements. For instance, "Rambla" comes from the Arabic word, *ramla*, which means "sand," a reference to the sandy riverbed that was on the site of Barcelona's iconic promenade.

■ **Architecture.** Barcelona showcases architecture with Arabic influence, but you'll find even stronger examples in Andalucía in the south, most notably the Alhambra in Granada, the Giralda in Sevilla, and Cordoba's Mosque.

■ **Food.** You can't visit Spain without indulging in paella, a famous dish meant to share. Its two key components, rice and spices, are both attributed to the Moors, who also introduced Spain to almonds, sugar cane, and eggplant.

■ **Music.** Muslim influence brought new instruments and melodies, such as the guitar and flamenco. Hence, traditional Spanish music has hints of northern African sounds and rhythm.

The poet-playwright Federico García Lorca noted that La Rambla was the only street in the world he wished would never end—and, in a sense, it doesn't. The promenade in the heart of pre-modern Barcelona was originally an *arroyo* (watercourse) that separated the walled Ciutat Vella from the Raval and was dry for most of the year. In the 14th century, the city walls were extended, and the arroyo was filled in, gradually becoming a thoroughfare where peddlers, farmers, and tradesmen hawked their wares.

The arroyo is still under the pavement, and, occasionally, a torrential rain fills it, pushing water up through the drains. Most of the time, however, it's a river of humanity that flows along La Rambla, where mimes, acrobats, jugglers, musicians, puppeteers, portrait artists, break dancers, rappers, and rockers compete for the crowd's attention.

Couples sit at café tables no bigger than tea trays as nimble-footed waiters dodge traffic while bringing food and drink from kitchens. With the din of taxis and motorbikes in the traffic lanes on either side of the promenade, the revelers and rubberneckers, and the Babel of languages, the scene is as animated at 3 am as it is at 3 pm.

Much as you might want to avoid the crush of visitors, and the touristy shops and eateries that cater to them, a stroll along the pedestrian strip down the middle of the city's most famous boulevard is essential to your Barcelona experience. There are many gems along this spinal column of street life—from Café Zurich, a rendezvous point at the head of La Rambla, to the produce market of La Boqueria to the Liceu opera house and La Rambla's lower reaches.

 Sights

Carrer dels Escudellers

STREET | Named for the *terrissaires* (earthenware potters) who worked here making *escudellas* (bowls or stew pots), this colorful loop is an interesting subtrip off La Rambla. Go left at Plaça del Teatre and you'll pass the landmark Grill Room at No. 8, an Art Nouveau saloon with graceful wooden decor and an ornate oak bar; next is La Fonda Escudellers,

Visit La Boqueria market early (it opens at 8 am) to avoid the crowds as you discover all this colorful institution has to offer.

another lovely, glass- and stone-encased dining emporium. (Alas, the food is not especially good at either.)

At Nos. 23–25 is Barcelona's most comprehensive ceramics display, Art Escudellers. Farther down, on the right, is Los Caracoles, once among the most traditional of Barcelona's restaurants and now mainly the choice of tourists with deep pockets. Still, the bar and the walk-through kitchen on the way in are picturesque, as are the dining rooms and the warren of little stairways between them. Another 100 yards down Carrer Escudellers is Plaça George Orwell, named for the author of *Homage to Catalonia,* a space created to bring light and air into this somewhat sketchy neighborhood. The little flea market that hums along on Saturday is a great place to browse.

Take a right on the narrow Carrer de la Carabassa—a street best known in days past for its houses of ill fame, and one of the few remaining streets in the city still entirely paved with cobblestones. It is arched over with two graceful bridges that once connected the houses with their adjacent gardens. At the end of the street, looming atop her own basilica, is Nostra Senyora de la Mercè (Our Lady of Mercy). This giant representation of Barcelona's patron saint is a 20th-century (1940) addition to the 18th-century Església de la Mercè; the view of La Mercè gleaming in the sunlight, babe in arms, is one of the Barcelona waterfront's most impressive sights.

As you arrive at Carrer Ample, note the 15th-century door with a winged Sant Miquel Archangel delivering a backhand blow to a scaly Lucifer. It's from the Sant Miquel church, formerly part of City Hall, torn down in the early 19th century. From the Mercè, a walk out Carrer Ample (to the right) leads back to the bottom of La Rambla. ⊠ *Carrer dels Escudellers, Barcelona* Ⓜ *Drassanes.*

Carrer Petritxol

STREET | Just steps from La Rambla, Carrer Petritxol is one of Barcelona's most popular streets. Lined with art galleries, *xocolaterías* (chocolate shops), and stationers, this narrow passageway dates from the 15th century, when it was used as a shortcut through the backyard of a local property owner.

Working up Petritxol from Plaça del Pi, stop to admire the late-17th-century sgraffito design (mural ornamentation made by scratching away a plaster surface), some of the city's best, on the facade over the Ganiveteria Roca knife store, *the* place for cutlery in Barcelona. Next on the right, at Petritxol 2 is the 200-year-old Dulcinea, with a portrait of the great Catalan playwright Àngel Guimerà (1847–1924) over the fireplace. Drop in for the house specialty, the *suizo* ("Swiss" hot chocolate and whipped cream).

Note the plaque to Àngel Guimerà over No. 4 and Sala Parès at No. 5, founded in 1840, the dean of Barcelona's art galleries, where major figures like Isidre Nonell, Santiago Rusiñol, and Picasso have shown their work, and its affiliated Galeria Trama, which shows more contemporary work. Look carefully at the "curtains" carved into the wooden door at No. 11 and the floral ornamentation around the edges of the ceiling inside; the store is Granja la Pallaresa, yet another enclave of chocolate and *ensaimada* (a light-looking but deadly sweet Mallorcan pastry, with confectioner's sugar dusted on top). ⊠ *Carrer Petrixol, Barcelona* Ⓜ *Liceu, Catalunya.*

Casa Bruno Cuadros

NOTABLE BUILDING | Like something out of an amusement park, this former umbrella shop was whimsically designed (assembled is more like it) by Josep Vilaseca in 1885. A Chinese dragon with a parasol, Egyptian balconies and galleries, and a Peking lantern all reflect the Eastern style that was very much in vogue at the time of the Universal Exposition of 1888. Now housing a branch office of the Banco Bilbao Vizcaya Artentaria (BBVA), this prankster of a building is much in keeping with Art Nouveau's eclectic playfulness, though it has never been taken very

seriously as an expression of Modernisme and is generally omitted from most studies of Art Nouveau architecture. ⊠ *La Rambla 82, La Rambla* Ⓜ *Liceu.*

Església de Betlem

CHURCH | The Church of Bethlehem is one of Barcelona's few baroque buildings, and hulks stodgily on La Rambla just above Rambla de les Flors. Burned out completely at the start of the Civil War in 1936, the church is unremarkable inside; the outside, spruced up, is made of what looks like quilted stone. If you find this less than a must-see, worry not: you have all of Barcelona for company, with the possible exception of Betlem's parishioners. This was where Viceroy Amat claimed the hand of the young virreina-to-be when in 1780 she was left in the lurch by the viceroy's nephew. In a sense, Betlem has compensated the city with the half century of good works the young widow was able to accomplish with her husband's fortune. ⊠ *Carme 2, La Rambla* ☎ *93/318–3823* Ⓜ *Catalunya.*

Font de Canaletes

FOUNTAIN | This fountain is a key spot in Barcelona, the place where all great *futbol* victories are celebrated by jubilant (and often unruly) Barça fans. It was originally known for the best water in Barcelona, brought in by *canaletes* (small canals) from the mountains. The bronze plaque on the pavement in front of the fountain explains in Catalan that if you drink from these waters, you will fall under Barcelona's spell and are destined to return. ⊠ *Rambla de Canaletes s/n, La Rambla* Ⓜ *Catalunya.*

★ Gran Teatre del Liceu

NOTABLE BUILDING | Barcelona's opera house has long been considered one of the most beautiful in Europe, a rival to La Scala in Milan. First built in 1848, this cherished cultural landmark was torched in 1861, later bombed by anarchists in 1893, and once again gutted by an accidental fire in early 1994. During that most recent fire, Barcelona's soprano

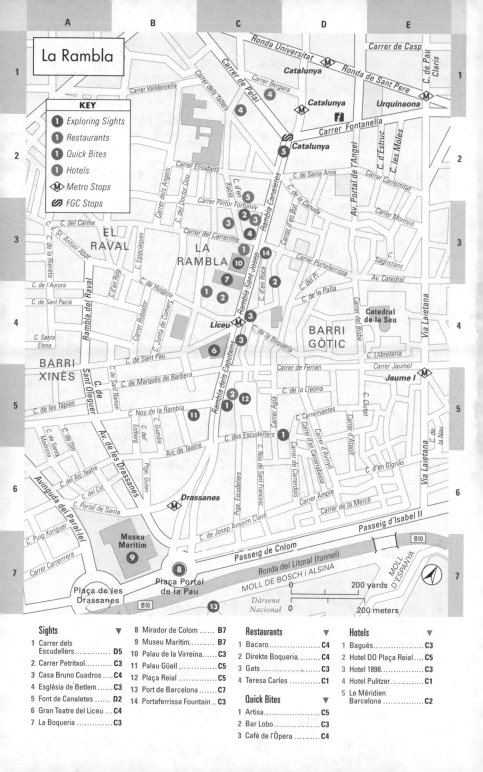

La Rambla

KEY

- 1 Exploring Sights
- 1 Restaurants
- 1 Quick Bites
- 1 Hotels
- Ⓜ Metro Stops
- FGC Stops

EL RAVAL

LA RAMBLA

BARRI XINÈS

BARRI GÒTIC

Catedral de la Seu

Museu Marítim

Drassanes

Plaça de les Drassanes

Plaça Portal de la Pau

Passeig de Colom

Ronda del Litoral (tunnel)

MOLL DE BOSCH i ALSINA

Dàrsena Nacional

MOLL D'ESPANYA

Passeig d'Isabel II

0   200 yards

0   200 meters

Montserrat Caballé stood on La Rambla in tears as her beloved venue was consumed. Five years later, a restored Liceu, equipped for modern productions, opened anew. Some of the Liceu's most spectacular halls and rooms, including the glittering foyer known as the Saló dels Miralls (Room of Mirrors), were untouched by the fire of 1994, as were those of Spain's oldest social club, El Círculo del Liceu—established in 1847 and restored to its pristine original condition after the fire. ⊠ La Rambla 51–59, La Rambla ☎ 93/485–9931 premium visit reservations ⊕ www.liceubarcelona.cat Ⓜ Liceu.

★ **La Boqueria**

MARKET | Barcelona's most spectacular food market, also known as the Mercat de Sant Josep, is an explosion of life and color. As you turn in from La Rambla, you're greeted by bar-restaurants serving tapas at counters and stall after stall selling fruit, herbs, veggies, nuts, candied preserves, cheese, ham, fish, poultry, and other types of provender. Although you can avoid the worst of the crowds by browsing before 8 am and after 5 pm, most of the time, you'll have to wade through throngs of both locals and visitors. Indeed, the market has become so popular, that tourist groups of 15 people or more are banned from entering between 8 am to 3 pm Monday through Saturday.

Under a Moderniste hangar of wrought-iron girders and stained glass, the market occupies a Neoclassical square built in 1840, after the original Sant Josep convent was torn down, by architect Francesc Daniel Molina. The Ionic columns around the edges of the market were part of the mid-19th-century square, uncovered in 2001 after more than a century of neglect.

Highlights include the sunny greengrocers' market outside (to the right if you enter from La Rambla), along with Pinotxo (Pinocchio), just inside to the

right, where owner Juanito Bayén and his family serve some of the best food in Barcelona. The secret? "Fresh, fast, hot, salty, and garlicky." If it's too crowded to find a seat, the Kiosko Universal, over toward the port side of the market, and Quim de la Boqueria, both offer delicious alternatives. Don't miss the *fruits del bosc* (fruits of the forest) specialty stand at the back of the market, with its display of wild mushrooms, herbs, nuts, and berries. ⊠ La Rambla 91, La Rambla ☎ 93/413–2345 market telephone, 93/304–0270 The Traders Association telephone ⊕ www.boqueria.info ⊗ Closed Sun. Ⓜ Liceu.

Mirador de Colom (*Columbus Monument*)

VIEWPOINT | This Barcelona landmark to Christopher Columbus sits grandly at the foot of La Rambla along the wide harbor-front promenade of Passeig de Colom, not far from the very shipyards (Drassanes Reials) that constructed two of the ships of his tiny but immortal fleet. Standing atop the 150-foot-high iron column—the base of which is aswirl with gesticulating angels—Columbus seems to be looking out at "that far-distant shore" he discovered; in fact he's pointing, with his 18-inch-long finger, in the general direction of Sicily.

The monument was erected for the 1888 Universal Exposition to commemorate the commissioning of Columbus's voyage in Barcelona by the monarchs Ferdinand and Isabella, in 1491. Since the royal court was at that time itinerant (and remained so until 1561), Barcelona's role in the discovery of the New World is at best circumstantial. In fact, Barcelona was consequently excluded from trade with the Americas by Isabella, so Catalonia and Columbus have never really seen eye to eye. For a bird's-eye view of La Rambla and the port, take the elevator to the small viewing platform (*mirador*) at the top of the column (open daily from 8:30 am to 8:30 pm). The entrance is on the harbor side. ⊠ Pl. Portal de la

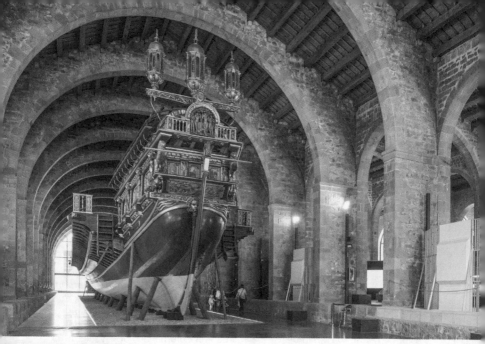

A shipshape collection of nautical wonders is on display at the Museu Marítim.

Pau s/n, Port Olímpic ☎ *93/285–3834* 🖃 *€6* ☞ *Last elevator ride is at 8 pm* Ⓜ *Drassanes.*

★ Museu Marítim

HISTORY MUSEUM | FAMILY | This superb museum is housed in the 13th-century Drassanes Reials (Royal Shipyards), at the foot of La Rambla adjacent to the harborfront. This vast covered complex launched the ships of Catalonia's powerful Mediterranean fleet directly from its yards into the port (the water once reached the level of the eastern facade of the building). Today, these are the world's largest and best-preserved medieval shipyards. Centuries ago, at a time when the region around Athens was a province of the House of Aragón (1311–90), they were of crucial importance to the sea power of Catalonia (then the heavyweight in an alliance with Aragón).

On the Avinguda del Paral·lel side of Drassanes is a completely intact section of the 14th- to 15th-century walls—Barcelona's third and final ramparts—that encircled El Raval along the Paral·lel and the Rondas de Sant Pau, Sant Antoni, and Universitat. (*Ronda,* the term used for the "rounds," or patrols soldiers made atop the defensive walls, became the name for the avenues that replaced them.)

The Museu Marítim is filled with vessels, including a spectacular collection of ship models. The life-size reconstruction of the galley of Juan de Austria, commander of the Spanish fleet in the Battle of Lepanto, is perhaps the most impressive display in the museum. Figureheads, nautical gear, early navigational charts, and medieval nautical lore enhance the experience, and headphones and infrared pointers provide a first-rate self-guided tour.

Concerts are occasionally held in this acoustic gem. The cafeteria-restaurant Norai, open daily 9 am to 8 pm, offers dining in a setting of medieval elegance, and has a charming terrace. Admission to the museum includes a visit to the schooner *Santa Eulàlia,* a meticulously restored clipper built in 1918, which is moored nearby at the Port Vell. 🖃 *Av. de*

les Drassanes s/n, La Rambla ☎ 93/342–
9920 ⊕ www.mmb.cat/en ◱ €10
(includes admission to Santa Eulàlia
clipper); free Sun. after 3 ☻ Santa Eulàlia
closed Mon. Ⓜ Drassanes.

Palau de la Virreina

ART GALLERY | This beautiful edifice right
on the bustling Rambla is an important
Barcelona art hub, resource, and outpost
of the Institut de Cultura, with photography on display at the Espai Xavier
Miserachs, temporary exhibits on the
patio, and cultural events held regularly
in the space. ✉ La Rambla 99, La Rambla
☎ 93/316–1000 ⊕ ajuntament.barcelona.
cat/lavirreina/en ◱ Free ☻ Closed Mon.
Ⓜ Catalunya, Liceu.

★ Palau Güell

HISTORIC HOME | Gaudí built this mansion
in 1886–90 for textile baron Count Eusebi
de Güell Bacigalupi, his most important
patron. (The prominent four bars of the
senyera, the banner of Catalunya, on the
facade between the parabolic arches
of the entrance attest to the nationalist
fervor the two men shared.) Gaudí's
principal obsession in this project was to
find a way to illuminate this seven-sto-
ry house, hemmed in as it is by other
buildings in the cramped quarters of El
Raval. The dark facade is a dramatic foil
for the brilliance of the inside, where
spear-shape Art Nouveau columns frame
the windows, rising to support a series
of detailed and elaborately carved wood
ceilings.

The basement stables are famous for the
"fungiform" (mushroom-like) columns
carrying the weight of the whole building.
Note Gaudí's signature parabolic arches
between the columns and the way the
arches meet overhead, forming a canopy
of palm fronds. (The beauty of the construction was probably little consolation
to the political prisoners held here during
the 1936–39 Civil War.) The patio where
the horses were groomed receives light
through a skylight, one of many devices
Gaudí used to brighten the space. Don't

miss the figures of the faithful hounds,
with the rings in their mouths for hitching
horses, or the wooden bricks laid down
in lieu of cobblestones in the entryway
upstairs and on the ramp down to the
basement grooming area, to deaden the
sound of horses' hooves.

Upstairs are three successive receiving
rooms; the wooden ceilings are progres-
sively more spectacular in the complexity
of their richly molded floral motifs. The
room farthest in has a jalousie in the balcony: a double grate through which Güell
was able to observe—and eavesdrop
on—his arriving guests. The main hall,
with the three-story-tall tower reaching
up above the roof, was for parties, dances, and receptions. Musicians played
from the balcony; the overhead balcony
window was for the principal singer. Double doors enclose a chapel of hammered
copper with retractable prie-dieu; around
the corner is a small organ, the flutes in
rectangular tubes climbing the central
shaft of the building.

The dining room is dominated by a beautiful mahogany banquet table seating 10,
an Art Nouveau fireplace in the shape
of a deeply curving horseshoe arch, and
walls with floral and animal motifs. From
the outside rear terrace, the polished
Garraf marble of the main part of the
house is exposed; the brick servants'
quarters are on the left. The passageway
built toward La Rambla was all that came
of a plan to buy an intervening property and connect three houses into one
grand structure, a scheme that never
materialized.

Gaudí is most himself on the roof, where
his playful, polychrome ceramic chimneys seem like preludes to later works
like the Park Güell and La Pedrera. Look
for the flying-bat weather vane over the
main chimney, a reference to the Catalan
king Jaume I, who brought the house of
Aragón to its 13th-century imperial apo-
gee in the Mediterranean. Jaume I's affinity for bats is said to have stemmed from

his Mallorca campaign, when, according to one version, he was awakened by a fluttering *rat penat* (literally, "condemned mouse") in time to stave off a Moorish night attack. ⊠ *Nou de la Rambla 3–5, La Rambla* ☎ *93/472–5775,* ⊕ *www.palau-guell.cat/en* 🖾 *€12 (€9 for students); free 1st Sun. of month for tickets purchased online* ☉ *Closed Mon.* ☞ *Guided tours (1 hr) in English Sat. at 10:30 am at no additional cost* Ⓜ *Drassanes, Liceu.*

★ Plaça Reial

PLAZA/SQUARE | Nobel Prize–winning novelist Gabriel García Márquez, architect and urban planner Oriol Bohigas, and Pasqual Maragall, former president of the Catalonian Generalitat, are among the many famous people said to have acquired apartments overlooking this elegant square, a chiaroscuro masterpiece in which neoclassical symmetry clashes with big-city street funk. Plaça Reial is bordered by stately ocher facades with balconies overlooking the wrought-iron Fountain of the Three Graces, and an array of lampposts designed by Gaudí in 1879. Cafés and restaurants line the square. Plaça Reial is most colorful on Sunday morning, when collectors gather to trade stamps and coins; after dark it's a center of downtown nightlife for the jazz-minded, the young, and the adventurous (it's best to be streetwise touring this area in the late hours). ⊠ *Plaça Reial, La Rambla* Ⓜ *Liceu.*

Port de Barcelona

MARINA/PIER | Beyond the Columbus monument—behind the ornate Duana (now the Barcelona Port Authority headquarters)—is La Rambla de Mar, a boardwalk with a drawbridge designed to allow boats into and out of the inner harbor. La Rambla de Mar extends out to the Moll d'Espanya, with its ultra-touristy Maremagnum shopping center (open on Sunday, unusual for Barcelona) and the excellent Aquàrium. Next to the Duana you can board a Golondrina boat for a tour of the port and the waterfront

or, from the Moll de Barcelona on the right, take a cable car to Montjuïc or Barceloneta. Trasmediterránea and Baleària passenger ferries leave for Italy and the Balearic Islands from the Moll de Barcelona; at the end of the quay is Barcelona's World Trade Center and the Eurostars Grand Marina Hotel. ⊠ *Port Olímpic* Ⓜ *Drassanes.*

Portaferrissa Fountain

FOUNTAIN | Both the fountain and the ceramic representation of Barcelona's second set of walls and the early Rambla are worth studying carefully. If you can imagine pulling out the left side of the ceramic scene and looking broadside at the amber yellow 13th-century walls that ran down this side of the Rambla, you will see a clear picture of what this spot looked like in medieval times. The sandy Rambla ran along outside the walls, while the portal looked down through the ramparts into the city. As the inscription on the fountain explains, the Porta Ferrica, or Iron Door, was named for the iron measuring stick attached to the wood and used in the 13th and 14th centuries to establish a unified standard for measuring goods. The fountain itself dates to 1680; the ceramic tiles are 20th century. ⊠ *Portaferrissa 2, La Rambla* Ⓜ *Liceu, Catalunya.*

🍴 Restaurants

Bacaro

$$ | ITALIAN | Tucked away in a quiet street off the Rambla, this cozy, rustic-chic Italian spot specializes in "cicchetti," which are sort of like Venetian tapas, so you can taste a number of things. There's plenty of wine, too; after all, "bacaro" means "wine bar" in Venetian. **Known for:** cozy atmosphere; good desserts; nice selection of Italian wines. $ *Average main: €18* ⊠ *Jerusalem 6, La Rambla* ☎ *93/115–6679* ⊕ *www.bacarobarcelona. com* ☉ *Closed Sun.* Ⓜ *Liceu.*

Barcelona's Lovers' Day

One of the best days to spend in Barcelona is April 23: St. George's Day, La Diada de Sant Jordi, Barcelona's "Valentine's Day." A day so sweet and playful, so goofy and romantic, that the whole of Catalonia goes giddy from dawn to dusk.

Legend has it that the patron saint of Catalonia, the knight-errant St. George (Sant Jordi in Catalan) slew a dragon that was about to devour a beautiful princess in the little village of Montblanc, south of Barcelona. From the dragon's blood sprouted a rosebush, from which the hero plucked the prettiest blossom for the princess. Hence the traditional Rose Festival celebrated in Barcelona since the Middle Ages, to honor chivalry and romantic love, and a day for men to present their true loves with roses. In 1923 the festival merged with International Book Day to mark the anniversary of the all-but-simulta-neous deaths of Miguel de Cervantes and William Shakespeare, on April 23, 1616; it then became the custom for the ladies to present their flower-bearing swains with a book in return.

Close to 7 million roses and close to 20 million euros worth of books (reportedly more than the rest of the year combined) are sold in Catalonia on Sant Jordi's Day. In Barcelona, bookstalls run the length of nearly every major thoroughfare, and although it's an official workday, nearly everybody manages to duck out for at least a while and go browsing. There is a 24-hour reading of *Don Quixote*. Authors come to bookstalls to sign their works. Given Barcelona's importance as a publishing capital, the literary side of the holiday gets special attention.

A Roman soldier martyred for his Christian beliefs in the 4th century, St. George is venerated as the patron saint of 15 European countries—England, Greece, and Romania among them. Images of St. George are everywhere in Barcelona—most notably, perhaps, on the facade of the Catalonian seat of government, the Generalitat. Art Nouveau sculptor Eusebi Arnau depicted Sant Jordi skewering the unlucky dragon on the facade of the Casa Amatller, and on the corner of Els Quatre Gats café. Gaudí referenced the story with an entire building, the Casa Batlló, with the saint's cross implanted on the scaly roof and the skulls and bones of the dragon's victims framing the windows.

Sant Jordi's Day roses are tied with a spike of wheat (for his association with springtime and fertility) and a little red and yellow *senyera*, the Catalonian flag.

In Sarrià there are displays of 45 varieties of rose, representing 45 different kinds of love, from impos-sible to unrequited, from platonic to filial and maternal. In the Plaça Sant Jaume the Generalitat, its patio filled with roses, opens its doors to the public. Choral groups sing love songs in the Barri Gòtic; jazz combos play in Plaça del Pi. La Rambla is packed solid from the Diagonal to the Mediter-ranean, with barcelonins basking in the warmth of spring and romance. Rare is the woman anywhere in town without a rose in hand, bound with a red-and-yellow ribbon that says "*t'estimo*": I love you.

Direkte Boqueria

$$$$ | CATALAN | Local gourmands pilgrimage to this tiny, unassuming-looking bar on the edge of the famous Boquería market, where Catalan chef Arnau Muñío flexes his culinary chops in full view of the diners at his chef's-table-style counter. There are two tasting menus, one long, one short, both of which showcase Muñío's unique approach to Catalan-Asian fusion food. **Known for:** need to book ahead; Asian-Catalan fusion; accessible fine dining. $ *Average main: €54* ✉ *Cabres 13, La Rambla* ☏ *93/114–6939* ⊕ *www.direkte.cat* ☉ *Closed Sun.* Ⓜ *Liceu.*

Gats

$$ | TAPAS | In a quiet square just off of La Rambla, you could easily pass by Gats without being lured inside, but that would be a mistake if you're looking for a casual spot for seasonal tapas. Expect to see some familiar staples, such as jamón ibérico, pan con tomato, and padrón peppers, along with more unexpected flavor combinations. **Known for:** modern, minimalist interior; good burger; small but nice wine list. $ *Average main: €16* ✉ *Xuclà 7, La Rambla* ☏ *93/144–0044* ⊕ *www.encompaniadelobos.com/gats* Ⓜ *Liceu.*

★ Teresa Carles

$$ | VEGETARIAN | Inspired by her Catalan roots, Teresa Carles Borrás has been creating inventive vegetarian fare for 40 years and counting but this namesake was her first restaurant. Both the space and the food are more sophisticated than the typical vegetarian restaurant. **Known for:** also runs Flax & Kale outlets around the city; sophisticated atmosphere for vegetarian food; great juices too. $ *Average main: €16* ✉ *Jovellanos 2, La Rambla* ☏ *93/317–1829* ⊕ *www.teresacarles.com* Ⓜ *Universitat.*

☕ Coffee and Quick Bites

Artisa

$ | CAFÉ | FAMILY | Started by two sisters, Marisol and Sofía, Artisa is a one-stop-shop for coffee, cakes, juices, and sandwiches, with a few outdoor and indoor tables. It's the perfect place for a light bite or a snack while sight-seeing. **Known for:** cozy inside; everything is house-made or sourced from local artisan providers; good coffee. $ *Average main: €8* ✉ *Colom 2, La Rambla* ☏ *65/887–9817* ⊕ *artisa.es/en* Ⓜ *Liceu.*

Bar Lobo

$ | TAPAS | Despite its location just off La Rambla, Bar Lobo's outdoor terrace overlooks a charming and usually quiet square, plus it's open for breakfast, lunch, and dinner. The menu covers all the bases: coffee, juice, wine, cocktails, traditional Catalan and Spanish tapas, and Western mains. **Known for:** busy brunch; great terrace; casual tapas. $ *Average main: €14* ✉ *Pintor Fortuny 3, La Rambla* ☏ *93/481–5346* ⊕ *grupotragaluz.com/restaurante/bar-lobo* Ⓜ *Liceu.*

Cafè de l'Òpera

$ | CAFÉ | Directly across from the Liceu opera house, this high-ceiling Art Nouveau café has welcomed operagoers and performers for more than 100 years. It's a central point on the Rambla tourist traffic pattern, so locals are increasingly hard to find, but the café has hung onto its atmosphere of faded glory nonetheless. **Known for:** late-night hours; good for a drink; Art Nouveau decor. $ *Average main: €14* ✉ *La Rambla 74, La Rambla* ☏ *93/317–7585* ⊕ *www.cafeoperabcn.com* Ⓜ *Liceu.*

Hotels

Bagués

$$$ | HOTEL | The luxury of the Eixample has worked its way down to La Rambla, as this boutique gem (formerly the shop and atelier of the well-known Art Nouveau jeweler of the same name) bears ample witness. **Pros:** steps from the opera house; free entrance to the Egyptian Museum of Barcelona; view of the cathedral and port from the rooftop terrace. **Cons:** street-facing rooms can be noisy; hectic location; rooms a bit small for the price. $ *Rooms from: €220* ⊠ *La Rambla 105, La Rambla* ☎ *93/343–5000* ⊕ *www.hotelbagues.com* ⤶ *31 rooms* ¶⊙¶ *No Meals* Ⓜ *Catalunya, Liceu.*

Hotel DO Plaça Reial

$$$$ | HOTEL | Just at the entrance to the neoclassical Plaça Reial, this charming boutique hotel—with its three separate dining areas—is a find for lovers of food and tasteful design. **Pros:** very central location; 24-hour room service; contactless check-in. **Cons:** street noise discernible in lower rooms; area can get busy; neighborhood can be rowdy at night. $ *Rooms from: €233* ⊠ *Pl. Reial 1, La Rambla* ☎ *61/856–7874* ⊕ *sonder.com* ⤶ *18 rooms* ¶⊙¶ *No Meals* Ⓜ *Liceu.*

Hotel 1898

$$$ | HOTEL | Overlooking La Rambla, this imposing mansion (once the headquarters of the Compañiá General de Tabacos de Filipinas) couldn't be better located for anyone who likes to be right in the thick of things—especially for opera fans, with the Liceu just around the corner. **Pros:** impeccable service; historic spaces plus modern amenities like a spa and roof deck; ideal location for exploring the Barri Gòtic. **Cons:** some street noise from the Rambla in lower rooms; some guests complain about water pressure; subway rumble discernible in lower rooms on the Rambla side. $ *Rooms from: €200* ⊠ *La Rambla 109, La Rambla* ☎ *93/552–9552*

⊕ *www.hotel1898.com* ⤶ *169 rooms* ¶⊙¶ *No Meals* Ⓜ *Catalunya, Liceu.*

Hotel Pulitzer

$$ | HOTEL | Hotel Pulitzer is an oasis of calm and appealingly located for those scouring the area's shops for the latest trends. **Pros:** hidden gem for this area; rooftop is a Barcelona hot spot; good value. **Cons:** some rooms could do with an upgrade; no gym, pool, or spa; crowded part of town. $ *Rooms from: €167* ⊠ *Bergara 8, La Rambla* ☎ *93/481-6767* ⊕ *www.hotelpulitzer.es/en* ⤶ *91 rooms* ¶⊙¶ *No Meals* Ⓜ *Catalunya.*

Le Méridien Barcelona

$$$$ | HOTEL | There's no dearth of hotels along La Rambla in the heart of the city, but few rival the upscale Le Méridien, popular with businesspeople and tourists alike for its suites overlooking the promenade and cozy amenities. **Pros:** central location; Mediterranean suites have large private terraces; soaker tubs in deluxe rooms. **Cons:** slightly sketchy location; rooms small for the price; no pool. $ *Rooms from: €250* ⊠ *La Rambla 111, La Rambla* ☎ *93/318–6200* ⊕ *www.marriott.com/hotels/travel/bcnmd-le-meridien-barcelona* ⤶ *231 rooms* ¶⊙¶ *No Meals* Ⓜ *Catalunya, Liceu.*

ⓨ Nightlife

The liveliest pedestrian promenade in the city bustles with a dizzying array of tourist-baiting shops, eateries, and arched paths to Plaça Reial's euphoric nightlife scene. Casual and unpretentious, the scene erupts nightly with a parade of rambunctious crowds of expats, curious interlopers, and assorted celebrations.

BARS

Boadas

COCKTAIL LOUNGES | Barcelona's oldest cocktail bar opened its doors in 1933 and quickly gained a reputation as the only place to enjoy a genuine mojito. The faithful—who still include a few of the city's luminaries—have been flocking ever since, despite the bar's decidedly lackluster decor. The space has the look and feel of an old-fashioned private club and is still the spot to watch old-school barmen in dapper duds mixing drinks the way tradition dictates. ⊠ *Tallers 1, La Rambla* ☎ *93/318–9592* ⊕ *boadascocktails.com* Ⓜ *Catalunya.*

Jamboree-Jazz and Dance-Club

LIVE MUSIC | This legendary nightspot has hosted some of the world's most influential jazz musicians since its opening in 1960. Decades later, the club continues to offer two nightly shows and remains a notable haven for new generations of jazz and blues aficionados. After the last performance, the spot transforms into a late-night dance club playing soul, hip-hop, and R&B. ⊠ *Pl. Reial 17, La Rambla* ☎ *93/304–1210* ⊕ *www.jamboreejazz. com/en* Ⓜ *Liceu.*

 Performing Arts

THEATER

Teatre Poliorama

THEATER | Originally built as a cinema in the late 1890s, Teatre Poliorama has also been immortalized in George Orwell's *Homage to Catalonia*, where the celebrated author describes it as the site of a shoot-out between opposing sides during the Spanish Civil War. In sharp contrast to its sinister past most of the productions offered focus on lighthearted comedy and musical plays in Spanish or Catalan, as well as flamenco and opera. ⊠ *Rambla del Estudis 115, La Rambla* ☎ *93/317–7599* ⊕ *www.teatrepoliorama. com* Ⓜ *Catalunya.*

Shopping

Although not exactly a shopping mecca— unless you're after a Sagrada Família snow globe from one of the dozens of souvenir shops—La Rambla has a few establishments that make up with convenience what they may lack in style. The

diamond in the rough is La Boqueria, one of the world's great food markets.

ART GALLERIES

Galería Maxó

ART GALLERIES | The popular Argentinian visual artist Maxó Rennella uses his adopted home of Barcelona as his muse and interprets the city using various mediums. There are several Galería Maxó locations sprinkled across downtown but this is the largest, spanning two floors. The 3D collages are especially popular and easily fit in carry-on luggage. ⊠ *Petritxol 18, La Rambla* ☎ *93/516–3792* ⊕ *galeriamaxo.co* Ⓜ *Liceu.*

DEPARTMENT STORES AND MALLS

El Triangle

DEPARTMENT STORE | The Triangle d'Or or Golden Triangle at the top end of the Rambla on Plaça Catalunya is a stylish and popular complex and home for, among other stores, FNAC, where afternoon book presentations and CD launches bring together crowds of literati and music lovers. ⊠ *Pl. Catalunya 1–4 and Pelai 13–39, La Rambla* ☎ *93/318–0108* ⊕ *www.eltriangle.es* Ⓜ *Catalunya.*

Maremàgnum

SHOPPING CENTER | This modern shopping complex sits on an artificial "island" in the harbor and is accessed by Rambla del Mar, a wooden swing bridge. The shops inside are fairly run-of-the-mill, but this mall is one of the few places in Barcelona where you can be sure to shop on Sunday. On the first floor, there's a good food court with fine water views. ⊠ *Moll d'Espanya 5, Port Vell, La Rambla* ☎ *93/225–8100* ⊕ *www.maremagnum. klepierre.es* Ⓜ *Drassanes.*

FOOD

Chök

CHOCOLATE | Catalans are pros when it comes to chocolate and Chök, the Chocolate Kitchen, is a local favorite thanks to their assortment of chocolates as well as their vegan cakes and pastries, all made daily, with natural ingredients. The shop on Carrer Carme is where it all began but the Barcelona-based brand has since added locations throughout the city and elsewhere in Spain. ✉ *Carme 3, La Rambla* ☎ *93/304–2360* ⊕ *www.chok.shop/en* Ⓜ *Liceu.*

Pastelería Escribà

FOOD | Barcelona's wave of creative cake makers owe a lot to Antoni Escribà, a pastry chef who elevated the craft to an art form, especially in the field of chocolate sculptures. His three sons—Cristian, Joan, and Jordi—keep his spirit alive in the Casa Figueras, a jewel box of a shop awash in mosaic murals, curly copper work, and other fanciful Art Nouveau detailing. Tortes, chocolate kisses, and candy rings are just some of the edible treasures here that delight and surprise. A second Escribà shop, which has a café area, is at Gran Vía 546 in the Eixample. ✉ *La Rambla 83, La Rambla* ☎ *93/454–7535* ⊕ *www.escriba.es* Ⓜ *Liceu.*

 ## Activities

SAILING

On any day of the week in Barcelona you can see midday regattas taking place off the Barceloneta beaches or beyond the *rompeolas* (breakwater) on the far side of the port. Believe it or not, Olympic-level sailors are being trained for competition just a stone's throw (or two) from La Rambla.

Reial Club Marítim de Barcelona

SAILING | Barcelona's most exclusive and prestigious yacht club can advise visitors on maritime matters, from where to charter yachts and sailboats to how to sign up for sailing programs. ✉ *Moll d'Espanya s/n, Port Vell* ☎ *93/221–7394* ⊕ *www.maritimbarcelona.org* Ⓜ *Drassanes.*

Chapter 4

THE BARRI GÒTIC

Updated by
Megan Eileen McDonough

👁 **Sights**
★★★★★

🍴 **Restaurants**
★★★★☆

🛏 **Hotels**
★★★☆☆

🛍 **Shopping**
★★★★☆

🍸 **Nightlife**
★★☆☆☆

NEIGHBORHOOD SNAPSHOT

TOP EXPERIENCES

- **Casa de l'Ardiaca:** Take in the 4th-century Roman wall, serene courtyard, and views of La Catedral de Barcelona from this 15th-century building.

- **The Jewish Quarter:** Discover one of Europe's oldest synagogues, secret Jewish baths, and the dark history of Barcelona's Jewish community in the fascinating quarter of El Call.

- **La Catedral de Barcelona:** Don't miss the cathedral's leafy 14th-century cloister with its tropical garden and pool populated by 13 white swans.

- **La Casa Martí–Els Quatre Gats:** Linger over a coffee at this historic café, once the meeting place for Barcelona's bohemians, such as Picasso and Gaudí.

- **Plaça Reial:** Wander the narrow streets off the Gothic Quarter, particularly the less-crowded area between Plaça Reial's square and the seafront.

- **Impromptu Opera:** On most evenings, opera singers gather behind La Catedral to sing classics, making great use of the acoustics.

GETTING HERE

The best way to get to the Barri Gòtic and the cathedral is to start down La Rambla from the Plaça de Catalunya metro stop. Take your first left on Carrer Canuda and walk past Barcelona's Ateneu Barcelonès at No. 6, through Plaça Villa de Madrid and its Roman tombstones, then through Passatge and Carrer Duc de la Victoria and out Carrer Boters (where the boot makers were located in medieval times) to Plaça Nova.

PLANNING YOUR TIME

Exploring the Barri Gòtic should take about three hours, depending on how often you stop and how long you linger. Allow another hour or two for the Museum of the History of the City. Plan to visit before 1:30 or after 4:30, or you'll miss a lot of street life; some churches are closed mid-afternoon as well.

FUN FACTS

While many of Barcelona's most important historical buildings are found in Barri Gòtic, pop culture has also made its mark.

- **Plaça de Sant Felip Neri:** Gothic rock band, Evanescence, shot their black and white music video for "My Immortal" here. If you remember the song, it's pretty fitting.

- **L'Arca Barcelona:** This family-owned vintage store unknowingly (at the time) supplied numerous costumes and props for James Cameron's iconic film, *Titanic*.

- **Plaça Reial:** The Barcelona-born-and-raised Instagram-star extraordinaire @marta__sierra films many of her signature outfit-changing reels right here.

No city in Europe has an ancient quarter to rival Barcelona's Barri Gòtic in terms of both historic atmosphere and the sheer density of monumental buildings. It's a stroller's delight, where you can expect to hear the strains of a flute or a classical guitar from around the next corner. Thronged with sightseers by day, the quarter can be eerily quiet at night, a stone oasis of silence at the eye of the storm.

A labyrinth of medieval buildings, squares, and narrow cobblestone streets, the Barri Gòtic comprises the area around La Catedral de Barcelona, built over Roman ruins you can still visit and filled with the Gothic structures that marked the zenith of Barcelona's power in the 15th century. On certain corners you feel as if you're making a genuine excursion back in time.

The Barri Gòtic rests squarely atop the first Roman settlement. Sometimes referred to as the *rovell d'ou* (the yolk of the egg), this high ground the Romans called Mons Taber coincides almost exactly with the early 1st- to 4th-century fortified town of Barcino. Sights to see here include the Plaça del Rei, the remains of Roman Barcino underground beneath the Museum of the History of the City, the Plaça Sant Jaume and the area around the onetime Roman Forum, the medieval Jewish Quarter, and the ancient Plaça Sant Just.

◉ Sights

Ajuntament de Barcelona
HISTORIC SIGHT | The 15th-century city hall on Plaça Sant Jaume faces the Palau de la Generalitat, with its mid-18th-century neoclassical facade, across the square once occupied by the Roman Forum. The Ajuntament is a rich repository of sculpture and painting by the great Catalan masters, from Marès to Gargallo to Clarà, from Subirachs to Miró and Llimona. Inside is the famous Saló de Cent, from which the Consell de Cent, Europe's oldest democratic parliament, governed Barcelona between 1373 and 1714. The Saló de les Croniques (Hall of Chronicles) is decorated with Josep Maria Sert's immense black-and-burnished-gold murals (1928) depicting the early-14th-century Catalan campaign in Byzantium and Greece under the command of Roger de Flor. The city hall is open to visitors on Sunday, with self-guided visits in English hosted at 10am (reserve online). Virtual 360° tours are available at

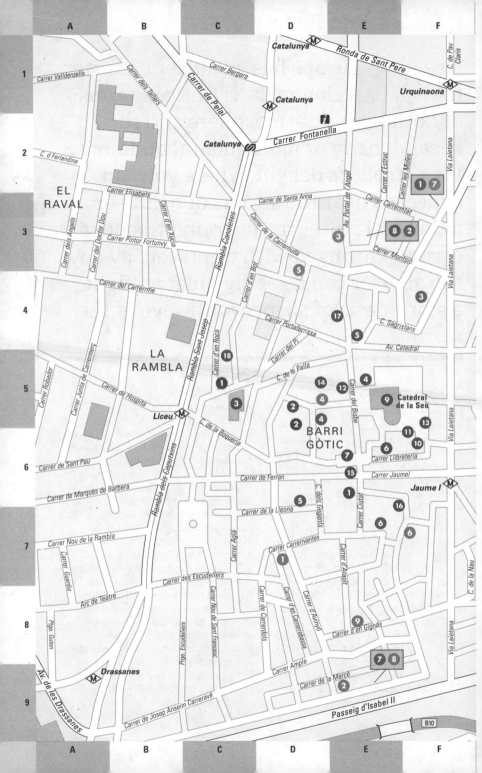

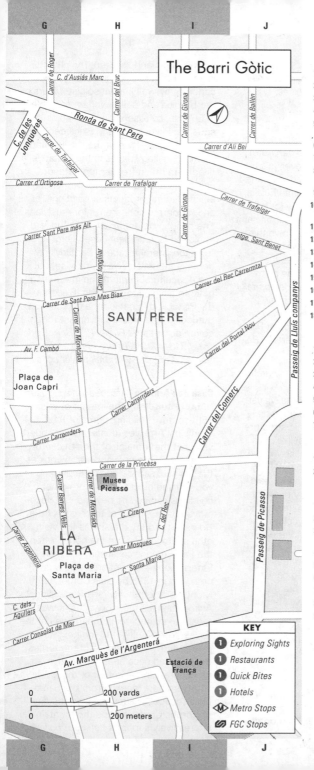

The Barri Gòtic

KEY

1 Exploring Sights
1 Restaurants
1 Quick Bites
1 Hotels
Ⓜ Metro Stops
🅵 FGC Stops

any time. ⊠ *Pl. Sant Jaume 1, Barri Gòtic* ☎ *93/402–7000* ⊕ *ajuntament.barcelona. cat/en* ⬛ *Free* Ⓜ *Jaume I, Liceu.*

Baixada de Santa Eulàlia

RELIGIOUS BUILDING | Down Carrer Sant Sever from the side door of the cathedral cloister, past Carrer Salomó ben Adret and the Església de Sant Sever, is a tiny shrine, in an alcove overhead, dedicated to the 4th-century martyr Santa Eulàlia, former patron saint of the city (before she was replaced by current patron saint Mare de Deu de la Mercè). Down this hill, or *baixada* (descent), Eulàlia was rolled in a barrel filled with—as the Jacint Verdaguer verse in ceramic tile on the wall reads—*glavis i ganivets de dos talls* (swords and double-edged knives), the final of the 13 tortures to which she was subjected before her crucifixion at Plaça del Pedró. ⊠ *Carrer Sant Sever s/n, Barri Gòtic* Ⓜ *Liceu, Jaume I.*

Basílica de Santa Maria del Pi (*Church of St. Mary of the Pine*)

CHURCH | Sister church to Santa Maria del Mar and to Santa Maria de Pedralbes, this early Catalan Gothic structure is perhaps the most fortresslike of all three: hulking, dark, and massive, and perforated only by the main entryway and the mammoth rose window, said to be the world's largest. Try to see the window from inside in the late afternoon to get the best view of the colors. The church was named for the lone *pi* (pine tree) that stood in what was a marshy lowland outside the 4th-century Roman walls. An early church dating back to the 10th century preceded the present Santa Maria del Pi, which was begun in 1319 and finally consecrated in 1453. The interior compares poorly with the clean and lofty lightness of Santa Maria del Mar, but there are two interesting things to see: the original wooden choir loft, and the Ramón Amadeu painting *La Mare de Deu dels Desamparats* (*Our Lady of the Helpless*), in which the artist reportedly used his wife and children as models

for the Virgin and children. The church is a regular venue for classical guitar concerts by well-known soloists. Tours of the basilica and bell tower are available in English, by reservation. The adjoining squares, Plaça del Pi and Plaça de Sant Josep Oriol, are two of the liveliest and most appealing spaces in the Ciutat Vella, filled with much-frequented outdoor cafés and used as a venue for markets selling natural products or paintings, or as an impromptu concert hall for musicians. The handsome entryway and courtyard at No. 4 Plaça de Sant Josep Oriol across from the lateral facade of Santa Maria del Pi is the Palau Fivaller, now seat of the Agricultural Institute, an interesting patio to have a look through. Placeta del Pi, tucked in behind the church, has outdoor tables and is convenient for a coffee or tapas. ⊠ *Pl. del Pi 7, Barri Gòtic* ☎ *93/318–4743* ⊕ *basilicadelpi.cat/en/ home* ⬛ *€5 (€10 with bell tower access)* Ⓜ *Liceu.*

Casa de l'Ardiaca (*Archdeacon's House*)

NOTABLE BUILDING | The interior of this 15th-century building, home of the Municipal Archives (upstairs), has superb views of the remains of the 4th-century Roman watchtowers and walls. Look at the Montjuïc sandstone carefully, and you will see blocks taken from other buildings carved and beveled into decorative shapes, proof of the haste of the Romans to fortify the site as the Visigoths approached from the north, when the Pax Romana collapsed. The marble letter box by the front entrance was designed in 1895 by Lluís Domènech i Montaner for the Lawyer's Professional Association; as the story goes, it was meant to symbolize, in the images of the doves, the lofty flight to the heights of justice and, in the images of the turtles, the plodding pace of administrative procedures. In the center of the lovely courtyard here, across from the Santa Llúcia chapel, is a fountain; on the day of Corpus Christi in June the fountain impressively supports *l'ou com balla,* or "the dancing egg," a Barcelona tradition in which eggs are set to bobbing atop jets of water in various places around the city. ⊠ *Santa Llúcia 1, Barri Gòtic* ☎ *93/256–2255 Barcelona City Archive* ⊕ *ajuntament.barcelona.cat/arxiumunicipal/arxiuhistoric/ca* ☾ *Closed Sun.* Ⓜ *Jaume I, Liceu.*

Col·legi Oficial d'Arquitectes de Catalunya (COAC)

ART MUSEUM | The architectural temporary exhibitions (see the website for details of the program) on the ground floor of the School of Architecture focus on urbanism and notable architects. The design and architecture bookshop in the basement is reason alone to visit. The stick figure frieze on the exterior of the building was designed by Picasso during his exile, and executed by the Norwegian artist Carl Nesjar in 1955. ⊠ *Pl. Nova 5, Barri Gòtic* ☎ *93/301–5000* ⊕ *www.arquitectes.cat* Ⓜ *Liceu, Catalunya.*

Columnes del Temple d'August (*Columns of the Temple of Augustus*)

RUINS | The highest point in Roman Barcelona is marked with a circular millstone at the entrance to the Centre Excursionista de Catalunya, a club dedicated to exploring the mountains and highlands of Catalonia on foot and on skis. Inside the entryway on the right are some of the best-preserved 1st- and 2nd-century Corinthian Roman columns in Europe. Massive, fluted, and crowned with the typical Corinthian acanthus leaves in two distinct rows under eight fluted sheaths, these columns remain only because Barcelona's early Christians elected, atypically, not to build their cathedral over the site of the previous temple. The Temple of Augustus, dedicated to the Roman emperor, occupied the northwest corner of the Roman Forum, which coincided approximately with today's Plaça Sant Jaume. ⊠ *Centre Excursionista de Catalunya, Carrer Paradís 10, Barri Gòtic* ☎ *93/315–2311 Centre Excursionista de Catalunya* ⊕ *ajuntament.barcelona.cat/*

museuhistoria/ca/muhba-temple-daugust Ⓜ *Jaume I.*

Generalitat de Catalunya

NOTABLE BUILDING | Opposite city hall, the Palau de la Generalitat is the seat of the autonomous Catalan government. Seen through the front windows of this ornate 15th-century palace, the gilded ceiling of the Saló de Sant Jordi (St. George's Hall), named for Catalonia's dragon-slaying patron saint, gives an idea of the lavish decor within. Carrer del Bisbe, running along the right side of the building from the square to the cathedral, offers a favorite photo op: the gargoyle-bedecked Gothic bridge overhead, connecting the Generalitat to the building across the street. The Generalitat opens to the public on the second and fourth weekends of the month, with free one-hour guided tours in English (request in advance), through the Generalitat website. The building is also open to visitors on Día de Sant Jordi (St. George's Day: April 23), during the Fiesta de la Mercé in late September, and on the National Day of Catalonia (September 11). ⊠ *Pl. de Sant Jaume 4, Barri Gòtic* ☎ *93/402–4600* ⊕ *www.gencat.cat* ⊠ *Free* Ⓜ *Jaume I, Liceu.*

La Casa Martí—Els Quatre Gats

NOTABLE BUILDING | Built by Josep Puig i Cadafalch for the Martí family, this Art Nouveau house was the fountainhead of bohemianism in Barcelona. It was here in 1897 that four friends, notable dandies all—Ramon Casas, Pere Romeu, Santiago Rusiñol, and Miguel Utrillo—started a café called the Quatre Gats (Four Cats), meaning to make it *the* place for artists and art lovers to gather. (One of their wisest decisions was to mount a show, in February 1900, for an up-and-coming young painter named Pablo Picasso.) The exterior was decorated with figures by sculptor Eusebi Arnau (1864–1934). The clientele may be somewhat tourist-heavy these days but the interior of Els Quatre Gats hasn't changed one iota: pride of

El Call: The Jewish Quarter

Barcelona's Jewish Quarter, El Call (a name derived from the Hebrew word *qahal, or* "meeting place"), is just to the Rambla side of the Palau de la Generalitat. Carrer del Call, Carrer de Salomó ben Adret, Carrer Marlet, and Arc de Sant Ramón del Call mark the heart of the medieval ghetto. Confined by law to this area at the end of the 7th century (one reason the streets in Calls or Aljamas were so narrow was that their inhabitants could only build into the streets for more space), Barcelona's Jews were the private bankers to Catalonia's sovereign counts (only Jews could legally lend money). The Jewish community also produced many leading physicians, translators, and scholars in medieval Barcelona, largely because the Jewish faith rested on extensive Talmudic and textual study, thus promoting a high degree of literacy. The reproduction of a plaque bearing Hebrew text on the corner of Carrer Marlet and Arc de Sant Ramón del Call was the only physical reminder of the Jewish presence here until the medieval synagogue reopened as a historical site in 2003.

In 2018, the name of Carrer de Sant Domènec was changed to Carrer de Ben Salomo Ben Adret to commemorate the 1391 attack on the Jewish community, in which 300 people were murdered on the feast day of Saint Dominic. The new name pays homage to Salomó ben Adret, a distinguished rabbi and leader of Catalan Judaism who served as an advisor to three monarchs.

The story of Barcelona's Jewish community came to a bloody end in August 1391, when during a time of famine and pestilence a nationwide outbreak of anti-Semitic violence reached Barcelona, with catastrophic results: nearly the entire Jewish population was murdered or forced to convert to Christianity. This resulted in a centuries-long end to public Jewish life in the city.

place goes to the Casas self-portrait, smoking his pipe, comically teamed up on a tandem bicycle with Romeu. Drop in for a café con leche and you just might end up seated in Picasso's chair. Venture to the dining room in back, with its unusual gallery seating upstairs; this room where Miró used to produce puppet theater is charming, but the food is nothing to rave about. *Quatre gats* in Catalan is a euphemism for "hardly anybody," but the four founders were each definitely somebody. ✉ *Montsió 3 bis, Barri Gòtic* ☎ *93/302–4140* ⊕ *www.4gats.com* Ⓜ *Catalunya, Jaume I, Urquinaona.*

★ **La Catedral de Barcelona** (*La Catedral de Santa Creu i Santa Eulàlia*) **CHURCH** | Barcelona's cathedral is a repository of centuries of the city's history and legend—although as a work of architecture visitors might find it a bit of a disappointment, compared to the Mediterranean Gothic Santa Maria del Mar and Gaudí's Moderniste Sagrada Família. It was built between 1298 and 1450; work on the spire and neo-Gothic facade began in 1892 and was not completed until 1913. Historians are not sure about the identity of the architect: one name often proposed is Jaume Fabre, a native of Mallorca. The building is perhaps most impressive at night, floodlit with the stained-glass windows illuminated from inside; book a room with a balcony at the Hotel Colon, facing the cathedral square, and make the most of it.

This is reputedly the darkest of all the world's great cathedrals—even at high noon the nave is enveloped in shadows, which give the appearance that it's larger than it actually is—so it takes a while for your eyes to adjust to the rich, velvety pitch of the interior. Don't miss the beautifully carved choir stalls of the Knights of the Golden Fleece; the intricately and elaborately sculpted organ loft over the door out to Plaça Sant Iu (with its celebrated Saracen's Head sculpture); the series of 60-odd wood sculptures of evangelical figures along the exterior lateral walls of the choir; the cloister with its fountain and geese in the pond; and, in the crypt, the tomb of Santa Eulàlia.

St. Eulàlia, originally interred at Santa Maria del Mar—then known as Santa Maria de les Arenes (St. Mary of the Sands)—was moved to the cathedral in 1339, and venerated here as its patron and protector. Eulalistas (St. Eulàlia devotees, rivals of a sort to the followers of La Mercé, or Our Lady of Mercy) celebrate the fiesta of La Laia (the nickname for Eulàlia) for a few days around her feast day on February 12.

Enter from the front portal (there are also entrances through the cloister and from Carrer Comtes down the left side of the apse), and the first thing you see are the high-relief sculptures of the story of St. Eulàlia, on the near side of the choir stalls. The first scene, on the left, shows St. Eulàlia in front of Roman Consul Decius with her left hand on her heart and her outstretched right hand pointing at a cross in the distance. In the next, she is tied to a column and being whipped by the consul's thugs. To the right of the door into the choir the unconscious Eulàlia is being hauled away, and in the final scene on the right she is being lashed to the X-shape cross upon which she was crucified in mid-February

in the year 303. To the right of this high relief is a sculpture of the martyred heroine, resurrected as a living saint.

Among the two dozen ornate and gilded chapels in the basilica, pay due attention to the Capella de Lepant, dedicated to Sant Crist de Lepanto, in the far right corner as you enter through the front door. According to legend, the 15th-century polychrome wood sculpture of a battle-scarred, dark-skinned Christ, visible on the altar of this 100-seat chapel behind a black-clad Mare de Deu dels Dolors (Our Lady of the Sorrows), was the bowsprit of the flagship Spanish galley at the battle fought between Christian and Ottoman fleets on October 7, 1571.

Outside the main nave of the cathedral to the right, you'll find the leafy, palm tree–shaded cloister surrounding a tropical garden and a pool said to be populated by 13 snow-white geese, one for each of the tortures inflicted upon St. Eulàlia in an effort to break her faith. Legend has it that they are descendants of the flock of geese from Rome's Capitoline Hill, whose honking alarms roused the city to repel invaders during the days of the Roman Republic. Don't miss the fountain with the bronze sculpture of an equestrian St. George, hacking away at his perennial foe, the dragon, on the eastern corner of the cloister. On the day of Corpus Christi, this fountain is one of the more spectacular displays of the traditional l'ou com balla (dancing egg).

In front of the cathedral is the grand square of Plaça de la Seu, where on occasion, barcelonins gather to dance the sardana, the circular folk dance performed for centuries as a symbol-in-motion of Catalan identity and the solidarity of the Catalan people. Nimble-footed oldsters share the space with young esbarts (dance troupes), coats and bags piled in the center of the ring, all dancing together to the reedy music of the cobla (band) in smooth, deceptively simple, heel-and-toe sequences of steps. This is

4

The Barri Gòtic

The ornate Gothic interior of La Catedral de Barcelona is always enveloped in shadow, even at high noon.

no tourist attraction: Catalans dance the sardana just for themselves. Check local listings for the annual series of evening organ concerts held in the cathedral. ☒ *Pl. de la Seu s/n, Barri Gòtic* ☎ *93/342–8262* ⊕ *www.catedralbcn.org* 🔲 *Free for worshippers; cultural/tourist visits €9 (includes cathedral, cloister, roof, and choir); Sunday tickets €15 and include entrance to the museum.* Ⓜ *Jaume I.*

★ **Museu d'Història de Barcelona (MUHBA)** (*Museum of the History of Barcelona*) **HISTORY MUSEUM** | This fascinating museum just off Plaça del Rei traces Barcelona's evolution from its first Iberian settlement through its Roman and Visigothic ages and beyond. The Romans took the city during the Punic Wars, and you can tour underground remains of their Colonia Favencia Iulia Augusta Paterna Barcino (Favored Colony of the Father Julius Augustus Barcino) via metal walkways. Some 43,000 square feet of archaeological artifacts, from the walls of houses, to mosaics and fluted columns, workshops (for pressing olive oil and salted fish

paste), and street systems, can be found in large part beneath the plaça. See how the Visigoths and their descendants built the early medieval walls on top of these ruins, recycling chunks of Roman stone and concrete, bits of columns, and even headstones. In the ground-floor gallery is a striking collection of marble busts and funerary urns discovered in the course of the excavations. Guided tours are available in English at 10:30 am daily, but have to be reserved in advance. The price of admission to the museum includes entry to the other treasures of the Plaça del Rei, including the Palau Reial Major, the splendid Saló del Tinell, and the chapel of Santa Àgata Also included are visits to other sites maintained by the museum: the most important and central of these are the Temple of Augustus, the Door of the Sea (the largest of the Roman-era city gates) and Dockside Thermal Baths, the Roman Funeral Way in the Plaça de la Vila de Madrid, and the Call (medieval Barcelona's Jewish quarter). ☒ *Palau Padellàs, Pl. del Rei s/n, Barri Gòtic* ☎ *93/256–2100* ⊕ *www.barcelona.cat/museuhistoria/en*

📷 *From €7; free with Barcelona Card, Sat. and the first Sun. of month* 🕙 *Closed Mon.* Ⓜ *Jaume I.*

Palau del Lloctinent (*Lieutenant's Palace*) CASTLE/PALACE | The three facades of the Palau face Carrer dels Comtes de Barcelona on the cathedral side, the Baixada de Santa Clara, and Plaça del Rei. Typical of late Gothic–early Renaissance Catalan design, it was constructed by Antoni Carbonell between 1549 and 1557, and remains one of the Gothic Quarter's most graceful buildings. The heavy stone arches over the entry, the central patio, and the intricately coffered wooden roof over the stairs are all good examples of noble 16th-century architecture. The door on the stairway is a 1975 Josep Maria Subirachs work portraying scenes from the life of Sant Jordi and the history of Catalonia. The Palau del Lloctinent was inhabited by the king's official emissary or viceroy to Barcelona during the 16th and 17th centuries; it now houses the historical materials of the Archivo de la Corona de Aragón (Archive of the Crown of Aragon), and offers an excellent exhibit on the life and times of Jaume I, one of early Catalonia's most important figures. The patio also occasionally hosts early-music concerts, and during the Corpus Christi celebration is one of the main venues for the ou com balla, when an egg "dances" on the fountain amid an elaborate floral display. ✉ *Carrer dels Comtes 2, Barri Gòtic* ☎ *93/485–4285 archives office* Ⓜ *Jaume I.*

Plaça de Garriga i Bachs
PLAZA/SQUARE | Ceramic murals depicting executions of heroes of the Catalan resistance to Napoleonic troops in 1809 flank this little space just outside the cloister of La Catedral de Barcelona. The first three scenes show the five resistance leaders waiting their turns to be garroted or hanged (the *garrote vil,* or vile garrote, was reserved for the clergymen, as hanging was considered a lower and less-humane form of execution). The fourth scene depicts the surrender of three agitators who attempted to rally a general Barcelona uprising to save the first five by ringing the cathedral bells. The three are seen here, pale and exhausted after 72 hours of hiding in the organ, surrendering after being promised amnesty by the French. All three were subsequently executed. The bronze statue of the five martyred insurgents (1929), in the center of the monument, is by the Moderniste sculptor Josep Llimona, whose prolific work in Barcelona also includes the frieze on the Arc de Triomf and the equestrian statue of Count Ramon Berenguer III (1068–1131) in the Plaça de Ramon Berenguer el Gran, between Via Laietana and the Cathedral. ✉ *Pl. de Garriga i Bachs, Barri Gòtic* Ⓜ *Jaume I.*

★ **Plaça del Rei**
PLAZA/SQUARE | This little square is a compact a nexus of history. Long held to be the scene of Columbus's triumphal return from his first voyage to the New World— the precise spot where Ferdinand and Isabella received him is purportedly on the stairs fanning out from the corner of the square (though evidence indicates that the Catholic Monarchs were at a summer residence in the Empordá)—the Palau Reial Major (admission included in the €7 entrance fee for the Museu d'Història de Barcelona; closed Monday) was the official royal residence in Barcelona. The main room is the Saló del Tinell, a magnificent banquet hall built in 1362. To the left is the Palau del Lloctinent (Lieutenant's Palace); towering overhead in the corner is the dark 15th-century Torre Mirador del Rei Martí (King Martin's Watchtower). The 14th-century Capella Real de Santa Àgueda (Royal Chapel of St. Agatha) is on the right side of the stairway, and behind and to the right as you face the stairs is the Palau Clariana-Padellàs, moved to this spot stone by stone from Carrer Mercaders in the early 20th century and now the entrance to

the Museu d'Història de Barcelona. ✉ *Pl. del Rei s/n, Barri Gòtic* Ⓜ *Jaume I.*

★ Plaça Sant Felip Neri

PLAZA/SQUARE | A tiny square just behind Plaça de Garriga Bachs off the side of the cloister of La Catedral de Barcelona, this was once a burial ground for Barcelona's executed heroes and villains, before all church graveyards were moved to the south side of Montjuïc, the present site of the municipal cemetery. The church of San Felip Neri here is a frequent venue for classical concerts. On January 30th, 1938, one of Franco's bombs fell in the square, taking the lives of 42 people, most of whom were children from the School of Sant Philip Neri. Fragments of a bomb made the pockmarks that are still visible on the walls of the church. These days, the schoolchildren still play in the square, which is cherished by locals for its silence and serenity (at least when the children are indoors), despite its tragic history. ✉ *Pl. Sant Felip Neri, Barri Gòtic* Ⓜ *Jaume I, Liceu.*

Plaça Sant Jaume

PLAZA/SQUARE | Facing each other across this oldest epicenter of Barcelona (and often on politically opposite sides as well) are the seat of Catalonia's regional government, the Generalitat de Catalunya, in the Palau de La Generalitat, and the City Hall, the Ajuntament de Barcelona, in the Casa de la Ciutat. This square was the site of the Roman forum 2,000 years ago, though subsequent construction filled the space with buildings. The square was cleared in the 1840s, but the two imposing government buildings are actually much older: the Ajuntament dates from the 14th century, and the Generalitat was built between the 15th and mid-17th century. Guided tours are temporarily suspended; check for availability. ✉ *Pl. Sant Jaume, Barri Gòtic* Ⓜ *Jaume I.*

Plaça Sant Just

PLAZA/SQUARE | To the left of city hall, down Carrer Hèrcules (named for the mythical founder of Barcelona) are this square and the site of the Església de Sant Just i Pastor, one of the city's oldest Christian churches. Although the present structure dates from 1342, and nothing remains of the original church, founded in 801 by King Louis the Pious, early Christian catacombs are reported to have been found beneath the plaça. The Gothic fountain was built in 1367 by the patrician Joan Fiveller, then the city's Chief Minister. (Fiveller's major claim to fame was to have discovered a spring in the Collserola hills and had the water piped straight to Barcelona.) The fountain in the square bears an image of St. Just, and the city and sovereign count-kings' coats of arms, along with a pair of falcons. The entryway and courtyard to the left of Carrer Bisbe Caçador are for the Palau Moixó, the town house of an important early Barcelona family; down Carrer Bisbe Caçador is the Acadèmia de Bones Lletres, the Catalan Academy of Arts and Letters. The church is dedicated to the boy martyrs Just and Pastor; the Latin inscription over the door translates into English as "Our pious patron is the black and beautiful Virgin, together with the sainted children Just and Pastore." ✉ *Pl. Sant Just, Barri Gòtic* Ⓜ *Jaume I.*

Reial Cercle Artístic

ART MUSEUM | This private fine-arts society, at the bottom of Portal de l'Angel, where it divides and leads off left to the Cathedral, has two art galleries (one with a permanent collection of works by Salvador Dalí; the other, upstairs, for themed exhibitions), as well as a restaurant and bar open to the public. It also offers drawing and painting classes and occasional film showings and concerts. Note the elegant Gothic details of the main entrance, with its heavy keystone arch, the stone carvings inside to the right in the Sala Güell, and the stairway sculptures. The El Cercle restaurant upstairs has an intimate feel, though the service can be inconsistent; best option here is a drink or a light lunch on the terrace, overlooking the passing throngs. ✉ *Carrer*

dels Arcs 5, Barri Gòtic ☎ *93/318–7866, 93/318–1774 Dalí collection* ⊕ *www. reialcercleartistic.cat* ⌨ *€10 to Dalí collection* ⊘ *Restaurant closed Sun. and Mon.* Ⓜ *Catalunya, Jaume I.*

Sala Parès

ART GALLERY | The dean of the city's art galleries is also the oldest one in Spain. It opened in 1840 as an art-supplies shop; as a gallery, it dates from 1877 and has shown every Barcelona artist of note since. Picasso, Dalí, and Miró exhibited their work here, as did Rusiñol before them. Nowadays, artists like Magí Puig and Carlos Morago get pride of place. ✉ *Petritxol 5, Barri Gòtic* ☎ *93/318–7020* ⊕ *salapares.com* ⊘ *Closed Sun. and Mon.* Ⓜ *Liceu, Catalunya.*

🍴 Restaurants

★ Caelis

$$$$ | **CATALAN** | This restaurant takes contemporary decor and fine-dining style and adds the pizzazz of open-kitchen cooking. It's known for its decadent tastings menus, and the star dish is a rich *mar i muntanya* macaroni with lobster, foie gras, and artichoke. **Known for:** Michelin star; tasting menus for carnivores and vegetarians; lunchtime menu option. $ *Average main: €98* ✉ *Via Laietana 49, Barri Gòtic* ⚜ *Inside Hotel Ohla Barcelona* ☎ *93/510–1205* ⊕ *www.caelis.com* ⊘ *Closed Sun.–Tues.* Ⓜ *Urquinaona.*

Els Quatre Gats

$$ | **CATALAN** | "The Four Cats" was founded in 1897 by a quartet of Moderniste artists—the bohemians of their day—whose work still graces the walls, and the building, Casa Martí (1896), by Modernista master Josep Puig i Cadafalch with sculptural detail by Eusebi Arnau, is a treat in itself. The restaurant in back offers a range of traditional Catalan dishes, but the cooking is uninspired and overpriced so stick to the front room café, where you can linger over a drink, order some of the simpler offerings like *pa de coca*

(thin country flatbreads with tomato and olive oil), cheese, cured ham, or *pebrots de Padrón* (fried green peppers), and enjoy a bit of local cultural history. **Known for:** keep a sharp eye on your valuables; Picasso's first exhibition was held here in 1899; it's about the history, not the food. $ *Average main: €20* ✉ *Montsió 3, Barri Gòtic* ☎ *93/302–4140* ⊕ *www.4gats.com* Ⓜ *Catalunya, Urquinaona.*

Koy Shunka

$$$$ | **JAPANESE** | The Japanese-Chinese team of master chefs Hideki Matsuhisa and Xu Zhangchao received a Michelin star for their tribute to Asian fusion cooking based on products from the Catalan larder. Dishes vary with the season but may include standouts such as *berberechos en salsa de sake* (cockles in sake sauce), *cerdo ibérico con ciruelas* (Ibérico pork with plums), and *ventresca de atun* (tuna belly with grated tomato and lemon) are several of the infinite variations on the Asia-meets-Catalonia theme in this sleek, contemporary setting. **Known for:** tasting menus only; not to be confused with the team's less adventurous Shunka restaurant nearby; inventive fusion cuisine. $ *Average main: €110* ✉ *Copons 7, Barri Gòtic* ☎ *93/412–7939* ⊕ *www.koyshunka.com* ⊘ *Closed Mon., Tues., 3 wks in Aug., and 2 wks at Christmas. No dinner Sun.* Ⓜ *Urquinaona.*

★ La Alcoba Azul

$$ | **TAPAS** | One of Barcelona's most beloved bars, La Alcoba Azul offers a wide selection of tapas with a full-on immersive atmosphere. The decor reflects the Moorish influence of Andalucía, mixed with the quirkiness of the original owners so you'll get illuminated lanterns and broken birdcages hang from the ceiling, while a years-old candle burns in a corner. **Known for:** selection of tapas-sized tostas (open-faced toasted sandwiches); the cod carpaccio is a must-try; wonderfully quirky decor. $ *Average main: €18* ✉ *Salomó ben Adret 14,*

A Primer on Barcelona's Cuisine 🍴

Menus in Catalan are as musical as they are aromatic, with rare ingredients such as *salicornia* (seawort, or sea asparagus) with *bacalao* (cod), or fragrant wild mushrooms such as *rossinyols* (chanterelles) and *moixernons* (St. George's mushroom) accompanying dishes like *mandonguilles amb sepia* (meatballs with cuttlefish).

Four sauces grace the Catalan table: *sofregit* (fried onion, tomato, and garlic—a base for nearly everything); *samfaina* (a ratatouille-like sofregit with eggplant and sweet red peppers); *picada* (garlic, almonds, bread crumbs, olive oil, pine nuts, parsley, saffron, or chocolate); and *allioli* (pounded garlic and virgin olive oil).

The three *e*'s deserve a place in any Catalan culinary anthology: *escalibada* (roasted red peppers, eggplants, and tomatoes served in garlic and olive oil); *esqueixada* (shredded salt-cod salad served raw with onions, peppers, olives, beans, olive oil, and vinegar); and *escudella* (a winter stew of meats and vegetables with noodles and beans).

Universal specialties are *pa amb tomaquet* (toasted bread with squeezed tomato and olive oil), *espinaques a la catalana* (spinach cooked with raisins, garlic, and pine nuts), and *botifarra amb mongetes* (pork sausage with white beans).

The *mar i muntanya* (Catalan "surf 'n' turf") has been a standard since Roman times. Rice dishes are simply called *arròs*, and range from standard seafood paella to the *arròs a banda* (paella with shelled prawns, shrimp, and mussels), to *arròs negre* (paella cooked in cuttlefish ink) or *arròs caldós* (a brothy risotto-like dish often made with lobster). *Fideuà* is a paella made of vermicelli noodles, not rice.

Fresh fish such as *llobarro* (sea bass, *lubina* in Spanish) or *dorada* (gilthead bream) cooked *a la sal* (in a shell of salt) are standards, as are grilled *llenguado* (sole) and *rodaballo* (turbot). Duck, goose, chicken, and rabbit frequent Catalan menus, as do *cabrit* (kid or baby goat), *xai* (lamb), *porc* (pork), *vedella* (veal), and *bou* (beef). Finally come the two Catalan classic desserts, *mel i mató* (honey and fresh cream cheese) and *crema catalana* (a crème brûlée–like custard with a caramelized glaze).

A typical session *à table* in Barcelona might begin with *pica-pica* (hors d'oeuvres), a variety of delicacies such as *jamón ibérico de bellota* (acorn-fed ham), *xipirones* (baby squid), *pimientos de Padrón* (green peppers, some spicy), or *bunyols de bacallà* (cod fritters or croquettes), and pa amb tomaquet. From here you can order a starter such as *canelones* (cannelloni) or you can go straight to your main course.

Barri Gòtic ☎ *93/302–8141* 🌐 *laalcobaazul.com/en* [M] *Liceu, Jaume I.*

La Cerería

$ | **VEGETARIAN** | Situated next to the birthplace of Catalan painter, Joan Miró, this café and musical instrument store is both humble and endearing. In summer, tables in the Passatge offer quiet, shady, breezy respite from the bustling streets. **Known for:** vegetarian menu (with vegan options); breezy outside tables; charming atmosphere. [$] *Average main: €12* ✉ *Baixada de Sant Miquel 3, Barri Gòtic* ☎ *93/301–8510* 🕒 *Closed Mon. No dinner Sun.* [M] *Liceu, Jaume I.*

Pla B

$$ | **CATALAN** | Filled with couples night after night, this candle-lit dining spot is an atmospheric spot that plays up the room's ancient stone, brick, and wood. The cuisine is light and contemporary, featuring inventive salads and fresh seafood, as well as options for vegetarians and vegans. **Known for:** lunch set menu; extensive wine list; romantic ambience. [$] *Average main: €18* ✉ *Bellafila 5, Barri Gòtic* ☎ *93/412–6552* 🌐 *www.restaurant-pla.cat* [M] *Jaume I.*

★ Restaurante Informal

$$$ | **CATALAN** | On the ground floor of the The Serras hotel, local star chef Marc Gascons has outdone himself with this superb bistro-style restaurant that serves upscale takes on tapas and modern twists on traditional Catalan food. The menu is like a hip, contemporary version of what a Barcelona grandma would serve for Sunday dinner. **Known for:** Michelin-starred chef; creative patatas bravas; contemporary twist on Catalan classics. [$] *Average main: €25* ✉ *Passeig de Colom 9, Barri Gòtic* ☎ *93/169–1869* 🌐 *restauranteinformal.com/en* ⏲ *Closed Mon. and Tues.* [M] *Barceloneta.*

Coffee and Quick Bites

Irati Taverna Basca

$$ | **BASQUE** | There's only one drawback to this lively Basque bar between Plaça del Pi and La Rambla: it's narrow at the street end, and harder to squeeze into than the metro at rush hour. Skip the pintxos (typical of San Sebastian) on the bar and opt instead for the plates brought out piping-hot from the kitchen. **Known for:** dinner and lunch are served, but it's more fun for tapas; refreshing txakoli sparkling wine; bustling atmosphere. [$] *Average main: €20* ✉ *Cardenal Casañas 17, Barri Gòtic* ☎ *93/302–3084* 🌐 *gruposagardi.com/restaurante/irati-taverna-basca* [M] *Liceu.*

Satan's Coffee Corner

$ | **CAFÉ** | Since opening in 2012, Barcelona's original specialty coffee bar has been serving high-quality roasts and small bites. Floor-to-ceiling windows create an indoor-outdoor feel, regardless of where you sit. **Known for:** hip vibe; Japanese-inspired pastries; closes at 5 pm or 6 pm depending on day of the week. [$] *Average main: €10* ✉ *l'Arc de Sant Ramon del Call 11, Barri Gòtic* ☎ *93/252-6249* 🌐 *satanscoffee.com* [M] *Liceu, Jaume I.*

Hotels

Arai Aparthotel 4*S

$$$$ | **HOTEL** | **FAMILY** | You couldn't ask for a more convenient location from which to explore Barcelona's Barri Gòtic—or for a lodging more elegant—than one of the aparthotel suites in this stunning restoration. **Pros:** warm and attentive service; free admission to Egyptian Museum of Barcelona; historic character retained in former palace. **Cons:** rooms on the top floor lack historic charm; on busy street; seedy area. [$] *Rooms from: €273* ✉ *Avinyó 30, Barri Gòtic* ☎ *93/320–3950* 🌐 *www.hotelarai.com* 🛏 *31 rooms* 🍴 *No Meals* [M] *Liceu.*

Duquesa de Cardona

$$$$ | **HOTEL** | A 16th-century town house, built when the Passeig de Colom in front was lined with the summer homes of the nobility, houses this waterfront hotel a five-minute walk from everything in the Barri Gòtic and Barceloneta and a 30-minute walk from the Eixample. **Pros:** pillow menu; room service until 10:30 pm; dreamy location. **Cons:** pricey for a four-star; no spa; rooms on the small side. [$] *Rooms from: €230* ✉ *Passeig de Colom 12, Barri Gòtic* ☎ *93/268–9090* 🌐 *www.hduquesadecardona.com* 🛏 *64 rooms* 🍴 *No Meals* [M] *Barceloneta, Drassanes.*

Hotel Catalonia Portal de l'Àngel

$ | **HOTEL** | Converted in 1998 from a historic stately home dating back to 1825, the Catalonia Portal d'Angel beckons with its neoclassic facade and original grand marble staircase. **Pros:** great location; pleasant breakfast pavilion in the garden; includes walking tours of the Old City and the Eixample. **Cons:** could use an all-around refresh; faces busy pedestrian mall; small rooms. [$] *Rooms from: €108* ✉ *Av. Portal d'Angel 17, Barri Gòtic* ☎ *93/318–4141* 🌐 *www.cataloniahotels.com/en/hotel/catalonia-portal-del-angel* 🛏 *83 rooms* 🍴 *No Meals* [M] *Catalunya.*

★ Hotel Neri

$$$$ | **HOTEL** | Just steps from the cathedral, in the heart of the city's old Jewish Quarter, this elegant, upscale, boutique hotel, part of the prestigious Relais & Chateaux hotel group, marries ancient and avant-garde designs. **Pros:** ideal, central location (in the middle of Barri Gòtic); very professional reception and staff; set in a restored medieval palace. **Cons:** very pricey; limited loungers by the rooftop pool; noisy on summer nights and school days. [$] *Rooms from: €374* ✉ *Sant Sever 5, Barri Gòtic* ☎ *93/304–0655* 🌐 *www.hotelneri.com/en* 🛏 *28 rooms* 🍴 *No Meals* [M] *Jaume I, Liceu.*

★ Kimpton Vividora Hotel

$$$$ | **HOTEL** | Every Kimpton hotel is designed to reflect the character of the city it inhabits and, in the case of Kimpton Vividora, that means Mediterranean blues and earthy terra-cotta hues mixed with bright splashes of color and a lush rooftop terrace with stunning views. **Pros:** rooftop bar with great views; a design-lover's dream; local partnerships sourced for toiletries, tea and coffee. **Cons:** no parking available; not all rooms have city views; touristy area (but on a quiet side street). [$] *Rooms from: €285* ✉ *Duc 15, Barri Gòtic* ☎ *93/642–5400* 🌐 *kimptonvividorahotel.com/en* 🛏 *156 rooms* 🍴 *No Meals* [M] *Catalunya.*

Mercer Hotel Barcelona

$$$$ | **HOTEL** | On a narrow side street near Plaça Sant Jaume, this romantic boutique hotel, a medieval town house, is among the most spectacular examples of Barcelona's signature genius for the redesign and rebirth of historical properties. **Pros:** in the heart of the Old City; breakfast in glassed-in patio with orange trees; comfortable rooftop terrace with a larger than usual pool and (in season) a bar-café. **Cons:** expensive breakfast; no gym or spa; very pricey. [$] *Rooms from: €437* ✉ *Carrer dels Lledó 5, Barri Gòtic* ☎ *93/310–7480* 🌐 *www.mercerbarcelona.com/en* 🛏 *28 rooms* 🍴 *No Meals* [M] *Jaume I.*

Ohla Barcelona

$$$$ | **HOTEL** | One of Barcelona's top design hotels (also with incredible food), the Ohla has a neoclassical exterior (not counting the playful eyeballs stuck to the facade) that belies its avant-garde interior, full of witty, design-conscious touches. **Pros:** rooftop terrace and pool; high-end wines at Vistro49; remarkable restaurant Caelis on-site. **Cons:** some rooms are small; uncomfortable furniture in lobby; adjacent to noisy Via Laietana. [$] *Rooms from: €239* ✉ *Via Laietana 49, Barri Gòtic* ☎ *93/341–5050* 🌐 *www.ohlabarcelona.com* 🛏 *74 rooms* 🍴 *Free Breakfast* [M] *Urquinaona.*

The Serras

$$$$ | **HOTEL** | If you're looking for an ultra-exclusive boutique hotel that offers superb comfort, discretion, and excellent facilities, then this is it. Picasso had his first studio here (on the sixth floor) when the building was all walk-up flats; today, designer Eva Martinez has found ingenious, tasteful ways to make the best of the space: a small lobby with a comfortable sofa suite leads back to the breakfast area, while a mezzanine hosts the 24-hour lounge bar and a small gym. **Pros:** dreamy "El Sueño" rooftop terrace with show-stopping views; excellent restaurant Informal; outstanding, personalized service. **Cons:** rooms on the smaller side; hard on the budget; no sauna or spa. [$] *Rooms from: €395* ✉ *Passeig Colom 9, Barri Gòtic* ☎ *93/169–1868*

⊕ www.hoteltheserrasbarcelona.com
↪ 28 rooms ¶○¶ No Meals Ⓜ Barceloneta,
Drassanes.

The Wittmore

$$$$ | HOTEL | The Wittmore is an adults-only romantic hideaway par excellence, tucked away in a tiny cul-de-sac in one of the Barri Gòtic's prettiest mazes of streets. **Pros:** ultra chic; plunge pool and bar on rooftop terrace; cocktail bar with fireplace. **Cons:** decor on the dark side; pricey; no spa or gym. Ⓢ Rooms from: €400 ✉ Riudares 7, Barri Gòtic ☎ 93/550–0885 ⊕ www.thewittmore. com ↪ 21 rooms ¶○¶ No Meals Ⓜ L3 Drassanes/L4 Jaume 1.

ⓨ Nightlife

The medieval Barri Gòtic is a wanderer's paradise filled with ancient winding streets, majestic squares, and myriad period-perfect wine bars and dimly lighted pubs found in the hidden corners of labyrinthine alleyways. It's a contrast with the adjoining La Rambla, the liveliest pedestrian promenade in the city, which bustles with a dizzying array of tourist-baiting shops and restaurants leading to Plaça Reial's euphoric nightlife scene.

BARS

Craft Barcelona

BARS | This tavern-esque basement spot hosts everything from open mic nights and comedy shows to jam sessions and monologues, and has dozens of handcrafted beer on offer, as well as a small food menu. There's a small outdoor terrace if you need a breath of air. ✉ Paradís 4, Barri Gòtic ☎ 93/625–4968 ⊕ craftbarcelona.com Ⓜ Jaume I. BARS/PUBS

El Paraigua

COCKTAIL LOUNGES | This restaurant's stunning Moderniste facade, an exquisite vintage cash register, and other delicate reminders of its former incarnation as a turn-of-the-20th-century umbrella shop— is usually enough to lure newcomers inside for a closer look but for fun-loving night owls, the real attraction is downstairs in the exposed-brick cocktail club, a former convent basement offering first-rate cocktails and often live music. ✉ Carrer del Pas de l'Ensenyança 2, Barri Gòtic ☎ 93/317–1479 ⊕ www.elparaigua. com Ⓜ Jaume I.

Harlem Jazz Club

LIVE MUSIC | Located on a rare tree-lined street with twinkling lights, this club attracts patrons of all ages and musical tastes for live Cuban salsa, swing, and reggae alongside creative cocktails in a relaxed and friendly atmosphere. Most concerts start around 10 or 11 pm. ✉ Comtessa de Sobradiel 8, Barri Gòtic ☎ 93/310–0755 ⊕ www.harlemjazzclub. es Ⓜ Jaume I, Liceu.

La Vinateria del Call

WINE BARS | In the heart of Barcelona's former Jewish Quarter, this rustic charmer serves a wide variety of hearty national wines paired with regional cheeses, meats, and tapas. The antique carved-wood furnishings and candlelit setting makes for an atmospheric respite from the area's chaotic pace. ✉ Salomó ben Adret 9, Barri Gòtic ☎ 93/302–6092 ⊕ www.lavinateriadelcall.com Ⓜ Jaume I, Liceu.

Ocaña

BARS | In a trio of ancient mansions on buzzy Plaça Reial's southern flank, this venue is dedicated to Jose Peréz Ocaña, a cross-dressing artist, LGBTQ activist, proud bohemian, and dominating figure of Barcelona's post-Franco, alternative-culture explosion. Ocaña also has an adjoining Mediterranean restaurant; a sizable café bar, club, and cocktail lounge; and the fiercest drag queen hostesses on the square. ✉ Pl. Reial 13–15, Barri Gòtic ☎ 93/676–4814 ⊕ www.ocana.cat Ⓜ Drassanes.

Pipa Club

COCKTAIL LOUNGES | Situated in an upstairs apartment, this somewhat secret bar is decorated in Victorian-style, with wood-paneled rooms and ornate chandeliers, but serves contemporary premium spirits. Enjoy a creative cocktail in a nook by the window overlooking Plaça Reial. It's technically a members club, but visitors are generally granted access in the evenings. ⊠ *Pl. Reial 3, Barri Gòtic* ☎ *65/258–9116* Ⓜ *Liceu.*

🎟 Performing Arts

FLAMENCO

★ Los Tarantos

FOLK/TRADITIONAL DANCE | Open since 1963, this small basement spot is the oldest tablao flamenco in Barcelona. It spotlights some of Andalusia's best flamenco in 40-minute shows of dance, percussion, and song. These shows are a good intro to the art, and feel much less touristy than most standard flamenco fare. Shows are daily and it's best to reserve online. ⊠ *Pl. Reial 17, Barri Gòtic* ☎ *93/304–1210* ⊕ *www.tarantosbarcelona.com/en* Ⓜ *Liceu.*

🛍 Shopping

The Barri Gòtic was built on trade and cottage industries, and there are plenty of nimble fingers producing artisan goods in the old-world shops along its stone streets.

ART GALLERIES

Artevistas

ART GALLERIES | In the same building where Joan Miró was born, Artevistas showcases a rotating collection of contemporary art, with an emphasis on young and emerging talent. Though many of the featured artists are from or based in Barcelona, notable international artists including actor and photographer Norman Reedus of *The Walking Dead* and The Libertines frontman, Peter Doherty, have exhibited here. ⊠ *Passatge del Crèdit 4, Barri Gòtic* ☎ *93/513–0465* ⊕ *www.artevistas.eu* ☉ *Closed Mon.* Ⓜ *Liceu, Jaume I.*

Catalan Flamenco

Barcelona has a burgeoning and erudite flamenco scene, even if the dance is imported from Andalusia. For the best flamenco in Barcelona, consult listings and concierges and don't be put off if the venue seems touristy—these venues often book the best artists. Barcelona-born *cantaors* (flamenco singers) include Mayte Martín and Miguel Poveda. Keep an eye on the billboards also for names like Estrella Morente (also a flamenco singer) and Chano Domínguez, a pianist who often appears at the Barcelona Jazz Festival.

Base Elements Urban Art Gallery

ART GALLERIES | The building may be from the 19th-century but the fine art here is very *now.* The focus is on street art, graffiti, and urban contemporary pieces. Originally from Los Angeles, painter and urban architect, Robert Burt, opened the creative space in 2003 as a workshop and hangout for young artists. The medieval basement is sometimes used as an event space. Paintings can be shipped all over the world. ⊠ *Palau 4, Barri Gòtic* ☎ *93/164–4772* ⊕ *www.baseelements.net* Ⓜ *Liceu, Jaume I.*

BOOKS AND STATIONERY

★ Espai Quera: Llibres i platillos

BOOKS | This is the bookstore to seek out if you're interested in the Pyrenees or in exploring any part of the Catalonian hinterlands. Maps, charts, and books detailing everything from Pyrenean ponds and lakes to Romanesque chapels are available in this diminutive giant of a resource. The space doubles as a restaurant, serving wine, cheese, and a few traditional Catalan dishes. It's been family owned and operated since 1916.

Petritxol 2, Barri Gòtic ☎ *93/318–0743* ⊕ *www.espaiquera.com* Ⓜ *Liceu.*

Raima

STATIONERY | Currently the largest stationery store in Europe, Raima opened in 1986 and continues to be a go-to spot for everything paper-related, from journals and travel notebooks to office supplies. The store covers three floors plus a rooftop terrace and bar. ✉ *Comtal 27, Barri Gòtic* ☎ *93/317–4966* ⊕ *raima.cat/en* Ⓜ *Urquinaona.*

CERAMICS AND GLASSWARE
★ **Art Escudellers**

CERAMICS | Ceramic pieces from all over Spain are on display at this large store across the street from the restaurant Los Caracoles; more than 140 different artisans are represented, with maps showing what part of Spain the work is from. There are several other branches of Art Escudellers in the old city. ✉ *Escudellers 23, Barri Gòtic* ☎ *93/412–6801* ⊕ *www. artescudellers.com* Ⓜ *Liceu, Drassanes.*

CLOTHING
★ **L'Arca**

MIXED CLOTHING | This family-owned (and women-owned) store sells vintage clothing, fabrics, jewelry, and accessories, with a focus on wedding dresses, veils, and lace. Despite the found-object attitude and ambience of the place, they're not giving away these vintage baubles, so don't be surprised at the hefty price tags. You'll also find a collection of their own bridal gowns, newly made but in romantic, old-fashioned styles. Notably, the shop supplied many costumes and props for the filming of *Titanic.* ✉ *Banys Nous 20, Barri Gòtic* ☎ *93/302–1598* ⊕ *larcabarcelona.com* Ⓜ *Liceu.*

Sombrereria Obach

HATS & GLOVES | This hat shop is as much part of the Barri Gòtic's landscape as any of its medieval churches. It occupies a busy corner in El Call (the old Jewish district) and has curved glass windows with displays of timeless, classic hats—from traditional Basque berets to Stetsons and Panamas—that have been dressing heads in Barcelona since 1924. ✉ *Call 2, Barri Gòtic* ☎ *93/318–4094* ⊕ *www.sombrereriaobach.com* Ⓜ *Liceu, Jaume I.*

FOOD
Caelum

FOOD | At the corner of Carrer de la Palla and Banys Nous, this café and shop sells wine and foodstuffs such as honey, biscuits, chocolates, and preserves made in convents and monasteries all over Spain. You can pop in to pick up an exquisitely packaged pot of jam, or linger over pastries and coffee in the tearoom. ✉ *Palla 8, Barri Gòtic* ☎ *93/302–6993* Ⓜ *Liceu, Jaume I.*

La Casa del Bacalao

FOOD | As you can guess from the name, which is decorated with cod-fishing memorabilia, this shop specializes in bacalao—salted and dried salt cod, whichis used in a wide range of Catalan recipes (such as *esqueixada*, in which shredded strips of raw salt cod are served in a marinade of oil and vinegar). Slabs of bacalao can be vacuum-packed for portability, and there are lots of recipe books if you're looking for inspiration. ✉ *Moles 11, just off Portal de l'Àngel, Barri Gòtic* ☎ *93/301–6539* ⊕ *lacasadelbacalao.es* Ⓜ *Catalunya.*

GIFTS AND SOUVENIRS
Centre d'Artesania Catalunya

CRAFTS | In 2010 the Catalan government created the registered trademark Empremtes de Catalunya to represent Catalan artisans and to make sure that visitors get the real deal when buying what they believe to be genuine products. The official shop now sells jewelry re-created from eras dating back to pre-Roman times, Gaudí-inspired sculptures, traditional Cava mugs, and some bravely avant-garde objects from young artisans—all officially sanctioned as fit to represent the city. ✉ *Banys Nous 11, Barri Gòtic* ☎ *93/467–4660* ⊕ *ccam. gencat.cat/ca/inici* Ⓜ *Liceu, Jaume I.*

Cereria Subirà

CRAFTS | Known as the city's oldest shop, having remained open since 1761 (though it was not always a candle store), this "waxery" (*cereria*) offers candles in all sizes and shapes, ranging from wild mushrooms to the Montserrat massif, home of the Benedictine abbey. ✉ *Baixada de la Llibreteria 7, Barri Gòtic* ☎ *93/315–2606* ⊕ *cereriasubira.cat/en* Ⓜ *Jaume I.*

★ Ganiveteria Roca

OTHER SPECIALTY STORE | Directly opposite the giant rose window of the Santa Maria del Pi church, the knife store (*ganivet* is Catalan for knife) beneath this lovely sgraffito-decorated facade takes cutlery culture to a new level. Knives, razors, scissors, hatchets, axes, swords, nail clippers, tweezers, and penknives are all displayed in this comprehensive, cutting-edge emporium. ✉ *Pl. del Pi 3, Barri Gòtic* ☎ *93/302–1241* ⊕ *www.ganiveteriaroca.cat* Ⓜ *Liceu.*

Guantería y Complementos Alonso

OTHER SPECIALTY STORE | The storefront and interiors of this ancient little glove and accessory shop is well worth the visit. Lovely antique cabinets painstakingly stripped of centuries of paint display gloves, fans, shawls, mantillas, and a miscellany of textile crafts and small gifts. ✉ *Santa Ana 27, Barri Gòtic* ☎ *93/317–6085* ⊕ *guanteria-alonso.com* Ⓜ *Catalunya.*

MARKETS
Mercat Gòtic

MARKET | A browser's bonanza, this interesting if somewhat pricey Thursday market (10 am–8 pm) for antique clothing, jewelry, and art occupies the plaza in front of the cathedral. In December, a Christmas market takes over the space. Most stalls aren't open during the vacation month of August. ✉ *Av. Plaça de la Catedral, Barri Gòtic* ⊕ *www.mercatgoticbcn.com* Ⓜ *Jaume I.*

Plaça del Pi

MARKET | The days for the natural-produce market are a bit unpredictable—usually the first and third Friday of the month—but when it happens, the little square fills with interesting tastes and aromas (look for local honey and cheese); the neighboring Plaça Sant Josep Oriol holds an art market every weekend. ✉ *Pl. del Pi, Barri Gòtic* Ⓜ *Liceu.*

SHOES AND LEATHER GOODS
BIBA

LEATHER GOODS | BIBA specializes in natural leather, cotton, organic fibers, and other sustainable materials, and their leather bags and accessories are are made using traditional artisan techniques such as vegetable tanning and hand braiding. There's even a line of products dedicated to travelers, including suitcases, toiletry bags, and wallets. The flagship shop is in Barcelona but they've expanded to other major cities across Spain. ✉ *Pl. del Pi 6, Barri Gòtic* ☎ *64/788–0823* ⊕ *bibashops.com/en* Ⓜ *Liceu.*

★ Handmade Barcelona

SHOES | Espadrille shoes evolved in different styles in different parts of Spain. In Cataluña, the most traditional espadrille, and the kind that Salvador Dalí loved, is called "Espardenya del Payes" (literally "the shoe of the peasant") and the style is open on the sides, and the typical colors are black and white. In Pamplona espadrilles are called "Pamplonicas" and they have super tight stitching (they're worn for the running of the bulls festivities so they can't be loose!), and they're traditionally white and red in color. On the island of Menorca, espadrilles are made using leather so that they can be in contact with water. When they have a heel, as is traditional in Valencia, they're called "Valencianas." Handmade Barcelona sells all of these styles and with lots of variety in terms of stitching, colors, and materials.

You can even custom-design your own at the shop's interactive 90-minute workshops, where participants choose the color, base, ribbon, and stitching style, and get to make them alongside an in-house artisan. You'll learn even more about the history of these versatile, comfortable shoes, made famous by Salvador Dalí, who wore them everywhere he went, including meetings with designers Yves Saint Laurent and Coco Chanel, both of whom later adapted the style for the international market. ✉ *Call 7, Barri Gòtic* ☎ *93/180–6768* ⊕ *www.barcelonahm.com* Ⓜ *Liceu.*

★ La Manual Alpargatera

SHOES | If you appreciate old-school craftsmanship in footwear and reasonable prices, visit this boutique just off Carrer Ferran. Handmade rope-sole sandals and espadrilles are the specialty, and this shop has sold them to everyone—including the pope. The flat, beribboned espadrilles model used for dancing the *sardana* is available, as are fashionable wedge heels with peep toes and comfy slippers. The price of a pair of espadrilles here start at $22, which is far less than the same quality shoes in the United States. They offer free shipping outside of Spain on orders of €250 or more. ✉ *Avinyó 7, Barri Gòtic* ☎ *93/301–0172* ⊕ *lamanual.com/en* Ⓜ *Liceu, Jaume I.*

 Activities

BICYCLING

Fat Tire Bike Tours

BIKING | Four-hour guided city tours with this well-reputed company start in Plaça Sant Jaume daily at 11 am and 4 pm (from mid-October to mid-April, morning tours only), and cover—with a lunch break—the usual areas: the Barri Gòtic, Sagrada Família, Ciutadella Park, the port, and Barceloneta. Reservations can be made on the website. ✉ *Marlet 4, Barri Gòtic* ☎ *93/342–9275* ⊕ *www.fattiretours.com/barcelona* 🚲 *€30 for adults* Ⓜ *Jaume I.*

Steel Donkey Bike Tours

BIKING | Groups of up to eight people can take unique four-hour bike tours with this outfit on Tuesday, Thursday, and Saturday mornings during winter, and daily from April through October, departing at 10 am from Carrer de Cervantes 5. The tours (€35 per person, including bike and helmet rentals) promise to be beyond the usual sights, offering visits to markets and sights that even some locals might not be familiar with. Call for reservations or book online. ✉ *Cervantes 5, Barri Gòtic* ☎ *65/728–6854* ⊕ *www.steeldonkeybiketours.com* Ⓜ *Jaume I.*

HIKING

The Collserola hills, just 20 minutes from downtown, offer well-marked trails, fresh air, and lovely views. Take the San Cugat, Sabadell, or Terrassa FGC train from Plaça de Catalunya and get off at Baixador de Vallvidrera; the information center, 10 minutes uphill next to the Jacint Verdaguer Museum, has maps of this mountain woodland. The walk back into town can take two to five hours depending on your speed and the trails you choose. For longer treks, try the 15-km (9-mile) Sant Cugat–to–Barcelona hike, or take the train south to Sitges and make the three-day pilgrimage walk to the Monastery of Montserrat.

Centre Excursionista de Catalunya

HIKING & WALKING | The center has information on hiking throughout Catalunya and the Pyrenees, gives mountaineering and technical climbing courses, organizes excursions, and provides guides for groups. ✉ *Carrer del Paradis 10, Barri Gòtic* ☎ *93/315–2311* ⊕ *www.cec.cat* Ⓜ *Jaume I.*

Chapter 5

EL RAVAL

Updated by
Megan Eileen McDonough

👁 **Sights**
★★★★☆

🍽 **Restaurants**
★★★☆☆

🛏 **Hotels**
★★☆☆☆

🛍 **Shopping**
★★★☆☆

🍸 **Nightlife**
★★★☆☆

NEIGHBORHOOD SNAPSHOT

TOP EXPERIENCES

- **Antic Hospital de la Santa Creu:** The 15th-century chapel of the hospital showcases the works of up-and-coming artists.

- **Sant Pau del Camp:** Catch a musical performance in Barcelona's oldest church and linger by the fountain at the tiny cloister.

- **Botero's bronze cat:** Stroke the famous bearlike and bronze El Gato del Raval, a favorite meeting spot on the Rambla del Raval.

- **Museu d'Art Contemporani de Barcelona:** Take a guided tour of MACBA's incredible collection of contemporary art and then watch the skateboarders performing outside on the plaza.

- **Bar crawl:** From Casa Almirall on lively Joaquin Costa to La Confitería's vintage bar in a former pastry shop to little-changed Marsella, a onetime haunt for artistic notables such as Gaudí, Picasso, and Hemingway, you'll want to pace yourself for a leisurely crawl of El Raval's bars.

GETTING HERE

Begin at Plaça de Catalunya, with its convenient metro stop. Walk down La Rambla and take your first right into Carrer Tallers, working your way through to the MACBA.

PLANNING YOUR TIME

The Raval covers a lot of ground. Plan on spending the day, exploring and stopping for a meal. The cloister of Sant Pau del Camp, not to be missed, is closed Monday morning, Saturday afternoon, and all day Sunday, except for during Mass. This is also a good area to spend the evening, with dinner and visiting a bar or two.

RAVAL STREET ART

If you walk around Raval, you're bound to notice building facades that have been decorated with tin cans that have been spray-painted with positive words and phrases. It's the work of Me Lata, an artist couple who describe themselves as "a couple in love who have been making street art since 2014: recycled cans painted with positive messages. We claim, with love, a better world and we practice ephemeral art, eternal love." Most of the messages are in Spanish (it's a great way to learn), but the Artevistas gallery in Barri Gòtic showcases English ones. Some pieces take excerpts from songs and poems, while others are short and sweet like a simple "amor" reminder—anything that instills optimism and spreads the love.

El Raval (from *arrabal*, meaning "suburb" or "slum") is the area to the west of La Rambla (it's on your right if you're walking toward the port). Originally a rough quarter outside the second set of city walls that ran down the left side of La Rambla, El Raval was once notorious for its Barri Xinès (or Barrio Chino) red-light district, which was known to have fascinated a young Pablo Picasso.

Gypsies, acrobats, prostitutes, and *saltimbanques* (clowns and circus performers) who made this area their home soon found immortality in the many canvases Picasso painted of them during his Blue Period. It was the ladies of the night on Carrer Avinyó, not far from the Barri Xinès, who may have inspired one of the 20th-century's most famous paintings, Picasso's *Les Demoiselles d'Avignon*, an important milestone on the road to Cubism. Not bad for a city slum.

El Raval, though still edgy, has certainly gentrified since 1980, largely as a result of the construction of the Museu d'Art Contemporani de Barcelona (MACBA) and other cultural institutions nearby, such as the Centre de Cultura Contemporània (CCCB), Filmoteca, and the Convent dels Àngels. The medieval Hospital de la Santa Creu, Plaça del Pedró, the Mercat de Sant Antoni, and Sant Pau del Camp are highlights of this funky, rough-edged part of Barcelona. The only area to consider avoiding is the lower part between Carrer de Sant Pau and the back of the Drassanes Reials shipyards on Carrer del Portal Santa Madrona.

Sights

★ Antic Hospital de la Santa Creu i Sant Pau

HISTORIC SIGHT | Founded in the 10th century as one of Europe's earliest medical facilities, the mostly 15th- and 16th-century complex contains some of Barcelona's most impressive Gothic architecture. From the grand entrance, the first building on the left is the 18th-century Reial Acadèmia de Cirurgia i Medicina (Royal Academy of Surgery and Medicine); the surgical amphitheater is kept just as it was in the days when students learned by observing dissections.

Through a gate to the left of the Casa de Convalescència is the garden-courtyard of the hospital complex, the Jardins de Rubió i Lluc, centered on a baroque cross and lined with orange trees. On the right is the Biblioteca Nacional de Catalunya, Catalonia's national library. The library is spectacular: two parallel halls—once the core of the hospital—230 feet long, with towering Gothic arches and vaulted ceilings, designed in the 15th century by the architect of the church of Santa Maria del

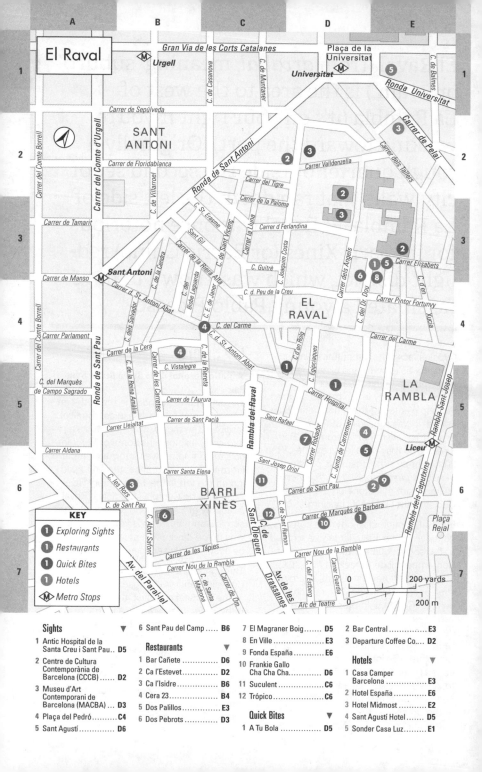

El Raval

KEY

- ① Exploring Sights
- ① Restaurants
- ① Quick Bites
- ① Hotels
- Ⓜ Metro Stops

One of the earliest medical complexes in Europe is the Antic Hospital de la Santa Creu i Sant Pau.

Pi, Guillem Abiell. This was the hospital where Antoni Gaudí was taken, unrecognized and assumed to be a pauper, after he was struck by a trolley on June 7, 1926. ⊠ Hospital 56 (or Carme 45), El Raval ☎ 93/317–1686 Reial Acadèmia de Medicina, 93/270–2300 Biblioteca de Catalunya ⊕ www.bnc.cat ⊠ €10 (Reial Acadèmia de Medicina de Catalunya tour) ⊙ Reial Acadèmia de Medicina de Catalunya: Closed Sun.–Tues., Thurs., and Fri; Biblioteca de Catalunya and Capella: Closed Sun. Ⓜ Liceu.

Centre de Cultura Contemporànea de Barcelona (CCCB) (CCCB)

ARTS CENTER | Just next door to the MACBA, this multidisciplinary gallery, lecture hall, and concert and exhibition space offers a year-round program of cultural events and projects. The center also has a remarkable film archive of historic shorts and documentaries, free to the public. Housed in the restored and renovated Casa de la Caritat, a former medieval convent and hospital, the CCCB, like the Palau de la Música Catalana, is one of the city's shining examples of contemporary flare added to traditional architecture and design. A smoked-glass wall on the right side of the patio, designed by architects Albert Villaplana and Helio Piñon, reflects out over the rooftops of El Raval to Montjuïc and the Mediterranean beyond. ⊠ Montalegre 5, El Raval ☎ 93/306–4100 ⊕ www.cccb.org ⊠ Exhibitions €6; Sun. 3–8, free (pre-book online). Admission to CCCB Film Archive is free with previous reservation ⊙ Closed Mon. Ⓜ Universitat, Catalunya.

★ Museu d'Art Contemporani de Barcelona (MACBA) (MACBA Museum of Contemporary Art Barcelona)

ART MUSEUM | FAMILY | Designed by American architect Richard Meier in 1992, this gleaming explosion of light and geometry in El Raval houses a permanent collection of contemporary art, and also regularly mounts special temporary exhibitions. Meier gives a nod to Gaudí (with the Pedrera-like wave on one end of the main facade), but his minimalist building otherwise looks unfinished.

That said, the MACBA is unarguably an important addition to the cultural capital of this once-shabby neighborhood. The MACBA's 20th-century art collection (Calder, Rauschenberg, Oteiza, Chillida, Tàpies) is excellent, while the free app offers a useful introduction to the philosophical foundations of contemporary art as well as the pieces themselves. The museum also offers wonderful workshops and activities for kids. ⊠ *Pl. dels Àngels 1, El Raval* ☎ *93/412–0810* ⊕ *www.macba.cat* ☒ *€11, free Sat. after 4* ⊙ *Closed Tues.* Ⓜ *Universitat, Catalunya.*

Plaça del Pedró
PLAZA/SQUARE | This landmark in medieval Barcelona was the dividing point where ecclesiastical and secular paths parted. The high road, Carrer del Carme, leads to the cathedral and the seat of the bishopric; the low road, Carrer de l'Hospital, heads down to the medieval hospital and the Boqueria market, a clear choice between body and soul. Named for a stone pillar, or *pedró* (large stone), marking the fork in the road, the square became a cherished landmark for Barcelona Christians after Santa Eulàlia, co-patron of Barcelona, was crucified there in the 4th century after suffering the legendary 13 ordeals designed to persuade her to renounce her faith—which, of course, she heroically refused to do. As the story goes, an overnight snowfall chastely covered her nakedness with virgin snow. The present version of Eulàlia and her cross was sculpted by Barcelona artist Frederic Marès and erected in 1951. The bell tower and vacant alcove at the base of the triangular square belong to the **Capella de Sant Llàtzer** church, originally built in the open fields in the mid-12th century and used as a leper hospital and place of worship after the 15th century when Sant Llàtzer (St. Lazarus) was officially named patron saint of lepers.

May 11 in Raval

El Raval's big day is May 11, when Carrer Hospital celebrates the Fira de Sant Ponç, a beloved Barcelona holiday. The feast day of Sant Ponç, patron saint of herbalists and beekeepers, brings Catalonia's *pagesos* (country folk) to Barcelona laden with every natural product they can haul. Everything from bees in glass cases to chamomile, rosemary, thyme, lavender, basil, pollens, mint, candied fruits, snake oil, headache remedies, and aphrodisiacs, and every imaginable condiment and savory takes over the city's streets and, more importantly, the air.

Flanked by two ordinary apartment buildings, the Sant Llàtzer chapel has a tiny antique patio and apse visible from the short Carrer de Sant Llàtzer, which cuts behind the church between Carrer del Carme and Carrer Hospital. ⊠ *Pl. del Pedró, El Raval* Ⓜ *Sant Antoni.*

Sant Agustí
NOTABLE BUILDING | This unfinished church is one of Barcelona's most unusual structures, with jagged stone sections projecting down the left side, and the upper part of the front entrance on Plaça Sant Agustí waiting to be covered with a facade. The church has had an unhappy history: originally part of an Augustinian monastery, it was first built between 1349 and 1700. It was later abandoned and rebuilt only to be destroyed in 1714 during the War of the Spanish Succession, rebuilt again, then burned in the antireligious riots of 1825 when the cloisters were demolished. The church was looted and torched once more in the closing days of the Civil War. Sant Agustí comes alive on May 22, feast day of Santa Rita, patron saint of *"los imposibles,"* meaning lost causes. Unhappily married

Skateboarders enjoy practicing in front of the Museu d'Art Contemporani de Barcelona.

women, unrequited lovers, and all-but-hopeless sufferers of every sort form long lines through the square and down Carrer Hospital. Each carries a rose that will be blessed at the chapel of Santa Rita on the right side of the altar. ⊠ *Pl. Sant Agustí s/n, El Raval* ☎ *93/318–3863* Ⓜ *Liceu.*

★ Sant Pau del Camp

CHURCH | Barcelona's oldest church was originally outside the city walls (*del camp* means "in the fields") and was a Roman cemetery as far back as the 2nd century, according to archaeological evidence. What you see now was built in 1127 and is the earliest Romanesque structure in Barcelona. Elements of the church—the classical marble capitals atop the columns in the main entry—are thought to be from the 6th and 7th centuries. The hulking, mastodonic shape of the church is a reminder of the church's defensive posture in the face of intermittent Roman persecution and, later, Moorish invasions and sackings. Check for musical performances here, as the church is an acoustical gem. The tiny cloister is Sant Pau del Camp's best feature and one of Barcelona's semisecret treasures. ⊠ *Sant Pau 101, El Raval* ☎ *93/441–0001* ⊕ *stpaudelcamp.blogspot.com* 🎫 *Free when Masses are celebrated; entrance €5, guided tours €9 (Sat. at 1pm)* ⊘ *Cloister closed Sun. during Mass; no tours in mid-Aug.* Ⓜ *Paral·lel.*

🍴 Restaurants

★ Bar Cañete

$$ | TAPAS | This spot just around the corner from the Liceu opera house is one of Barcelona's best tapas restaurants, with a long bar overlooking the burners and part of the kitchen that leads down to the 20-seat communal tasting table at the end of the room. Specialists in Ibérico products, they serve obscure cuts of Ibérico pork, such as *pluma ibérica* and *secreto ibérico* (nuggets of meat found on the inside of the shoulder blade and much-prized by Ibérico fanatics), though the real highlight of the menu is the market-fresh seafood that ranges from oysters, to grilled baby scallops and house special dishes like the baby squid (*chipirones*) with white Santa Pau beans. **Known for:** fresh seafood; superb tapas; boisterous atmosphere. $ *Average main: €18* ✉ *Unió 17, El Raval* ☎ *93/270–3458* ⊕ *www.barcanete.com/en* Ⓜ *Liceu.*

Ca l'Estevet

$$ | **CATALAN** | This restaurant has been serving old-school Catalan cuisine to local and loyal customers since 1940 (and under a different name for 50 years before that), and the practice has been made perfect. Standouts include *butifarra* sausage with spinach and chickpeas, meatballs with squid and shrimp, or veal stew with wild mushrooms. **Known for:** historic location; large, hearty portions; Catalan specialties. $ *Average main: €16* ✉ *Valldonzella 46, El Raval* ☎ *93/301–2939* ⊕ *www.restaurantestevet.com* ◔ *No dinner Sun. and Mon.* Ⓜ *Universitat.*

Ca l'Isidre

$$$$ | **CATALAN** | Since the early 1970s, Ca l'Isidre has elevated simplicity to the level of the spectacular, with traditional Catalan dishes prepared to an extraordinarily high standard (and at a rather high price tag by Barcelona standards). Ignore the menu—just follow the recommendations and order whatever's in season. **Known for:** art collection; locally sourced produce; once frequented by Miró and Dalí, whose work is on the walls, as well as current celebrities and politicians. $ *Average main: €32* ✉ *Flors 12, El Raval* ☎ *93/441–1139* ⊕ *www.calisidre.com* ◔ *Closed Mon., and 1st 2 wks of Aug.; No dinner Tues., Wed., Sun.* Ⓜ *Paral·lel.*

Cera 23

$$ | **SPANISH** | A gem among a crop of modern restaurants putting the razzle back into the run-down Raval, Cera 23 offers a winning combination of great service and robust cooking in a fun, friendly setting; stand at the bar and enjoy a blackberry mojito while you wait for your table. The focus of the dining area is the open kitchen, so guests can watch the cooks create contemporary presentations of traditional Spanish dishes. **Known for:** exceptional service; slow-cooked pork ribs with honey and soy sauce; "volcano" of black rice. $ *Average main: €15* ✉ *Cera 23, El Raval* ☎ *93/442–0808* ⊕ *www.cera23.com* ◔ *Closed Wed. and Thurs. No lunch* Ⓜ *Sant Antoni.*

Dos Palillos

$$$$ | **ECLECTIC** | After 10 years as the chief cook and favored disciple of pioneering chef Ferran Adrià, Albert Raurich opened this outstanding Asian-fusion restaurant that focuses on an eclectic assortment of tastes and textures. There are several tasting menus to choose from; an à la carte menu is available at the bar. **Known for:** gin- and chocolate-filled doughnuts; Michelin star; creative pan-Asian cooking with interesting wine pairings. $ *Average main: €32* ✉ *Elisabets 9, El Raval* ☎ *93/304–0513* ⊕ *www.dospalillos.com* ◔ *Closed Sun. and Mon., 3 wks Aug., and 2 wks at Christmas. No lunch Tues. and Wed.* Ⓜ *Catalunya, Universitat.*

Dos Pebrots

$$ | **MEDITERRANEAN** | Albert Raurich of the upscale Dos Palillos restaurant, transformed his favorite neighborhood haunt, Bar Raval, into a cutting-edge tapas bar that explores the history of Mediterranean cuisine. The gleaming makeover hasn't robbed the space of its old-town feel, though, thanks to little touches like the restored original facade and vintage cutlery. **Known for:** restored original exterior; unusual ingredients; unique tapas. $ *Average main: €20* ✉ *Doctor Dou 19, El Raval* ☎ *93/853–9598* ⊕ *www.dospebrots.com* ◔ *Closed Mon. and Tues., and 2 wks at Christmas* Ⓜ *Catalunya.*

El Magraner Boig

$ | **GREEK** | Chef Andreas Christodoulides's intent here is to recreate the dishes he grew up eating as a kid in Athens but don't expect a setting of clichéd blue and white Greek Island decor. Instead, the setting is bright and casual, allowing the classic food to speak for itself. **Known for:** saganaki (fried cheese) always a good starter; good selection of Greek wine and beer; delicious meze. $ *Average main: €12* ⊠ *Robador 22, El Raval* ☎ *93/011–8605* ⊕ *www.elmagranerboig. com* ☉ *Closed Mon. No lunch Tues.–Fri.* Ⓜ *Liceu.*

En Ville
$$ | BISTRO | With pan-Mediterranean cuisine and reasonable prices, this attractive bistro 100 yards west of the Rambla is perennially popular. The inexpensive lunch menu attracts in-the-know locals, and à la carte choices like scallops with pea foam are tempting and economical. **Known for:** value lunch menu; romantic setting; very good gluten-free offerings. $ *Average main: €17* ⊠ *Doctor Dou 14, El Raval* ☎ *93/302–8467* ⊕ *www.envillebarcelona.es/en* ☉ *Closed Sun. and 1 wk in Jan. No dinner Mon.–Wed.* Ⓜ *Catalunya, Liceu, Universitat.*

★ Fonda España
$$$ | CATALAN | The sumptuous glory of this restored late-19th-century Art Nouveau dining room has food to match, courtesy of chef German Espinosa, who spent many years working under superstar Martín Berasategui. **Known for:** the tasting menus; satisfying traditional dishes; Art Nouveau decor. $ *Average main: €23* ⊠ *Hotel España, Sant Pau 9, El Raval* ☎ *93/550–0010* ⊕ *www.hotelespanya. com* ☉ *Closed Mon.–Wed. and Aug. No dinner Sun.* Ⓜ *Liceu.*

Frankie Gallo Cha Cha Cha
$ | PIZZA | There are days when only a pizza will do and this might be the best spot in Barcelona to satisfy the craving, with a combination of wood-fired sourdough pizzas, craft beer, top-notch artisanal ingredients, and a buzzing atmosphere. The eggplant parmigiana pizza is a best seller, as is the tiramisú for dessert. **Known for:** eggplant parmigiana pizza; great atmosphere; some of the best pizza joint in town. $ *Average main: €13* ⊠ *Marquès de Barberà, 15, El Raval* ☎ *93/159–4250* ⊕ *frankiegallochachacha. com* ☉ *Closed Mon.* Ⓜ *Drassanes.*

★ Suculent
$$ | CATALAN | This is a strong contender for the crown of Barcelona's best bistro, where chef Toni Romero turns out Catalan tapas and dishes that have roots in rustic classics but reach high modern standards of execution. The name is a twist on the Catalan *sucar lent* (to dip slowly), and excellent bread is duly provided to soak up the sauces, which you won't want to let go to waste. **Known for:** big, bold flavors; must-try steak tartare on marrow bone; set menus but à la carte available at the bar. $ *Average main: €18* ⊠ *Rambla del Raval 45, El Raval* ☎ *93/443–6579* ⊕ *www.suculent. com* ☉ *Closed Sat. and Sun.* Ⓜ *Liceu.*

★ Trópico
$ | LATIN AMERICAN | This lively brunch spot is a breath of fresh air in a neighborhood perhaps best described as "up and coming." The name "trópico" (or tropical) refers to both the bright decor and the menu that takes inspiration from the tastes of the tropics—from Colombian *arepas* to Brazilian chicken *coxinhas,* Thai dragon fruit smoothies, Peruvian *ají,* and Indian-style curries. Founders Leonardo Tristancho from Colombia and Rodrigo Marco from Brazil have created a space that reflects their love of vibrant, unapologetic flavors, blended with all the warmth of Latin hospitality. **Known for:** Colombian arepas; Latin hospitality; vibrant decor and atmosphere. $ *Average main: €14* ⊠ *Marquès de Barberà 24, El Raval* ☎ *93/667–7552* ⊕ *www.tropicobcn.com* Ⓜ *Drassanes.*

☕ Coffee and Quick Bites

A Tu Bola

$ | ISRAELI | Fresh, falafel-like balls of meat, fish, and vegetables in unique, mouthwatering combinations are prepared with laser-sharp focus by the Israeli chef helming A Tu Bola. Everything from the *harissa* (spicy chili paste) to the hummus is made by hand, elevating the standard far beyond that of typical street food in the surrounding Raval. **Known for:** quality street food; quick snacks; amazing chocolate ball dessert. $ *Average main: €12* ✉ *Hospital 78, El Raval* ☎ *93/315–3244* ⊕ *www.atubolarest.com* Ⓜ *Liceu.*

Bar Central

$ | CAFÉ | If you're looking for a calm respite in which to enjoy a mid-morning coffee or a laid-back lunch, you can't beat a patio table at this café in the lush gardens of Casa de la Misericòrdia (a former orphanage), replete with palm trees, ferns, moss, and a small waterfall that mutes the street noise. In the evening, twinkling lights add a touch of romance to the already magical space. **Known for:** quiet surroundings; good croissants; romantic ambience in the evening. $ *Average main: €12* ✉ *d'Elisabets 6, El Raval* ☎ *93/270–3314* ⊕ *barcentral.bar* Ⓜ *Catalunya.*

Departure Coffee Co.

$ | CAFÉ | Tucked away in a small alley that's easy to miss, Departure Coffee is a neighborhood go-to for freshly brewed coffee any way you like it, plus a selection of toasts and pastries. There's an eclectic mix of old and new here: the building dates to 1867, when it was horse stables for the Valldonzella convent, and the entrance doors, which are the original stable doors, feature a mural by Barcelona urban artist, SM172. **Known for:** good coffee; bright, light-filled spot; modern space. $ *Average main: €8* ✉ *Verge 1, El Raval* ⊕ *www.instagram. com/departurecoffeeco* ⊘ *Closed Sun.* Ⓜ *Universitat.*

Hotels

Casa Camper Barcelona

$$$ | HOTEL | A marriage between the Camper footwear empire and the (now defunct) Vinçon design store produced this 21st-century hotel halfway between La Rambla and the MACBA (Barcelona Museum of Contemporary Art), with a focus on sustainability (think solar panels and water recycling). **Pros:** great breakfast with dishes cooked to order; complimentary 24-hour snack bar; just steps from the MACBA and the Boqueria. **Cons:** no in-room minibar; extra per person charge for children over three years old; expensive for what you get. $ *Rooms from: €220* ✉ *Elisabets 11, El Raval* ☎ *93/342–6280* ⊕ *www.casacamper.com* ⇆ *40 rooms* ⦿| *Free Breakfast* Ⓜ *Catalunya, Liceu.*

★ Hotel España

$$ | HOTEL | This beautifully renovated Art Nouveau gem is the second oldest (after the nearby Sant Agustí) and among the best of Barcelona's smaller hotels. **Pros:** near Liceu opera house and La Rambla; lavish breakfast; alabaster fireplace in the bar lounge. **Cons:** rooftop has restricted views; could use a refresh; lower rooms facing Carrer Sant Pau get some street noise. $ *Rooms from: €160* ✉ *Sant Pau 9–11, El Raval* ☎ *93/550–0000* ⊕ *www. hotelespanya.com* ⇆ *83 rooms* ⦿| *No Meals* Ⓜ *Liceu.*

Hotel Midmost

$$ | HOTEL | This handsome Moderniste property has gone through several incarnations, the most recent resulting in a rather serene setting (quite welcome in this busy neighborhood) and reasonably priced rooms, some with a terrace or balcony. **Pros:** near La Rambla and the MACBA; "superior doubles" have private terrace; small "Wellness" room for massages and treatments. **Cons:** tiny

lobby; small rooms, but good value; noisy avenue in front of hotel. *$* *Rooms from: €145* ✉ *Pelai 14, El Raval* ☏ *93/505–1100* ⊕ *www.hotelmidmost.com* ⇌ *56 rooms* ⭐ *No Meals* Ⓜ *Universitat.*

Sant Agustí Hotel

$$ | HOTEL | FAMILY | In a leafy square just off La Rambla, the Sant Agustí bills itself as the oldest billet in Barcelona—it was built in the 1720s for the library of the adjacent convent and reborn as a hotel in 1840. **Pros:** steps from the Boqueria market, La Rambla, and the Liceu opera house; intimate breakfast room; very good value for price. **Cons:** not enough closet space; safe boxes too small for laptops; Plaça Sant Agusti can be a homeless hangout. *$* *Rooms from: €156* ✉ *Pl. Sant Agustí 3, El Raval* ☏ *93/318–1658* ⊕ *www.hotelsa.com* ⇌ *80 rooms* ⭐ *Free Breakfast* Ⓜ *Liceu.*

Sonder Casa Luz

$$ | HOTEL | Just above Raval, the Casa Luz stands out for its larger than average rooms, most with with balconies that open up to let in lots of natural light. **Pros:** single rooms are an option; majority of rooms include balconies; good on-site restaurant with panoramic views. **Cons:** some rooms face inner courtyard (could be preferred for some); reception is on the second floor; no pool or spa. *$* *Rooms from: €131* ✉ *Ronda de la Universitat 1, El Raval* ☏ *67/690–9310* ⊕ *www.sonder.com* ⇌ *65* Ⓜ *Universitat.*

☯ Nightlife

El Raval has slowly evolved from a forgotten, somewhat seedy no-man's-land into one of the choicest districts to enjoy a boho-glam party scene. Though not to everyone's taste, hippie students, tattooed misfits, artists, and trend-seekers routinely bar crawl up and down a stretch of nightlife-friendly streets (like Joaquin Costa) featuring a wide assortment of divey dens, music bars, pubs, and funky *coctelerias.*

BARS

Ambar

BARS | Right off the tree-lined Rambla del Raval, the clientele at this popular watering hole is as colorful as the snazzy, red-quilted bar and moody green-blue lighting: expat students and pierced young artists rub shoulders with visiting rabble-rousers warming up for a wild night out. With its basic menu of classic cocktails and long drinks, the main attraction is arguably the space itself—the epitome of shabby chic (with an emphasis on shabby) with its calculated mix of modern and retro. ✉ *Sant Pau 77, El Raval* ☏ *93/441–3725.*

Casa Almirall

BARS | The twisted wooden fronds framing the bar's mirror, an 1888 vintage bar-top iron statue of a muse, and Art Nouveau touches such as curvy door handles make this one of the most atmospheric bars in Barcelona. It's also the second oldest, dating from 1860. (The oldest is the Marsella, another Raval favorite.) It's a good spot for evening drinks after hitting the nearby MACBA (Museu d'Art Contemporani de Barcelona) or for a pre-lunch *vermut* (vermouth) on weekends. ✉ *Joaquín Costa 33, El Raval* ☏ *93/318–9917* ⊕ *www.casaalmirall.com/en* Ⓜ *Universitat.*

El Jardí

BARS | El Raval has its gritty side, but there's bits of glamor, too, and El Jardí gets a good dose of it. In the gardens of the former Hospital de la Santa Creu, during the summer months, El Jardí is the perfect reprieve from the heat and heavy foot traffic, serving a selection of classic cocktails and vermouth, as well as a hot and cold tapas. The place closes shortly before midnight, so consider squeezing in a visit around sunset or for a round of post-dinner drinks. ✉ *Hospital 56, El Raval* ☏ *93/681–9234* ⊕ *www.eljardi.com* Ⓜ *Liceu.*

La Confitería

BARS | In a former pastry shop, this vintage bar has retained so much of the 19th-century Moderniste facade and interior touches (onetime cake display cases are now filled with period memorabilia) that visitors might experience the sensation of time standing still. Divided into two equally inviting spaces, the front is usually packed with regulars, while the granite-and-metal tables in the back are popular with couples. ☒ *Sant Pau 128, El Raval* ☎ *93/140–5435* ⊕ *www.confiteria. cat* Ⓜ *Paral·lel.*

Manchester

BARS | There's no doubt about what the name of this laid-back Raval hangout pays tribute to: that of the early '80s Manchester scene, with the Joy Division and Happy Mondays and the Stone Roses. The sheer number of people (both locals and foreigners) crowding around the wood tables and dancing in the spaces in between suggest that a tribute is welcome. ☒ *Valldonzella 40, El Raval* ☎ *62/773–3081* ⊕ *www.manchesterbar. com* Ⓜ *Catalunya.*

Marsella

BARS | Inaugurated in 1820, this historic venue, a favored haunt for artistic notables such as Gaudí, Picasso, and Hemingway, has remained remarkably unchanged since its celebrated heyday. The chipped paint on the walls and ceiling, cracked marble tables, and elaborate spiderwebs on chandeliers and bottles all add to the charm, but the main reason patrons linger is one special shot: Marsella is one of few establishments serving homemade absinthe (*absenta* in Spanish), a potent aniseed-flavored spirit meant to be savored and rumored to enhance productivity. ☒ *Sant Pau 65, El Raval* ☎ *93/442–7263* ⊕ *www.facebook. com/Bar-Marsella-148097715525039* Ⓜ *Liceu.*

33/45

BARS | From the street, this indie-cool spot might seem too brightly lighted for gritty-glam Raval, but the mismatched sofas with oversize pillows and the eclectic selection of flavored gins, tequila blends, and imported beer attracts a steady flow of lounge lizards. ☒ *Joaquin Costa 4, El Raval* ☎ *93/187–4138* ⊕ *www.3345.es* Ⓜ *Sant Antoni.*

Two Schmucks

BARS | One of the Barcelona cocktail bars to make it onto the "World's 50 Best Bars" list, Two Schmucks is the kind of fun-filled neighborhood bar that's hard to resist. The vibe is laid-back, but never boring, and it's spawned spin-offs Two Schmucks on a Terrace and the rock-'n'-roller Lucky Schmuck, also in Raval. ☒ *Joaquín Costa 52, El Raval* ☎ *67/448–0073* ⊕ *www.two-schmucks. com* Ⓜ *Universitat.*

DANCE CLUBS

Sala Apolo

DANCE CLUBS | Set across three levels and multiple rooms, Sala Apolo offers a variety of house/techno nights and intimate live music concerts. Two Sunday afternoons a month, it turns into Barcelona's hottest LGBTQ destination, playing host to the immensely popular Churros con Chocolate and VenTú! tea dances. ☒ *Nou de la Rambla, 113, El Raval* ☎ *93/441–4001* ⊕ *www.sala-apolo.com* Ⓜ *Paral·lel.*

MUSIC CLUBS

Jazz Sí Club

LIVE MUSIC | Run by the Barcelona contemporary music school next door, this workshop and (during the day) café is a forum for musicians, teachers, and fans to listen to and debate their art. Most weeks, the schedule offers jazz on Monday and Wednesday; pop, blues, and rock jam sessions on Tuesday; Cuban salsa on Thursday; flamenco on Friday; and rock and pop on weekends. The small cover charge (€6–€10, depending on which night you visit) includes a drink.

Gigs start between 6:30 and 8:45 pm.
✉ *Requesens 2, El Raval* ☎ *93/329–0020*
⊕ *tallerdemusics.com/en/jazzsi-club*
Ⓜ *Sant Antoni.*

Shopping

Shopping in the Raval reflects the district's multicultural and bohemian vibe. Around MACBA (Barcelona Museum of Contemporary Art) you'll find dozens of designer-run start-ups selling fashion, crafts, and housewares, while the edgier southernmost section has lots of food shops (along Calles Hospital and Carme) and vintage clothing (on Calle Riera Baixa).

ART GALLERIES
Miscelanea
ART GALLERIES | As the name suggests, Miscelanea shows a mix of art disciplines, including both emerging and established artists. The window display features a new artist every month. ✉ *Carrer Dr. Dou 16, El Raval* ☎ *93/317–9398* ⊕ *miscelanea.info* Ⓜ *Catalunya.*

BOOKS
La Central del Raval
BOOKS | This bookstore in the former chapel of the Casa de la Misericòrdia sells books amid stunning architecture and holds regular cultural events. You can sift through books of various genres, from anthropology and architecture to photography and poetry, and the English-language section showcases both best-sellers and lesser-known works. Behind the bookstore is Bar Central's lush garden restaurant, which is still a bit of a local secret. ✉ *Elisabets 6, El Raval* ☎ *90/080–2109* ⊕ *www.lacentral.com* Ⓜ *Catalunya.*

CLOTHING
Holala! Plaza
SECOND-HAND | Holala! is more a lifestyle than a vintage store. The owners travel the world in search of garments for the next trend or wave of nostalgia and the

Barcelona Jazz ⓨ

Barcelona has loved jazz ever since Sam Wooding and his Chocolate Kiddies triumphed here in 1929. Jack Hilton's visits in the early 1930s paved the way for Benny Carter and the Hot Club of Barcelona in 1935 and 1936. In the early years of the post–Spanish civil war Franco dictatorship, jazz was viewed as a dangerous influence from beyond, but by 1969 Duke Ellington's Sacred Concerts smuggled jazz into town under the protective umbrella of the same Catholic Church whose conservative elements cautioned the Franco regime against the perils of this "degenerate music."

the huge space is chockablock with clothing, furniture, objects, knickknacks, and other flotsam of the distant and not-so-distant past. Hawaiian surfboards, high-waisted Levis, nubby 1980s knits—it's all put into a postmodern context at Holala! There's a smaller Holala! selling clothes only at Tallers 73, also in the Raval. ✉ *Valldonzella 2, El Raval* ☎ *93/302–0593* Ⓜ *Catalunya.*

GIFTS AND HOME DECOR
Fusta'm
HOUSEWARES | Old meets new at this small but stylish shop. Restorer Lídia Matos and carpenter Oriol Viñas put their skills to good use when opening Fusta'm. Matos, for her part, collects and restores unique objects from around the peninsula. In addition to decorative pieces and original furniture from the '60s and '70s, Fusta'm sells a selection of glassware, ceramics, macrame, and other home decor items. ✉ *Joaquín Costa 62, El Raval* ☎ *63/952–7076* ⊕ *fustam. cat/en* Ⓜ *Universitat.* Household Items and Furniture

Grey Street

OTHER SPECIALTY STORE | If you're looking for unique local gifts, this is the spot. The owner, Amy Cocker, hails from Australia and named her store after the address of her grandparents house in Canberra but the shop mainly showcases local talent, with items that include ceramics, jewelry, essential oils, candles, and other thoughtful pieces you'd never think to get but now want ten of. There's also a dedicated bookshelf on everything from astrology and Tarot to crystals and travel notebooks. ⊠ *Peu de la Creu 25, El Raval* ⊕ *www.greystreetbarcelona.com/en* Ⓜ *Sant Antoni, Liceu.*

JEWELRY
Bagana

JEWELRY & WATCHES | This family-run jewelry shop has an on-site workshop where you can see the jewelry being made. There are several collections, including one inspired by travelers and another that celebrates cultures around the world. ⊠ *Carrer de Ferlandina, 33, El Raval* ☎ *93/172–8836* ⊕ *baganabcn.com* Ⓜ *Universitat.*

MARKETS
Flea Market Barcelona

SECOND-HAND | Barcelona's love for retro and vintage reaches its pinnacle twice a month in two different squares. In Plaça Blanquerna, on the second Sunday of the month, Flea Market Barcelona (aka "El Flea") bring together the hipsters and the hippies, the dads and the dealers, who empty out their wardrobes and garages so that you can walk away with art-deco wall clocks or a 1970s hand mixer. Over in Plaça Salvador Seguí, on the first Sunday of the month, is the so-called "Fleadonia." ⊠ *Pl. Blanquerna* ⊕ *fleamarketbcn.com* Ⓜ *Drassanes.*

Mercat de Sant Antoni

MARKET | A mammoth hangar at the junction of Ronda de Sant Antoni and Comte d'Urgell, designed in 1882 by Antoni Rovira i Trias, the Mercat de Sant Antoni is considered the city's finest example of wrought-iron architecture. The Greek-cross-shaped market covers an entire block on the edge of the Eixample, and some of the best Moderniste stall facades in Barcelona distinguish this exceptional space. Fully functioning as of 2017 after years of painstaking restoration to incorporate medieval archaeological remains underneath, the market is a foodie paradise of fruit, vegetables, fish, cheeses, and more. The indoor food market is closed on Sunday but this is when, in the morning, you can wander the outdoor stalls of the weekly flea market full of stamps and coins, comic books and trading cards, VHS, CDs, vinyl, and vintage clothing. ⊠ *Comte d'Urgell 1, El Raval* ☎ *93/426–3521* ⊕ *www.mercatde-santantoni.com* Ⓜ *Sant Antoni.*

MUSIC
Discos Paradiso

MUSIC | Sifting through the new and second-hand vinyl is part of the fun at Discos Paradiso. Since opening in 2010, the store has done well curating a large selection of electronic music: techno, house, IDM, experimental, and everything in between..There's plenty of disco, soul, hip-hop, and rock recordings as well. If you're lucky, your visit may coincide with one of their exhibitions or musical events. ⊠ *Ferlandina 39, El Raval* ☎ *93/329–6440* ⊕ *www.discosparadiso.com* Ⓜ *Universitat, Sant Antoni.*

Chapter 6

SANT PERE AND LA RIBERA

Updated by
Isabelle Kliger

⊙ Sights	🍴 Restaurants	🛏 Hotels	👜 Shopping	🍸 Nightlife
★★★★★	★★★★★	★★★★☆	★★★★★	★★★★★

NEIGHBORHOOD SNAPSHOT

TOP EXPERIENCES

■ **Streets of El Born:** Get lost in the narrow alleyways of El Born, exploring the tiny designer stores and hidden sun-kissed squares along Carrer dels Flassaders, Carrer dels Banys Vells, and Carrer dels Mirallers.

■ **Santa Maria del Mar:** Attend a concert or requiem Mass in this surprisingly light and serene church.

■ **Snare a seat in the sun:** The outdoor terraces in the squares surrounding Santa Caterina market, as well as Plaça de Sant Pere square and Plaça de Sant Agustí Vell, are great for enjoying a cold beer or coffee in the sun.

■ **Cal Pep:** Squeeze through the door and enjoy a glass (or share a bottle) of Albariño while you eat some of the city's best tapas.

■ **Casa Gispert:** Browse the olive oils, spices, chocolates, and fruits at this venerated food shop—we strongly suggest purchasing some of the roasted nuts that have been prepared in the same wood-fired roaster for more than 160 years.

GETTING HERE

From the central Plaça de Catalunya metro hub, it's a 10-minute walk over and down to the Palau de la Música Catalana for the beginning of this tour. The yellow L4 metro stop at Jaume I is closer to Santa Maria del Mar, but it's a hassle if you have to change trains; Plaça de Catalunya is close enough, and makes for a pleasant stroll.

PLANNING YOUR TIME

Depending on the number of museum visits and stops, exploring these neighborhoods can take a full day. Count on at least four hours of actual walking time. Catching Santa Maria del Mar open is key (it's closed daily 1:30–4:30). If you make it to Cal Pep for tapas before 1:30, you might get a place at the bar; if you don't, it's well worth the wait. The Picasso Museum is at least a two-hour visit.

DON'T MISS

La Boqueria may be Barcelona's most famous food market, but most Barcelonians find less busy alternative for their day-to-day shopping. With its undulating multicolored mosaic roof, Mercat de Santa Caterina is as enticing from the outside as it is inside: The original covered market here was erected in 1848 but it was redesigned in the early 2000s and the colorful roof, designed to look like fruit and vegetables when seen from the sky, is by artist Toni Comella. Grab lunch in one of the food stalls or stock up on tins of salted anchovies from Rosa Marina, ceramics from Niu d'Art, or local olive oil from Olisoliva (✉ *Avenida de Francesc Cambó, 16, Sant Pere*).

Nowadays, these districts are, arguably, the trendiest parts of Barcelona's old town, or Ciutat Vella. A few hundred years ago, however, when Barceloneta was still an island, the ancient Sant Pere textile district was better known as Barcelona's well-to-do waterfront neighborhood. No surprise, then, that these areas have some of the city's most iconic buildings, from the Gothic 14th-century basilica of Santa Maria del Mar to the over-the-top Moderniste Palau de la Música Catalana. At the Museu Picasso, works of the 20th-century master are displayed in five adjoining Renaissance palaces.

Sant Pere, which borders Barceloneta, is centered on its eponymous church. A half mile closer to the port, the Barri de la Ribera and the former market of El Born, now known as La Ribera/El Born, were at the center of Catalonia's great maritime and economic expansion of the 13th and 14th centuries.

Surrounding the basilica of Santa Maria del Mar, La Ribera/El Born area includes Carrer Montcada, lined with 14th- to 18th-century Renaissance palaces; Passeig del Born, where medieval jousts were held; Carrer Flassaders and the area around the early mint; the antiques shop- and restaurant-rich Carrer Banys Vells; and Plaça de les Olles. The district is also home to Pla del Palau, where La Llotja, Barcelona's early maritime exchange, housed the fine-arts school where Picasso, Gaudí, and Domènech i Montaner all studied, as did many more of Barcelona's most important artists and architects.

La Ribera began to experience a revival in the 1980s and is now full of intimate bars and cafés, as well as trendy boutiques. An open excavation in the center of El Born offers a fascinating view of pre-1714 Barcelona, dismantled by the victorious troops of Felipe V at the end of the War of the Spanish Succession. The Passeig del Born, medieval Barcelona's version of La Rambla, is once again a pleasant, leafy promenade.

Sights

Biblioteca Francesca Bonnemaison (Women's Public Library)

LIBRARY | Barcelona's (and probably the world's) first library established exclusively for women, the Biblioteca Popular de la Dona was founded in 1909, evidence of the city's early-20th-century progressive attitudes and tendencies. Over the opulently coffered main reading room, the stained-glass skylight reads "Tota dona val mes quan letra apren" (Any woman's worth more when she learns how to read), the first line of a ballad by the 13th-century Catalan troubadour Severí de Girona.

Once Franco's Spain composed of church, army, and oligarchy had restored law and order after the Spanish Civil War, the center was taken over by Spain's one legal political party, the Falange, and women's activities were reoriented toward more domestic pursuits such as sewing and cooking. Today, the library is open to all genders, and the complex includes a small theater that has a program of theatrical and cultural events. ⊠ Centro de Cultura, Sant Pere Més Baix 7, Sant Pere ☎ 93/268–7360 ⊕ ajuntament.barcelona.cat/biblioteques/bibfbonnemaison/ca ۞ Closed Sun. Ⓜ L1/L4 Urquinaona.

Capella d'en Marcús (Marcús Chapel)

CHURCH | This Romanesque hermitage looks as if it had been left behind by some remote order of hermit-monks who meant to take it on a picnic in the Pyrenees. The tiny chapel, possibly—along with Sant Llàtzer—Barcelona's smallest religious structure, and certainly one of its oldest, was originally built in the 12th century on the main Roman road into Barcelona, the one that would become Cardo Maximo just a few hundred yards away as it passed through the walls at Portal de l'Àngel.

Bernat Marcús, a wealthy merchant concerned with public welfare and social issues, built a hospital here for poor travelers; the hospital chapel that bears his name was dedicated to the Mare de Déu de la Guia (Our Lady of the Guide). As a result of its affiliation, combined with its location on the edge of town, the chapel eventually became the headquarters of the Confraria del Correus a Cavall (Brotherhood of the Pony Express), also known as the troters (trotters), that made Barcelona the key link in overland mail between the Iberian Peninsula and France. ⊠ Carders 2 (Placeta d'en Marcús), Born-Ribera ☎ 93/310–2390 Ⓜ Jaume I.

Carrer Flassaders

STREET | Named for the weavers and blanket makers to whom this street belonged in medieval times, Carrer Flassaders is best approached from Carrer Montcada, at **El Xampanyet**, one of La Ribera's most popular bars for tapas and cava. Duck into the short, dark Carrer Arc de Sant Vicenç. At the end, you'll find yourself face to face with La Seca, what used to be the Royal Mint (officially, the Reial Fàbrica de la Moneda de la Corona d'Aragó), where money was manufactured until the mid-19th century. Coins bearing the inscription, in Castilian, "Principado de Cataluña" (Principality of Catalonia) were made here as late as 1836.

Turn left on Carrer de la Seca to Carrer de la Cirera. Overhead to the left is the image of Santa Maria de Cervelló, one of the patron saints of the Catalan fleet, on the back of the Palau Cervelló on Carrer Montcada. Turn right on Carrer de la Cirera, and arrive at the corner of Carrer dels Flassaders. Walk left past several shops. Wander down Flassaders through a gauntlet of elegant clothing, furnishings, and jewelry design boutiques, and you'll pass the main entry to Escenari Joan Brossa at Number 40, with the gigantic Bourbon coat of arms over the imposing archway.

Look up to your right at the corner of the gated Carrer de les Mosques, famous as Barcelona's narrowest street. The mustachioed countenance peering down at you was once a medieval advertisement for a brothel. **Pasteleria Hofmann**, at Number 44, is the excellent pastry shop (don't pass up the mascarpone croissants) of famous Barcelona chef, the late Mey Hofmann, whose cooking school is over on nearby Carrer Argenteria. A right on Passeig del Born will take you back to Santa Maria del Mar. ⊠ *Flassaders, Born-Ribera* Ⓜ *Jaume I.*

Fossar de les Moreres (*Cemetery of the Mulberry Trees*)
HISTORIC SIGHT | This low marble monument runs across the eastern side of the church of Santa Maria del Mar. It honors the defenders of Barcelona who gave their lives in the final siege that ended the War of the Spanish Succession on September 11, 1714, and who are buried in the cemetery that lies beneath the square.

The inscription (in English: "in the cemetery of the mulberry trees no traitor lies") refers to the graveyard keeper's story. He refused to bury those on the invading side, even when one turned out to be his son. This is the traditional gathering place for the most radical elements of Catalonia's nationalist (separatist) movement, on the Catalonian national day, which celebrates the heroic defeat.

From the monument, look back at Santa Maria del Mar. The lighter-color stone on the lateral facade was left by the 17th-century Pont del Palau (Palace Bridge), erected to connect the Royal Palace in the nearby Pla del Palau with the Tribuna Real (Royal Box) over the right side of the Santa Maria del Mar altar, so that nobles and occupying military officials could get to Mass without the risk of walking in the streets. The bridge, regarded as a symbol of imperialist oppression, was finally dismantled in 1987. The steel arch with its eternal flame that honors the fallen Catalans was erected in 2002. ⊠ *Pl. de Santa Maria, Born-Ribera* Ⓜ *L4 Jaume I.*

La Llotja (*Maritime Exchange*)
NOTABLE BUILDING | Barcelona's maritime trade center, the Casa Llotja de Mar, was designed to be the city's finest example of civil architecture, built in the Catalan Gothic style between 1380 and 1392. At the end of the 18th century, the facades were (tragically) covered in the neoclassical uniformity of the time, but the interior, the great Saló Gòtic (Gothic Hall), remained unaltered, and was a grand venue for balls and celebrations throughout the 19th century.

The Gothic Hall was used as the Barcelona stock exchange until 1975, and until late 2001 as the grain exchange. The hall, with its graceful arches and columns and floors of light Carrara and dark Genovese marble, has now been brilliantly restored. The building, which can only be seen on a guided tour, now houses the Barcelona Chamber of Commerce.

The Escola de Belles Arts (School of Fine Arts) occupied the southwestern corner of the Llotja from 1849 until 1960. Many illustrious Barcelona artists studied here, including Gaudí, Miró, and Picasso. The Reial Acadèmia Catalana de Belles Arts de Sant Jordi (Royal Catalan Academy of Fine Arts of St. George) still has its seat in the Llotja, and its museum is one of Barcelona's semisecret collections of art, from medieval paintings by unknown artists to modern works by members of the Academy itself; a 17th-century *Saint Jerome* by Joan Ribalta is especially fine. To slip into the Saló Gòti, walk down the

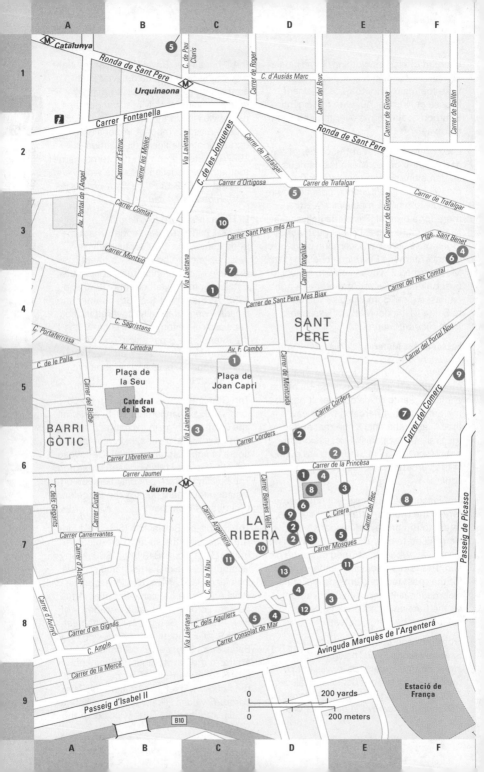

Map: Sant Pere and La Ribera

EL FORT PIUS

Arc de Triomf
Arc de Triomf
Antic Estació del Nord
Parc de l'Estacio del Nord
Parc de la Ciutadella
Universitat Pompeu Fabra
Parlament de Catalunya
Parc Zoològic

Passeig de Saint Joan
Carrer d'Ausiás Marc
C. de Nápols
C. de Sicilia
Carrer d'Ali Bei
Carrer de Roger de Flor
Av. Vilanova
Passeig de Lluís companys
Passeig de Lluís companys
Carrer des Almogàvers
Carer de Buenaventura Muñoz
Passeig de Pujades
Av. Meridiana
Carrer de Wellington
Pg. Circumval·lació

Sights ▼

1 Biblioteca Francesca Bonnemaison C4
2 Capella d'en Marcús D6
3 Carrer Flassaders...................E6
4 Fossar de les Moreres D8
5 La Llotja B1
6 Moco Museum Barcelona D7
7 Museu de la Xocolata.............F5
8 Museu Picasso D6
9 Palau Dalmases...................D7
10 Palau de la Música Catalana......C3
11 Passeig del Born....................E7
12 Plaça de les Olles..................D8
13 Santa Maria del Mar D7

Restaurants ▼

1 Bar del Pla..........................D6
2 Bodega La Puntual D7
3 Cal Pep..............................E8
4 Cremat 11...........................D6
5 El Passadís d'en Pep C8
6 Fismuler..............................F3
7 Le Cucine Mandarosso C3
8 Llamber F6
9 Picnic F5
10 Proper...............................D7
11 Sagardi..............................C7

Quick Bites ▼

1 Brunells.............................D6
2 El Xampanyet.......................D7
3 Euskal Etxea........................D7
4 Gocce di Latte......................D8
5 Pastelería Hofmann E7

Hotels ▼

1 The Barcelona EDITION C5
2 Ciutat de Barcelona E6
3 H10 Montcada C6
4 Hotel Rec F3
5 Hotel Yurbban Trafalgar...........D3

KEY

1 Exploring Sights
1 Restaurants
1 Quick Bites
1 Hotels
 Metro Stops

stairs from the museum to the second floor, then take the marble staircase down and turn right. ✉ *Casa Llotja, Passeig d'Isabel II 1, Born-Ribera* ☎ *93/319–2432 Reial Acadèmia, 670/466260 guided visits to museum* ⊕ *www.racba.org* ✆ *Guided tours €12 (English tours Sat. at 11 am)* Ⓜ *L4 Barceloneta.*

Museu de la Xocolata (*Museum of Chocolate*)

OTHER MUSEUM | FAMILY | The elaborate, painstakingly detailed chocolate sculptures, which have included everything from La Sagrada Família to Don Quixote's windmills, delight both youthful and adult visitors to this museum, set in an imposing 18th-century former monastery and developed by the Barcelona Provincial Confectionery Guild. Other exhibits here touch on Barcelona's centuries-old love affair with chocolate, the introduction of chocolate to Europe by Spanish explorers from the Maya and Aztec cultures in the New World, and both vintage and current machinery and tools used to create this sweet delicacy.

The "Bean To Bar" experience showcases the full production process for making artisanal chocolate using traceable cocoa from different parts of the world. You can buy the finished products, including boxes and bars of chocolate, in the museum shop. The beautiful café offers rich hot and cold chocolate drinks and house-made cakes and pastries. Tasting sessions and classes on making chocolate are offered, too. ✉ *Comerç 36, Born-Ribera* ☎ *93/268–7878* ⊕ *www.museuxocolata.cat* ✆ *€6* ⊘ *Closed Mon.* Ⓜ *L4 Jaume 1, L1 Arc de Triomf.*

★ **Museu Picasso** (*Picasso Museum*)

ART MUSEUM | The Picasso Museum is housed in five adjoining 13th- to 15th-century palaces on Carrer Montcada, a street known for its elegant medieval mansions. Picasso spent his formative years in Barcelona (1895–1904), and although this collection doesn't include

a significant number of his most famous paintings, it's strong on his early work, especially showcasing the link between Picasso and Barcelona.

The museum opened in 1963 on the suggestion of Picasso's friend Jaume Sabartés, and the initial donation was from the Sabartés collection. Later, Picasso donated his early works, and in 1982 his widow, Jacqueline Roque, added 41 ceramic pieces. Displays include childhood sketches, works from the artist's Rose and Blue periods, and the famous 1950s cubist variations on Velázquez's *Las Meninas* (in Rooms 12–16).

On the lower-floor, the sketches, oils, and schoolboy caricatures from Picasso's early years in A Coruña are perhaps the most fascinating part of the whole museum, showing the facility he seemed to possess from birth. His *La Primera Communión* (*First Communion*), painted at the age of 15, gives an idea of his early accomplishments. On the second floor you see the beginnings of the mature Picasso and his Blue Period in Paris. Stop at the terrace café and restaurant for a light Mediterranean meal to break up the day.

It is always best to book tickets online ahead of time, especially for visits on the first Sunday of the month and every Thursday after 4 p.m., when admission is free. Online tickets are typically released four days in advance. ✉ *Montcada 15–19, Born-Ribera* ☎ *93/256–3000, 93/256–3022 guided tour and group reservations* ⊕ *www.museupicasso.bcn.cat* ✆ *€12; free Thurs. from 4 pm, and 1st Sun. of month. Tours €6* ⊘ *Closed Mon.* ☞ *Guided tours of permanent collection (in English) are Sun. at 11* Ⓜ *L4 Jaume I, L1 Arc de Triomf.*

Palau Dalmases

NOTABLE BUILDING | If you can get through the massive wooden gates that open onto Carrer Montcada (at the moment,

the only opportunity is when the first-floor café-theater is open), you'll find yourself in Barcelona's best 17th-century Renaissance courtyard, built into a former 15th-century Gothic palace. Note the door knockers up at horseback level, and then scrutinize the frieze—featuring *The Rape of Europa*—that runs up the stone railing of the elegant stairway at the end of the patio. It's a festive abduction: Neptune's chariot, cherubs, naiads, dancers, tritons, and musicians accompany Zeus, in the form of a bull, as he carries poor Europa up the stairs and off to Crete.

The stone carvings in the courtyard, the 15th-century Gothic chapel, with its reliefs of angelic musicians, and the vaulting in the reception hall and salon are all that remain of the original 15th-century palace. The ground-floor Espai Barroc café features baroque-era flourishes and period furniture. It also hosts jazz, opera *concertante*,and other musical performances, as well as nightly (at 6, 7:30, and 9:30) flamenco shows. ⊠ *Montcada 20, Born-Ribera* ☎ *66/076–9865 Espai Barroc* ⊕ *www.flamencopalaudalmases.com* ⊠ *Shows from €25 (includes 1 drink)* Ⓜ *L4 Jaume I.*

★ **Palau de la Música Catalana**
NOTABLE BUILDING | On Carrer Amadeus Vives, just off Via Laietana, a 10-minute walk from Plaça de Catalunya, is one of the world's most extraordinary music halls, a flamboyant tour de force designed in 1908 by Lluís Domènech i Montaner. Its sponsors, the Orfeó Català musical society, wanted it to celebrate the importance of music in Catalan culture and the life of its ordinary people (as opposed to the Liceu opera house, with its Castilian-speaking, monarchist, upper-class patrons, and its music from elsewhere), but the Palau turned out to be anything but commonplace. It and the Liceu were, for many decades, opposing crosstown forces in Barcelona's musical as well as philosophical discourse. If you

can't fit a performance into your itinerary, you owe it to yourself to at least take a tour of this amazing building.

The exterior is a remarkable riot of color and form. The Miquel Blay sculptural group over the corner of Amadeu Vives and Sant Pere Més Alt is a hymn in stone to Catalonia's popular traditions, with hardly a note left unsung: St. George the dragon-slayer (at the top), women and children at play and work, fishermen with oars over their shoulders—a panoply of everyday life.

Inside, the decor of the Palau assaults your senses before the first note of music is ever played. Wagner's Valkyries burst from the right side of the stage over a heavy-browed bust of Beethoven; Catalonia's popular music is represented by the graceful maidens of Lluís Millet's song *Flors de Maig* (Flowers of May) on the left. Overhead, an inverted stained-glass cupola seems to channel the divine gift of music straight from heaven. Painted rosettes and giant peacock feathers adorn the walls and columns, and, across the entire back wall of the stage, is a relief of muse-like Art Nouveau musicians in costume. The visuals alone make music sound different here, be it a chamber orchestra, a renowned piano soloist, a gospel choir, or an Afro-Cuban combo.

A variety of tours are available. The standard guided tour in English takes place at 10 am and 3 pm, and you can add a 20-minute live piano or organ recital on select dates (check availability and book online in advance). Self-guided audio tours, downloaded to your personal device, are €14. ⊠ *Palau de la Música 4–6, Born-Ribera* ☎ *93/295–7200, 90/247–5485 box office* ⊕ *www.palaumusica.cat/en* ⊠ *Standard guided tour €18* Ⓜ *L1/L4 Urquinaona.*

★ **Passeig del Born**
PLAZA/SQUARE | Once the site of medieval jousts and the Inquisition's autos-da-fé,

the passeig, at the end of Carrer Montcada behind the church of Santa Maria del Mar, was early Barcelona's most important square. Nowadays, late-night cocktail bars and small restaurants with tiny spiral stairways line the narrow, elongated plaza.

The numbered cannonballs under the public benches are 20th-century works by the late poet, playwright, and designer, Joan Brossa—the so-called poet of space, whose visual-arts pieces incorporated numbers and/or letters and words. These sculptures are intended to evoke the 1714 siege of Barcelona, which concluded the 14-year War of the Spanish Succession, when Felipe V's conquering Castilian and French troops attacked the city ramparts at their lowest, flattest flank.

After their victory, the Bourbon forces obliged residents of the Barri de la Ribera (Waterfront District) to tear down nearly a thousand of their own houses, some 20% of Barcelona at that time, to create fields of fire so that the occupying army of Felipe V could better train its batteries of cannon on the conquered populace and discourage any nationalist uprisings. Thus began Barcelona's "internal exile" as an official enemy of the Spanish state.

Walk down to the Born itself—a great iron hangar that was once a produce market designed by Josep Fontseré and is in the Plaça Comercial, across from the end of the promenade. The initial stages of the construction of a public library here uncovered the remains of the lost city of 1714, complete with blackened fireplaces, taverns, wells, and the canal that brought water into the city.

The streets of 14th- to 18th-century Born-Ribera now lie open in the sunken central square of the old market. Around it, at ground level, are a number of new, multifunctional, exhibition and performance spaces that make this area one

of the city's newest and liveliest cultural hubs. Among the attractions is the Museu d'Història de la Ciutat's El Born Centre de Cultura i Memòria (closed Monday, free to upper galleries, €4 to the archaeological site). ⊠ *Passeig del Born, Born-Ribera* ☎ *93/256–6851 El Born Centre de Cultura i Memòria* ⊕ *elbornculturaimemoria.barcelona.cat* Ⓜ *L4 Jaume I/Barceloneta.*

Plaça de les Olles

PLAZA/SQUARE | This pretty little square named for the makers of *olles,* or pots, has been known to host everything from topless sunbathers to elegant Viennese waltzers to the overflow from the popular nearby tapas bar Cal Pep. Notice the balconies at No. 6 over Café de la Ribera, oddly with colorful blue and yellow tile on the second and top floors. The house with the turret over the street on the right at the corner leading out to Pla del Palau (at No. 2 Plaça de les Olles) is another of Enric Sagnier i Villavecchia's retro-Moderniste works. ⊠ *Pl. de les Olles, Born-Ribera* Ⓜ *L4 Jaume I/Barceloneta.*

★ Santa Maria del Mar

CHURCH | An example of early Catalan Gothic architecture, Santa Maria del Mar is extraordinary for its unbroken lines and elegance. At what was then the water's edge, the church was built by stonemasons who chose, fitted, and carved each stone hauled down from the same Montjuïc quarry that provided the sandstone for the 4th-century Roman walls. The medieval numerological symbol for the Virgin Mary, the number eight (or multiples thereof), runs through every element: the 16 octagonal pillars are 2 meters in diameter and spread out into rib vaulting arches at a height of 16 meters; the painted keystones at the apex of the arches are 32 meters from the floor; and the central nave is twice as wide as the lateral naves (8 meters each).

A wooden door leads to Barcelona's best 17th-century patio in the Palau Dalmases.

The church survived the fury of anar- chists who, in 1936, burned nearly all of Barcelona's churches as a reprisal against the alliance of army, church, and oligarchy during the military rebellion. The basilica, then filled with ornate side chap- els and choir stalls, burned for 11 days, nearly crumbling. Restored after the Civil War by a series of Bauhaus-trained archi- tects, the church is now an architectural gem.

The paintings in the keystones overhead represent the Coronation of the Virgin, the Nativity, the Annunciation, the eques- trian figure of the father of Pedro IV, King Alfons, and the Barcelona coat of arms. The 34 lateral chapels are dedicated to different saints and images. The first chapel to the left of the altar (No. 20) is the Capella del Santo Cristo (Chapel of the Holy Christ), its stained-glass window an allegory of Barcelona's 1992 Olympic Games. An engraved stone riser beside the door onto Carrer Sombrerers com- memorates where San Ignacio de Loyola,

founder of the Jesuit Order, begged for alms in 1524 and 1525.

Set aside at least a half-hour to see Santa Maria del Mar, and be sure to check out *La Catedral del Mar* (*The Cathedral of the Sea*), by Ildefonso Falcons, which chronicles the construction of the basil- ica and 14th-century life in Barcelona. Consider joining a guided tour to climb the towers for magnificent rooftop views or to access the crypt. Die-hard enthu- siasts will want to sign up for the Santa Maria del Mar at Dusk Tour, an exclusive, 1½-hour experience for small groups that not only lets you visit spaces normally closed to the public, but also enables you to fully appreciate the lighting of the building in addition to its silence and enormity.

■ TIP→ **Scan weekly magazines to see if there are any concerts being held in the basilica during your visit. The setting and the acoustics make performances here truly memorable.** ⊠ *Pl. de Santa Maria*

Picasso's Barcelona

Barcelona's claim to Pablo Picasso (1881–1973) has been contested by Málaga (the painter's birthplace), as well as by Madrid, where *Guernica* hangs, and by the town of Gernika, victim of the 1937 Luftwaffe saturation bombing that inspired the famous canvas. Fervently anti-Franco, Picasso refused to return to Spain after the Civil War; in turn, the regime allowed no public display of his work until 1961, when the artist's *Sardana* frieze on Barcelona's Architects' Guild building was unveiled. Picasso did not set foot on Spanish soil for his last 39 years.

Picasso spent a sporadic but formative period of his youth in Barcelona between 1895 and 1904, after which he moved to Paris. His father was an art professor at the Reial Acadèmia de Belles Arts in La Llotja—where his son, a precocious draftsman, began advanced classes at the age of 15. The 19-year-old Picasso first exhibited at Els Quatre Gats, a tavern on Carrer Montsió that looks today much as it did then. His early Cubist painting *Les Demoiselles d'Avignon* was inspired not by the French town but by the Barcelona street Carrer d'Avinyó, then infamous for its brothels. After moving to Paris, Picasso returned occasionally to Barcelona until his last visit in 1934.

The company **Iconoserveis Culturals** (✉ *Av. Portal de l'Àngel 38, 4º–2ª, Born-Ribera* ☎ *93/410–1405* 🎫 *€335 for 1–3 people*) arranges private walking tours through the key spots in Picasso's Barcelona life, covering studios, galleries, family apartments, and the painter's favorite haunts and hangouts.

1, Born-Ribera ☎ *93/310–2390* 🌐 *www.santamariadelmarbarcelona.org* 🎫 *From €5* [M] *L4 Jaume I.*

🍴 Restaurants

★ Bar del Pla

$ | CATALAN | Specializing in Catalan bar food and local, organic, biodynamic, and natural wine, this sometimes-rowdy bar may not look like much from the outside but the hordes of people waiting to be seated give it away. Top choices include the mushroom carpaccio with wasabi vinaigrette and strawberries, the black squid-ink croquettes and the spicy *patatas bravas*. **Known for:** totally on-trend despite the old-school appearance; excellent tapas; Catalan natural wines. [$] *Average main: €15* ✉ *Montcada 2, Born-Ribera* ☎ *93/268–3003* 🌐 *www.bardelpla.cat* 🕐 *Closed Sun.* [M] *Jaume I L4.*

★ Bodega La Puntual

$$ | CATALAN | Just down the road from the Picasso Museum, Bodega La Puntual might look like a tourist trap, but it's a classic, specializing in hearty portions of Catalan fare, made from seasonal, locally sourced produce. Top menu choices include the fresh marinated anchovies, the plate of premium hand-cut Iberian *jamón*, and *trinxat*: a traditional Catalan dish made with potatoes, cabbage, and pork meat, served with a fried egg. **Known for:** great for lunch after the Picasso Museum; seasonal, locally sourced ingredients; traditional Catalan food. [$] *Average main: €22* ✉ *Montcada 22, Born-Ribera* ☎ *93/310–3545* 🌐 *grupovarela.es/bodega-la-puntual-barcelona* [M] *Jaume I L4.*

★ Cal Pep

$$ | **TAPAS** | It's has been in a permanent feeding frenzy for more than 30 years, intensified by hordes of tourists, but this loud, hectic bar manages to keep delivering the very highest quality tapas, year in year out. Be prepared to wait up to an hour for a place at the counter; reservations for the tables in the tiny back room and on the outdoor terrace are accepted, but the counter is where the action is. **Known for:** lively counter scene; delicious tortilla de patatas; excellent fish fry. $ *Average main: €20* ✉ *Pl. de les Olles 8, Born-Ribera* ☎ *93/310–7961* ⊕ *www.calpep.com* ⊘ *Closed Sun. and 3 wks in Aug. No lunch Mon.* Ⓜ *Jaume I, Barceloneta.*

Cremat 11

$ | **FRENCH FUSION** | Brunch spots may be ten a penny these days but few can compete with the superb, French-owned Cremat 11, almost hidden down this tiny street behind the Picasso Museum. The dining room is small but cozy, and there is also a shady outdoor patio on what is arguably one of the prettiest squares in the city. **Known for:** killer cocktails; steak and eggs; leafy patio on a pretty square. $ *Average main: €12* ✉ *Cremat Gran 11, Born-Ribera* ☎ *682/038377* ⊕ *cremat11. business.site* ⊘ *Closed Tues. and Wed.* Ⓜ *Jaume I L4.*

El Passadís d'en Pep

$$$$ | **SEAFOOD** | Hidden away at the end of a narrow unmarked passageway off the Pla del Palau, near the Santa Maria del Mar church, this restaurant is a favorite with well-heeled and well-fed gourmands who tuck in their napkins before devouring some of the city's best traditional seafood dishes. Don't bother asking for a menu—there isn't one (although you can prebook a set menu in advance online if you prefer), rather, you can either place yourself completely in the hands of the team, or tell your server what your budget is (starting from €50 per person). **Known for:** no actual menu; tapas served in rapid-fire succession; fresh seafood and Iberian ham. $ *Average main: €50* ✉ *Pl. del Palau 2, Born-Ribera* ☎ *93/310–1021* ⊕ *www.passadis.com* ⊘ *Closed Sun., public holidays, and 3 wks in Aug.* Ⓜ *Jaume I.*

Fismuler

$$$ | **SPANISH** | The cosmopolitan crowd here doesn't just come for hip vibe and stylish decor: Fismuler Barcelona re-creates its Madrid-based mothership's precise, market-based cooking and adds interesting local touches. Star dishes include a translucent, semi-cured carpaccio of gilthead bream with grapes and almonds, and an unctuous, complex cheesecake that tastes more like cheese than cake and is an utterly sinful, gooey delight. **Known for:** killer cheesecake; inventive cooking; trendy atmosphere. $ *Average main: €25* ✉ *Rec Comtal 17, Born-Ribera* ☎ *93/514–0050* ⊕ *www. fismuler.com* Ⓜ *Arc de Triomf.*

Le Cucine Mandarosso

$$ | **ITALIAN** | This no-frills, big-flavor southern-Italian restaurant near the Via Laietana is a favorite with locals for its friendly prices, boisterous atmosphere, and generous portions of burrata, lasagne, ragù, carbonara, and so on, featuring authentic ingredients from the in-store deli. Leave room for the excellent tiramisu. **Known for:** great homemade pastas; hidden gem; always packed. $ *Average main: €15* ✉ *Verdaguer i Callís 4, Born-Ribera* ☎ *93/269–0780* ⊕ *www. lecucinemandarosso.com* ⊘ *Closed Mon.* Ⓜ *Urquinaona.*

Llamber

$$ | **TAPAS** | This dapper, friendly space attracts a crowd with its excellent wine list and the well-crafted tapas based on classic Catalan and Asturian recipes, as interpreted by chef Francisco Heras, who has earned his chops in Spain's top restaurants. Consider the pig's trotters with rice, and potatoes stuffed with Cabrales cheese and hazelnut praline.

Known for: good option for late-night eats; pig's trotters with rice; well-crafted tapas. $ *Average main: €18* ✉ *Fusina 5, Born-Ribera* ☎ *93/319–6250* ⊕ *www. llamber.com* Ⓜ *Jaume 1.*

★ Picnic

$ | LATIN AMERICAN | Between the buzzing indoor dining room, the breezy outdoor patio, and the strongest Bloody Mary game in town, there's a reason why Picnic has reigned supreme on the Barcelona brunch scene for more than a decade. House specials include the quinoa and potato hash browns, the fried green tomatoes with feta and fresh corn salsa, and, of course, the killer eggs Benedict. **Known for:** top brunch choice in town; the Bloody Marys; breezy outdoor patio. $ *Average main: €12* ✉ *Comerç 1, Born-Ribera* ☎ *93/511–6661* ⊕ *www. picnic-restaurant.com* Ⓜ *Arc de Triomf L1.*

Proper

$$ | ARGENTINE | The menu at this "gastronomic tavern" run by Argentinian chef Augusto Mayer is simple and affordable, with unfussy dishes of local, seasonal produce, mostly prepared in the wood-fired oven and meant for sharing. The steak is outstanding, of course, but other, more delicate choices are also worth exploring, like the eggplant with ricotta, figs, and lemon preserves or the tuna confit with kefir tartar sauce. **Known for:** wood-fired oven; local produce; Argentinian-style steak. $ *Average main: €20* ✉ *Banys Vells 20, Born-Ribera* ☎ *93/295–5307* ⊕ *www.properbcn.com* ☽ *Closed Sun. and Mon. No lunch.* Ⓜ *Jaume I L4.*

Sagardi

$$ | BASQUE | FAMILY | An attractive wood-and-stone cider-house replica, Sagardi piles the counter with a dazzling variety of cold Basque-style pintxos served on toothpicks; even better, though, are the hot offerings from the kitchen. The restaurant in back serves Basque delicacies like veal sweetbreads with artichokes and *txuletas de buey* (beef steaks) grilled

over coals. **Known for:** busy outdoor patio; veal sweetbreads and steak; multiple locations, all equally good. $ *Average main: €22* ✉ *Argenteria 62, Born-Ribera* ☎ *93/319–9993* ⊕ *www.gruposagardi. com* Ⓜ *Jaume I.*

☕ Coffee and Quick Bites

Brunells

$ | CAFÉ | One of the oldest bakeries in the city, Brunells has occupied the same corner in El Born since 1852. Recently remodeled, it now sports a contemporary look worthy of a Wes Anderson movie, while its flakey butter croissants filled with everything from ham and cheese to salted caramel, regularly win awards as some of the best in the city. **Known for:** historic bakery; award-winning pastries; Instagram-worthy interior. $ *Average main: €9* ✉ *Princesa, 22, Born-Ribera* ☎ *93/653–6468* ⊕ *www.brunells.barcelona* Ⓜ *Jaume 1, L4.*

El Xampanyet

$ | TAPAS | Just down the street from the Museu Picasso, dangling *botas* (leather wineskins) announce one of Barcelona's liveliest and most visually appealing taverns, with marble-top tables and walls decorated with colorful ceramic tiles, some of which may look like they've been here since the joint opened in 1929. It's usually packed to the rafters with a rollicking mob of local and out-of-town celebrants. **Known for:** real cava; mouth-watering pa amb tomàquet; perfect Iberian ham. $ *Average main: €12* ✉ *Montcada 22, Born-Ribera* ☎ *93/319–7003* ☽ *Closed Mon. and 2 wks in Aug. No dinner Sun.* Ⓜ *Jaume I.*

Euskal Etxea

$ | BASQUE | FAMILY | One of the better grazing destinations in El Born (it's part of the Sagardi group of Basque restaurants) the bar here is topped with a colorful array of tapas and *pintxos* (bite-sized snacks typical of the Basque country, served on a toothpick). The restaurant section (which also houses an art gallery) is usually completely booked, but it's more fun to sip and nibble in the bar anyway. **Known for:** lively bar section for a quick snack; art gallery on-site; Basque pintxos. [$] *Average main: €15* ✉ *Placeta de Montcada 1–3, Born-Ribera* ☎ *93/310–2185* 🌐 *www.gruposagardi.com* [M] *Jaume I.*

★ Gocce di Latte

$ | **ICE CREAM** | If you're looking to freshen up after a long, sweaty day of sightseeing, this artisanal Italian-owned *gelateria* is just the ticket. In addition to a broad range of dairy-based flavors, there are plant-based options and fresh-fruit sorbets, plus gluten-free cones. **Known for:** open until midnight; dairy-free options, like vegan dark chocolate; Italian-style gelato. [$] *Average main: €6* ✉ *Pla de Palau 4, Born-Ribera* ☎ *61/798–6186* 🌐 *www.facebook.com/heladeriagoccedilatte* [M] *Barceloneta L4.*

★ Pastelería Hofmann

$ | **BAKERY** | The late Mey Hofmann, a constellation in Barcelona's gourmet galaxy for the last three decades through her restaurant and cooking courses, established this sideline dedicated exclusively to pastry. Everything from the lightest, flakiest croissants to the cakes, tarts, and ice creams are about as good they get in this legendary sweets emporium. **Known for:** croissants filled with mascarpone or almond cream; tiny shop; legendary pastry shop. [$] *Average main: €8* ✉ *Flassaders 44, Born-Ribera* ☎ *93/268–8221* 🌐 *www.hofmann-bcn.com* [M] *Jaume I.*

Hotels

★ The Barcelona EDITION

$$$$ | **HOTEL** | The Edition hotels are known for their sleek, minimalist design and top-notch food and drink options and the Barcelona outpost adds a breezy 10th-floor terrace with sweeping views. **Pros:** excellent service; great food and drink options; dreamy views from the rooftop. **Cons:** tiny swimming pool; only upgraded rooms have balconies; pricey. [$] *Rooms from: €380* ✉ *Av. de Francesc Cambó 14, Born-Ribera* ☎ *93/626–3330* 🌐 *www.editionhotels.com/es/barcelona* 🛏 *100 rooms* 🍴 *No Meals* [M] *Jaume I L4.*

Ciutat de Barcelona

$$ | **HOTEL** | Ciutat de Barcelona is a no-frills hotel with a bit of an edge, in the trendy El Born quarter of the Old City. **Pros:** close to Picasso Museum, Santa Maria del Mar, and the Gothic quarter; decent value for price; friendly, helpful staff. **Cons:** somewhat sketchy neighborhood; Carrer Princesa gets a lot of pedestrian traffic; no spa, gym, or sauna. [$] *Rooms from: €150* ✉ *Princesa 35, Born-Ribera* ☎ *93/269–7475* 🌐 *www.ciutatbarcelona.com* 🛏 *78 rooms* 🍴 *No Meals* [M] *L4 Jaume I.*

H10 Montcada

$$ | **HOTEL** | A short walk from the attractions of the Gothic Quarter and the Born-Ribera district, the Montcada is a good choice for comfort and convenience. **Pros:** inviting rooftop deck with Jacuzzi; pleasant breakfast room; great location. **Cons:** no pool or spa; bed lighting could improve; a bit pricey for what it is. [$] *Rooms from: €180* ✉ *Via Laietana 24, Born-Ribera* ☎ *93/268–8570* 🌐 *www.h10hotels.com* 🛏 *80 rooms* 🍴 *No Meals* [M] *Jaume I.*

★ Hotel Rec

$ | **HOTEL** | Within an easy stroll of many of Barcelona's best restaurants and top sights, this is an affordable urban adults-only hotel in an unbeatable location. **Pros:** great value; great location; top restaurant downstairs. **Cons:** rooms on the small side; area can be sketchy at night; noisy street outside. [$] *Rooms from: €99* ✉ *Rec Comtal 17–19, Sant Pere* ☎ *93/556–9960* 🌐 *www.hotelrecbarcelona.com* 🛏 *99 rooms* 🍴 *No Meals* [M] *Arc de Triomf L1.*

Hotel Yurbban Trafalgar

$$ | HOTEL | Guests and locals alike rave about the rooftop terrace at the Yurbban Trafalgar, and with good reason: the panoramic view is hands down one of the best in the city at this hip, casual hotel, which offers some of the best value accommodation in the city. **Pros:** superb rooftop terrace; outstanding breakfast; spa access at next-door property. **Cons:** small shower stalls; room service ends at 11 pm; small, basic rooms. [$] *Rooms from: €144* ✉ *Trafalgar 30, Eixample Dreta* ☎ *93/268–0727* 🌐 *yurbban.com/en* 🛏 *56 rooms* 🍴 *No Meals* [M] *L1/L3 Urquinaona.*

🍸 Nightlife

La Ribera, home to some of the city's loveliest ancient architecture, is home to a number of atmospheric bars, galleries, and eateries dotted around the narrow, winding streets and arched stone passageways. Meanwhile, the fashionable El Born district has become popular with the international party-all-night crowd in recent years and, as a result, provides a more eclectic collection of bars and lounge spots offering everything from craft beer to cocktails and organic wines. Although few people really known where La Ribera/El Born ends and Sant Pere begins, the upper part of the area, around the Sant Pere streets tends to be quieter (and rather sketchy) at night.

BARS

Ale&Hop

BREWPUBS | A slick microbrewery with exposed brick walls and indie beats, Ale&Hop was a trailblazer in the city's craft-beer-bar invasion. There are plenty of artisanal brews, plus wine and vegetarian snacks. ✉ *Basses de Sant Pere 10, Sant Pere* ☎ *93/126–9094* 🌐 *www.facebook.com/aleandhop* [M] *Arc de Triomf.*

★ Eldiset

WINE BARS | Specializing in local wine from Catalonia, this charming wine bar—an escape from the rowdy watering holes in nearby Passeig del Born and Plaça Comercial—also has an impressive food menu. ✉ *Antic de Sant Joan 3, Born-Ribera* ☎ *93/268–1987* 🌐 *www.facebook.com/eldiset* [M] *Barceloneta L4.*

La Vinya del Senyor

WINE BARS | Ambitiously named "The Lord's Vineyard," this romantic wine bar directly across from the entrance to the Santa Maria del Mar has an extensive wine list featuring more than 350 wines by the bottle, and a rotating selection of 20 by the glass. Watch your step on the rickety ladder leading to the pint-size mezzanine. ✉ *Pl. de Santa Maria 5, Born-Ribera* ☎ *93/310–3379* 🌐 *www.lavinyadelsenyor.es* [M] *Jaume I.*

Paradiso

COCKTAIL LOUNGES | Hidden behind the fridge door in an unassuming-looking pastrami bar, this speakeasy is one of the city's worst-kept secrets. Cocktail maestro Giacomo Giannotti's creations are works of art, bursting with fire, smoke, and dry ice. And they taste absolutely delicious. Prepare to stand in line for up to an hour to get in. ✉ *Rera Palau 4, Born-Ribera* 🌐 *paradiso.cat/en* [M] *Barceloneta L4.*

Paspartú

COCKTAIL LOUNGES | Dark and inviting, the bar stocks 25 gin flavors and has plenty of comfortable seating in which to try them. ✉ *Basses de Sant Pere 12, Barcelona* ☎ *699/546252* 🌐 *www.facebook.com/paspartubar* [M] *Arc de Triomf.*

Rubí Bar

BARS | The whimsical apothecary-like spirits cabinet, exposed-stone wall, and dramatic red lighting will be the first things to catch your eye, but the relaxed atmosphere and inventive selection of cocktails bring locals and expats back again and again. Check out the choice of home-brewed flavored gins tantalizingly displayed on the bar shelves in hand-labeled bottles. ✉ *Banys Vells 6, Born-Ribera* ☎ *697/673802* Ⓜ *Jaume I.*

⭐ Performing Arts

La Puntual (*Putxinel·lis de Barcelona*)
THEATER | **FAMILY** | As one of the city's pioneering puppet (in Catalan, *putxinel·li*) theaters, this beloved venue features entertaining marionette, puppet, and shadow puppet performances. Weekend matinee performances are major kid magnets and tend to sell out fast, so arrive early or reserve a ticket in advance online. ✉ *Allada Vermell 15, Born-Ribera* ☎ *639/305353* ⊕ *www.lapuntual.info* ⏣ *From €9* Ⓜ *Jaume I.*

🛍 Shopping

The tiny streets of La Ribera and El Born are all about artisanal food, fashion, and design. Stroll along Carrer Argenteria and Plaça de Santa Maria, then head over to Carrer Banys Vells.

Two streets north of Carrer Montcada, there is Carrer Rec for designer haute couture clothing, jewelry, and knick-knacks of all kinds, while Carrer Vidrieria is lined with shops all the way over to Plaça de les Olles. Carrer Banys Vells and Mirallers are known for their local designers and boutiques with ethically sourced fashion. Over in the edgier Sant Pere neighborhood, shopkeepers and artisans provide different, but no less essential, services: this is where the people of Barcelona go to get their hair cut, their dresses mended, and their boots reheeled.

CERAMICS AND GLASSWARE
Baraka

CRAFTS | Barcelona's prime purveyor of Moroccan goods, ceramics chief among them, the wares here are generally of good price and great quality. Other African countries are represented, too, such as spectacular busts covered in tiny beads from Cameroon. ✉ *Canvis Vells 2, Born-Ribera* ☎ *93616/268–4220* ⊕ *www.barakaweb.com* Ⓜ *Jaume I.*

CLOTHING
Anna Povo

WOMEN'S CLOTHING | Look for an elegant and innovative selection of relaxed knits, coats, and dresses at this stylish boutique. Anna Povo's designs tend to sleek and minimalist, in cool tones of gray and beige. ✉ *Providència 75, Gràcia* ☎ *93/319–3561* ⊕ *www.annapovo.com* Ⓜ *Joanic.*

Angle Store

MIXED CLOTHING | Ethical fashion is all the rage in Barcelona and perhaps nowhere more so than at Angle Store. Here you can discover clothing and accessories by the in-house brand and a selection of local and international designers that share its responsible, ethical values and views. ✉ *Mirallers 10, Born-Ribera* ☎ *93/501–6602* ⊕ *anglestore.com* Ⓜ *Jaume 1, L4.*

Coquette

WOMEN'S CLOTHING | Coquette specializes in understated feminine beauty, with a small but careful selection of mainly French designers, like Souur, Des Petits Hauts, and Spain's own Hoss Intrópia. Whether it's a romantic or a seductive look you're after, Coquette makes sure you'll feel both comfortable and irresistible. ✉ *Madrazo 153, Sant Gervasi* ☎ *93/310–3535* ⊕ *coquettebcn.com/en* Ⓜ *La Bonanova.*

El Ganso

MIXED CLOTHING | Who would have thought that two Madrid-born brothers could out-Brit the Brits? One of Spain's more recent fashion success stories, El Ganso makes very appealing preppy-inspired men's, women's, and children's wear—striped blazers, pleated skirts, and tailored suits made for upper-class frolics. ✉ *Rambla de Catalunya, 116, Eixample*

☎ 93932/368–2069 ⊕ www.elganso.com Ⓜ Diagonal.

★ Ivori

MIXED CLOTHING | This ultra-chic clothing store stocks both men's and women's clothing and accessories, all made by young Catalan designers. A labor of love that is spearheaded by local designer Carola Alexandre, who sells her own designs as well as pieces by the likes of Name BCN, Lubochka, and Mus Roew. ✉ Mirallers, 7, Born-Ribera ☎ 93/137–0264 ⊕ www.ivoribarcelona. com Ⓜ Jaume 1, L4.

La Comercial

MIXED CLOTHING | This mini-agglomeration of boutiques spreads out over three streets, together defining El Born's penchant for the achingly à la mode. Menswear can be found at Bonaire 7, Rec 73 and 75, with the latter entirely dedicated to the natty threads of U.K. designer Paul Smith. Women can choose from predominantly French designers such as Isabel Marant and Sonia Rykiel at Rec 52. ✉ Rec 52–75, Carrer Rec, Born-Ribera ☎ 93/319–3463 ⊕ www.lacomercial.info/ en Ⓜ Jaume I.

La Condicional

WOMEN'S CLOTHING | Spotlighting ethical designers from Barcelona, slow fashion in the name of the game at this ladies' clothing store. Expect warm, earthy tones and fabrics that are either organic or up-cycled. ✉ Abaixadors 9, Born-Ribera ☎ 93/488–6879 ⊕ lacondicional.com Ⓜ Jaume 1, L4.

FOOD

La Botifarreria de Santa Maria

FOOD | This busy emporium next to the church of Santa Maria del Mar stocks excellent cheeses, hams, pâtés, and homemade sobrassadas (pork pâté with paprika). Catalan botifarra sausage is the main item here, with a wide range of varieties, including egg sausage for meatless Lent and sausage stuffed with spinach, asparagus, cider, cinnamon, and Cabrales cheese. ✉ Santa Maria 4, Born-Ribera ☎ 93/319–9123 ⊕ www. labotifarreria.com Ⓜ Jaume I.

★ Casa Gispert

FOOD | This shop is one of the most aromatic and picturesque in Barcelona, bursting with teas, coffees, spices, saffron, chocolates, and nuts. The star is an almond-roasting stove in the back of the store—purportedly the oldest in Europe, dating from 1851 like the store itself, so make sure to pick up a bag of freshly roasted nuts to take with you. ✉ Sombrerers 23, Born-Ribera ☎ 93/319–7535 ⊕ www.casagispert.com Ⓜ Jaume I.

Demasié

FOOD | The shop's motto, "galetes Exageradament Bones" (biscuits that are exaggeratedly good) may seem like a bit of hype, but these rich colorful cookies are exceptionally tasty. They are best enjoyed with a cup of coffee at the bar inside, or you can have them wrapped up in a pretty duck-egg-blue box to take home with you. ✉ Princesa 28, Born-Ribera ☎ 93/269–1180 ⊕ www.demasie.es Ⓜ Jaume I.

★ El Magnífico

FOOD | Just up the street from Santa Maria del Mar, this coffee emporium is famous for its sacks of coffee beans from all over the globe and is said to serve the best cup of coffee in Barcelona, also available to go. El Magnífico's best-kept secret is its nearby "Mag by El Magnífico" coffee shop, open Friday through Sunday only (✉ Carrer de Grunyí 10). ✉ Argenteria 64, Born-Ribera ☎ 93/319–3975 ⊕ www.cafeselmagnifico.com Ⓜ Jaume I.

★ Vila Viniteca

WINE/SPIRITS | Near Santa Maria del Mar, this is perhaps the best wine treasury in Barcelona, with a truly massive catalog, tastings, courses, and events, including a hugely popular street party to welcome in new-harvest wines (usually late October or early November). Under the same ownership, the tiny grocery store next door offers exquisite artisanal cheeses ranging from French goat cheese to Extremadura's famous *Torta del Casar*. There are a few tables inside, and, for a corkage fee, you can enjoy a bottle of wine together with a tasting platter. ⊠ *Agullers 7–9, Born-Ribera* ☎ *9390/777–7017* ⊕ *www.vilaviniteca.es* Ⓜ *Jaume I.*

GIFTS AND SOUVENIRS
Natura
CRAFTS | The Spanish Natura chain has branches around the city and stocks a good selection of global crafts, including incense, clothing, tapestries, candles, shoes, gadgets, and surprises of all kinds. ⊠ *Argenteria 78, Born-Ribera* ☎ *93/268–2525* ⊕ *www.naturaselection. com* Ⓜ *Jaume I.*

HOUSEHOLD ITEMS AND FURNITURE
Pachulí
HOUSEWARES | Hidden away down one if the tiniest alleyways behind the Santa María del Mar basilica you will find this delightful treasure trove of interior design, photography, and craftsman-ship. From the Balinese furnishings to the Moroccan rugs and Cuban artwork, everything in this concept store has been sustainably made and carefully selected to shine the light on the work of local artisans from all over the world. ⊠ *Brosolí 4, Born-Ribera* ☎ *60/3528–386* ⊕ *pachu-linterior.com/en/home/* Ⓜ *Jaume 1, L4.*

 Activities

BICYCLING
Bike Tours Barcelona
BIKING | This company offers 2.5-hour bike tours (in English) for €27 (e-Bikes are €39; depending on availability), daily at 11am, all year. They can also organize pri-vate guided tours around the city, to Port Olímpic and Barceloneta, the Ruta Mod-erniste, and other itineraries on request. ⊠ *Sant Agustina Vell 16, Born-Ribera* ☎ *93/268–2105* ⊕ *biketoursbarcelona. com* Ⓜ *Jaume I.*

Chapter 7

LA CIUTADELLA, BARCELONETA, PORT OLÍMPIC, AND POBLENOU

7

Updated by
Jennifer Ceaser

◉ Sights	🍴 Restaurants	🛏 Hotels	🛍 Shopping	🍸 Nightlife
★★★☆☆	★★★★★	★★★☆☆	☆☆☆☆☆	★★★★☆

NEIGHBORHOOD SNAPSHOT

TOP EXPERIENCES

■ **Ciutadella Park:** Wander the shady paths, admire the ornate Catalan Parliament building, and be wowed by the monumental two-tiered fountain, complete with a waterfall and gleaming gold sculptures, at Barcelona's central green space.

■ **Museu d'Història de Catalunya:** After learning about Catalan history at this state-of-the-art museum, head to the rooftop restaurant for harbor views.

■ **Beachfront drinks:** Chill at one of the many casual beach bars (chiringuitos), that dot the urban shoreline.

■ **Passeig Marítim:** Walk or bike along the broad, palm tree-lined seafront promenade.

■ **Rambla del Poblenou:** This pedestrian thorough-fare is a less-touristy alternative to La Rambla and is packed with cafés; it's perfect for a weekend stroll.

GETTING HERE

The Barceloneta stop on the metro's yellow line (L4) is the nearest subway stop to Barceloneta and its beaches. For La Ciutadella, the Arc de Triomf stop on the red line (L1) is the most central. Most of Poble-nou is served by the L4 but for popular attractions like the Museu del Disseny, the L1 Glòries stop is best. To get to Glòries and the upper end of Rambla del Poblenou from La Ciutadella, hop on the tram (T4), with stops all along Avenue Diagonal.

PLANNING YOUR TIME

Exploring Ciutadella Park and Barceloneta can take from three to four hours. Add at least another hour if you're stopping for lunch and more if you're heading to the beach. For Poblenou, allow at least an hour to explore the excellent Museu del Disseny and build in a couple more hours for a leisurely stroll along the Rambla del Poblenou or dinner and bar-hopping around the barrio.

FUN FACT

Walking along the waterfront avenue of Passeig de Colom, it's hard to miss the large, brightly colored sculpture that dominates the entrance to Port Vell. "El Cap de Barcelona" (Barcelona's Head) is the work of American pop artist Roy Lichtenstein; it was one of many public artworks commissioned by the city for the 1992 Olympic Games. The concrete sculpture stands 60 feet high and is covered with fragments of ceramic tile, a technique known as *trencadís*, a clear homage to Antoni Gaudí who famously used it in his designs for Parc Güell. While abstract in style, the sculpture features an animated face, with "brush-strokes" of red, blue, and black that hint at the eyes, nose, and mouth.

Each of Barcelona's waterfront districts has its own flavor: Barceloneta, once the city's sea-farers' neighborhood, is cheerfully authentic and down-to-earth, while the Port Olimpic and Poblenou feel more modern, the former known for its restaurants, beaches, and nightlife, and the latter having become the city's modern tech hub.

Barceloneta and La Ciutadella fit together historically. In the early 18th century, some 1,000 houses in the Barrio de la Ribera, then the waterfront neighborhood around Plaça del Born, were ordered torn down, to create fields of fire for the cannon of La Ciutadella, the newly built fortress that kept watch over the rebellious Catalans.

Barceloneta, then a marshy wetland, was filled in and developed almost four decades later, in 1753, to house the families who had lost homes in La Ribera. Open water in Roman times, and gradually silted in only after the 15th-century construction of the port, it became Barcelona's fishermen's and stevedores' quarter. Originally composed of 15 longitudinal and three cross streets and 329 two-story houses, this was Europe's earliest planned urban development, built by the military engineer Juan Martin Cermeño under the command of El Marquès de la Mina, Juan Miguel de Guzmán Dávalos Spinola (1690–1767). With its tiny original apartment blocks, and its history of seafarers and gypsies, Barceloneta even now maintains its spontaneous, carefree flavor.

Poblenou, meanwhile, came about in the mid-19th century, amid Barcelona's industrial boom. Today, its former factories and warehouses have been converted into offices for digital start-ups, and rrendy restaurants, bars, art galleries, and design shops dot its broad streets. The long, leafy Rambla del Poblenou is the heart of the neighborhood's social and commercial life.

 Sights

Arc de Triomf

NOTABLE BUILDING | This exposed-redbrick arch was built by Josep Vilaseca as the grand entrance for the 1888 Universal Exhibition. Similar in size and sense to the traditional triumphal arches of ancient Rome, this one refers to no specific military triumph anyone can recall. In fact, Catalonia's last military triumph of note may have been Jaume I el Conqueridor's 1229 conquest of the Moors in Mallorca—as suggested by the bats (always part of Jaume I's coat of arms) on either side of the arch itself. The Josep Reynés sculptures adorning the structure represent Barcelona hosting visitors to the exhibition on the western side (front),

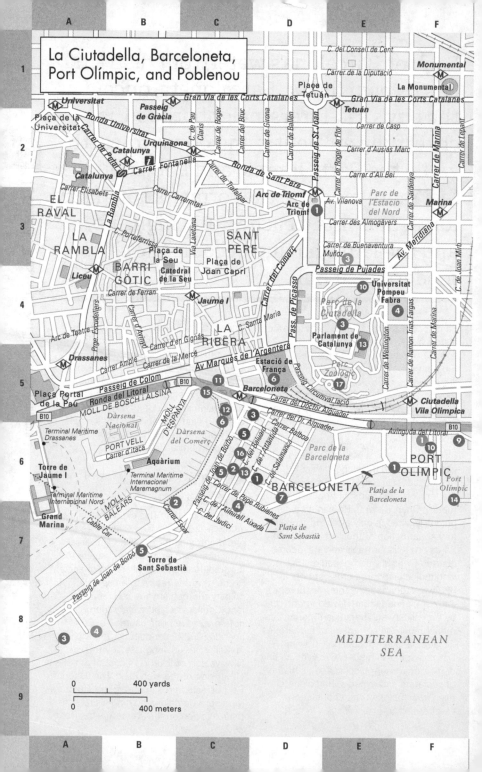

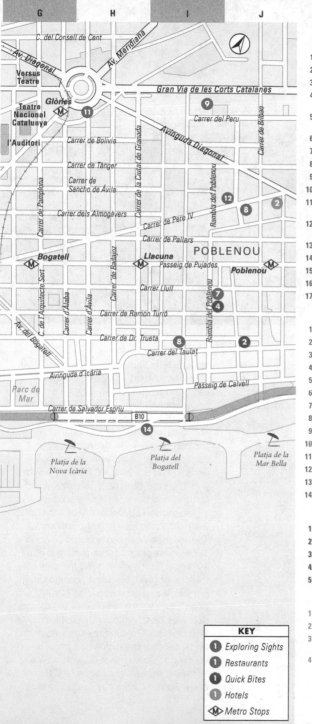

Sights ▾

1 Arc de Triomf...................... D3
2 Carrer Sant Carles No. 6........... C6
3 Ciutadella Park..................... E4
4 Dipòsit de les Aigües–
   Universitat Pompeu Fabra......... E4
5 El Transbordador
   Aeri del Port...................... B7
6 Estació de França D5
7 Fuente de Carmen Amaya........ D7
8 IDEAL Centre d'Arts Digitals...... I5
9 KBr Photography Center........... F6
10 La Cascada........................ E4
11 Museu del Disseny
   de Barcelona...................... H2
12 Museu d'Història
   de Catalunya C5
13 Parlament de Catalunya E4
14 Port Olímpic F6
15 Port Vell C5
16 Sant Miquel del Port C6
17 Zoo E5

Restaurants ▾

1 Agua................................ E6
2 Barceloneta........................ B7
3 Camping Mar....................... A8
4 Can Majó C7
5 Can Solé C6
6 1881 per Sagardi...................C5
7 El 58 .... I4
8 El Menjador de la Beckett.........J3
9 Els Tres Porquets I2
10 Enoteca Paco Pérez................ F6
11 Green Spot C5
12 L' Artesana Poblenou..............J3
13 La Cova Fumada C6
14 Xiringuito Escribà................. H6

Quick Bites ▾

1 Bar Bodega l'Electricitat.......... D6
2 The Cake Man Bakery J5
3 El Vaso de Oro..................... D5
4 Horchatería El Tío Ché I4
5 La Bombeta......................... C6

Hotels ▾

1 Hotel Arts Barcelona.............. F6
2 Meliá Barcelona Sky...............J3
3 Motel One Barcelona-
   Ciutadella......................... E3
4 W Barcelona A8

KEY

1 Exploring Sights
1 Restaurants
1 Quick Bites
1 Hotels
Ⓜ Metro Stops

Formerly an obsolete harbor, Port Vell is a modern yacht-basin and lively entertainment center.

while the Josep Llimona sculptures on the eastern side depict the prizes being given to its outstanding contributors. ⊠ *Passeig de Sant Joan, La Ciutadella* Ⓜ *L1 Arc de Triomf.*

Carrer Sant Carles No. 6

HISTORIC HOME | The last Barceloneta house left standing in its original 1755 two-story entirety, this low, boxlike structure was planned as a single-family dwelling with shop and storage space on the ground floor and the living space above. Overcrowding soon produced split houses and even quartered houses, with workers and their families living in tiny spaces. After nearly a century of living under Madrid-based military jurisdiction, Barceloneta homeowners were given permission to expand vertically, and houses of as many as five stories began to tower over the lowly original dwellings. The house is not open to the public. ⊠ *Carrer Sant Carles 6, Barceloneta* Ⓜ *Barceloneta.*

★ **Ciutadella Park** (*Parc de la Ciutadella*) CITY PARK | FAMILY | Once a fortress designed to consolidate Madrid's military occupation of Barcelona, the Ciutadella is now the city's main downtown park. The clearing dates from shortly after the War of the Spanish Succession in the early 18th century, when Felipe V demolished some 1,000 houses in what was then the Barri de la Ribera to build a fortress and barracks for his soldiers and a *glacis* (open space) between rebellious Barcelona and his artillery positions. The fortress walls were pulled down in 1868 and replaced by gardens laid out by Josep Fontseré. In 1888 the park was the site of the Universal Exposition that put Barcelona on the map as a truly European city; today it is home to the Castell dels Tres Dragons, built by architect Lluís Domènech i Montaner as the café and restaurant for the exposition (the only building to survive that project, now a botanical research center), the Catalan parliament, and the city zoo. ⊠ *Passeig* de Picasso 21, La Ciutadella Ⓜ L4 Barceloneta, Ciutadella–Vila Olímpica, L1 Arc de Triomf.

Dipòsit de les Aigües–Universitat Pompeu Fabra

NOTABLE BUILDING | The Ciutadella campus of Barcelona's private Universitat Pompeu Fabra contains a contemporary architectural gem worth seeking out. It's two blocks up from the Ciutadella–Vil·la Olímpica metro stop, just beyond where the tramline out to the Fòrum begins. Once the hydraulic cistern for the Ciutadella waterworks, built in 1880 by Josep Fontseré, the Dipòsit de les Aigües was converted to the school's Central Library in 1999 by the design team of Lluís Clotet and Ignacio Paricio. The massive, 3-foot-thick walls, perforated and crowned with tall brick arches, are striking; the trompe-l'oeil connecting corridor between the reading rooms is a brilliant touch. Even in humble Barceloneta, there are opportunities for really gifted architects to take a historical property in hand and work magic. ✉ Ramon Trias Fargas 25–27, La Ciutadella ☎ 93/542-2000 ⊕ www.upf.edu/en/web/campus/historia-del-diposit-de-les-aigues ▨ Free Ⓜ L4 Ciutadella–Vil·la Olímpica.

El Transbordador Aeri del Port (Port Cable Car)

TRANSPORTATION | FAMILY | This hair-raising cable-car ride over the Barcelona harbor, from Barceloneta to Montjuïc hill, is a serious adrenaline rush. Swaying 100 feet or so in the air, the windowed gondola, which holds 19 people, travels the mile-long route in about 10 minutes—every one of them packed with fabulous bird's-eye views. Cable-car access is from both ends, though most people leave from the Torre de San Sebastián (San Sebastian tower) in Barceloneta heading to the Torre de Miramar on Montjuïc.
■ TIP→ The Torre de Altamar restaurant in the tower at the Barceloneta end serves excellent food and wine. ✉ Passeig Joan de Borbó 88, Barceloneta ☎ 93/430–4716 ⊕ www.telefericodebarcelona.com ▨ €11 one-way; €16.50 round-trip Ⓜ Barceloneta.

Estació de França

TRAIN/TRAIN STATION | Barcelona's main railroad station until about 1980, and still in use, the elegant Estació de França is outside the west gate of the Ciutadella. Rebuilt in 1929 for the International Exhibition and restored in 1992 for the Olympics, this mid-19th-century building overshadows Estació de Sants, the city's main intercity and international terminus. The marble and bronze, the Moderniste decorative details, and the delicate tracery of its wrought-iron roof girders make this one of the most beautiful buildings of its kind. Stop in for a sense of the bygone romance of European travel. ✉ Av. Marquès de l'Argentera s/n, La Ciutadella ☎ 902/320–230 RENFE office Ⓜ L4 Barceloneta.

Fuente de Carmen Amaya (Carmen Amaya Fountain)

FOUNTAIN | At the eastern end of Carrer Sant Carles, where Barceloneta joins the beach, is the monument to the famous Gypsy flamenco dancer Carmen Amaya (1913–63). Amaya was born in the Gypsy settlement known as Somorrostro, part of Barceloneta until 1920 when development sent the Gypsies farther east to what is now the Fòrum grounds (from which they were again displaced in 2003). Amaya achieved universal fame in 1929 at the age of 16, when she performed at Barcelona's International Exposition and later starred in films such as La hija de Juan Simón (1934) and Los Tarantos (1962). The fountain, and its high-relief representations of cherubic children as flamenco performers (two guitarists, three dancers—in the nude, unlike real flamenco dancers), has been poorly maintained since it was placed here in 1959, but it remains an important reminder of Barceloneta's roots as a

7

La Ciutadella, Barceloneta, Port Olímpic, and Poblenou

rough-and-tumble enclave of free-living sailors, stevedores, Gypsies, and fishermen. ⊠ *Carrer Sant Carles s/n, Barceloneta* Ⓜ *L4 Barceloneta.*

IDEAL Centre d'Arts Digitals

ARTS CENTER | A defunct old Poblenou movie theater that was rescued and reimagined for the digital age, the IDEAL space combines 360-degree projections with virtual reality and cutting-edge light and sound effects for an immersive experience. Recent shows have explored the works of Monet, Gustav Klimt, and Frida Kahlo. ⊠ *Dr. Trueta 196–198, Poblenou* ☎ *93/395–7412* ⊕ *idealbarcelona. com/en* 🖾 *From €14.50* ⊙ *Closed Tues.* Ⓜ *Llacuna.*

★ KBr Photography Center

ART MUSEUM | Set inside the glassy MAP-FRE Tower near the Port Olímpic, this new venue for photography, supported by the MAPFRE Foundation, showcases comprehensive temporary exhibits of international photographers such as Lee Friedlander, Paul Strand, and Catalan photojournalist Adolf Mas. ⊠ *Ave. Litoral 30, Port Olímpic* ☎ *93/272–3180* ⊕ *kbr. fundacionmapfre.org* 🖾 *€5* ⊙ *Closed Mon.* Ⓜ *Ciutadella/Vila Olímpica.*

La Cascada

FOUNTAIN | The sights and sounds of Barcelona seem far away when you stand near this monumental two-tiered fountain by Josep Fontseré, presented as part of the 1888 Universal Exhibition. The waterfall's somewhat overwrought arrangement of rocks was the work of a young architecture student named Antoni Gaudí—his first public work, appropriately natural and organic, and certainly a hint of things to come. ⊠ *Parc de la Ciutadella, La Ciutadella* Ⓜ *L1 Arc de Triomf.*

★ Museu del Disseny de Barcelona

(*Design Museum of Barcelona*)
ARTS CENTER | This eye-catching center for design is home to six permanent collections covering everything from textiles, historical clothing, and haute couture to ceramics (with a number of pieces by Miró and Picasso), decorative arts, and graphic design. The product design and modern and contemporary furniture collections are particularly outstanding. Temporary exhibits run the gamut, with recent shows devoted to the graffiti art of Banksy, Balenciaga's exquisite hats, and COVID design initiatives. The building itself, by MBM Arquitectes (Oriol Bohigas, doyen of the firm, was the prime mover in much of Barcelona's makeover for the 1992 Olympics), juts out like a multistoried wedge into the Plaça de les Glòries. ⊠ *Pl. de les Glòries Catalans 37–8, Poblenou* ☎ *93/256–6800* ⊕ *www. museudeldisseny.cat* 🖾 *€6; free Sun. 3–8 and all day 1st Sun. every month; temporary exhibit cost varies* ⊙ *Closed Mon.* Ⓜ *L1 Glòries, Glòries (Tram).*

Museu d'Història de Catalunya (*Museum of the History of Catalonia*)

HISTORY MUSEUM | Established in what used to be a port warehouse, this state-of-the-art interactive museum makes you part of Catalonian history, from prehistoric times to the contemporary democratic era. After centuries of "official" Catalan history dictated from Madrid (from 1714 until the mid-19th century Renaixença, and from 1939 to 1975), this offers an opportunity to revisit Catalonia's autobiography. Audioguides are available in English. The rooftop restaurant (1881 Per Sagardi) has fabulous harbor views. ⊠ *Pl. de Pau Vila 3, Barceloneta* ☎ *93/254–700* ⊕ *www.mhcat.cat* 🖾 *From €6 (free on the first Sun. of every month, 10 am–2:30 pm)* ⊙ *Closed Sun. afternoon and Mon.* Ⓜ *L4 Barceloneta.*

Parlament de Catalunya

NOTABLE BUILDING | Once the arsenal for the Ciutadella—as evidenced by the thickness of the building's walls—this is the only surviving remnant of Felipe V's fortress. For a time it housed the city's museum of modern art, before it was repurposed to house the unicameral Catalan Parliament. Under Franco, the Generalitat—the regional government—was suppressed, and the Hall of Deputies was shut fast for 37 years. Book a free 45-minute guided tour (Mon.–Fri.) of the building via the website at least two days in advance; it includes the grand "Salon Rose," which is worth a visit in itself. ✉ *Pl. de Joan Fiveller, Parc de la Ciutadella s/n, La Ciutadella* ☎ *93/304–6645* ⊕ *www.parlament.cat* ✉ *Free* Ⓜ *L4 Ciutadella/Vila Olímpica.*

Port Olímpic

MARINA/PIER | The Olympic Port is 2 km (1 mile) up the beach from Barceloneta and is marked by the mammoth shimmering goldfish sculpture by starchitect Frank Gehry, with the towering five-star Hotel Arts just behind. A swath of swanky beachfront nightclubs line the promenade here and farther up is a marina packed with oversized yachts. Much of the area is undergoing a significant overhaul, with renovations scheduled to last into 2023. These include a reimagining of the various docks and piers to make them more accessible to the public and replacing the glut of seedy bars along the Moll de Mestral with a wider variety of businesses. ✉ *Port Olímpic, Port Olímpic* ⊕ *www.portolimpic.barcelona/ca* Ⓜ *Ciutadella/Vila Olímpica.*

Port Vell (Old Port)

MARINA/PIER | **FAMILY** | From Pla del Palau, cross to the edge of the port, where the Moll d'Espanya, the Moll de la Fusta, and the Moll de Barceloneta meet (*Moll* means docks). Just beyond the colorful Roy Lichtenstein sculpture, the modern Port Vell complex—home to the aquarium and Maremagnum shopping mall—stretches seaward to the right on the Moll d'Espanya. The Palau de Mar, with rows of pricey, tourist-oriented quayside terrace restaurants (La Gavina or Merendero de la Mari are okay if you must), stretches down along the Moll

de Barceloneta to the left. The rather soulless Maremagnum complex is noteworthy if only for being one of very few shopping options that remains open on Sunday. ✉ *Port Vell, Barceloneta* Ⓜ *L4 Barceloneta.*

Sant Miquel del Port

CHURCH | Have a close look at this baroque church with its modern (1992), pseudo-bodybuilder version of the winged archangel Michael himself, complete with sword and chain, in the alcove on the facade. (The figure is a replica; the original was destroyed in 1936.) One of the first buildings to be completed in Barceloneta, Sant Miquel del Port was begun in 1753 and finished by 1755 under the direction of architect Damià Ribes. Due to strict orders to keep Barceloneta low enough to fire La Ciutadella's cannon over, Sant Miquel del Port had no bell tower and only a small cupola until Elies Rogent added a new one in 1853. Interesting to note are the metopes: palm-sized gilt bas-relief sculptures around the interior cornice and repeated outside at the top of the facade. These 74 Latin-inscribed allegories each allude to different attributes of St. Michael. For example, the image of a boat and the Latin inscription "iam in tuto" (finally safe), alludes to the saint's protection against the perils of the sea. ✉ *Carrer de Sant Miquel 39, Barceloneta* ☎ *93/221–6550* ⊕ *santmiqueldelport.org* Ⓜ *L4 Barceloneta.*

Zoo

ZOO | **FAMILY** | Barcelona's zoo occupies the whole eastern end of the Parc de la Ciutadella. There's a superb reptile house and a full assortment of African animals. ✉ *Parc de la Ciutadella s/n, La Ciutadella* ☎ *93/706–5656* ⊕ *www.zoobarcelona. cat/en* ✉ *€21.40* Ⓜ *L4 Ciutadella–Vila Olímpica, Barceloneta; L1 Arc de Triomf.*

☺ Beaches

Barcelona's *platges* (beaches) stretch from Barceloneta's W Hotel north to the Fòrum site at the northeastern end of Diagonal. At Barceloneta's southwestern end is the Platja de Sant Sebastià, followed northward by the Platges de Sant Miquel, Barceloneta, Passeig Marítim, Port Olímpic, Nova Icària, Bogatell, Mar Bella, and La Nova Mar Bella (the last football-field length of which is a nudist enclave), and Llevant. The Sant Miquel and Barceloneta beaches form the most popular stretch, easily accessible by several bus lines, notably the No. V15 bus (which runs all the way from Tibidado at the top of the city), and the L4 metro stop at Barceloneta. The best surfing stretch is at the northeastern end of the Barceloneta beach, and the boardwalk itself (Passeig Marítim) offers miles of runway for walkers, skaters, bicyclers, and runners. Topless bathing is the norm on all beaches in and around Barcelona. There are public toilets, but people often stop into a nearby bar to use the facilities. There are free outdoor showers at the edge of most beaches. ■TIP➔ **Never leave your belongings unattended on any of Barcelona's beaches.**

Most city beaches get crowded, especially in summer and on weekends. If you want a bit more space between your blanket and your neighbors', consider heading to the beaches northeast of the city in the Maresme province: Montgat, Ocata, Vilasar de Mar, Arenys de Mar, Canet de Mar, and Sant Pol de Mar are all accessible by train from the RENFE station in Plaça de Catalunya. Sant Pol is a good pick, with clean sand, a lovely old town, and the beachfront restaurant Banys Lluis, which serves a flavorful paella. Another beach with a top-notch gastronomical opportunity is Arenys de Mar, with the famous Hispania restaurant a minute's walk from the beach across the NII road. Canet de Mar's beach extends for 10 km (6 miles), and offers rental options for surfboards or windsurfers, as well as beach restaurants such as El Parador de Canet.

Platja de la Barceloneta

BEACH | FAMILY | Reached by walking down Passeig Joan de Borbó and turning left at Plaça del Mar, the adjacent beaches of Barceloneta and Sant Miquel are the easiest to get to and hence the busiest—though they're also the most fun for people-watching. Note that itinerant beach vendors can be a nuisance, and pickpocketing has become increasingly problematic in recent years. The calm waters are easy for swimming, and there are several companies that provide surfing and paddle board rentals and lessons. Take note of Rebecca Horn's iconic sculpture of towering, rusting cubes, *L'Estel Ferit*, a popular meeting spot on Sant Miquel beach. **Amenities:** food and drink; lifeguards; showers; toilets; water sports. **Best for:** partiers; swimming; walking; paddle boarding; surfing (mostly in winter). ⊠ *Passeig Marítim de la Barceloneta s/n, Barceloneta* Ⓜ *Ciutadella/Vila Olímpica.*

Platja de la Mar Bella

BEACH | Closest to the Poblenou metro stop, this is a thriving gay enclave and the unofficial nudist beach of Barcelona (although clothed bathers are welcome, too). The water-sports center Base Nàutica de la Mar Bella rents equipment for sailing, surfing, and windsurfing. Outfitted with showers, drinking fountains, and a children's play area, La Mar Bella also has lifeguards who warn against swimming near the breakwater. **Amenities:** food and drink; lifeguards; showers; toilets; water sports. **Best for:** partiers; nudists; LGBTQ beachgoers; swimming; windsurfing. ⊠ *Passeig Marítim del Bogatell, Poblenou* Ⓜ *Poblenou.*

Platja de la Nova Icària

BEACH | FAMILY | One of Barcelona's most popular beaches, this strand is just east of Port Olímpic, with a full range of entertainment and refreshment venues close at hand. The wide beach is directly across from the neighborhood built as the residential Olympic Village for Barcelona's 1992 Olympic Games, an interesting housing project that has now become a popular residential neighborhood. Vendors prowl the sand, offering everything from sunglasses to cold drinks to massages. Pickpocketing has been an issue here, too, so keep an eye on your belongings. **Amenities:** food and drink; lifeguards; showers; toilets; water sports. **Best for:** partiers; swimming; walking; windsurfing. ✉ *Passeig Marítim del Port Olímpic s/n, Port Olímpic* Ⓜ *Ciutadella/Vila Olímpic.*

Platja de Sant Sebastià

BEACH | Barceloneta's most southwestern platja (at the very end of Passeig Joan de Borbó), Sant Sebastià is the oldest and most historic of the city beaches; it was here that 19th-century locals cavorted in bloomers and bathing costumes. Despite repeated attempts to "clean up" Sant Sebastià, it remains a popular unofficial nudist spot. The famous sail-shaped W Barcelona hotel stands at the far south end. **Amenities:** food and drink; lifeguards; showers; toilets. **Best for:** partiers; swimming. ✉ *Passeig Marítim de la Barceloneta s/n, Barceloneta* Ⓜ *Barceloneta.*

🍴 Restaurants

Barceloneta, Port Olímpic, and Poblenou have little in common beyond their seaside location. While Barceloneta has retained its traditional character, with classic seafood restaurants and cozy, old-school tapas bars, the newer Port Olímpic is home to large, modern, upscale eateries and slick dinner lounges/nightclubs that mostly cater to tourist crowds. Given its less-central location, Poblenou has a more local-oriented dining scene, with many restaurants and cafés in converted warehouses and along the leafy pedestrian boulevard Rambla del Poblenou.

Agua

$$ | **MEDITERRANEAN** | Hit Agua's beachfront terrace on warm summer nights and sunny winter days, or just catch rays inside through immense windows; either way you'll have a prime spot for people-watching and fresh seafood-eating. Expect good-if-not-spectacular fare and hit-or-miss service at this popular tourist favorite. **Known for:** popular tourist spot; beachfront location; fresh seafood. $ *Average main: €21* ✉ *Passeig Marítim de la Barceloneta 30, Port Olímpic* ☎ *93/225-1272* ⊕ *restauranteagua.com* Ⓜ *Ciutadella–Vila Olímpica.*

Barceloneta

$$$ | **SEAFOOD** | This restaurant in an enormous riverboat-like building at the end of the yacht marina in Barceloneta is geared for high-volume business, but the paellas and grilled fish dishes are reliably excellent. The hundreds of fellow diners make the place feel like a cheerful celebration. **Known for:** fresh grilled fish; excellent rice and paella; lively waterside spot. $ *Average main: €27* ✉ *Escar 22, Moll de Pescadors, Barceloneta* ☎ *93/221-2111* ⊕ *www.restaurantbarceloneta.com* Ⓜ *Barceloneta.*

Camping Mar

$$ | **MEDITERRANEAN** | Slightly hidden in the exclusive yachting marina behind the W Barcelona hotel, this is a restaurant that only attracts those in the know, which might explain why it is largely devoid of tourists. The menu includes healthy starters like red tuna and eggplant tartare and grilled avocado salad, and there's a nice selection of both seafood- and meat-based paellas. **Known for:** paellas; healthy options; hidden gem. $ *Average main: €21* ✉ *Pg. Joan de Borbó 103, Marina Vela, Barceloneta* ☎ *93/408-8901* ⊕ *www.encompaniadelobos.com/en/camping-mar* ⊗ *Closed Mon.–Wed.* Ⓜ *Barceloneta.*

Can Majó

$$ | **SEAFOOD** | **FAMILY** | Can Majó doesn't consistently reach the standards that once made it famous but the food is still a notch above most of the touristy haunts nearby. Specialties include *caldero de bogavante* (a cross between paella and lobster bouillabaisse) and *suquet* (fish stewed in its own juices), and the terrace overlooking Barceloneta Beach is a pleasantly upscale alternative to the surrounding beach bars. **Known for:** excellent paella; fish dishes; terrace overlooking the Mediterranean. [$] *Average main: €22* ✉ *Emília Llorca Martín 23, (also an entrance at Carrer de l'Almirall Aixada, 23), Barceloneta* ☎ *93/221–5455* 🌐 *www.canmajo.es* 🕓 *Closed Mon; No dinner Tues., Wed., and Sun.* [M] *Barceloneta.*

Can Solé

$$$$ | **SEAFOOD** | With no sea views or terrace to attract diners, Can Solé has to rely on its reputation as one of Barceloneta's best options for seafood. Faded photos of half-forgotten local celebrities line the walls of this nearly 120-year-old establishment, but there's nothing out-of-date about the exquisitely fresh seafood. **Known for:** historical atmosphere; traditional Spanish rice dishes; fresh fish daily. [$] *Average main: €30* ✉ *Sant Carles 4, Barceloneta* ☎ *93/221–5012* 🌐 *restaurantcansole.com* 🕓 *Closed Mon. No dinner Sun.* [M] *Barceloneta.*

1881 per Sagardi

$$$ | **MEDITERRANEAN** | Enjoy fabulous views of yachts sailing out into the glittering Mediterranean while dining on fresh seafood—caught by local fisherman or sourced at the Barceloneta market—and expertly prepared on the wood-fired grill. This stylish restaurant is perched atop a renovated warehouse that now houses the Museum of the History of Catalonia. **Known for:** locally sourced seafood; all-day kitchen; terrace with great harbor and city views. [$] *Average main: €24* ✉ *Pl. de Pau Vila 3, Barceloneta* ☎ *93/221–0050* 🌐 *www.gruposagardi.com* [M] *Barceloneta.*

★ El 58

$$ | **TAPAS** | A long list of seasonal Mediterranean small plates, ranging from coal-grilled octopus to vegetarian risotto to traditional Catalan sausage stew, is chalked up on the boards here each day. Inside it's casually hip, with exposed brick walls and vintage furniture; there's a small back patio for al fresco dining as well as tables out front on the Rambla del Poblenou for excellent people-watching. **Known for:** wide range of tapas; charming back patio; nicely presented dishes. [$] *Average main: €20* ✉ *Rambla del Poblenou 58, Poblenou* ☎ *93/601–3903* 🌐 *facebook.com/el58poblenou* 🕓 *Closed Sun.* [M] *Poblenou.*

El Menjador de la Beckett

$$ | **CATALAN** | Part of Poblenou's Sala Beckett cultural center, this restaurant's vast, high-ceilinged dining room fills up with locals at lunchtime, thanks to its excellent, well-priced menu del dia of classic Catalan dishes. Reserve a table for the popular Sunday afternoon vermouth hour, featuring live jazz. **Known for:** affordable prix-fixe lunch (around €13); Sunday live jazz; cool industrial vibe. [$] *Average main: €18* ✉ *Pere IV 228, Poblenou* ☎ *93/599–1794* 🌐 *www.salabeckett.cat/espai/el-menjador-de-la-beckett/* [M] *Llacuna, Pere IV (Tram).*

Els Tres Porquets

$$ | **TAPAS** | Tucked behind the modern outdoor Glòries shopping mall, Els Tres Porquets (The Three Little Pigs) packs in foodies and bon vivants with a wide range of seasonal tapas and small dishes. The interesting wine list includes lesser-known but noteworthy selections from Spain and around the world. **Known for:** interesting wine list; delicious cheeses; Iberian specialties. [$] *Average main: €16* ✉ *Rambla del Poblenou 165, Poblenou* ☎ *93/300–8750* 🌐 *www.elstresporquets.es* 🕓 *Closed Sun.* [M] *Glòries, Clot.*

La Barceloneta, Land of Paella

Paella is Valencian, not Catalan, but it's typical for Barcelona families to go out for paella in Barceloneta on Sunday. Paella *de marisco*, or rice with mixed seafood (usually clams, mussels, octopus, and prawns) is the most popular, though you can also find meat and vegetarian versions. You'll generally see paella listed under rice dishes, which include many variations like *arroz negro* (black rice), cooked in squid ink, and *arroz caldoso*, a soupier rice. Catalan *fideuá* is made with vermicelli noodles mixed with the standard paella ingredients. Paella is for a minimum of two diners—it's usually enough for three. Don't go to any place where they have a photo of paella on a menu outside—it's a sure sign that the dish isn't made in-house.

★ Enoteca Paco Pérez

$$$$ | **MEDITERRANEAN** | The sleek white-on-white dining room sets the tone for chef Pérez's contemporary take on Mediterranean cuisine. Tasting menus present around a dozen courses, most with a seasonal, seafood-centric focus, like a sea cucumber pasta with bone marrow and young artichokes. **Known for:** creative wine list; tasting menus; two-Michelin-starred cuisine. Ⓢ *Average main: €196* ✉ *Hotel Arts, Carrer de la Marina 19-21, Port Olímpic* ☎ *93/221–1000* ⊕ *enotecapacoperez.com/en* ☾ *Closed Mon. and Tues. No dinner Sun. and Wed. Special €95 lunch menu available Sun. and Wed. only* Ⓜ *Ciutadella–Vila Olímpica.*

Green Spot

$$ | **VEGETARIAN** | The vegan and vegetarian options in Barcelona have improved remarkably in recent years, led by the likes of Green Spot, with its extensive menu of flavor-packed plant-based dishes designed to please non-meat-eaters and carnivores alike. The dining room's pale oak paneling elegantly frames an open kitchen and airy dining room. **Known for:** stylish space; craft beer and natural wine; vegan and vegetarian pizzas. Ⓢ *Average main: €16* ✉ *Reina Cristina 12, Barceloneta* ☎ *93/802–5565* ⊕ *www.encompaniadelobos.com/the-green-spot/* Ⓜ *Barceloneta.*

L'Artesana Poblenou

$$ | **TAPAS** | A top-notch natural wine list and an ever-changing menu of inventive tapas like pumpkin-ginger soup, cuttlefish "meatballs," and fig pastry with yogurt draw a devoted local crowd to this casual neighborhood eatery. **Known for:** well-priced menu del dia (around €13); local favorite; excellent croquetas. Ⓢ *Average main: €20* ✉ *Sant Joan de Malta 148, Poblenou* ☎ *93/002–2039* ⊕ *l-artesana-poblenou.negocio.site* ☾ *Closed Sun. and Mon.* Ⓜ *Poblenou, Pere IV (Tram).*

★ La Cova Fumada

$ | **TAPAS** | There's no glitz, no glamour, and not even a sign outside, but the battered wooden doors of this old, family-owned tavern hide a tapas bar to be treasured. Loyal customers and hordes of tourists queue for the market-fresh seafood, served from the furiously busy kitchen. **Known for:** lunch only; "bomba" (fried potato croquette); blink and you'll miss it. Ⓢ *Average main: €12* ✉ *Baluard 56, Barceloneta* ☎ *93/221–4061* ☾ *Closed Sun.* Ⓜ *Barceloneta.*

Xiringuito Escribà

$$ | **SEAFOOD** | Of the many restaurants that dot the Barcelona seafront, this is one of the better mid-range options. Seafood is the focus here—raw, grilled, or fried—and there's also an extensive menu of paellas and fideuàs, any of which are best enjoyed on the breezy terrace, overlooking Bogatell Beach and the Mediterranean. **Known for:** variety of paella and fideuà; weekend reservations for terrace essential; sea views. $ *Average main: €21* ⊠ *Av. del Litoral 62, Poblenou* ☎ *93/221–0729* ⊕ *restaurantsescriba. com/xiringuitoescriba* Ⓜ *Llacuna.*

😋 Coffee and Quick Bites

Bar Bodega l'Electricitat
$ | TAPAS | Don't let the slightly dingy atmosphere dissuade you; this Barceloneta bar serves reliably good tapas and an excellent house vermouth, making it a local favorite since its founding in 1908. The best seats are out on the plaza-fronting terrace. **Known for:** ensaladilla rusa (Russian potato salad with tuna); affordable tapas; house vermouth and by-the-barrel wines. $ *Average main: €12* ⊠ *Sant Carles 15, Barceloneta* ☎ *93/221–5017* ⊕ *facebook.com/BarBodegaElectricitat* ⊗ *Closed Mon. No dinner Sun.* Ⓜ *Barceloneta.*

★ The Cake Man Bakery
$ | BAKERY | This Poblenou bakery's ever-changing selection of delectable homemade cakes, tarts, and cookies—including many vegan and gluten-free options—hits the sweet spot. The Saturday-only brunch features savory egg sandwiches served on house-baked brioche buns. **Known for:** English- and Australian-style baked goods; seasonal specialties; Saturday brunch. $ *Average main: €4* ⊠ *Amistat 18, Poblenou* ☎ *66/440–5965* ⊕ *the-cake-man-bakery. business.site* ⊗ *Closed Sun. and Mon.* Ⓜ *Poblenou.*

★ El Vaso de Oro
$$ | TAPAS | A favorite with visiting gourmands, this often overcrowded little counter serves some of the best beer and tapas in town. The house-brewed artisanal draft beer—named after the

Fort family who owns and runs the bar—is drawn and served with loving care by veteran, epauletted waiters who have it down to a fine art. **Known for:** beef fillet is a favorite; stand-up dining; old-school service. $ *Average main: €15* ⊠ *Balboa 6, Barceloneta* ☎ *93/319–3098* Ⓜ *Barceloneta.*

Horchatería El Tío Ché
$ | ICE CREAM | Cool down with handmade ice cream or *horchata* (a creamy, sweet, tiger milk concoction) at this 110-year-old family-owned ice cream parlor on the Rambla del Poblenou. The queue can be long, especially on hot days, but it's worth the wait. **Known for:** Valencia-style horchata; granizados (iced fruit drinks); artisanal ice cream. $ *Average main: €4* ⊠ *Rambla del Poblenou 44-46, Poblenou* ☎ *93/309–1872* ⊕ *www.eltioche.es/en* Ⓜ *Poblenou.*

La Bombeta
$$ | CATALAN | Its proximity to Barceloneta's bustling Passeig de Joan de Borbó makes this old-school tapas restaurant popular with tourists, but that doesn't keep the locals away. Traditional Catalan small plates, including a delicious version of *bombas*—potato balls stuffed with meat, deep fried, and topped with a spicy sauce—are delivered by gruff but efficient waiters. **Known for:** bombas; no-frills ambience; seafood tapas. $ *Average main: €16* ⊠ *Maquinista 3, Barceloneta* ☎ *93/319–9445* ⊗ *Closed Wed.* Ⓜ *Barceloneta.*

🛏 Hotels

★ Hotel Arts Barcelona
$$$$ | HOTEL | This luxurious Ritz-Carlton-owned, 44-story hotel is just steps from the beach and all the nightlife of Port Olímpic. **Pros:** superb restaurant on-site; seafront pool area with loungers; fantastic views from rooms, especially on higher floors. **Cons:** reception area can get quite busy; very pricey; far from

the city center. Ⓢ *Rooms from: €420* ✉ *Carrer de la Marina 19–21, Port Olímpic* ☎ *93/221–1000* ⊕ *www.hotelartsbarcelona.com* ⇨ *483 rooms* ☺ *No Meals* Ⓜ *L4 Ciutadella–Vila Olímpica.*

Meliá Barcelona Sky

$$$ | **HOTEL** | **FAMILY** | This glassy 29-story skyscraper hotel rises high above Avenue Diagonal in the less-touristy Poblenou district. **Pros:** great views from the 24th-floor bar; variety of room configurations, including family-sized suites; friendly and helpful staff. **Cons:** outdoor pool lacks views; upper-floor "Level" rooms are costlier; a bit far from Barcelona's main attractions. Ⓢ *Rooms from: €175* ✉ *C. de Pere IV 272, Poblenou* ☎ *93/367–2050* ⊕ *www.melia.com* ⇨ *261 rooms* ☺ *No Meals* Ⓜ *L4 Poblenou, Pere IV (Tram).*

Motel One Barcelona-Ciutadella

$ | **HOTEL** | This stylish budget hotel fits the bill for well-designed, no-frills accommodations in a great location. **Pros:** great value; optimal location for exploring the city; rooftop terrace and bar. **Cons:** no pool, gym, or spa; no minibars; rooms are very small. Ⓢ *Rooms from: €99* ✉ *Passeig de Pujades 11–13, La Ciutadella* ☎ *93/626–1900* ⊕ *www.motel-one.com* ⇨ *301 rooms* ☺ *No Meals* Ⓜ *Àrc de Triomf, Wellington (Tram).*

W Barcelona

$$$$ | **RESORT** | The city's only true beachfront hotel, this towering sail-shape monolith is more of a self-contained urban resort, with multiple restaurants and bars, indoor and outdoor pools, lounge decks, plus a sprawling spa and gym—and just about every space has sea views. **Pros:** unrivaled views; beachfront setting; multiple bars and restaurants on-site. **Cons:** pricey rates; loud music in public areas; far from public transportation. Ⓢ *Rooms from: €400* ✉ *Pl. de la Rosa dels Vents 1, Barceloneta* ☎ *93/295–2800* ⊕ *www.marriott.com* ⇨ *473 rooms* ☺ *No Meals* Ⓜ *L4 Barceloneta.*

Nightlife

Barceloneta buzzes on weekends and throughout the summer, when beachgoers make their way from the sea to the narrow streets of this former fishing village. The neighborhood's casual, no-frills restaurants and *chiringuitos* (beachside bars) are packed, with the terraces along the seafront promenade being prime territory.

Though it's a short stroll along the waterfront from Barceloneta, the nightlife scene in Port Olímpic couldn't be more different. Here, a swath of posh lounges and DJ-driven dance clubs cater to fashionable tourists and the city's glitterati; everyone dresses smartly and pays handsomely for cocktails.

Once Barcelona's industrial hub, Poblenou has morphed into its hippest enclave: home to retro-chic cocktail lounges, cozy wine bars, and craft beer pubs. Far from the hustle and bustle of the city's main attractions, the neighborhood attracts locals who lean more toward a relaxed evening out rather than hardcore partying.

BARS

Absenta Bar

COCKTAIL LOUNGES | Checkerboard floors, mismatched antique furniture, and a profusion of vintage lamps and quirky paintings set the appropriately esoteric scene at this absinthe-themed bar, with more than 20 types of the potent spirit on offer. Beer, wine, and cocktails are also available. It's a favorite late-night Barceloneta haunt, staying open until 3 am on Fridays and Saturdays. ✉ *Sant Carles 36, Barceloneta* ☎ *93/221–3638* ⊕ *facebook.com/Absenta-Bar-185131778207493* Ⓜ *Barceloneta.*

★ Balius Bar

COCKTAIL LOUNGES | Sporting the original sign and glass shelving of the pharmacy that once stood here, Balius Bar has retro-chic decor, great music (check out the live jazz sessions on Sunday evenings), and top-notch cocktails. ✉ *Pujades 196, Poblenou* ☎ *93/315–8650* ⊕ *baliusbar.com* Ⓜ *Poblenou.*

Eclipse

COCKTAIL LOUNGES | The sweeping Mediterranean views from the 26th floor of the seaside W Barcelona hotel are no doubt Eclipse's biggest appeal. But toss in a slick, sexy interior, fancy cocktails, good sushi, and DJs spinning house and techno, and it's no wonder this is one of the city's most see-and-be-seen spots. ✉ *W Barcelona, Plaça de la Rosa dels Vents 1, Barceloneta* ☎ *93/295–2800* ⊕ *www.eclipse-barcelona.com* Ⓜ *Barceloneta.*

La Cervecita Nuestra de Cada Día

BREWPUBS | A must for craft beer lovers, this modern high-ceilinged bar and shop is filled to the brim with more than 200 international craft brands plus around 15 rotating artisanal beers on tap. Claim your spot early as regulars routinely dominate the seating at the long bar or the cozy corner tables up front. ✉ *Llull 184, Poblenou* ☎ *616/318–430* ⊕ *www.facebook.com/Lacervecitanuestradecadadia* Ⓜ *Llacuna.*

★ La Violeta Bar de Vinos Naturales

WINE BARS | Serving natural wines mainly from France and Spain, with many varieties from the nearby Penedes and Alella regions, this delightful bar also offers a nice selection of upscale tapas. The waitstaff is friendly, multilingual, and highly knowledgeable about the history and terroir of the wines. The cozy interior has an attractive rustic-chic design, but try for a seat on the terrace, right on Barceloneta's lively market square. ✉ *Baluard 58, Barceloneta* ☎ *93/221–9581* ⊕ *facebook.com/lavioletavinosnaturales* Ⓜ *Barceloneta.*

Madame George

COCKTAIL LOUNGES | Everything about this stylish bar is a happy contradiction: the chandeliered space has large gilded mirrors and polished chocolate brown stools that curiously complement the rickety antiques and quirky touches (check out the bathtub sofa in the back room). Cocktails run the full gamut from classic to creative. ✉ *Pujades 179, Poblenou* ☎ *93/500–5151* ⊕ *www.madamegeorgebar.com* Ⓜ *Poblenou.*

Més de Vi

WINE BARS | The brainchild of two Catalan sommeliers, Més de Vi is a chic wine bar with a purpose: to educate visitors on the art of Spanish wines, with a particular focus on regional vintages. There are plenty of seating options: a tasting table for serious aficionados, romantic tête-à-tête tables, and a bar area for socializing. ✉ *Marià Aguiló 123, Poblenou* ☎ *93/007–9151* ⊕ *www.restaurantemesdevi.es/en* Ⓜ *Poblenou.*

CASINOS

Casino de Barcelona

THEMED ENTERTAINMENT | Situated underneath the Hotel Arts, Barcelona's modern casino has everything from slot machines to roulette, plus restaurants, a bar, and a dance club. The casino regularly hosts Texas Hold'em poker tournaments, which add an air of Vegas-style excitement. ✉ *Marina 19–21, Port Olímpic* ☎ *900/225–7878* ⊕ *www.casinobarcelona.com/en* ☞ *For non-EU citizens, a passport is required for entry.* Ⓜ *Ciutadella–Vila Olímpica.*

DANCE CLUBS

CDLC

DANCE CLUBS | Among the glitziest of Barcelona's waterfront clubs, the CDLC (Carpe Diem Lounge Club) embraces all the clichés of Ibizan over-the-top decor. The music is electronic and cocktails are exotic—and pricey. ✉ *Passeig Maritim 32, Marina Beach, Port Olímpic*

☎ *64/777–9999* ⊕ *www.cdlcbarcelona.com* Ⓜ *Ciutadella–Vila Olímpica.*

Shôko

DANCE CLUBS | Located just below Frank Gehry's famous *Fish* sculpture, this swanky Asian-inspired restaurant and lounge morphs into a late-night party paradise featuring theme nights with international DJs ready to spin into the wee hours. ⊠ *Passeig Marítim de la Barceloneta 36, Port Olímpic* ☎ *93/225–9200* ⊕ *www.shoko.biz/en* Ⓜ *Ciutadella–Vila Olímpica.*

MUSIC CLUBS

Razzmatazz

LIVE MUSIC | Drawing crowds from all over the city, this enormous industrial warehouse turned dance club and concert hall is multiple clubs in one: RazzClub plays indie rock; The Loft and Lolita are all about techno and electronica; and the smaller, more relaxed Pop Bar and and Rex Room focus on pop tunes and urban music, respectively. DJs spin nightly and live acts run from local bands to huge international names in rock and pop. ⊠ *Almogàvers 122, Poblenou* ☎ *93/320–8200* ⊕ *www.salarazzmatazz.com* Ⓜ *Marina, Bogatell.*

🛍 Shopping

Poblenou has become something of a shopping destination, with lots of independent fashion boutiques along the Rambla del Poblenou, and cutting-edge concept stores and art galleries elsewhere around the district.

ART GALLERIES

La Plataforma

ART GALLERIES | Paintings, sculpture, and graphic artwork by emerging contemporary artists mainly based in Barcelona are on view (and for sale) at this combination gallery, studio workspace, and events venue. ⊠ *Pujades 99, Poblenou* ☎ *93/485–6519* ⊕ *laplataformabcn.com* Ⓜ *Llacuna.*

BOOKS AND MUSIC

Ultra-Local Records

RECORDS | Specializing in vinyl from independent record labels, especially Catalan labels, this is a great place to discover local music. You can also catch regular in-store performances by area bands. ⊠ *Pujades 113, Poblenou* ☎ *93/667–7788* ⊕ *ultralocalrecords.blogspot.com* Ⓜ *Llacuna.*

FOOD AND WINE

Bodega Alaparra

FOOD | Choose from the vast selection of Catalan and Spanish wines at this high-ceilinged bodega, which also sells fancy cheeses, pâté, Iberian ham, and other gourmet fare to go. It's also a wine and tapas bar, so you can sample a bit of everything before you buy. ⊠ *Pujades 136, Poblenou* ☎ *69/376–0805* ⊕ *facebook.com/people/Bodega-Alaparra/100013888817148* Ⓜ *Llacuna.*

HOUSEHOLD ITEMS AND FURNITURE

Espai Joliu

OTHER SPECIALTY STORE | Part café and part plant store, with pottery, prints, and design magazines also for sale, Espai Joliu is worth a visit to check out the cool raw space—distressed walls, exposed ceilings, concrete floors—prettified with greenery. ⊠ *Badajoz 95, Poblenou* ⊕ *espaijoliu.tumblr.com* Ⓜ *Llacuna.*

Noak Room

FURNITURE | Even if you're not in the market for retro-style furniture, it's worth popping into this large, loftlike space to check out all the sleek Scandinavian designs, from upcycled and renovated lamps to sofas, chairs, and mirrors from the 1950s to the present day. International shipping can be arranged. ⊠ *Roc Boronat 69, Poblenou* ☎ *93/309–5300* ⊕ *www.noakroom.com* Ⓜ *Llacuna.*

Unusual Store Barcelona

OTHER SPECIALTY STORE | Cool design objects and housewares, edgy

Barcelona-based fashion labels, and locally made artwork are among the many unique offerings at this well-curated concept store. ⊠ *Ramón Turró 147, Poblenou* ☎ *65/510–1069* ⊕ *unusualconcept.store* Ⓜ *Llacuna.*

MARKETS
★ Palo Alto Market

MARKET | This sprawling 19th-century factory complex—with its gorgeous brick architecture, towering chimney, multiple courtyards, and verdant garden—now serves as creative studio space for designers and artists. On the first weekend of every month, the Palo Alto Market invites the public to step inside the gates and experience the vast, very cool space. There's live music and DJs, street food trucks, and dozens upon dozens of stalls selling a range of goods, from crafts to clothing. ⊠ *Pellaires 30, Poblenou* ☎ *93/159–6670* ⊕ *www.palomarketfest.com/en* ⌕ *€5 entry fee; tickets must be purchased online* Ⓜ *Selva del Mar.*

 Activities

BIKING
Barcelona By Bike

BIKING | FAMILY | Gather at the meeting point next to the main entrance of the Barcelona Casino for a three-hour guided bike tour (€24 with a complimentary drink en route) of the Old City, Gaudí architecture, and the port. ⊠ *Calle Marina 16, Port Olímpic* ☎ *67/130–7325* ⊕ *www.barcelonabybike.com* Ⓜ *Ciutadella/Vila Olimpica.*

WATERSPORTS
SEA YOU Surf School

WATER SPORTS | FAMILY | Located right on Sant Sebastià Beach, this company offers lessons and rentals for all types of watersports, including surfing, windsurfing, and sailing. Try a sunset SUP (stand-up paddleboarding) outing, when the sea is often at its calmest. ⊠ *Passeig del Mare Nostrum 14, Barceloneta* ☎ *66/167–3702* ⊕ *seayoubarcelona.com* Ⓜ *Barceloneta.*

Chapter 8

THE EIXAMPLE

8

Updated by
Isabelle Kliger

👁 **Sights**
★★★★★

🍴 **Restaurants**
★★★★★

🛏 **Hotels**
★★★★★

🛍 **Shopping**
★★★★★

🍸 **Nightlife**
★★★★★

NEIGHBORHOOD SNAPSHOT

TOP EXPERIENCES

■ **Casa Milà:** Visit the wavy, curving stone rooftop of one of Gaudí's most celebrated designs on a night tour which includes a spectacular son et lumière projection.

■ **Temple Expiatori de la Sagrada Família:** Reserve timed tickets in advance for Barcelona's most emblematic architectural icon. Choose the "Top Views" ticket for access to the bell towers, and bring binoculars to zoom in on incredible details.

■ **Consell de Cent:** The best art galleries in Barcelona are gathered around a few blocks on Consell de Cent.

■ **La Rambla de Catalunya:** Stroll the leafy promenade of one of Barcelona's trendiest streets.

GETTING HERE

The metro stops at Plaça de Catalunya and Provença nicely bracket this quintessential Barcelona neighborhood; the Diagonal and Passeig de Gràcia stations are right in the center.

Barcelona's unnumbered Eixample (Expansion), the post-1860 grid, is a perfect place to get lost, but fear not: the Eixample is vertebrate. Carrer Balmes divides the working-class *Esquerra* (left, looking uphill) from its bourgeois *Dreta* (right). Even the blocks are divided by flats *davant* (front) or *darrera* (behind). The sides of the streets are either *mar* (seaward) or *muntanya* (facing the mountain).

PLANNING YOUR TIME

Exploring the Eixample can take days, but three hours will be enough to cover the most important sites. Add another two or three hours (including the wait in line) for the Sagrada Família. Look for the *passatges* (passageways) through some of the Eixample blocks; Passatge Permanyer, Passatge de la Concepció, and Passatge Mendez Vigo are three of the best. Beware of the tapas emporia on Passeig de Gràcia; almost all of them microwave previously prepared bits and are not the best.

GAIXAMPLE

Barcelona has long been a hub for the LGBTQ+ community and, while the whole city is pretty open-minded and gay friendly, nowhere personifies Barcelona's queer credentials more than Gaixample. The small enclave within Eixample Esquerra—spanning three blocks up from Gran Via to Aragó, and six across from Comte d'Urgell to Balmes—is where you'll find the city's highest concentration of rainbow flags per square foot. Brimming with drag queens, gay bars and clubs, and LGBTQ-owned shops and businesses, Gaixample is one of the liveliest, most colorful and welcoming parts of Barcelona.

The "Eixample" (pronounced ay-shompla) means "Expansion" in Catalan and this late-19th-century urban development is one of Barcelona's best known neighborhoods, famed for its dazzling Art Nouveau architecture. The upscale shops, art galleries, facades of the Moderniste town houses, and the venues for some of the city's finest cuisine are the main attractions.

Though designed as a grid, the Eixample, which is almost three square miles, is oddly difficult to navigate; the builders seldom numbered the buildings and declined to alphabetize the streets. Even Barcelona residents can get lost here. The easiest orientation to grasp is the basic division between the historically well-to-do Eixample Dreta, to the right of Rambla Catalunya looking inland, and where you'll find find many of the most beautiful Moderniste facades, upscale boutiques, and classic *grand dame* hotels—and Eixample Esquerra, left of Passeig de Gràcia and traditionally more working-class, and today cooler and far more happening, with lots of natural wine bars, vegan eateries, and art galleries. Eixample locations are also either *mar* (on the ocean side of the street) or *muntanya* (facing the mountains). The neighborhood of Sant Antoni is technically also part of Eixample, and has recently become one of Barcelona's hippest *barrios* for eating and drinking.

The Eixample was created when the Ciutat Vella's city walls were demolished in 1860, and Barcelona embarked on a vast expansion, financed by the return of rich colonials from the Americas, aristocrats who had sold their country estates, and the city's industrial magnates. They expected their investment to trumpet not only their own wealth and influence, but also the resurgence of Barcelona itself and its unique cultural heritage— not Spanish, but Catalan, and modern European. The grid was the work of engineer Ildefons Cerdà, and much of the construction was done in the peak years of the Moderniste movement by a who's who of Art Nouveau architects, starring Gaudí, Domènech i Montaner, and Puig i Cadafalch; rising above it all is Gaudí's Sagrada Família church. The Eixample's principal thoroughfares are La Rambla de Catalunya and the Passeig de Gràcia, where many of the city's most elegant shops occupy the ground floors of the most interesting Art Nouveau buildings. The name of Eixample's most famous block of houses, the Manzana de la Discordia, is a pun on the Spanish word *manzana*, which means both "apple" and "city block," alluding to the three-way architectural counterpoint on this street and to the classical myth of the Apple of Discord, which played a part in that legendary tale about the Judgment of Paris and the subsequent Trojan War. The houses here are spectacular and encompass three monuments of Modernisme—Casa Lleó Morera, Casa Amatller, and Casa Batlló—in significantly different styles.

By far the largest of Barcelona's neighborhoods, Eixample is more than three miles wide, with a total area of just under three square miles. We've divided the neighborhood into its three sub-districts: Eixample Dreta, Eixample Esquerra, and Sant Antoni.

Sights

Casa Amatller
HISTORIC HOME | The neo-Gothic Casa Amatller was built by Josep Puig i Cadafalch in 1900, when the architect was 33 years old. Eighteen years younger than Domènech i Montaner and 15 years younger than Gaudí, Puig i Cadafalch was one of the leading statesmen of his generation, once the mayor of Barcelona, and in 1917, president of Catalonia's first home-rule government since 1714. Puig i Cadafalch's architectural historicism sought to recover Catalonia's proud past, in combination with eclectic elements from Flemish and Dutch architectural motifs. Note the Eusebi Arnau sculptures—especially his St. George and the Dragon, and the figures of a drummer with his dancing bear. The flowing-haired "Princesa" is thought to be Amatller's daughter; the animals above the motif are depicted pouring chocolate, a reference to the source of the Amatller family fortune. The first-floor apartment, where the Amatller family lived, is a museum, with original furniture and decor; self-guided tours are available with an English audioguide. A quick visit will give you a sense of what the rest of the building is like and a chance to buy some chocolate *de la casa* at the boutique. ✉ *Passeig de Gràcia 41, Eixample Dreta*

☎ *93/216–0175* ⊕ *amatller.org/en* ✉ *From €19* ✆ *15% admission discount if you book online through the website* Ⓜ *L2/ L3/L5 Passeig de Gràcia, FGC Provença.*

★ Casa Batlló
HISTORIC HOME | **FAMILY** | Gaudí at his most spectacular, the Casa Batlló is actually a makeover: it was originally built in 1877 by one of Gaudí's teachers, Emili Sala Cortés, and acquired by the Batlló family in 1900. Batlló wanted to tear down the undistinguished Sala building and start over, but Gaudí persuaded him to remodel the facade and the interior, and the result is astonishing. The facade—with its rainbow of colored glass and *trencadís* (polychromatic tile fragments) and the toothy masks of the wrought-iron balconies projecting outward toward the street—is an irresistible photo op. Nationalist symbolism is at work here: the scaly roof line represents the Dragon of Evil impaled on St. George's cave, and the skulls and bones on the balconies are the dragon's victims, allusions to medieval Catalonia's code of chivalry and religious piety. Gaudí is said to have directed the composition of the facade from the middle of Passeig de Gràcia, calling instructions to workmen on the scaffolding. Inside, the translucent windows on the landings of the central staircase light up the maritime motif and the details of the building; as everywhere in his oeuvre, Gaudí opted for natural shapes and rejected straight lines.

A visit to Casa Batlló is more than a traditional tour of a museum or monument. The fully restored house is packed with state-of-the-art technologies, including immersive rooms, surprising audiovisual productions, and an intelligent audio guide available in 15 languages. Children especially will enjoy an Augmented Reality SmartGuide: a fun, interactive way to discover the genius of Gaudí. From May to October, finish your visit with an open-air concert on the roof (starts at 8

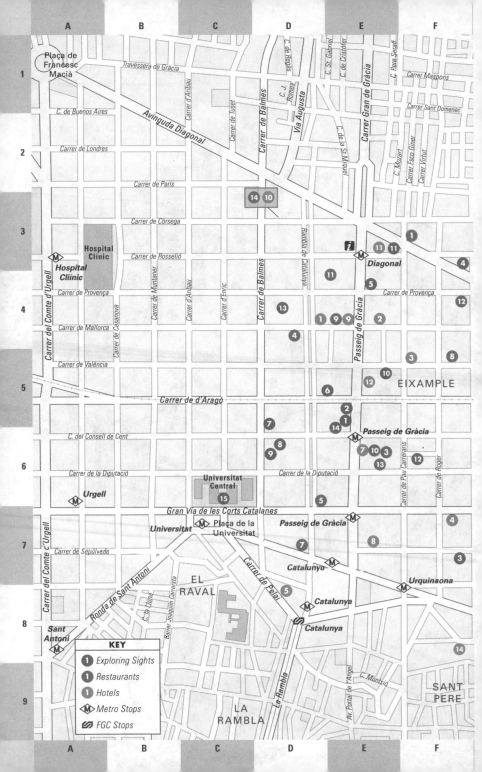

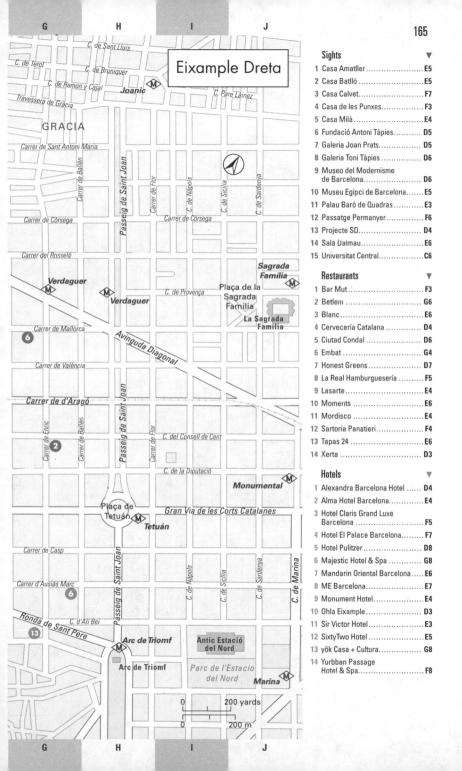

Eixample Dreta

Sights ▼

1 Casa Amatller E5
2 Casa Batlló E5
3 Casa Calvet........................... F7
4 Casa de les Punxes................. F3
5 Casa Milà............................. E4
6 Fundació Antoni Tàpies........... D5
7 Galeria Joan Prats................. D5
8 Galeria Toni Tàpies D6
9 Museo del Modernisme
   de Barcelona...................... D6
10 Museu Egipci de Barcelona....... E5
11 Palau Baró de Quadras E3
12 Passatge Permanyer.............. F6
13 Projecte SD........................ D4
14 Sala Dalmau........................ E6
15 Universitat Central................. C6

Restaurants ▼

1 Bar Mut F3
2 Betlem G6
3 Blanc................................. E6
4 Cervecería Catalana D4
5 Ciutad Condal D6
6 Embat G4
7 Honest Greens D7
8 La Real Hamburguesería F5
9 Lasarte.............................. E4
10 Moments E6
11 Mordisco E4
12 Sartoria Panatieri.................. F4
13 Tapas 24 .... E6
14 Xerta D3

Hotels ▼

1 Alexandra Barcelona Hotel D4
2 Alma Hotel Barcelona............. E4
3 Hotel Claris Grand Luxe
   Barcelona F5
4 Hotel El Palace Barcelona........ F7
5 Hotel Pulitzer..................... D8
6 Majestic Hotel & Spa G8
7 Mandarin Oriental Barcelona..... E6
8 ME Barcelona...................... E7
9 Monument Hotel................... E4
10 Ohla Eixample..................... D3
11 Sir Victor Hotel.................... E3
12 SixtyTwo Hotel E5
13 yök Casa + Cultura................. G8
14 Yurbban Passage
   Hotel & Spa....................... F8

Sights ▼

1 Casa de la Papallona
  (Casa Fajol)........................ A6
2 Casa Golferichs................... D6
3 Marlborough Gallery............. G4
4 N2................................. G4

Restaurants ▼

1 Benzina D9
2 Besta.............................. G4
3 Cinc Sentits....................... B6
4 Cruix.............................. B6
5 Deliri.............................. G3
6 Disfrutar E4
7 Gresca G4
8 Igueldo............................ G3
9 La Taverna del Clínic E3
10 Mont Bar.......................... F6
11 Paco Meralgo...................... F3
12 Slow & Low........................ D7
13 Taktika Berri...................... F5

Quick Bites ▼

1 Bar Alegria D7
2 DeLaCrem G6
3 L' Atelier.......................... D6
4 La Flauta G6
5 La Pastisseria G5

Hotels ▼

1 The Corner Hotel................... F4
2 Hotel Astoria G2
3 Hotel Cram........................ G5
4 Villa Emilia C6

KEY

1 Exploring Sights
1 Restaurants
1 Quick Bites
1 Hotels
Ⓜ Metro Stops
Ⓕ FGC Stops

pm) and a drink, as part of the "Magic Nights" program.

Budget-conscious visitors take note: The admission fee is rather high but there are discounts for booking in advance online; you can also just take in the view from outside the Casa Batlló and instead visit the Casa Milà, up the Passeig de Gràcia on the opposite side. ⊠ *Passeig de Gràcia 43, Eixample Dreta* ☎ *93/216–0306* ⊕ *www.casabatllo.es* ✉ *From €35* Ⓜ *L2/L3/L4 Passeig de Gràcia, FGC Provença.*

Casa Calvet
NOTABLE BUILDING | This exquisite but more conventional town house (for Gaudí, anyway) was the architect's first commission in the Eixample (the second was the dragon-like Casa Batlló, and the third, and last—he was never asked to do another—was the stone quarry–esque Casa Milà). Peaked with baroque scroll gables over the unadorned (no ceramics, no color, no sculpted ripples) Montjuïc sandstone facade, Casa Calvet compensates for its structural conservatism with its Art Nouveau details, from the door handles to the benches, chairs, vestibule, and spectacular glass-and-wood elevator. Built between 1898 and 1900 for the textile baron Pere Calvet, the house includes symbolic elements on the facade, ranging from the owner's stylized letter "C" over the door to the cypress, symbol of hospitality, above. The wild mushrooms on the main (second) floor reflect Pere Calvet's (and perhaps Gaudí's) passion for mycology, while the busts at the top of the facade represent St. Peter, the owner's patron saint, and St. Genis of Arles and St. Genis of Rome, patron saints of Vilassar, the Calvet family's hometown in the coastal Maresme north of Barcelona. Note that the only part of the building accessible to visitors is the ground-floor China Crown restaurant, originally the suite of offices for Calvet's textile company, with its exuberant Moderniste decor. ⊠ *Carrer Casp 48, Eixample Dreta*

☎ *93/315 8095 (China Crown restaurant)* Ⓜ *L1/L4 Urquinaona.*

Casa de la Papallona (Casa Fajol)
NOTABLE BUILDING | This extraordinary apartment house crowned with an enormous yellow butterfly (*papallona*) made of *trencadís* (broken ceramic chips used by the Modernistes to add color to curved surfaces) was built between 1911 and 1929 by Josep Graner i Prat. Technically called Casa Fajol, it is more commonly referred to as Casa de la Papallona (butterfly house). Next to Plaça de Espanya, directly overlooking the Arenes de Barcelona (the former bullring, now a multilevel shopping mall), the building displays lines of a routine, late-19th-century design—that is, until your eye reaches the top of the facade. ⊠ *Carrer Llançà 20, Eixample Esquerra* Ⓜ *L1 Rocafort.*

Casa de les Punxes (*House of the Spikes*)
NOTABLE BUILDING | Also known as Casa Terrades for the family that owned the house and commissioned Puig i Cadafalch to build it, this extraordinary cluster of six conical towers ending in impossibly sharp needles is another of Puig i Cadafalch's inspirations, this one rooted in the Gothic architecture of northern European countries. One of the few freestanding Eixample buildings, visible from 360 degrees, this ersatz Bavarian or Danish castle in downtown Barcelona is composed entirely of private apartments, some of them built into the conical towers themselves on three circular levels, connected by spiral stairways. Casa de les Punxes currently functions as a co-working space and is not open to visitors. ⊠ *Av. Diagonal 420, Eixample Dreta* ☎ *93/018–5242* ⊕ *www.barcelona.de/en/barcelona-casa-de-les-punxes.html* Ⓜ *L4/L5 Verdaguer, L3/L5 Diagonal.*

Casa Golferichs (*Golferichs Civic Center*)
HISTORIC HOME | Gaudí disciple Joan Rubió i Bellver built this extraordinary house, known as El Xalet (The Chalet), for the Golferichs family when he was

only 30. The rambling wooden eaves and gables of the exterior enclose a cozy and comfortable dark-wood-lined interior with a pronounced verticality. The top floor, with its rich wood beams and cerulean walls, is often used for intimate concerts; the ground floor exhibits paintings and photographs. The building serves now as the quarters of the Golferichs Centre Civic, which offers local residents a range of conferences and discussions, exhibitions and adult education courses, and organizes various thematic walking tours of the city. ✉ *Gran Via 491, Eixample Esquerra* ☎ *93/323-7790* ⊕ *www.golferichs.org* ⊗ *Closed Sat.–Sun.* Ⓜ *L1 Rocafort, Urgell.*

★ **Casa Milà**

NOTABLE BUILDING | Usually referred to as "La Pedrera" (the Stone Quarry), this building, with its curving stone facade undulating around the corner of the block, is one of Gaudí's most celebrated yet initially reviled designs. Topped by chimneys so eerie they were nicknamed *espantabruixes* (witch scarers), the Casa Milà was unveiled in 1910 to the horror of local residents. The exterior has no straight lines; the curlicues and wrought-iron foliage of the balconies, sculpted by Josep Maria Jujol, and the rippling, undressed stone, made you feel, as one critic put it, "as though you are on board a ship in an angry sea."

Gaudí's rooftop chimney park, alternately interpreted as veiled Saharan women or helmeted warriors, is as spectacular as anything in Barcelona, especially in late afternoon when the sunlight slants over the city into the Mediterranean. Inside, the handsome Àtic de la Balena (Whale Attic) has excellent critical displays of Gaudí's works from all over Spain, as well as explanations of his theories and techniques. The Pis dels veïns (Tenants' Apartment) is an interesting look into the life of a family that lived in La Pedrera in the early 20th century. People still occupy the other apartments.

In the summer, lines of visitors waiting to see the Pedrera can stretch a block or more; if you sign up for "Gaudí's Pedrera: Night Experience" you'll tour the building by night, with a spectacular illuminated projection. Check the website for tour times and book online. Bookings are essential. On *La Pedrera Jazz* (Friday and Saturday summer nights) the Àtic de la Balena and the roof terrace are open for drinks and jazz concerts; the doors open at 8:15 pm and concerts begin at 8:45. Priced at €38, admission includes a visit to the whole attic, the concert, and a drink. ✉ *Passeig de Gràcia 92, Eixample Dreta* ☎ *93/214-2576* ⊕ *www.lapedrera.com/en* 💶 *From €24* Ⓜ *L2/L3/L5 Diagonal, FGC Provença.*

Fabra i Coats–Fàbrica de Creació

ARTS CENTER | This self-proclaimed artist social club—remodeled from an old textile factory on the outer limits of the Poblenou district—is a great place for emerging young visual artists to find their footing. Part of the complex accommodates work spaces for resident artists and creatives; live performances and festivals are hosted here as well. ✉ *Sant Adrià 20, Sant Andreu* ☎ *93/256-6150* ⊕ *www.barcelona.cat/fabraicoats* Ⓜ *Sant Andreu.*

Fundació Antoni Tàpies

ART MUSEUM | This foundation created in 1984 by Catalonia's then-most important living artist, Antoni Tàpies, continues to promote the work of important Catalan artists and writers. Tàpies, who died in 2012, was an abstract painter who was influenced by surrealism, and his passion for art and literature still echoes in the halls of this enchanting Modernist building by esteemed architect Domènech i Montaner. There are thought-provoking temporary exhibitions, a comprehensive lecture series, and film screenings. The modern split-level gallery also has a bookstore that's strong on Tàpies, Asian art, and Barcelona art and architecture. ✉ *Carrer Aragó 255, Eixample Esquerra*

☎ 93/487–0315 ⊕ www.fundaciotapies. org ⊠ €8 ⊙ Closed Sun. afternoon and Mon. Ⓜ L2/L3/L4 Passeig de Gràcia.

Galeria Joan Prats

ART GALLERY | One of several galleries on or around Consell de Cent in Eixample Esquerra, "La Prats" has been one of the city's top galleries since the 1920s, showing international painters and sculptors from Henry Moore to Antoni Tàpies. Barcelona painter Joan Miró was a prime force in the founding of the gallery when he became friends with Joan Prats. The motifs of bonnets and derbies on the gallery's facade are callbacks to the trade of Prats's father. José Maria Sicilia and Juan Ugalde have shown here, while Erick Beltrán, Hannah Collins, and Eulàlia Valldosera are among the regular artists on display. ⊠ Balmes 54, Eixample Esquerra ☎ 93/216–0290 ⊕ www.galeriajoanprats. com ⊙ Closed Sun. and Mon. Ⓜ Passeig de Gràcia.

Galeria Toni Tàpies

ART GALLERY | After the prolific Catalan painter Antoni Tàpies died in 2012, his son Toni decided to change the direction of his successful gallery and, as a touching homage, only show his late father's work, which is now on show permanently. This is complemented by periodic smaller shows and events from other leading artists, sometimes of one single piece, which have been chosen to create a "dialogue" with the Tàpies oeuvre. ⊠ Consell de Cent 282, Eixample Esquerra ☎ 93/487–6402 ⊕ www. tonitapies.com ⊙ Closed Sat. and Sun. Ⓜ Catalunya, Passeig de Gràcia.

Marlborough Gallery

ART GALLERY | This international giant occupies an important position in Barcelona's art-gallery galaxy with exhibits of major contemporary artists from around the world, as well as local stars. Recent shows featured the hyperrealist collages of Antonio López García and the contemporary designer and painter Alberto Corazón. ⊠ Enric Granados 68, Eixample

Esquerra ☎ 93/467–4454 ⊕ www. galeriamarlborough.com ⊙ Closed Sun. Ⓜ Passeig de Gràcia.

Museu del Modernisme de Barcelona

(Museum of Catalan Modernism: MMBCN)
ART MUSEUM | Though often unjustly bypassed in favor of rival displays in the Casa Milà, Casa Batlló, and the DHUB Design Museum in Plaça de les Glòries, this museum houses a small but rich collection of Moderniste furnishings, paintings and posters, sculpture (including works by Josep Limona), and decorative arts. Don't miss the section devoted to Gaudí-designed furniture. ⊠ Carrer Balmes 48, Eixample Esquerra ☎ 93/272–2896 ⊕ www.gothsland.com ⊠ €12 ⊙ Closed Sun. Ⓜ L1/L2 Universitat.

Museu Egipci de Barcelona

HISTORY MUSEUM | FAMILY | Presumably you came to Barcelona to learn about Catalonia, not ancient Egypt, but you might be making a mistake by skipping this major collection of art and artifacts. This museum takes advantage of state-of-the-art curatorial techniques, with exhibitions showcasing everything from mummies to what the ancient Egyptians had for dinner. The museum offers free guided tours, but only in Catalan or Spanish. ⊠ Fundació Arqueòlogica Clos, Valencia 284, Eixample Dreta ☎ 93/488–0188 ⊕ www.museuegipci.com ⊠ €12 Ⓜ L2/L3/L4 Passeig de Gràcia.

N2

ART GALLERY | Since it opened, the Galería N2 has established its position as a beacon at the crossroads of tradition and modernity, of high- and low-brow art. The experimental but careful selection of artists featured in several annual solo shows includes the street artist Sixeart and the Argentine surrealist Mauricio Vergara. Since N2 specializes in up-and-coming and mid-career artists, works are generally affordable yet safe to invest in, and browsing here makes for a lighthearted change from the

Eixample's more serious art houses.
✉ *Enric Granados 61, Eixample Esquerra*
☎ *93/452–0592* ⊕ *www.n2galeria.com*
🕑 *Closed Sat. and Sun.*

Palau Baró de Quadras

NOTABLE BUILDING | The neo-Gothic and plateresque (intricately carved in silver-smith-like detail) facade of this house built for textile magnate Baron Manuel de Quadras and remodeled (1904–06) by Moderniste starchitect Puig i Cadafalch, has one of the most spectacular collections of Eusebi Arnau sculptures in town (other Arnau sites include the Palau de la Música Catalana, Quatre Gats–Casa Martí, and Casa Amatller). Look for the theme of St. George slaying the dragon once again, this one in a spectacularly vertiginous rush of movement down the facade. Across the top floor is an intimate-looking row of alpine chalet–like windows. The Palau currently houses the Institut Ramon Llull, a nonprofit organization dedicated to spreading the knowledge of Catalan culture worldwide.
✉ *Av. Diagonal 373, Eixample Dreta*
☎ *93/467–8000* ⊕ *www.llull.cat* 🔲 *Group guided tours €10/person* Ⓜ *L2/L3/L5 Diagonal.*

Passatge Permanyer

STREET | Cutting through the middle of the block bordered by Pau Claris, Roger de Llúria, Consell de Cent, and Diputació, this charming, leafy mid-Eixample sanctuary is one of 46 passatges (alleys or passageways) that cut through the blocks of this gridlike area. Once an aristocratic enclave and hideaway for pianist Carles Vidiella and poet, musician, and illustrator Apel·les Mestre, Passatge Permanyer is, along with the nearby Passatge Méndez Vigo, the best of these through-the-looking-glass downtown Barcelona alleyways.
✉ *Passatge Permanyer, Eixample Dreta*
Ⓜ *L2/L3/L4 Passeig de Gràcia.*

Projecte SD

ART GALLERY | This gallery, located in one of the Eixample's most beautiful little passages, doesn't go easy on its visitors.

No show at Projecte SD can be grasped without the explanatory booklet; no piece of art can be fully appreciated in isolation. The pieces exhibited and sold here are complex, philosophical, challenging, and bleedingly conceptual—anything but simply decorative. Projecte SD is really more of a museum than a gallery. That makes every visit an experience and every purchase an audacious act of faith.
✉ *Passatge Mercader 8, Baixos 1, Eixample Esquerra* ☎ *93/488–1360* ⊕ *www.projectesd.com* 🕑 *Closed Sun. and Mon.*
Ⓜ *Diagonal, Provença.*

★ Recinte Modernista de Sant Pau

NOTABLE BUILDING | Among the more recent tourist attractions in Barcelona, the Sant Pau Art Nouveau Site is set in what was surely one of the most beautiful public projects in the world: the Hospital de la Santa Creu i Sant Pau. A UNESCO World Heritage site, the complex is extraordinary in its setting and style. The story behind it as fascinating as the site itself: architect Lluis Domènech i Montaner believed that trees, flowers, and fresh air were likely to help people recover from what ailed them more than anything doctors could do in emotionally sterile surroundings. The hospital wards were set among gardens, their brick facades topped with polychrome ceramic tile roofs in extravagant shapes and details. Domènech also believed in the therapeutic properties of form and color, and decorated the hospital with sculptures by Eusebi Arnau and colorful mosaics, replete with motifs of hope and healing and healthy growth. One of the most famous, by Mario Maragliano, describes the history of the institution and can be found in the main facade of the building. Begun in 1902, this monumental production won Domènech i Montaner his third Barcelona "Best Building" award in 1912. (His previous two prizes were for the Palau de la Música Catalana and Casa Lleó Morera.)

8

The Eixample

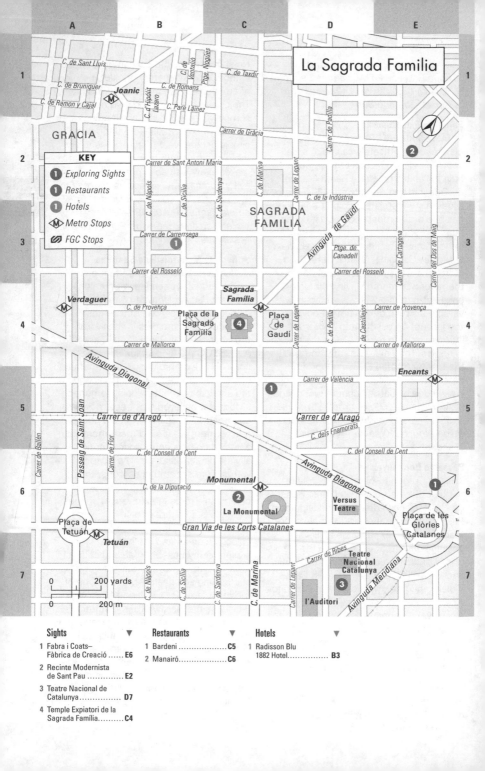

La Sagrada Familia

KEY

- **1** Exploring Sights
- **1** Restaurants
- **1** Hotels
- **M** Metro Stops
- **Ⓕ** FGC Stops

No longer a functioning hospital (the new Sant Pau—comparatively soulless but fully functional and state-of-the-art—is uphill from the complex), many of the buildings have been taken over for other purposes. The Sant Manuel Pavillion, for example, now houses the Barcelona Health Hub, a platform for startups working in the fields of e-health and innovation. The center offers self-guided tours with audio guides in the form of an app that can be downloaded to your personal devices, for maximum safety and hygiene. ⊠ *Carrer Sant Antoni Maria Claret 167, Eixample Dreta* ☎ *93/553–7801* ⊕ *www.santpaubarcelona.org/en* ⊠ *From €15; free 1st Sun. of month* Ⓜ *L5 Sant Pau/Dos de Maig.*

Sala Dalmau
ART GALLERY | An old-timer in the established Consell de Cent gallery scene, Sala Dalmau shows an interesting and heterodox range of Catalan and international artists. ⊠ *Consell de Cent 349, Eixample Esquerra* ☎ *93/215–4592* ⊕ *www.saladalmau.com* ⊗ *Closed Sun.* Ⓜ *Passeig de Gràcia.*

Teatre Nacional de Catalunya
ARTS CENTER | This grandiose glass-enclosed classical theater was designed by Ricardo Bofill, architect of Barcelona's airport and the sail-shaped W Barcelona hotel. Programs cover everything from Shakespeare to avant-garde theater. Most productions, as the name suggests, are in Catalan but beautiful to witness all the same. ⊠ *Plaça de les Arts 1, Eixample Dreta* ☎ *93/306–5700* ⊕ *www.tnc.cat* Ⓜ *Glóries, Monumental.*

★ Temple Expiatori de la Sagrada Família
NOTABLE BUILDING | Barcelona's most emblematic architectural icon, Antoni Gaudí's Sagrada Família, is still under construction close to 140 years after it was begun. This striking and surreal creation was conceived as nothing short of a Bible in stone, a gigantic representation of the entire history of Christianity, and it continues to cause responses from surprise to consternation to wonder. Plan to spend at least a few hours here to take it all in. However long your visit, it's a good idea to bring binoculars.

Looming over Barcelona like a magical mid-city massif of needles and peaks, the Sagrada Família can at first seem like piles of caves and grottoes heaped on a labyrinth of stalactites, stalagmites, and flora and fauna of every stripe and sort. The sheer immensity of the site and the energy flowing from it are staggering. The scale alone is daunting: the current lateral facades will one day be dwarfed by the main Glory facade and central spire—the Torre del Salvador (Tower of the Savior), which will be crowned by an illuminated polychrome ceramic cross and soar to a final height 1 yard shorter than Montjuïc (564 feet) guarding the entrance to the port (Gaudí felt it improper for the work of man to surpass that of God). You can take an elevator skyward to the top of the bell towers for some spectacular views (choose the "Top Views" ticket). Back on the ground, visit the museum, which displays Gaudí's scale models, photographs showing the progress of construction, and images of the vast outpouring at Gaudí's funeral; the architect is buried under the basilica, to the left of the altar in the crypt.

Soaring skyward in intricately detailed and twisted carvings and sculptures, part of the Nativity facade is made of stone from Montserrat, Barcelona's cherished mountain sanctuary and home of Catalonia's patron saint, La Moreneta, the Black Virgin of Montserrat. Gaudí himself was fond of comparing the Sagrada Família to the shapes of the sawtooth massif 50 km (30 miles) west of the city; a plaque in one of Montserrat's caverns reads *"Lloc d'inspiració de Gaudí"* ("Place of inspiration for Gaudí").

"My client is not in a hurry," Gaudí was fond of replying to anyone curious about the timetable for the completion of his mammoth project. The Sagrada Família was begun in 1882 under architect

Francisco de Paula del Villar, passed on in 1883 to Gaudí (who worked on the project until his death in 1926). After the church's neo-Gothic beginnings, Gaudí added Art Nouveau touches to the crypt (the floral capitals) and in 1891 went on to begin the Nativity facade of a new and vastly ambitious project. At the time of his death in 1926, however, only one tower of the Nativity facade had been completed.

Gaudí's plans called for three immense facades, the Nativity and Passion facades on the northeast and southwest sides of the church, and the even larger Glory facade designed as the building's main entry, facing east over Carrer de Mallorca. The four bell towers over each facade would together represent the 12 apostles. The first bell tower, in honor of Barnabas and the only one Gaudí lived to see, was completed in 1925. The towers of Barnabas, Simon, Judas, and Matthias (from left to right) stand over the Nativity facade, with James, Bartholomew, Thomas, and Phillip over the Passion facade. The four larger towers around the central Tower of the Savior will represent the evangelists Mark, Matthew, John, and Luke. Between the central tower and the reredos at the northwestern end of the nave rises the 18th and second-highest tower, crowned with a star, in honor of the Virgin Mary. The naves are not supported by buttresses but by treelike helicoidal (spiraling) columns.

Reading the existing facades is a challenging course in Bible studies. The three doors on the Nativity facade are named for Charity in the center, Faith on the right, and Hope on the left. (Gaudí often described the symbolism of his work to visitors, but because he never wrote any of it down much of the interpretation owes to oral tradition.) In the Nativity facade Gaudí addresses nothing less than the fundamental mystery of Christianity: why does God the Creator become, through Jesus Christ, a mortal

creature? The answer, as Gaudí explained it in stone, is that God did this to free man from the slavery of selfishness, symbolized by the iron fence around the serpent of evil at the base of the central column of the Portal of Charity. The column is covered with the genealogy of Christ going back to Abraham. Above the central column is a portrayal of the birth of Christ; above that, the Annunciation is flanked by a grotto-like arch of water. Overhead are the constellations in the Christmas sky at Bethlehem.

To the right, the Portal of Faith chronicles scenes of Christ's youth: Jesus preaching at the age of 13, and Zacharias prophetically writing the name of John. Higher up are grapes and wheat, symbols of the Eucharist, and a sculpture of a hand and an eye, symbols of divine providence.

The left-hand Portal of Hope begins at the bottom with flora and fauna from the Nile; the slaughter of the innocents; the flight of the Holy Family into Egypt; Joseph surrounded by his carpenter's tools, contemplating his son; and the marriage of Joseph and Mary. Above this is a sculpted boat with an anchor, representing the Church, piloted by St. Joseph assisted by the Holy Spirit in the form of a dove.

Gaudí planned these slender towers to house a system of tubular bells (still to be created and installed) capable of playing more complete and complex music than standard bell-ringing changes had previously been able to perform. At a height of one-third of the bell tower are the seated figures of the apostles.

The Passion facade on the Sagrada Família's southwestern side, over Carrer Sardenya and the Plaça de la Sagrada Família, is a dramatic contrast to the Nativity facade. In 1986, sculptor Josep Maria Subirachs was chosen by project director Jordi Bonet to finish the Passion facade. Subirachs was picked for his starkly realistic, almost geometrical sculptural style, which many visitors and devotees of Gaudí find gratingly off the mark. Subirachs pays double homage to the great Moderniste master in the Passion facade: Gaudí himself appears over the left side of the main entry, making notes or drawings, while the Roman soldiers farther out and above are modeled on Gaudí's helmeted warriors from the roof of La Pedrera. Art critic Robert Hughes calls the homage "sincere in the way that only the worst art can be: which is to say, utterly so."

Following an S-shape path across the Passion facade, the scenes represented begin at the lower left with the Last Supper. The faces of the disciples are contorted in confusion and dismay, especially that of Judas, clutching his bag of money behind his back. The next sculptural group to the right represents the prayer in the Garden of Gethsemane and Peter awakening, followed by the kiss of Judas.

In the center, Jesus is lashed to a pillar during his flagellation. Note the column's top stone is out of kilter, reminder of the stone soon to be removed from Christ's sepulcher. To the right of the door is a rooster, as well as Peter, who is lamenting his third denial of Christ: "ere the cock crows." Farther to the right are Pilate and Jesus with the crown of thorns, while just above, starting back to the left, Simon of Cyrene helps Jesus with the cross after his first fall.

Over the center is the representation of Jesus consoling the women of Jerusalem and a faceless St. Veronica (because her story is considered legendary, not historical fact), with the veil she gave Christ to wipe his face with on the way to Calvary. To the left is the likeness of Gaudí taking notes, and farther to the left is the equestrian figure of a centurion piercing the side of the church with his spear, the church representing the body of Christ. Above are the soldiers rolling dice for Christ's clothing and the naked,

crucified Christ at the center. To the right are Peter and Mary at the sepulcher. At Christ's feet is a figure with a furrowed brow, thought to be a self-portrait of Subirachs, characterized by the sculptor's giant hand and an "S" on his right arm.

Over the door will be the church's 16 prophets and patriarchs under the cross of salvation. Apostles James, Bartholomew, Thomas, and Phillip appear at a height of 148 feet on their respective bell towers. Thomas, the apostle who demanded proof of Christ's resurrection (hence the expression "doubting Thomas"), is visible pointing to the palm of his hand, asking to inspect Christ's wounds. Bartholomew, on the left, is turning his face upward toward the culminating element in the Passion facade, the 26-foot-tall gold metallic representation of the resurrected Christ on a bridge between the four bell towers at a height of 198 feet.

The apse of the basilica, consecrated by Pope Benedict XVI in November 2010, has space for close to 15,000 people and a choir loft for 1,500. The towers still to be completed over the apse include those dedicated to the four evangelists— Matthew, Mark, Luke, and John—and the highest of all, dedicated to Christ the Savior. In 2021, the Tower of the Virgin Mary was inaugurated, complete with a star made of textured glass and stainless steel, weighing 5.5 tons. Once completed, the great central tower and dome, resting on four immense columns of Iranian porphyry, considered the hardest of all stones, will soar to a height of 564 feet, making the Sagrada Família Barcelona's tallest building. Prior to the outbreak of the COVID-19 pandemic, the Sagrada Família was due to be completed by 2026, the 100th anniversary of Gaudí's death, after 144 years of construction. A new official date is yet to be announced.

■ TIP➔ Lines to enter the church can stretch around the block. Buy your tickets online, with a reserved time of entry, and

8

The Example

jump the queue. ✉ *Pl. de la Sagrada Família, Carrer Mallorca 401, Eixample Dreta* ☎ *93/207–3031, 93/208–0414 visitor info* 🌐 *sagradafamilia.org* 🎟 *From €26* [M] *L2/L5 Sagrada Família.*

Universitat Central

NOTABLE BUILDING | Barcelona's Central University was built between 1863 and 1882 by Elies Rogent. In its neo-Romanesque style alluding, no doubt, to classical knowledge, the university's two-tiered Pati de Lletres (Literary Patio) is its most harmonious element, along with the vestibule, gardens, and Paraninfo (main assembly hall). Originally founded as a medical school in 1401 by King Martí I (dubbed "the Humane"), the university was exiled to the town of Cervera 100 km (62 miles) west of Barcelona in 1717 by Felipe V as part of his reprisal for Catalonia supporting the Habsburg contender in the War of the Spanish Succession. The town became Catalonia's version of Oxford or Cambridge until the university was invited back to Barcelona in 1823. ✉ *Gran Via 585, Eixample Esquerra* ☎ *93/402–1100* 🌐 *www.ub.es* [M] *L1/L2 Universitat.*

🍴 Restaurants

The sprawling blocks of the Eixample contain Barcelona's finest selection of restaurants, from upscale and elegant traditional cuisine in Moderniste houses to high-concept fare in sleek minimalist spaces. Many chefs with experience in multi-star kitchens have opened their own restaurants here, offering limited menus of humble ingredients cooked to exacting standards—these stellar experiences at relatively budget prices are as close as you can still get to a bargain in Barcelona.

★ Bar Mut

$$$ | CATALAN | Just above Diagonal, this elegant retro space serves first-rate products ranging from wild sea bass to the best Ibérico hams. Crowded, noisy, chaotic, delicious—it's everything a great tapas bar or restaurant should be. **Known for:** snacks at nearby spin-off Entrepanes Diaz; great wine list; upmarket tapas. [$] *Average main: €26* ✉ *Pau Claris 192, Eixample Dreta* ☎ *93/217–4338* 🌐 *www.barmut.com* 🕒 *Closed Mon.* [M] *Diagonal.*

Bardeni

$$ | TAPAS | FAMILY | This "meat bar" doesn't take reservations; instead it offers a walk-in-and-graze tapas menu of items like steak tartare and aged filet mignon in a tiled, industrially chic dining room that doesn't invite lingering but is rarely empty—arrive early for a table. Former Catalan Chef of the Year Dani Lechuga throws in the occasional fine-dining dish to lighten things up. **Known for:** aged filet mignon; good for tapas lunch; excellent steak tartare. [$] *Average main: €22* ✉ *València 454, Eixample Dreta* ☎ *93/232–5811* 🌐 *www.bardeni.es* 🕒 *Closed Sun., No dinner Mon.–Thurs.* [M] *Sagrada Família.*

★ Benzina

$$ | ITALIAN | Named for the car-mechanic shop that once stood here, Benzina blends industrial-chic elements with splashes of color and excellent music (on vinyl, naturally) to create a hip but cozy Italian restaurant. The food, however, is center stage: the freshly made pasta is among the best in the city, and other must-eats include the melt-in-the-mouth eggplant parmigiana with Parmesan ice cream and the *fritto misto*of calamari, shrimp, and fresh anchovies with curry mayo. **Known for:** chic decor; "Sferamisu" chocolate bomb of deconstructed tiramisú; best spaghetti carbonara in the city. [$] *Average main: €18* ✉ *Passatge Pere Calders 6, Sant Antoni* ☎ *93/659–5583* 🌐 *www.benzina.es* 🕒 *Closed Mon.–Tues., No lunch Wed.–Thur.* [M] *Poble Sec.*

★ Besta

$$ | CATALAN | The atmosphere is relaxed but sophisticated and the constantly changing menu is a melting pot of seasonal produce from the Spanish regions

of Catalonia and Galicia. Freshly caught fish and seafood take pride of place, as do the seasonal vegetables. **Known for:** cosmopolitan vibe; seafood dishes; Catalan-Galician cuisine. [$] *Average main: €20* ✉ *Aribau 106, Eixample* ☎ *93/019–8294* 🌐 *bestabarcelona.com* 🕑 *Closed Tues.–Wed. No dinner Mon.* [M] *Universitat L1, L2.*

★ Betlem

$$ | CATALAN | Set In a charming Moderniste space dating back to 1892, this bar hits the perfect balance of quality, price, service, and ambiance. The menu mixes classic dishes like deep-fried calamari and spicy *patatas bravas,* with house specials like the steak tartare and show-stopping omelet with black pudding (or *butifarra negra*) and seasonal mushrooms. **Known for:** Moderniste interior; sunny terrace; omelet with black pudding and mushrooms. [$] *Average main: €15* ✉ *Girona 70, Eixample* ☎ *93/265–5105* [M] *Girona L4.*

Blanc

$$$$ | CATALAN | Blanc's menu couples traditional Catalan cuisine with fresh, seasonal products, and the three-course lunch menu, and the ever changing, five-course "Sundays at Blanc" tasting menu are popular. The dining room is in an airy atrium at the heart of the Mandarin Oriental and feels lively most of the day, starting when the first hotel guests come in for the (excellent) breakfast. **Known for:** lovely atrium setting; excellent prix-fixe menu options; Classic Catalan fused with contemporary touches. [$] *Average main: €38* ✉ *Passeig de Gràcia 38–40, Eixample Dreta* ✣ *Entrance via Hotel Mandarin Oriental* ☎ *93/151–8783* 🌐 *www.mandarinoriental.com/barcelona/fine-dining/bars/blanc* [M] *Passeig de Gràcia.*

Cervecería Catalana

$ | TAPAS | FAMILY | A bright and booming tapas bar with a few tables outside, this spot is always packed for a reason: good food at reasonable prices. Try the small *solomillos* (filets mignons), mini-morsels that will take the edge off your carnivorous appetite without undue damage to your wallet, or the jumbo shrimp brochettes. **Known for:** lively atmosphere; perfect jumbo shrimp brochettes; affordable tapas. [$] *Average main: €13* ✉ *Mallorca 236, Eixample Esquerra* ☎ *93/216–0368* [M] *Diagonal, Provença (FGC).*

Cinc Sentits

$$$$ | CATALAN | Obsessively local, scrupulously sourced, and masterfully cooked, the dishes of Catalan-Canadian chef Jordi Artal put the spotlight on the region's finest ingredients in an intimate, sophisticated setting. It's hard to believe that this garlanded restaurant is Jordi's first, but there's no arguing with the evidence of your *cinc sentits* (five senses). **Known for:** tasting menu only; awarded two Michelin stars; excellent chef. [$] *Average main: €119* ✉ *Entença 60, Eixample Esquerra* ☎ *93/323–9490* 🌐 *cincsentits.com* 🕑 *Closed Sun., Mon., and public holidays* [M] *Provença.*

Ciudad Condal

$$ | TAPAS | FAMILY | At the bottom of Rambla de Catalunya, this scaled-up tapas bar draws a throng of mostly international clients and has tables outside on this busy part-pedestrianized street all year round. The *solomillo* (miniature beef fillet) is a winner here, as is the *broqueta d'escamarlans* (brochette of jumbo shrimp). **Known for:** reliable quality; central location; long wait times. [$] *Average main: €15* ✉ *Rambla de Catalunya 18, Eixample* ☎ *93/318–1997* 🌐 *ciudadcondal.cat* [M] *Passeig de Gràcia, Catalunya.*

★ Cruix

$$$ | CATALAN | With an eight-course tasting menu priced at just €35, Cruix is the fine-dining restaurant for people who don't want to spend 200 euros on a meal. Everything here is laid-back and unpretentious, including the exposed-brick interior, but the quality speaks to

Continued on page 187

TEMPLE EXPIATORI DE LA
SAGRADA FAMÍLIA

Antoni Gaudí's striking and surreal masterpiece was conceived as nothing short of a Bible in stone, an arresting representation of the history of Christianity. Today, this Roman Catholic church is Barcelona's most emblematic architectural icon. Looming over the city like a manmade massif of grottoes and peaks, La Sagrada Família strains skyward in piles of stalagmites. Construction is ongoing and continues to stretch toward the heavens.

CONSTRUCTION, PAST AND PRESENT

"My client is not in a hurry," was Gaudí's reply to anyone curious about his project's timetable . . . good thing, too, because La Sagrada Família was begun in 1882 under architect Francesc Villar, passed on in 1891 to Gaudí, and is still thought to be several years from completion. Gaudí added Art Nouveau touches to the crypt and, in 1883, started the Nativity facade. Conceived as a symbolic construct encompassing the complete story and scope of the Christian faith, the church was intended by Gaudí to impress the viewer with the full sweep and force of the Gospel. At the time of his death in 1926 only one tower of the Nativity facade had been completed.

By 2026, the 100th anniversary of Gaudí's death, after 144 years of construction in the tradition of the great medieval and Renaissance cathedrals of Europe, La Sagrada Família may well be complete enough to call finished. Architect Jordi Bonet continues in the footsteps of his father, architect Lluís Bonet, to make Gaudí's vision complete as he has since the 1980s.

(left) Sagrada Família interior. (top) Shepherds gather to witness the birth of Christ in the Nativity facade.

BIBLE STUDIES IN STONE: THE FACADES

Gaudí's plans called for three immense facades. The northeast-facing **Nativity facade** and the southwest-facing **Passion facade** are complete. The much larger southeast-facing **Glory facade,** the building's main entry, is still under construction. The final church will have 18 towers: The four **bell towers** over each facade represent the 12 apostles; the four **larger towers** represent the evangelists Mark, Matthew, John, and Luke; the **second-highest tower** in the reredos behind the altar honors the Virgin Mary; and, in the center, the **Torre del Salvador** (Tower of the Savior) will soar to a height of 564 feet.

THE NATIVITY FACADE

Built during Gaudí's lifetime, this facade displays his vision and sculptural style, the organic or so-called "melting wax" look that has become his signature. The facade is crowned by **four bell towers,** representing the apostles Barnabas, Jude, Simon, and Matthew and divided into three sections around the doors of **Charity** in the center, **Faith** on the right, and **Hope** on the left.

(left) The ornamental Nativity facade. (above, top right) A figure in the Portal of Faith. (above, center right) The spiraling staircase. (above, bottom right) A decorative cross..

The focal point in the Nativity facade: Joseph and Mary presenting the infant Jesus.

Over the central **Portal of Charity** is the birth of Christ, with a representation of the Annunciation overhead in an ice grotto, another natural element. Above that are the signs of the zodiac for the Christmas sky at Bethlehem, with two babies representing the Gemini and the horns of a bull for Taurus. The evergreen cypress tree rising above symbolizes eternity, with the white doves as souls seeking life everlasting.

The **Portal of Faith** on the right shows Christ preaching as a youth. Higher up are the Eucharistic symbols of grapes and wheat and a hand and eye, symbols of divine Providence.

The **Portal of Hope** on the left shows a series of biblical scenes including the slaughter of the innocents, the flight into Egypt, Joseph surrounded by his carpenter's tools looking down at his infant son, and the marriage of Joseph and Mary with Mary's parents, Joaquin and Anna, looking on. Above is a boat, representing the Church, piloted by Joseph, with the Holy Spirit represented as a dove.

THE PASSION FACADE

On the **Passion facade**, Gaudí intended to dramatize the abyss between the birth of a child and the death of a man. In 1986, Josep Maria Subirachs, an artist known for his atheism and his hard-edged and geometrical sculptural style, was commissioned to finish the Passion facade. The contrast is sharp, in content and in sculptural style, between this facade and the Nativity facade. Framed by leaning columns of tibia-like bones, the Passion facade illustrates the last days of Christ and his Resurrection. The scenes are laid out chronologically in an S-shape path beginning at the bottom left and ending at the upper right.

At bottom left is the **Last Supper**, the disciples' faces contorted in confusion and anguish, most of all Judas clutching his bag of money behind his back over a reclining hound, the contrasting symbol of fidelity. To the right is the Garden of Gethsemane and Peter awakening, followed by the **Kiss of Judas**.

Judas kissing Jesus while a cryptogram behind contains a numerical combination adding up to 33, the age of Christ's death.

The stark, geometric Passion facade.

To the right of the door is **Peter's Third Denial** of Christ "ere the cock crows." Farther to the right are **Pontius Pilate and Jesus** with the crown of thorns.

Above on the second tier are the **Three Marys** and Simon helping Jesus lift the cross. Over the center, **Jesus carries the cross.** To the left, Gaudí himself is portrayed, pencil in hand, the evangelist in stone, while farther left a **mounted centurion** pierces the side of the church with his spear, the church representing the body of Christ. At the top left, **soldiers gamble for Christ's clothing** while at the top center is the **crucifixion**, featuring Subirachs's controversial (in 1971 when it was unveiled) naked and anatomically complete Christ. Finally to the right, Peter and Mary grieve at **Christ's entombment**, an egg overhead symbolizing rebirth and the resurrection. At a height of 148 feet are the four Apostles on their bell towers. Bartholomew, on the left, looks upward toward the 26-foot risen Christ between the four bell towers at a height of 198 feet.

THE GLORY FACADE

The Glory facade, still under construction, will have a wide stairway and esplanade or porch leading up to three portals dedicated, as in the other facades, to Charity, Faith, and Hope. The doors are inscribed with the Lord's Prayer in bronze in 50 languages, with the Catalan version in the center in relief. Carrer Mallorca will be routed underground, and the entire city block across the street will be razed to make space for the esplanade and park. Present predictions are between 2026 and 2030 for the completion of this phase, but progress has slowed due to Covid.

A new element in La Sagrada Família: the bronze doorway of the Glory facade.

THE INTERIOR: "TEMPLE OF HARMONIOUS LIGHT"

(top) Above the altar, supporting columns form a canopy of light. (below) Towering columns and stained-glass windows keep the interior bright.

Until 2010, La Sagrada Família was able to be adequately appreciated without going inside. But since the interior was completed for the Papal consecration, it's become Barcelona's most stunning space, comparable to the breathtaking upsweep of the finest soaring Gothic architecture but higher, brighter, and carved in a dazzling fusion of hard-edged Subirachs over organic Gaudí.

DESIGN

The floor plan for the church is laid out in the form of a **Latin cross** with five longitudinal naves intersected by three transepts. The **apse** has space for 15,000 people, a choir loft for 1,500, and is large enough to encompass the entire Santa Maria del Mar basilica. From the Glory Façade, the Baptistry Chapel is to the left and the Chapel of the Sacrament and Penitence is to the right. The Chapel of the Assumption is at the back of the apse. Over the main altar is the figure of the crucified Christ, suspended in mid-air under a diaphanous canopy.

LIGHT

The basilica's main nave and the apse create an immense, immaculate space culminating in the highest point: the main alter's hyperboloid skylight 75 meters (250 feet) above the floor. The vaulting is perforated with 288 skylights admitting abundant light. The sharp-edged, treelike leaning columns shape the interior spaces and will support the six towers being built above them. Vaults are decorated with green and gold Venetian mosaics that diffuse the light as if they were leaves in a forest, making the basilica, in the words of Gaudí, "the temple of harmonious light."

DETAILS TO DISCOVER: THE EXTERIOR

GAUDÍ IN THE PASSION FACADE

Subirachs pays double homage to the great Moderniste master in the Passion facade: Gaudí himself appears over the left side of the main entry making notes or drawings, the evangelist in stone, while the Roman soldiers are modeled on Gaudí's helmeted, Star Wars–like warriors from the roof of La Pedrera.

Gaudí in the Passion facade

TOWER TOPS

Break out the binoculars and have a close look at the pinnacles and peaks of La Sagrada Família's towers. Sculpted by Japanese artist Etsuro Sotoo, these clusters of grapes and different kinds of fruit are symbols of fertility, of rebirth, and of the Resurrection of Christ.

Sotoo's ornamental fruit

SUBIRACHS IN THE PASSION FACADE

At Christ's feet in the entombment sculpture is a blocky figure with a furrowed brow, thought to be a portrayal of the agnostic's anguished search for certainty. This figure is generally taken as a self-portrait of Subirachs, characterized by the sculptor's giant hand and an "S" on his massive right arm.

DONKEY ON THE NATIVITY FACADE

On the left side of the Nativity facade over the Portal of Hope is a *burro*, a small donkey, known to have been modeled from a donkey that Gaudí saw near the work site. The *ruc català* (Catalan donkey) is a beloved and iconic symbol of Catalonia, often displayed on Catalonian bumpers as a response to the Spanish fighting bull.

The donkey in the Nativity facade

THE ROSE TREE DOOR

The richly sculpted Rose Tree Door, between the Nativity facade and the cloisters, portrays Our Lady of the Rose Tree with the infant Jesus in her arms, St. Dominic and St. Catherine of Siena in prayer, with three angels dancing overhead. The sculptural group on the wall, known as *The Death of the Just*, portrays the Virgin and Child comforting a moribund old man, as in the Spanish prayer "*Jesús, José, y María, asistidme en mi última agonía*" (Jesus, Joseph, and María, help me in my final agony). The accompanying inscriptions in English, "Pray for us sinners now and at the hour of our death, Amen" are the final words of the Ave María prayer.

The heavily embellished Rose door

COLUMN FROM THE PORTAL OF CHARITY

The column, dead center in the Portal of Charity, is covered with the genealogy of Christ going back through the House of David to Abraham. At the bottom of the column is its snake of evil, complete with the apple of temptation in his mouth, closed in behind an iron grate, symbolic of Christianity's mission of neutralizing the sin of selfishness.

The column in the Portal of Charity

FACELESS ST. VERONICA

Because her story is considered legendary, not historical fact, St. Veronica appears faceless in the Passion facade. Also shown is the veil she gave Christ to wipe his face with on the way to Calvary that was said to be miraculously imprinted with his likeness. The veil is torn in two overhead and covers a mosaic that Subirachs allegedly disliked and elected to conceal.

St. Veronica with the veil

STAINED-GLASS WINDOWS

The stained-glass windows of La Sagrada Família are the work of Joan Vila-Grau. Those in the west central part of the nave represent the light of Jesus and a bubbling fountain in a bright chromatic patchwork of shades of blue with green and yellow reflections. The main window on the Passion facade represents the Resurrection. Gaudí left express instructions that the central nave's windows be translucent, to let in as much light as possible, and colorless, as a symbol of purity and to prevent altering the hues of the tiles and trencadís (mosaics of broken tile) in green and gold representing palm leaves.

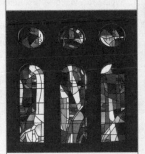

Stained-glass windows

TORTOISES AND TURTLES

Nature lover Gaudí used as many elements of the natural world as he could in his stone Bible. The sea tortoise beneath the column on the Mediterranean side of the Portal of Hope and the land turtle supporting the inland Portal of Faith symbolize the slow and steady stability of the cosmos and of the church.

ST. THOMAS IN THE BELL TOWER

Above the Passion facade, St. Thomas demanding proof of Christ's resurrection (thus the expression "doubting Thomas") and perched on the bell tower is pointing to the palm of his hand asking to inspect Christ's wounds.

CHRIST RESURRECTED ABOVE PASSION FACADE

High above the Passion facade, a gilded Christ sits resurrected, perched between two towers.

Christ resurrected

MAKING THE MOST OF YOUR TRIP

Sagrada Família

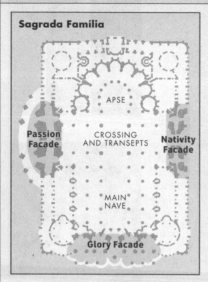

APSE

Passion Façade

CROSSING AND TRANSEPTS

Nativity Façade

MAIN NAVE

Glory Façade

BUYING TICKETS

Tickets, with a set entry time, can only be purchased online. Reservations (available up to two months in advance) are essential. For more context, it's a good idea to book a private tour.

VISITOR INFORMATION

✉ Pl. de la Sagrada Família, Eixample
☎ 93/207–3031 ⊕ www.sagradafamilia.org
🎫 From €26
🕐 Apr.–Sept.: Mon.–Sat. 9–8, Sun. 10:30–8.
Oct. and Mar: Mon.–Sat. 9–7, Sun. 10:30–7.
Nov.–Feb.: Mon.–Sat. 9–6, Sun. 10:30–6.
Ⓜ Sagrada Família.

WHICH TOWER?

Only the Nativity and Passion towers are currently accessible, and even they might be temporarily closed owing to construction work. Both have elevators for going up and (very narrow) stairs for going down. We recommend the richly decorated Nativity Tower, the only one on which Gaudí actually worked. Although the views are jaw dropping, avoid visiting the towers if you have a fear of heights or enclosed spaces. Note, too, that there's a small bridge affording better views and close-up looks at the facade.

WHEN TO VISIT

To avoid crowds, come first thing in the morning. Or, plan to visit during mid-morning and mid-to-late afternoon, when golden light streams through the stained-glass windows.

WHAT TO WEAR AND BRING

You're encouraged not to wear shorts and to cover bare shoulders. It's a good idea to bring binoculars to absorb details all the way up.

TIMING

An hour or two is plenty of time to walk around the exterior. If you'd like to go inside to the crypt, visit the museum, visit the towers, and walk down the spiraling stairway, you'll need three to four hours.

BONUS FEATURES

The **museum** displays Gaudí's scale models and shows photographs of the construction. The **crypt** holds Gaudí's remains. The excellent gift shop has a wide selection of Gaudi-related articles, including sculptures, jewelry, miniature churches, and beautiful books.

Dining with Children?

If you have children in tow, Barcelona's dining scene has several types of options that should make meal times easy. For instance, the miniature scale and finger-food aspects of tapas usually appeals to kids, many of whom are happy to munch on commonly found dishes, like croquettes, cured meats, toasted almonds, and maybe even fried squid rings.

Most cafés, bars, and terraces can whip up sandwiches on the go, served on fresh bread—an inexpensive and respectable snack—or the Catalan staple *pa amb tomaquet*, crushed tomatoes on toast. For dessert, Barcelona's ubiquitous ice-cream parlors and vendors are another favorite.

Note, too, that Barceloneta's beach-front paella specialists are popular with families at Sunday lunch, with children free to get up and run, skate, cycle, or generally race up and down the boardwalk while their parents linger over brandies and coffee.

8

The Eixample

the Chef Miquel Pardo's pedigree: he worked under Spanish superstar chefs like Albert Adrià and Jordi Cruz before opening Cruix in 2017. **Known for:** excellent rice with shrimp and garlic; creative food; fine dining on a budget. $ *Average main: €28* ⊠ *Entença 57, Eixample* ☎ *93/525–2318* ⊕ *www.cruixrestaurant.com* ☉ *Closed Mon. and Tues. No dinner Sun.* Ⓜ *Rocafort L1.*

★ Deliri

$$$ | CATALAN | Elevated sharing plates made from locally sourced, seasonal ingredients are the bottom line at this trendy Eixample eatery. The menu features unlikely combos: artichoke salad with parmesan cream and bottarga, or glazed mackerel with pumpkin—blends that shouldn't work, but yet they really do—along with nods to the most classic of Catalan "grandma" dishes, like the decadently meaty macaroni covered in cheese. **Known for:** "grandma"-style macaroni; top-notch seasonal produce; dining room showcases local artists. $ *Average main: €29* ⊠ *Còrsega, 242, Eixample Esquerra* ☎ *93/611–3927* ⊕ *www.deliri.es* ☉ *Closed Mon. and Tues.* Ⓜ *Diagonal L3, L5.*

★ Disfrutar

$$$$ | ECLECTIC | Three former head chefs from the now-closed "World's Best Restaurant" El Bulli combined their considerable talents to create this roller-coaster ride of culinary fun (the word "disfrutar" is Spanish for "to enjoy") spotlighting tasting menus of dazzling inventiveness and good taste. Bowls are swirled to reveal beetroot meringues emerging from sesame-seed "earth" (the seeds are made to look like soil), and jellied truffle-and-egg tempura hit the bull's-eye of pure pleasure; desserts are otherworldly. **Known for:** surprisingly accessible wine list; tasting menus only; inventive food. $ *Average main: €210* ⊠ *Villarroel 163, Eixample Esquerra* ☎ *93/348–6896* ⊕ *www.disfrutarbarcelona.com* ☉ *Closed Sat.–Sun., 2 wks in Aug., and 1 wk after Christmas* Ⓜ *Hospital Clínic.*

Embat

$$ | CATALAN | An *embat* is a puff of wind in Catalan, and this little bistro is a breath of fresh air in the sometimes stuffy Eixample. The highly affordable market cuisine is always impeccably fresh and freshly conceived, from the great-value three-course lunch selection to the

more elaborate evening menu. **Known for:** market-fresh Catalan dishes; stylish minimalist interior; modern, unfussy fare. [$] *Average main: €17* ✉ *Mallorca 304, Eixample Dreta* ☎ *93/458–0855* 🌐 *embatrestaurant.com* ⏲ *Closed Mon. No dinner Sun. and Tues.* [M] *Verdaguer.*

Gresca

$$$$ | **CATALAN** | Chef-owner Rafa Peña applies the skills he honed in the world's most celebrated kitchens at this excellent-value restaurant and its adjacent wine-tapas bar. Expect a well-chosen wine list and some of the most delightful dishes you can find in Barcelona: the tasting menu is the best way to sample what's on offer. **Known for:** tapas of the day; adjacent wine-tapas bar; great, affordable cuisine. [$] *Average main: €45* ✉ *Provença 230, Eixample Esquerra* ☎ *93/451–6193* ⏲ *Closed 1 wk in Aug.* [M] *Provença (FGC).*

Honest Greens

$$ | **VEGETARIAN** | There are a few fish and meat options on the menu but most visitors skip the animal proteins and opt for the impressive selection of plant-based foods. Delicious salads, tasty vegetarian curries, and fresh grilled vegetables are a hit with the health-conscious and the vegan desserts are even tastier than regular versions. **Known for:** several outposts around the city; great desserts; healthy but delicous food. [$] *Average main: €18* ✉ *Rambla de Catalunya 3, Eixample* ☎ *93/122–7664* 🌐 *honestgreens.com/en* [M] *Catalunya L1, L3.*

Igueldo

$$ | **BASQUE** | Basque dishes are competently updated and delivered with a dash of style at this smart, white-walled Eixample establishment. A fiery grill turns out excellent regional meat specialties, but don't overlook fish dishes such as baby squid with cured ham and caramelized onions. **Known for:** Basque cuisine; excellent service; great wine pairings. [$] *Average main: €20* ✉ *Rosselló 186, Eixample Esquerra* ☎ *93/452–2555* 🌐 *restauranteigueldo.com* ⏲ *Closed Sun. and 1 wk in Aug. No dinner Tues.* [M] *Diagonal.*

La Real Hamburguesería

$ | **BURGER** | If you're jonesing for a burger, this laid-back, Venezuelan-owned fast-food spot is the place to go. The burgers are great, of course, but so are sides like deep-fried cheese sticks (*tequeños*) with sweet chili sauce. **Known for:** vegan and vegetarian options available; Latin-American-style sides; small outdoor terrace. [$] *Average main: €14* ✉ *València 285, Tienda 03, Eixample* ☎ *93/832–8694* 🌐 *larealbcn.com* [M] *Girona L4.*

★ Lasarte

$$$$ | **BASQUE** | While Martin Berasategui, one of San Sebastián's corps of master chefs, no longer runs the day-to-day operations of this Barcelona kitchen (it's in the capable hands of chef Paolo Casagrande) the restaurant continues to be a culinary triumph. Expect an eclectic selection of Basque, Mediterranean, and off-the-map creations, a hefty bill, and fierce perfectionism apparent in every dish. **Known for:** heavenly grilled pigeon; magnificent tasting menu; inventive cuisine at one of the best restaurants in Barcelona. [$] *Average main: €70* ✉ *Mallorca 259, Eixample* ☎ *93/445–3242* 🌐 *www.restaurantlasarte.com* ⏲ *Closed Sun., Mon., Tues., 2 wks in Jan., 1 wk at Easter, and 3 wks in Aug./Sept.* [M] *Diagonal, Passeig de Gràcia, Provença (FGC).*

La Taverna del Clínic

$$ | **CATALAN** | Just outside the main entrance to Barcelona's largest hospital (Hospital Clínic), La Taverna del Clínic is a place you would (hopefully) never stumble upon by accident, but discerning locals and serious food lovers know this is a great spot for modern twist on classic Catalan fare. The truffle cannelloni is especially good, as is the *patatas bravas.* **Known for:** sunny outdoor patio; good wine list; contemporary tapas. [$] *Average main: €20* ✉ *Rosselló 155, Eixample Esquerra* ☎ *93/410–4221* 🌐 *www.*

latavernadelclinic.com ⏲ *Closed Sun.* [M] *Hospital Clinic.*

Manairó

$$$ | **CATALAN** | A *manairó* is a mysterious Pyrenean elf, and Jordi Herrera may be the culinary version: his ingenious cooking methods—such as filet mignon *al faquir* (heated from within on red-hot spikes) or blowtorched on a homemade centrifuge—may seem eccentric but produce undeniably good results. Melt-in-your-mouth meat dishes form the centerpiece of Manairó's menus, but they are ably supported by a bonanza of bold and confident creations that aren't frightened of big flavors. **Known for:** food that's fun to look at and even better to eat; delicious meat dishes; innovative contemporary cuisine. [$] *Average main: €26* ✉ *Diputació 424, Eixample Dreta* ☎ *93/231–0057* 🌐 *www.manairo.com* ⏲ *Closed Sun., Mon., and 1st wk of Jan.* [M] *Monumental.*

★ **Moments**

$$$$ | **CATALAN** | Inside the ultrasleek Hotel Mandarin Oriental Barcelona, this restaurant, with food by Raül Balam and his mother—the legendary Carme Ruscalleda—lives up to its stellar pedigree, with original preparations that draw on deep wells of Catalan culinary traditions. Dishes display a masterful lightness of touch and come to the table so exquisitely presented that putting a fork into them feels almost like wanton vandalism; the reward, however, is sublime, with treasures of taste revealed in every astonishing bite. **Known for:** outstanding wine list; tasting menus are the only option; chef's table in the kitchen. [$] *Average main: €189* ✉ *Passeig de Gràcia 38–40, Eixample Dreta* ☎ *93/151–8781* 🌐 *www.mandarinoriental.com* ⏲ *Closed Mon.–Wed. and 2 wks in Jan. No dinner Sun., no lunch Thurs.–Fri.* [M] *Passeig de Gràcia.*

Mont Bar

$$$$ | **CATALAN** | Mont Bar's cramped interior belies the size of the flavors delivered from its kitchen. Star-quality morsels such as an oyster with apple and beetroot, and mochi stuffed with Mallorcan sobrassada (cured sausage) are complemented by an immense wine list. **Known for:** pricier than the laid-back ambience might lead you to think; mix of fine-dining dishes and barroom snacks; upmarket bistro atmosphere. [$] *Average main: €40* ✉ *Diputació 220, Eixample* ☎ *93/323–9590* 🌐 *www.montbar.com* ⏲ *Closed Mon. and Tues.* [M] *Universitat.*

Mordisco

$$ | **MEDITERRANEAN** | The columns and skylights of this former high-class jewelry shop now frame a Mediterranean restaurant that emphasizes wholesome, market-fresh produce in dishes such as artichoke hearts and veal carpaccio that comes sizzling from the charcoal grill. Cocktails are served until late in the elegant upstairs bar from Thursday to Saturday. **Known for:** enclosed patio; cocktails at the upstairs bar; veal carpaccio. [$] *Average main: €16* ✉ *Passatge de la Concepció 10, Eixample Esquerra* ☎ *93/487–9656* 🌐 *www.mordisco.com* [M] *Diagonal.*

Paco Meralgo

$$ | **TAPAS** | The name, a pun on *para comer algo* ("to eat something" with an Andalusian accent), may be only marginally amusing, but the tapas here are no joke, from the classical *calamares fritos* to the *pimientos de Padrón* (green peppers, some fiery, from the Galician town of Padrón). Whether at a table, at the counter, or in the private dining room upstairs, this modern space does traditional tapas that reliably hit the spot. **Known for:** traditional tapas; excellent wine list; montaditos (baguette slices with varied toppings). [$] *Average main: €16* ✉ *Muntaner 171, Eixample Esquerra* ☎ *9393/430–9027* 🌐 *www.restaurant-pacomeralgo.com* ⏲ *Closed Christmas* [M] *Hospital Clínic, Provença (FGC).*

Sartoria Panatieri

$ | **PIZZA** | "Farm to pizza" is the tagline at this urban chic pizzeria specializing in home-cured artisanal charcuteries and pizzas made in a wood-fired oven. The dough for the Neapolitan-style pizzas is made with organic hand-milled flour, and all the ingredients are fresh, organic, seasonal, and local (some are grown on-site at the restaurant). **Known for:** chic crowd; Neapolitan-style pizza made in a wood-fired oven; home-cured artisanal charcuteries. $ *Average main:* *€14* ✉ *Provença 330, Eixample* ☎ *93/105–5795* ⊕ *www.sartoriapanatieri.com* Ⓜ *Diagonal L3, L5.*

★ Slow & Low

$$$$ | FUSION | The energetic young team behind Slow & Low is a blend of many different cultures and it shows in the menu, which combines Mediterranean, Mexican, Peruvian, and even some Southeast Asian influences. Better still, they make it look effortless in standout dishes like a green curry with seasonal green peas and Basque-style *pil-pil* cod tripe, or the Mediterranean red shrimp Thai salad with som tam sorbet. **Known for:** creative tasting menu; young, international team; fresh seafood and seasonal veggies. $ *Average main: €72* ✉ *Comte Borrell, 119, Sant Antoni* ☎ *93/625–4512* ⊕ *slowandlowbcn.com* ☾ *Closed Sun. and Mon.* Ⓜ *Urgell L1.*

Taktika Berri

$$ | BASQUE | Specializing in San Sebastián's favorite dishes, this Basque restaurant has only one drawback: a table is hard to score unless you call well in advance. A good backup plan, though, is the tapas served at the first-come, first-served bar. **Known for:** Basque pintxos; convivial tavern atmosphere; hospitable service. $ *Average main: €18* ✉ *València 169, Eixample Esquerra* ☎ *93/453–4759* ⊕ *www.taktikaberri.net/* ☾ *Closed Sun., 2 wks in Jan., 2 wks at Easter, and 3 wks in Aug. No dinner Sat.* Ⓜ *Hospital Clinic, Provença (FGC).*

Tapas 24

$$ | TAPAS | FAMILY | The tapas emporium of celebrity chef Carles Abellán shows us how much he admires traditional Catalan and Spanish bar food, from patatas bravas to *croquetes de pollastre rostit* (roast chicken croquettes), although the star dish is the truffled "bikini," or ham and cheese toastie. The counter and terrace are constantly crowded and the service can be iffy at times, but the food is worth elbowing your way through the crowd for. **Known for:** bikini Carles Abellán (truffled ham-and-cheese toastie); all-day kitchen; traditional tapas with a twist. $ *Average main: €16* ✉ *Diputació 269, Eixample Dreta* ☎ *9393/488–0977* ⊕ *www.carlesabellan.com/tapas24-diputacio* Ⓜ *Passeig de Gràcia.*

★ Xerta

$$$$ | CATALAN | Much of Xerta's menu is the expected swanky fine-dining fare, but stand-out options use unique produce from the deltas and rivers of the Terres de l'Ebre region, such as sweet miniature *canyuts* (razor clams), oysters, and fresh eel. The superb weekday four-course lunch menu is a steal at €42. **Known for:** midweek lunch menu; outstanding seafood and rice dishes; regional produce. $ *Average main: €55* ✉ *Ohla Eixample hotel, Còrsega 289, Eixample* ☎ *9393/737–9080* ⊕ *www.xertarestaurant.com* ☾ *Closed Sun. and Mon.* Ⓜ *Provença.*

☕ Coffee and Quick Bites

Bar Alegria

$$ | CATALAN | Alegria translates as "joy" and nothing is more joyful than finding a sunny spot on Alegria's popular patio for a glass of iced *vermút* and a *tapa* of spicy patatas bravas or the famous truffled ham and cheese toastie. Vermouth culture is all about bar hopping from place to place until you are full (and tipsy) and suddenly realize the sun set a long time ago and you have no idea what time it is—nor do you care. **Known for:** delicious tapas; sunny patio; popular vermouth spot. $ *Average main: €15* ✉ *Comte*

Barcelona's Must-Eats

Top priorities for a trip to Barcelona might just read: see great art and architecture, enjoy the nightlife, eat ham. In all seriousness, you shouldn't pass up the opportunity to eat Spain's exquisite artisanal ham—known in Catalan as *pernil* and in Spanish as *jamón*—made from acorn-fed native black pigs whose meat is salt-cured and then air-dried for two to four years. The best kind, *jamón ibérico de bellota*, comes from carefully managed and exercised pigs fed only acorns. This lengthy process results in a silky, slightly sweet and nutty meat that is contradictorily both light and intensely rich.

You can casually approach the quest for this delicacy at nearly any bar or restaurant across Barcelona, feasting on different qualities of hams, including jamón ibérico's lesser but still stellar cousin, *jamón serrano*.

Catalonia's love affair with cured pork isn't restricted to jamón. Sausages and other pork derivatives, known as *embutits* (*embutidos* in Spanish), are equally common sandwich-fillers, and are regularly served as starters in even high-end restaurants. For an authentic experience, try some with a cold glass of *vermut* and a side of

potato chips, ideally as a light snack on a terrace before a full lunch.

Chorizo is, of course, the best-known and most ubiquitous sausage in Spain. Pork and paprika are the two key ingredients, but styles and quality vary widely, ranging from cheap, mass-produced batons for stews to handmade *chorizo ibérico*, best savored in wafer-thin slices.

Local Catalan favorites include the chewy but tasty *llonganissa* (cured sausages), and *fuet*. The latter can be almost too tough to eat or wonderfully delicious, depending on the quality, so don't rush to judgment after your first experience. *Bull* (pronounced, more or less, "boo-eey") comes in *blanc* (white) and *negre* (black) varieties—the latter is made with blood. Served cold in thin slices, bull is often served with salads.

Botifarra sausages are important components of Catalan cuisine. Most are served hot, typically with *mongetes* (white haricot beans), but cold *botifarra blanc* and negre are also common. A third variety, *botifarra d'ou*, includes eggs and has an unusual yellow hue. For a truly Catalan taste experience, look for *botifarra dolça*—this decidedly odd dessert sausage incorporates lemon and sugar.

8

The Eixample

Borrell, 133, Sant Antoni ☎ 93/032–6720 Ⓜ Urgell L1.

★ **DeLaCrem**

$ | ICE CREAM | For a cool pick-me-up on a hot Barcelona afternoon, you can't beat the seasonal, locally sourced, Italian-style ice cream from DeLaCrem. Expect classics like vanilla, chocolate, and dulce de leche as well as more unconventional combinations like mandarin and orange blossom yogurt, pear and Parmesan,

or pumpkin and toasted butter. **Known for:** pumpkin and toasted butter gelato; unconventional flavors; Italian-style ice cream. Ⓢ *Average main: €5* ✉ *Enric Granados, 15, Eixample* ☎ 93/004–1093 ⊕ *delacrem.cat* Ⓜ *Universitat L1, L2.*

★ **L' Atelier**

$ | BAKERY | This superb café, bakery, and pastry school has set a new standard for sweet treats in the city. The glazed cinnamon rolls are a standout, as is the to-die-for brioche filled with red berries and mascarpone, while the fresh croissant cone overflowing with soft-serve ice cream, praline, and salted caramel is a rare thing of great beauty. **Known for:** there are a few tables to eat at; creative desserts; breakfast pastries. [$] *Average main: €10* ✉ *Viladomat 140, Eixample* ☎ *93/828–7373* 🌐 *latelierbarcelona.com* 🕒 *Closed Sun. afternoon* [M] *Urgell L1.*

La Flauta

$ | **TAPAS** | The name of this boisterous bar refers to the flutelike baguettes used for sandwiches but there's also a seemingly infinite number of tapas and small portions of everything from wild mushrooms in season to wild asparagus or *xipirones* (baby cuttlefish). Although the food is fresh and flavorsome, service can be brusque—perhaps a result of the sheer number of customers—and you may feel pressure to eat quickly when the queue outside is particularly long. A second branch—the original but perhaps not as good—is at Carrer Balmes 171. **Known for:** tightly packed space; can get very busy; delicious in-season vegetables. [$] *Average main: €10* ✉ *Aribau 23, Eixample* ☎ *93/323–7038* 🌐 *laflauta.cat* 🕒 *Closed Sun. and 3 wks in Aug.* [M] *Diagonal.*

La Pastisseria

$ | **BAKERY** | **FAMILY** | This stylish *pastisseria* looks more like a designer jewelry store than a bakery, with rows of world-class cakes and pastries gleam temptingly in glass cases, ready to be taken away or enjoyed in-store with coffee or a glass of cava. Owner Josep Rodríguez learned his craft in Michelin-starred kitchens before winning the 2011 world pastry chef of the year award for his *rosa dels vents* (rose of the winds) cake. **Known for:** high-quality ingredients; handmade delicacies; award-winning cakes. [$] *Average main: €10* ✉ *Aragó 228, Eixample Esquerra* ☎ *93/451–8401* 🌐 *www.lapastisseriabarcelona.com* 🕒 *Closed Sun. evening* [M] *Passeig de Gràcia.*

Calçots from Heaven 🍴

Since the late 19th century, *calçots*, long-stemmed, twice-planted white onions cooked over grapevine clippings, have provided a favorite outing from Barcelona to the Collserola hills or on the beaches of Gavá and Casteldefells from November to April. Some in-town restaurants also serve calçots, usually eaten with romescu sauce and accompanied by lamb chops, botifarra sausage, and copious quantities of young red wine poured from a long-spouted *porró* held overhead.

🛏 Hotels

★ Alexandra Barcelona Hotel

$$$ | **HOTEL** | **FAMILY** | Part of Hilton's upscale Curio Collection, the real draw about the Hotel Alexandra are the spectacular—and surprisingly affordable—suites with private terraces. **Pros:** relatively affordable; on-site restaurant serves some of the the best steak in town; great-value suites have terraces and outdoor tubs. **Cons:** doesn't have much local character; standard rooms on the small side; interior is rather dark. [$] *Rooms from: €207* ✉ *Mallorca 251, Eixample* ☎ *93/467–7166* 🌐 *www.hilton.com/en/hotels/bcnmaqq-alexandra-barcelona-hotel* 🔑 *116* 🍴 *No Meals* [M] *Diagonal L3, L5.*

★ Alma Hotel Barcelona

$$$$ | **HOTEL** | The facade recalls the Moderniste origins of this wonderful building but the redesigned inside spaces make the Alma one of Barcelona's sleekest mid-Eixample hotels. **Pros:** impressive design; no keys or cards; you access your room with your fingerprint (taken when you check in); gorgeous garden with a restaurant. **Cons:** pricey breakfast; no

outdoor pool; budget-stretching room rates. $ *Rooms from: €312* ✉ *Carrer Mallorca 271, Eixample* ☎ *9393/216–4490* ⊕ *www.almahotels.com* ⇨ *72 rooms* ↿⃝↾ *No Meals* Ⓜ *L3/L5 Diagonal, L4 Girona, FGC Provença.*

The Corner Hotel

$$ | **HOTEL** | This hip hotel, positioned (yes, you guessed it) on a corner, has been fashioned from a handsome, turn-of-the-century building within a few blocks of Gaudí's key sights on Passeig de Gràcia. **Pros:** walking distance to Passeig de Gràcia; cool decor; rooftop terrace with great views. **Cons:** breakfast expensive for what you get; interior-facing rooms lack natural light; common areas can get rather busy. $ *Rooms from: €154* ✉ *Mallorca 178, Eixample Esquerra* ☎ *93/554–2400* ⊕ *www.thecornerhotel-barcelona.com* ⇨ *72 rooms* ↿⃝↾ *No Meals* Ⓜ *FGC Provença; L5 Hospital Clinic.*

Hotel Astoria

$ | **HOTEL** | Three blocks west of Rambla Catalunya, near the upper middle of the Eixample, this renovated classic property, part of the Derby Hotels Collection group of fabulous artistic restorations, is a treasure for the budget-minded. **Pros:** convenient location; free entrance to the Egyptian Museum of Barcelona; excellent value for price. **Cons:** rooftop terrace pool is small; rooms on lower floors on the street side can be noisy; limited gym facilities. $ *Rooms from: €114* ✉ *Carrer Paris 203, Eixample Esquerra* ☎ *9393/209–8311* ⊕ *www.derbyhotels. es/en/hotels/astoria-hotel* ⇨ *117 rooms* ↿⃝↾ *No Meals* Ⓜ *Provença (FGC), L3/L5 Diagonal.*

Hotel Claris Grand Luxe Barcelona

$$$$ | **HOTEL** | In the heart of Eixample and within walking distance of most of the city, the legendary Hotel Claris, with its vast collection of antiques, is an icon of design, tradition, and connoisseurship. **Pros:** impressive design and antiques collection; rooms in a variety of styles; Mayan Secret Spa with temazcal and pure chocolate skin treatment. **Cons:** capacity bookings can sometimes overwhelm the staff; rooftop terrace noise at night can reach down into sixth-floor rooms; basic ("Superior") rooms small for the price. $ *Rooms from: €250* ✉ *Carrer Pau Claris 150, Eixample Dreta* ☎ *9393/487–6262* ⊕ *www.hotelclaris.com* ⇨ *124 rooms* ↿⃝↾ *No Meals* Ⓜ *L2/L3/L4 Passeig de Gràcia.*

★ Hotel Cram

$$ | **HOTEL** | A short walk from La Rambla, this Eixample design hotel offers impeccable midcity accommodations with cheerful avant-garde decor and luxurious details. **Pros:** Jordi Cruz's Angle restaurant on-site; great location; dolly slides under the bed for suitcase storage. **Cons:** rooms are a bit small, with quirky shapes; no gym or spa; Aribau is a major uptown artery, noisy at all hours. $ *Rooms from: €130* ✉ *Carrer Aribau 54, Eixample* ☎ *93/216–7700* ⊕ *www. hotelcram.com* ⇨ *67 rooms* ↿⃝↾ *No Meals* Ⓜ *L1/L2 Universitat, Provença (FGC).*

★ Hotel El Palace Barcelona

$$$$ | **HOTEL** | Founded in 1919 by Caesar Ritz, the original Ritz (the grande dame of Barcelona hotels) was renamed in 2005 but kept its lavish, timeless style intact blending its grand style with contemporary experiences, from the liveried doorman in top hat and lobby's massive crystal chandelier to seasonal immersive pop-up experiences on the seventh floor rooftop garden. **Pros:** historic grand-dame luxury; Mayan-style sauna in the award-winning spa; legendary cocktail bar. **Cons:** formal atmosphere; painfully pricey; may feel slightly intimidating. $ *Rooms from: €339* ✉ *Gran Vía de les Corts Catalanes 668, Eixample Dreta* ☎ *93/510–1130* ⊕ *www.hotelpalacebarcelona.com* ⇨ *120 rooms* ↿⃝↾ *No Meals* Ⓜ *L2/L3/L4 Passeig de Gràcia.*

Hotel Pulitzer

$$ | **HOTEL** | Built squarely over the metro's central hub and within walking distance of everything in town, this

8

The Eixample

breezy clubhouse-hotel could not be better situated. **Pros:** rooftop terrace has live music or DJ on weekends; bicycle rentals for guests; breakfast room bright and cheery. **Cons:** no pool or gym (but privileges at nearby fitness center); pricey surcharge for pets (dogs only); narrow standard rooms. $ *Rooms from: €160* ✉ *Bergara 8, Eixample Esquerra* ☎ *93/481-6767* ⊕ *www.hotelpulitzer.es* ⇨ *91 rooms* ⦿ *No Meals* Ⓜ *Catalunya.*

★ Majestic Hotel & Spa

$$$$ | **HOTEL** | With an unbeatable location on Barcelona's most stylish boulevard—steps from Gaudí's La Pedrera and near the area's swankiest shops—and a stunning rooftop terrace with killer views of the city's landmarks, this hotel is a near-perfect place to stay. **Pros:** very good restaurant and spa; superb, personalized service; beloved city landmark with interesting history. **Cons:** street outside often bustling; pricey but excellent buffet breakfast; some standard rooms a bit small for the price. $ *Rooms from: €323* ✉ *Passeig de Gràcia 68-70, Eixample Dreta* ☎ *93/488-1717* ⊕ *majestichotel-group.com/en/barcelona/hotel-majestic* ⇨ *275 rooms* ⦿ *No Meals* Ⓜ *L2/L3/L4 Passeig de Gràcia, Provença (FGC).*

★ Mandarin Oriental Barcelona

$$$$ | **HOTEL** | A carpeted ramp leading from the elegant Passeig de Gràcia lends this hotel the air of a privileged—and pricey—inner sanctum. **Pros:** outstanding Moments restaurant; exceptional, discreet service; babysitters and parties for the kids, on request. **Cons:** painfully expensive; Wi-Fi free in rooms only if booked online; lower room categories small for a five-star accommodation. $ *Rooms from: €475* ✉ *Passeig de Gràcia 38-40, Eixample Dreta* ☎ *93/151-8888* ⊕ *www.mandarinoriental.com/barcelona* ⇨ *120 rooms* ⦿ *No Meals* Ⓜ *L2/L3/L4 Passeig de Gràcia, L3/L5 Diagonal, Provença (FGC).*

★ ME Barcelona

$$$$ | **HOTEL** | "Location, location, location" has become such an overused trope but, in the case of the ultra-swanky ME Barcelona, it simply can't be denied. **Pros:** spacious rooftop and heated year-round pool; strong sustainability profile; unbeatable central location. **Cons:** a bit pricey; far from the beach; rooms don't have balconies. $ *Rooms from: €350* ✉ *Casp 1–13, Eixample Dreta* ☎ *93/122-8278* ⊕ *www.melia.com/en/hotels/spain/barcelona/me-barcelona* ⇨ *164 rooms* ⦿ *No Meals* Ⓜ *Catalunya L1, L3.*

★ Monument Hotel

$$$$ | **HOTEL** | Originally the home of Enric Battló, a brother of the textile magnate who commissioned Gaudí to redesign the Moderniste masterpiece Casa Battló, and a minute's walk away on the Passeig de Gràcia, the historic 1898 building that houses the Monument went through several incarnations before it was transformed into the elegant upmarket hotel it is today. **Pros:** superbly professional multilingual staff; outstanding dining options; ideal mid-Eixample location. **Cons:** pricey breakfast; most "junior suites" are in effect large doubles with seating areas; hard on the budget. $ *Rooms from: €280* ✉ *Passeig de Gràcia 75, Eixample* ☎ *93/548-2000* ⊕ *www.monumenthotel.com* ⇨ *158 rooms* ⦿ *No Meals* Ⓜ *L3/L5 Diagonal, Provença (FGC).*

Ohla Eixample

$$$$ | **HOTEL** | With its location just off Passeig de Gràcia and Rambla de Catalunya, Ohla Eixample is ideally situated for designer shopping and gawking at Gaudí, but it's still within easy reach of the Ciutat Vella and the beach. **Pros:** outstanding food; sleek design; well located for shopping and Gaudí. **Cons:** lack of privacy with open plan room/shower; more modern than cozy; a bit far from the Old Town. $ *Rooms from: €239* ✉ *Còrsega 289, Eixample* ☎ *93/737-7977* ⊕ *www.ohlaeixample.com/en* ⇨ *94 rooms* ⦿ *Free Breakfast* Ⓜ *Diagonal L3, L5.*

★ Radisson Blu Hotel 1882

$$$ | **HOTEL** | Just a few minutes' walk from Gaudí's unfinished masterpiece, la Sagrada Família, this eco-conscious hotel may be named for the year in which work on that project began but the feel is distinctly contemporary. **Pros:** private parking (at a cost); strong sustainability profile; affordable designer hotel. **Cons:** no bar on the rooftop; no restaurant (except breakfast); quite far from downtown attractions and beaches. [$] *Rooms from: €208* ✉ *Còrsega 482, Barcelona* ☎ *93/347–8486* 🌐 *www.hotelbarcelona1882.com* 🛏 *182 rooms* 🍴 *No Meals* [M] *Sagrada Familia L2, L5.*

Sir Victor Hotel

$$$$ | **HOTEL** | Named after Catalan poet and playwright Caterina Albert i Paradís, who became a prominent member of the Modernisme movement under her pseudonym Victor Català, the uptown, upmarket Sir Victor Hotel will appeal to design lovers with its modern, ultra-elegant look. **Pros:** on-point design; rooftop overlooking La Pedrera; excellent food and drinks. **Cons:** expensive public parking; standard rooms on the small side; quite pricey. [$] *Rooms from: €246* ✉ *Rosselló 265, Eixample* ☎ *93/271–1244* 🌐 *www.sirhotels.com/en/victor* 🛏 *91 rooms* 🍴 *No Meals* [M] *Diagonal L3, L5.*

SixtyTwo Hotel

$$$ | **HOTEL** | Across from Gaudí's Casa Batlló and just down Passeig de Gràcia from his Casa Milà (La Pedrera), this boutique hotel is surrounded by Barcelona's top shopping addresses and leading restaurants. **Pros:** ideal location; good deals on parking; free coffee, tea, and snacks in the lounge, 24/7. **Cons:** noise can be an issue in lower-level rooms; no pool, gym, or spa; some rooms a bit small. [$] *Rooms from: €185* ✉ *Passeig de Gràcia 62, Eixample Dreta* ☎ *93/272–4180* 🌐 *www.sixtytwohotel.com* 🛏 *44 rooms* 🍴 *No Meals* [M] *L2/L3/L4 Passeig de Gràcia.*

Villa Emilia

$$ | **HOTEL** | The stylish, comfortable Villa Emilia is a bit removed from the tourist attractions of the Eixample and the Old City, but a mere five minutes' walk to the Fira de Barcelona exposition grounds, Las Arenas shopping center, and the airport shuttle bus stop in Plaça Espanya. **Pros:** convenient for Plaça Espanya and Fira de Barcelona; excellent wines at on-site bistro; barbecue and drinks on the opulent rooftop terrace (May–October). **Cons:** smallish rooms; no gym or spa; no pool. [$] *Rooms from: €162* ✉ *Carrer Calàbria 115, Eixample Esquerra* ☎ *93/252–5285* 🌐 *www.hotelvillaemilia.com* 🛏 *53 rooms* 🍴 *No Meals* [M] *L1 Rocafort.*

yök Casa + Cultura

$$$ | **APARTMENT** | Ideally located at the edge of the Eixample and Sant Pere neighborhoods, yök is made up of only three renovated boutique apartments that date back to 1900 and the time of the Catalan Moderniste movement. **Pros:** sleek design; great option for families or groups; stunning rooftop. **Cons:** minimum two-night stay; no pool or spa; no restaurant. [$] *Rooms from: €210* ✉ *Trafalgar 39, Eixample* ☎ *64/062–5313* 🌐 *www.helloyok.com* 🛏 *3 apartments* 🍴 *No Meals* [M] *Arc de Triomf L1.*

★ Yurbban Passage Hotel & Spa

$$$ | **HOTEL** | On the edge of the hip Sant Pere neighborhood, right where it meets the Eixample, this is the more sophisticated sister property to the Yurbban Trafalgar next door. **Pros:** good value; rooftop with views and a pool; outstanding spa. **Cons:** small rooftop pool; area can be a bit sketchy at night; no parking. [$] *Rooms from: €214* ✉ *Trafalgar 26, Eixample* ☎ *93/882–8977* 🌐 *www.yurbbanpassage.com* 🛏 *60 rooms* 🍴 *No Meals* [M] *Urquinaona L1, L4.*

🅨 Nightlife

The Eixample district is the largest and most diverse nightlife destination in town, with truly something for all tastes. On any given night you can find expat students blowing off steam at themed pubs and dance clubs catering to their likes, the LGBTQ community partying in the fashionable area affectionately known as "Gaixample," and the posh set rushing from high-end restaurants and chandeliered hotel bars to find a place at VIP tables in the city's swankiest clubs and lounges.

BARS

★ Banker's Bar

COCKTAIL LOUNGES | With decor details from its past life as a bank (like the safety deposit boxes on the wall), the swank cocktail bar of the Mandarin Oriental Hotel lounge is an atmospheric spot for an opulent night out. There's an "East meets West" menu for classic cocktail favorites—the Banker's Martini is the house specialty—and light food. DJs play mellow jazz, swing, and blues tunes on weekends. ✉ *Hotel Mandarin Oriental, Passeig de Gràcia 38–40, Eixample Dreta* ☎ *9393/151–8782* ⊕ *www.mandarinoriental.es/barcelona* Ⓜ *Passeig de Gràcia.*

Bitter Cocktail Bar

COCKTAIL LOUNGES | The only thing bitter about this place is the name. Excellent cocktails and friendly service are what keep guests coming back to this cute neighborhood joint in trendy Sant Antoni. ✉ *Viladomat, 17, Sant Antoni* ☎ *93/532–7199* ⊕ *bitter-bar.com/en* Ⓜ *Poble Sec L3.*

Dry Martini

COCKTAIL LOUNGES | An homage to the traditional English martini bar of decades past, this stately spot by local mixology maestro Javier de las Muelas is paradise for cocktail aficionados seeking expertly mixed drinks. ✉ *Aribau 162, Eixample Esquerra* ☎ *9393/217–5072* ⊕ *www. drymartiniorg.com* Ⓜ *Provença.*

Jonny Aldana

BARS | This cheery technicolor bar-resto, featuring a tiled facade and open-window bar with stools inside and out, is bursting with 1950s iconography. Wines are sold by the glass and beer is served from the tap, but it's the superb vermouths and cocktails combined with vegetarian tapas that keep patrons coming back. ✉ *Aldana 9, Sant Antoni* ☎ *93/250–7005* ⊕ *www. jonnyaldana.com* Ⓜ *Paral·lel.*

Les Gens que J'aime

COCKTAIL LOUNGES | Bohemia meets the Moulin Rouge at this intimate, below-street-level bordello-inspired bar with turn-of-the-20th-century memorabilia like fringed lampshades, faded period portraits, and comfy wicker sofas cushioned with lush red velvet. There's usually jazz playing in this laid-back spot where guests linger over reasonably priced cocktails (whiskey sours are popular). ✉ *València 286, bajos, Eixample Dreta* ☎ *93/215–6879* ⊕ *www.lesgensque-jaime.com* Ⓜ *Passeig de Gràcia.*

★ Morro Fi

BARS | Opened by a trio of vermouth aficionados, Morro Fi (loosely translates as "refined palate") began as a food blog that morphed into a bar determined to educate people about enjoying vermouth (they even produce their own brand) with select tapas. The result? Locals and the odd expat routinely spilling out into the streets, drink in hand while indie music blares. ✉ *Consell de Cent 171, Eixample Esquerra* ⊕ *www.morrofi.cat* Ⓜ *Urgell.*

★ Pepa Bar a Vins

WINE BARS | When it comes to wine, the team at Pepa really know their grapes, and they excel with natural wines, though there's also vermouth and artisanal beer if you're in the mood for that. The food is excellent, too, and it's all served in an old converted library. ✉ *Aribau 41, Eixample* ☎ *93/611–1885* Ⓜ *Universitat L1, L2.*

Priscilla Cafe
BARS | This friendly LGBTQ+ bar in the heart of the "Gaixample" neighborhood opens in the morning and stays busy until late. Expect strong drinks and a fun, eclectic crowd of locals, visitors, and fabulous drag queens. ✉ *Consell de Cent, 273, Eixample Esquerra* ☎ *67/911–5105* ⊕ *www.priscillacafe.com* Ⓜ *Universitat L1, L2.*

Senyor Vermut
BARS | This snazzy, high-ceilinged *vermuteria* has guests lining up to sample a generous selection of more than 40 *vermuts* served with traditional tapas. From bitter to earthy or aged in a barrel, the classic aperitif is the star attraction though other offerings include wine, beer, and juices. ✉ *Carrer de Provença 85, Eixample Esquerra* ☎ *93/532–8865* Ⓜ *Entença.*

SIPS
COCKTAIL LOUNGES | Perhaps more akin to a laboratory than a cocktail bar, SIPS draws from a menu influenced by seasonal ingredients and uses state-of-the-art techniques to mix a range of classic recipes and signature concoctions. ✉ *Muntaner 108, Eixample* ☎ *6193/964–1402* ⊕ *sips.barcelona* Ⓜ *Hospital Clínic L5.*

Solange Cocktails and Luxury Spirits
COCKTAIL LOUNGES | This sleek, luxurious lounge space is named after Solange Dimitrios, 007's original Bond girl, and the homage includes signature cocktails that reference Bond films, characters, and even a "secret mission" concoction for the more daring. ✉ *Aribau 143, Eixample Esquerra* ☎ *93/164–3625* ⊕ *www.solangecocktail.com* Ⓜ *Hospital Clínic, Diagonal.*

Xixbar
COCKTAIL LOUNGES | The interior of this Alice in Wonderland–like venue of checkered half-walls, a marble bar, and contemporary objets d'art rarely seen on ceilings is the first clue that you've landed somewhere special. Beyond that, with 50-plus flavors of gins and infusions, and a lounge-friendly 3 am last call on weekends, Xix turns conventional cocktail drinkers into card-carrying gin lovers. ✉ *Rocafort 19, Sant Antoni* ☎ *93/423–4314* ⊕ *www.xixbar.com* Ⓜ *Poble Sec.*

DANCE CLUBS

Antilla Salsa Barcelona
DANCE CLUBS | You'll find this exuberant Caribbean spot sizzling with salsa, son cubano, and merengue from the moment you step in the door. From 10 to 11 on Wednesday, enthusiastic dance instructors teach bachata for free. After that, the dancing begins and the dancers rarely stop to draw breath. This self-proclaimed "Caribbean cultural center" cranks out every variation of salsa ever invented. There are regular live concerts, and on Friday and Saturday, the mike gives way to animated Latin DJs. ✉ *Aragó 141, Eixample Esquerra* ☎ *610610/900588* ⊕ *www.antillasalsa. com* Ⓜ *Urgell, Hospital Clínic.*

Bikini Barcelona
DANCE CLUBS | This sleek megaclub, which was reborn as part of the L'Illa shopping center, boasts the best sound system in Barcelona. A smaller space puts on concerts of emerging and cult artists— the Nigerian singer-songwriter Asa, local soulsters The Pepper Pots, and Gil Scott-Heron (in one of his final performances) among them. When gigs finish around midnight, the walls roll back, and the space ingeniously turns into a sweaty nightclub. ✉ *Diagonal 547, Eixample Esquerra* ☎ *93/322–0800* ⊕ *www.bikinibcn.com* Ⓜ *Maria Cristina.*

City Hall
DANCE CLUBS | Nightly parties starring electro house music and guest DJs from neighboring clubs guarantee dancing till you drop at this raging mid-city favorite, set in a gorgeously revamped turn-of-the-20th-century theater. ✉ *Rambla Catalunya 2–4, Eixample Dreta* ☎ *66093/769–865* ⊕ *cityhallbarcelona.com* Ⓜ *Catalunya.*

8

The Eixample

La Chapelle

BARS | This busy LGBTQ bar, decked out in quasi-religious memorabilia, attracts locals and visitors of all persuasions, tastes, and age ranges. ✉ *Muntaner 67, Eixample Esquerra* ☎ *939/453–3076* Ⓜ *Universitat.*

Luz de Gas

DANCE CLUBS | Luz de Gas, an ornate 19th-century theater, offers everything from live performances (mostly world music and Latin) to wild late-night dancing (expect soul and standards). ✉ *Muntaner 246, Eixample Esquerra* ☎ *93/209–7711* ⊕ *www.luzdegas.com* Ⓜ *Muntaner, Diagonal.*

MUSIC CLUB: JAZZ AND BLUES
Milano

LIVE MUSIC | For more than a decade, this "secret" basement bar, in an area otherwise dominated by student pubs and tourist traps, has had a rotating line-up of international acts including blues, soul, jazz, flamenco, swing, and pop. The space resembles a 1940s cabaret, with a brass bar, spot-lit photos of previous acts, and red banquette-style seating. ✉ *Ronda Universitat 35, Eixample Esquerra* ☎ *93/112–7150* ⊕ *www.camparimilano.com/en* Ⓜ *Catalunya, Universitat.*

 Performing Arts

CONCERTS
L'Auditori de Barcelona

CONCERTS | Functional, sleek, and minimalist, the Rafael Monco-designed Auditori has a full calendar of classical music performances—with regular forays into jazz, flamenco, and pop—near Plaça de les Glòries. Orchestras that perform here include the Orquestra Simfònica de Barcelona i Nacional de Catalunya (OBC) and the Orquestra Nacional de Cambra de Andorra. The excellent Museu de la Música is on the first floor. ✉ *Lepant 150, Sant Martí* ☎ *93/247–9300* ⊕ *www.auditori.cat* Ⓜ *Marina, Monumental, Glòries.*

DANCE
Teatre Tívoli

THEATER | FAMILY | One of the city's most beloved traditional theater and dance venues, the century-old Tívoli has staged timeless classics and has hosted everyone from the Ballet Nacional de Cuba to flamenco and teeny-bopper treats. ✉ *Casp 8, Eixample Dreta* ☎ *93/215–9570* ⊕ *www.grupbalana.com* Ⓜ *Catalunya.*

 Shopping

Beginning with the Triangle d'Or at the top of La Rambla and up Passeig de Gràcia, now rightly considered one of the world's greatest shopping streets, the Eixample is a compendium of design and fashion stores that could take years to fully explore.

Passeig de Gràcia, with reportedly the most expensive retail floor space in Spain, accommodates a lengthy and luxurious list of fashionista showcases, such as Prada, Stella McCartney, and Loewe, with more down-to-earthling brands such as Zara and Mango situated at the southern end. Also in the Eixample, Moderniste grocery stores such as Queviures Murria dazzle foodies. Other targets of opportunity include Rambla de Catalunya (which runs parallel to Passeig de Gràcia and is less uptight) and Carrer Enric Granados. This is just the tip of the shopping iceberg: turn yourself loose and discover the factory outlet stores along Carrer Girona, or wander into the Bermuda Triangle of antiques shopping in Bulevard dels Antiquaris at Passeig de Gràcia 55–57.

ANTIQUES AND COLLECTIBLES
Bulevard dels Antiquaris

ANTIQUES & COLLECTIBLES | Look carefully for the stairway leading one flight up to this 73-store antiques arcade off Passeig de Gràcia. You never know what you might find: dolls, icons, Roman or Visigothic objects, paintings, furniture, cricket kits, fly rods, or toys from a century ago. Bargaining is common practice—but Catalan antiques dealers are tough nuts to crack. ⊠ *Passeig de Gràcia 55, Eixample Dreta* ☎ *93/215–4499* ⊕ *www.bulevarddelsantiquaris.com* Ⓜ *Passeig de Gràcia.*

El Recibidor
ANTIQUES & COLLECTIBLES | Like a scene from *Mad Men*, El Recibidor oozes mid-century modern elegance. This large split-level showroom deals in furniture and objects, mainly of European provenance, from the art deco period onward. From small ceramic figurines to dining tables, table lamps, and vintage TVs, each item has been curated and restored with a deep understanding of the period's aesthetic and value. ⊠ *Carrer de Calàbria 85, Eixample Esquerra* ☎ *93/530–4221* ⊕ *www.elrecibidor.com* Ⓜ *Sant Antoni.*

Novecento
ANTIQUES & COLLECTIBLES | A standout primarily for being so out of place among all the design emporiums and fashion denizens on this great white way of high commerce, Novecento is an antique jewelry store with abundant items from all epochs and movements from Victorian to Art Nouveau to Belle Époque. ⊠ *Passeig de Gràcia 75, Eixample Dreta* ☎ *93/215–1183* Ⓜ *Passeig de Gràcia.*

BOOKS AND STATIONERY
Altaïr
BOOKS | Barcelona's premier travel and adventure bookstore stocks many titles in English. Book presentations and events scheduled here feature a wide range of notable authors from Alpinists to Africanists. ⊠ *Gran Via 616, Eixample Esquerra* ☎ *93/342–7171* ⊕ *www.altair.es* Ⓜ *Catalunya.*

Casa del Llibre
BOOKS | On Barcelona's most important shopping street, Casa del Llibre is a major book feast with a wide variety of English titles. ⊠ *Passeig de Gràcia 62, Eixample Dreta* ☎ *9102/1793–463* ⊕ *www.casadellibro.com* Ⓜ *Passeig de Gràcia.*

FNAC
BOOKS | For musical recordings and the latest book publications, this is one of Barcelona's most dependable and happening addresses. Regular concerts, presentations of new recordings, and art exhibits take place in FNAC, both here at the branch in the Triangle Shopping Center on Plaça Catalunya and one on Diagonal in the L'Illa shopping center. Much more than a bookstore, it's an important cultural resource. ⊠ *Centro Comercial El Triangle, Pl. Catalunya 4, Eixample Esquerra* ☎ *902/100632* ⊕ *www.fnac.es* Ⓜ *Maria Cristina, Les Corts.*

La Central
BOOKS | Hands-down, Barcelona's best bookstore for years, La Central has creaky, literary wooden floors and piles of recent publications with many interesting titles in English. ⊠ *Carrer Mallorca 237, Eixample Esquerra* ☎ *900/802–109* ⊕ *www.lacentral.com* Ⓜ *Diagonal, Passeig de Gràcia.*

Laie
BOOKS | Though it doesn't have a lot of English-language titles, this bookstore has a very pleasant café-restaurant upstairs; the space is often used for readings and other cultural events. Other branches of Laie are located around Barcelona, including major museums such as the Museu Picasso and Cosmocaixa. ⊠ *Pau Claris 85, Eixample Dreta* ☎ *93/302–7310* ⊕ *www.laie.es* Ⓜ *Catalunya.*

CERAMICS AND GLASSWARE
★ Lladró
CERAMICS | This Valencia company is famed worldwide for the beauty and quality of its ceramic figures. Barcelona's only Lladró factory store, this location has exclusive pieces of work, custom-designed luxury items of gold and porcelain, and classic and original works. Look for the cheeky figurines by Jaime Hayon,

a Spanish designer, and the spectacular chandeliers by Bodo Sperlein. ⊠ *Passeig de Gràcia 101, Eixample Dreta* ☎ *93/270–1253* ⊕ *www.lladro.com* Ⓜ *Diagonal.*

CLOTHING

Adolfo Domínguez

MIXED CLOTHING | One of Barcelona's long-time fashion giants, this is one of Spain's leading clothing designers, with many locations around town. Famed as the creator of the Iberia Airlines uniforms, Adolfo Domínguez has been in the not-too-radical mainstream of Spanish couture for the past quarter century. ⊠ *Passeig de Gràcia 32, Eixample Dreta* ☎ *93/487–4170* ⊕ *www.adolfodominguez.com* Ⓜ *Passeig de Gràcia.*

Aílanto

WOMEN'S CLOTHING | Twin brothers Iñaki and Aitor Muñoz are the creative and business force behind Aílanto, an avant-garde fashion brand renowned for sculptural silhouettes and daring prints. Winners of various accolades and regulars at Madrid's Fashion Week, their Barcelona shop is as drama-filled as their collections, with flowering metallic lamps dangling from double-height ceilings and dressing rooms swathed in fringes and velvet. Oversized coats, heavily textured fabrics, and patterns inspired by major artistic movements have become the brand's signatures. ⊠ *Enric Granados 46, Eixample Esquerra* ☎ *93/451–3106* ⊕ *www.ailanto.com* Ⓜ *Provença.*

The Avant

WOMEN'S CLOTHING | Under her own label, Silvia Garcia Presas—the creator of El Avant—offers quietly elegant and effortlessly chic clothing for women in her simple boutique at the top end of Enric Granados. Fabrics are 100% natural (organic cotton, alpaca wool, etc.), and the generous and easy cuts are transgenerational and flattering. ⊠ *Enric Granados 114, Eixample Esquerra* ☎ *9393/601–0430* ⊕ *www.theavant.com* Ⓜ *Diagonal.*

Carolina Herrera

WOMEN'S CLOTHING | Originally from Venezuela but professionally based in New York, Carolina Herrera and her international CH logo have become Barcelona mainstays. (Daughter Carolina Herrera Jr. is a Spanish resident and married to former bullfighter Miguel Báez.) Fragrances for men and women and clothes with a simple, elegant line—a white blouse is the CH icon—are the staples here. Herrera's light ruffled dresses and edgy urban footwear add feminine flourishes. ⊠ *Passeig de Gràcia 87, Eixample Dreta* ☎ *93/272–1584* ⊕ *www.carolinaherrera.com* Ⓜ *Diagonal.*

★ Cortana

WOMEN'S CLOTHING | A sleek and breezy Balearic Islands look for women is what this designer from Mallorca brings to the fashion scene of urban Barcelona in a whitewashed shop reminiscent of an art gallery. Her dresses transmit a casual, minimalistic elegance and have graced many a red carpet all over Spain. ⊠ *Provença 290, Eixample Esquerra* ☎ *93/487–2070* ⊕ *www.cortana.es* Ⓜ *Provença.*

Erre de Raso

WOMEN'S CLOTHING | Popular with the uptown crowd, Erre de Raso makes clothes in bright and breezy shades and patterns. With colors ranging from electric fuchsias to bright indigo blues and materials ranging from satin (raso) to cottons and silks, the objective is to outfit stylish women in chameleonic outfits that look equally appropriate picking up the kids from school, dropping by an art gallery opening, and hitting a cocktail party in the same sortie. ⊠ *Aribau 69, Eixample* ☎ *9393/452–3754* Ⓜ *Diagonal L3, L5.*

Furest

MEN'S CLOTHING | This well-established menswear star, with four stores in town and another at the airport, markets selections from Armani Jeans, Scotch & Soda, Hugo Boss, and Blackstone, as well as its own collection of dapper suits, shirts, and gentlemen's accessories. ✉ *Diagonal 468, Eixample* ☏ *9393/416–0665* ⊕ *www.furest.com* Ⓜ *Diagonal L3, L5.*

Loewe

MIXED CLOTHING | Occupying the ground floor of Lluís Domènech i Montaner's Casa Lleó Morera, Loewe is Spain's answer to Hermès, a classical clothing and leather emporium for men's and women's fashions and luxurious handbags that whisper status (at eye-popping prices). ✉ *Passeig de Gràcia 35, Eixample* ☏ *93/216–0400* ⊕ *www.loewe.com* Ⓜ *Passeig de Gràcia.*

Purificación García

MIXED CLOTHING | Known as a gifted fabric expert whose creations are invariably based on the qualities and characteristics of her raw materials, Galicia-born Purificación García enjoys solid prestige in Barcelona. Understated hues and subtle combinations of colors and shapes place this contemporary designer squarely in the camp of the less-is-more school, and, although her women's range is larger and more diverse, she understands men's tailoring. ✉ *Provença 292, Eixample Esquerra* ☏ *93/496–1336* ⊕ *www.purificaciongarcia.com* Ⓜ *Diagonal.*

Santa Eulalia

MIXED CLOTHING | The history of this luxury fashion superstore, which moved into its 2,000-square-meter premises designed by William Sofield in 2011, goes back to 1843. That year Domingo Taberner Prims opened the first shop, which would soon evolve into one of the city's first and foremost haute couture tailoring houses. Today it's run by the fourth generation of the founding family and features one of the best luxury brand selections in the country. It also regularly teams up with designers and design schools to present special collections or awards. When you're done browsing everything from Agent Provocateur to Vera Wang, refresh with some tea and cake at the fabulous café-terrace on the first floor, or head to the basement to see the in-house tailors at work on bespoke suits and men's shirts. ✉ *Passeig de Gràcia 93, Eixample Dreta* ☏ *93/215–0674* ⊕ *www.santaeulalia.com* Ⓜ *Diagonal.*

Sita Murt

WOMEN'S CLOTHING | The local Catalan designer Sita Murt produces smart, grown-up women's wear under her own label in this minimalist space in the Eixample. Colorful chiffon dresses and light, gauzy tops and knits characterize this line of clothing popular with professional women and wedding goers. ✉ *Mallorca 242, Eixample Esquerra* ☏ *93/215–2231* ⊕ *www.sitamurt.com* Ⓜ *Passeig de Gràcia, Diagonal.*

Teresa Helbig

WOMEN'S CLOTHING | A regular at Madrid Fashion Week, Teresa Helbig designs feminine and elegant pret-a-porter women's collections. Yet she is better known, and worth visiting, for her bespoke bridal wear and evening gowns, timeless haute couture she concocts for her well-heeled clients at her Barcelona studio-showroom. It may not come cheap, but you'll be able to hand it down through generations. ✉ *Mallorca 184, Loft, Eixample Esquerra* ☏ *93/451–5544* ⊕ *www.teresahelbig.com* Ⓜ *Diagonal L3, L5.*

Trait

MIXED CLOTHING | A store as trendy as the street on which it lies, Trait is *the* place for Sant Antoni's fashionistas to pick up the latest looks. From global brands like Carhartt WIP to Danish style favorites Samsoe Samsoe and Basic Apparel, as well as a selection of ethical local Catalan designers, Trait is where you'll find many of the hottest men's and women's labels around. ✉ *Parlament, 28, Sant Antoni* ☏ *93/667–1631* ⊕ *traitstore.com/en* Ⓜ *Poble Sec L3.*

8

The Eixample

DEPARTMENT STORES AND MALLS

El Corte Inglés

DEPARTMENT STORE | Iconic and ubiquitous, this Spanish department store has its main Barcelona branch on Plaça de Catalunya, with one annex close by in Porta de l'Àngel for younger fashion and sporting goods. You can find just . about anything here—clothing, shoes, perfumes, electronics—and there is a wonderful supermarket and food mall on the lower-ground floor. With branches in all major cities, El Corte Inglés is Spain's only large department store and has leagues of heritage fans. Service is inconsistent, but the sale season in August is worth fighting the crowds for. ⊠ *Pl. de Catalunya 14, Eixample* ☎ *93/306–3800* ⊕ *www.elcorteingles.es* Ⓜ *Catalunya.*

L'Illa Diagonal

DEPARTMENT STORE | This rangy complex buzzes with shoppers swarming through more than 100 stores and shops, including food specialists, Decathlon sports gear, and Imaginarium toys, plus FNAC, Zara, Benetton, and all the usual international brands. ⊠ *Av. Diagonal 557, Eixample Esquerra* ☎ *93/444–0000* ⊕ *www.lilla.com* Ⓜ *Maria Cristina.*

FOOD

★ Cacao Sampaka

CHOCOLATE | While it's perfectly possible to dash in and fill your bags with boxes of Cacao Sampaka's exquisite cocoa creations to take home with you (or nibble on the way back to your hotel), consider setting aside 30 minutes to sit down in the pleasant in-store café and order an "Azteca" hot chocolate drink. Quite possibly the best hot chocolate in Spain, a sip of this thick, rich, heaven-in-a-cup is the highlight of any Barcelona shopping spree. ⊠ *Carrer del Consell de Cent 292, Eixample Esquerra* ☎ *93/272–0833* ⊕ *www.cacaosampaka.com* Ⓜ *Passeig de Gràcia.*

Oriol Balaguer

CHOCOLATE | Oriol Balaguer is surely running out of room to store all the "Spain's Best…" trophies he's collected over the years. He's a consultant to some of the world's most famous restaurants, and the heart of his empire is this little shop of chocolate-making magic. Bring your credit card and prepare to have your mind blown. Some of the confectionery creations are so beautiful you'll feel bad about biting into them—at least until you taste them. There's a second boutique at Travessera de les Corts 340, which also sells bread and pastries. ⊠ *Pl. de Sant Gregori Taumaturg 2, Eixample* ☎ *93/201–1846* ⊕ *www.oriolbalaguer.com* Ⓜ *La Bonanova.*

Queviures Murria

FOOD | Founded in 1890, this historic Moderniste shop, its windows decorated with reproductions of Catalan artist Ramón Casas paintings, has a superb selection of some 200 cheeses, sausages, wines, and conserves from Spain, Catalunya, and beyond. This work of art–cum–grocery store (*queviures* means foodstuffs, literally, "things to keep you alive") is definitely worth a stop. ⊠ *Roger de Llúria 85, Eixample Dreta* ⊹ *Near metro Passeig de Gràcia* ☎ *93/215–5789* ⊕ *www.colmadomurria.com* Ⓜ *Passeig de Gràcia.*

Reserva Ibérica

FOOD | Purveyor of fine hams in Spain and abroad for more than 30 years, Reserva Ibérica has a shop in the Eixample where it not only sells a selection of its best, all-acorn-fed products, but also offers the opportunity for customers to taste the hams, accompanied by a glass of wine. ⊠ *Rambla de Catalunya 61, Eixample Esquerra* ☎ *93/215–5230* ⊕ *www.reservaiberica.com* Ⓜ *Passeig de Gràcia.*

GIFTS AND SOUVENIRS

Servei Estació

HOUSEWARES | It's a hardware store, yes, but one like you've never seen before. Servei Estació is situated in a rationalist-style landmark building dating from 1962. For decades it served the city's builders and handymen with tools and materials, but more recently the huge inventory has expanded to modern design and housewares, and sells everything from ropes of string to designer shopping carts. ⊠ *Aragó 270–272, Eixample Esquerra* ☎ *93/393-2410* ⊕ *www. serveiestacio.com* Ⓜ *Passeig de Gràcia.*

HOUSEHOLD ITEMS AND FURNITURE

Azul Tierra

HOUSEWARES | If you're looking for a one-of-a-kind statement piece for your home, look no further than Azul Tierra. This 1,400-square-foot showroom is filled with weird and wonderful interior design from all around the world, from sculptures, to ornaments, knick-knacks and furniture—all carefully selected by owner and designer Toni Espuch on his travels. ⊠ *Còrsega, 276–282, Eixample Esquerra* ☎ *93/217-8356* Ⓜ *Diagonal L3, L5.*

Gothsland

FURNITURE | Art Nouveau furniture, art objects, and decorative paraphernalia share space here with sculpted terra-cotta figures, vases, mirrors, and furniture, nearly all in Barcelona's signature Moderniste style. Paintings by Art Nouveau stars from Santiago Rusiñol to Ramón Casas might turn up here, along with lamps, clocks, and curios of all kinds. Modern pieces, particularly sculpture, are also represented. ⊠ *Consell de Cent 331, Eixample Esquerra* ☎ *93/488-1922* ⊕ *www.gothsland.com* Ⓜ *Passeig de Gràcia.*

Mar de Cava

HOUSEWARES | This Aladdin's Cave of design, housewares, furniture, clothing, and accessories bursts with creativity and color. The carefully curated collection includes everything from vases by cult ceramics maker Apparatu, cabinets rendered in Technicolor lacquers, African bead necklaces, and tables covered in antique tiles. The emphasis is more on craftsmanship than the latest trends—just about every item has an intriguing backstory. ⊠ *Valencia 293, Eixample* ☎ *93/458-5333* ⊕ *www.mardecava.com* Ⓜ *Girona.*

Nanimarquina

FURNITURE | A lover of both traditional methods and exuberant design, Nani Marquina makes textural rugs that look just as good on a wall as they do on the floor. Some of her rugs re-create ancient Persian or Hindu styles; others are trendy compositions by designers like Sybilla or the Bouroullec brothers. ⊠ *Rosselló 256/Av. Diagonal, Eixample Dreta* ☎ *93/487-1606* ⊕ *www.nanimarquina. com* Ⓜ *Diagonal.*

JEWELRY

Bagués Masriera

JEWELRY & WATCHES | The Bagués dynasty has bejeweled barcelonins since 1839. While they stock much that glitters, the Lluís Masriera line of original Art Nouveau pieces is truly unique; intricate flying nymphs, lifelike golden insects, and other easily recognizable motifs from the period take on a new depth of beauty when executed in the translucent enameling process that Masriera himself developed. The location in Moderniste architect Puig i Cadafalch's Casa Amatller in the famous Mansana de la Discòrdia on Passeig de Gràcia is worth the visit alone, although sadly, the interior of the shop bears little of the building's exuberance. ⊠ *Passeig de Gràcia 41, Eixample Dreta* ☎ *93/216-0174* ⊕ *bagues-masriera.com* Ⓜ *Catalunya, Passeig de Gràcia.*

Zapata Joyeros

JEWELRY & WATCHES | The Zapata family, with several stores around town, has been prominent in Barcelona jewelry design and retail for the last half century. With original designs of their own and a savvy selection of the most important Swiss and international watch designers, this family business is now in its second generation and makes a point of taking good care of clients with large or

8

The Eixample

small jewelry needs. Their L'Illa store, for example, specializes in jewelry accessible to the budgets of younger clients. ✉ *Buenos Aires 60, Eixample Esquerra* ☎ *93/430–6238* ⊕ *www.zapatajoyeros. com* Ⓜ *Provença.*

MARKETS

★ Els Encants Vells

MARKET | Though one of Europe's oldest flea markets, Els Encants has a new home—a stunning, glittering metal canopy that protects the rag-and-bone merchants (and their keen customers) from the elements. Stalls, and a handful of stand-up bars, have become a bit more upscale, too, although you'll still find plenty of oddities to barter over in the central plaza. It's open Monday, Wednesday, Friday, and Saturday—the latter is the busiest day so if you want a more relaxed rummage, go during the week. ✉ *Av. Meridiana 69, Pl. de Les Glòries Catalans, Sant Martí* ☎ *9393/245–2299* ⊕ *encantsbarcelona.com* Ⓜ *Glòries.*

SHOES

Camper

SHOES | This internationally famous Spanish shoe emporium (which also now includes several boutique hotels) has offers a large line of funky boots, heels, and shoes of all kinds. Men's, women's, and children's shoes are displayed against an undulating chrome-and-wood backdrop designed by architect Benedetta Tagliabue. ✉ *Passeig de Gràcia 2–4, Eixample Dreta* ☎ *9393/521–6250* ⊕ *www.camper.com* Ⓜ *Catalunya.*

★ Norman Vilalta

SHOES | Norman Vilalta was a lawyer in Buenos Aires before he decided to do something rather unusual: learn the trade of a traditional cobbler. He moved to Florence, Italy, to apprentice and learn the trade, and then set up shop in Barcelona. Today he is one of a handful of people in the world who produce artisanal bespoke shoes, which take three months to make (and can be shipped worldwide). The shoes come complete with a video showing the entire making of, and will set you back somewhere between €2,500 and €5,000. However, you will also join the ranks of the chef Ferran Adrià, the architect Oscar Tusquets, and members of the Spanish royal family as owner of a pair of Norman Vilalta shoes. And since they fit like no other and last a lifetime, you might consider it a worthy investment. For a more affordable option, Vilalta's ready-to-wear footwear is available at the high-fashion emporium Santa Eulàlia on the Passeig de Gràcia. ✉ *Enric Granados 5, Eixample Esquerra* ☎ *93/323–4014* ⊕ *www.normanvilalta. com* Ⓜ *Universitat.*

★ The Outpost

SHOES | A shop dedicated exclusively to men's accessories of the finest kind, the Outpost was created by a former Prada buyer who considers it his mission to bring stylishness to Barcelona men with this oasis of avant-garde fashion. The constantly changing window displays are works of art, providing a first taste of what's to be found inside: Robert Clergerie shoes, Albert Thurston suspenders, Roland Pineau belts, Yves Andrieux hats, Balenciaga ties. You enter the Outpost as a mere mortal, but leave it as a gentleman—provided you carry the necessary cash. ✉ *Rosselló 283, bis, Eixample Dreta* ☎ *93/457–7137* ⊕ *www.theoutpostbcn.com* Ⓜ *Diagonal, Verdaguer.*

Tascón

SHOES | International footwear designers and domestic shoemakers alike fill these stores with trendy urban footwear from brands such as Camper, United Nude, and Audley, as well as more sturdy models from Timberland and the like. Models designed in-house and made locally offer high style at reasonable prices. You'll find other branches of Tascón in strategic shopping hubs. ✉ *Passeig de Gràcia 64, Eixample Dreta* ☎ *93/487–9084* ⊕ *www. tascon.es* Ⓜ *Passeig de Gràcia.*

Chapter 9

GRÀCIA

Updated by
Jennifer Ceaser

◉ Sights	🍽 Restaurants	🛏 Hotels	⬤ Shopping	🍸 Nightlife
★★☆☆☆	★★★★☆	★★☆☆☆	★★★☆☆	★★★★☆

NEIGHBORHOOD SNAPSHOT

TOP EXPERIENCES

■ **Gran de Gràcia:** This central thoroughfare is lined with buildings of great architectural interest.

■ **Mercat de la Llibertat:** A great place to wander and snack, this lively market is also an occasional concert venue.

■ **Park Güell:** Gaudí's delightfully eccentric constructions make this hilly park one of the city's top tourist attractions.

■ **Historic plazas:** Dozens of squares dot the neighborhood, and their café terraces are popular gathering spots for a coffee, beer, or vermouth.

■ **Late-night dining and drinking:** Wander the maze of alleyways and side streets, hopping between wine bars, cocktail lounges, and tapas spots.

GETTING HERE

The metro's green line (L3) station at Fontana puts you in the heart of Gràcia, while the L3 at Lesseps is within walking distance of Park Güell. The yellow line (L4) Joanic stop is a short stroll from Gràcia's northeast side. Both the green line and the blue line (L5) stop at Diagonal, just to the south of Gràcia. The Gràcia stop on the FGC (Ferrocarril de la Generalitat de Catalunya) trains, part of the metro system that connects Sarrià, Sabadell, Terrassa, and Sant Cugat with Plaça de Catalunya, is yet another option.

PLANNING YOUR TIME

Exploring Gràcia is at least a several-hours outing, though you can easily spend an entire day here. From morning until late in the evening, the barrio's café-filled plazas hum with activity. Shoppers flock to its boutique-lined streets and the venerable Llibertat market, except Sunday, when stores are closed.

Evening sessions at the popular Verdi cinema (showing films in their original languages) usually get out just in time for a late-night dining or drinking in any of a number of bars and restaurants. Park Güell is best in the morning to avoid the heat and the crowds.

FUN FACT

August's weeklong Festa Major de Gràcia is the biggest and best of Barcelona's summer festivals and it transforms the neighborhood into a giant, colorful party. The streets and plazas become fantastical themed worlds, featuring canopies of lights, ribbons, flowers, found objects, and enormous papier-mâché constructions. Local residents work for months on end, crafting everything by hand, in the hope of winning the competition for "best decorated street." More than a million people flock here for the festival, which also includes live music, parades, dancing, fireworks, and traditional creating human towers. The event kicks off on August 15th, Assumption Day, a national holiday in Spain.

Gràcia is a state of mind. More than a neighborhood, it's a village republic that has periodically risen in armed rebellion against city, state, and country. Its jumble of streets have names (Llibertat, Fraternitat, Progrès) that invoke the ideological history of a once fiercely progressive, working-class enclave. Nowadays, it's where younger generations want to live; it's also where they come to party.

The site of Barcelona's first factory collectives, it was fertile ground for all sorts of radical reform movements, as workers organized and developed into groups ranging from anarchists to feminists to Esperantists. Once an independent village that joined the municipality of Barcelona only under duress, Gràcia attempted to secede from the Spanish state in 1856, 1870, 1873, and 1909.

Covering the area above the Diagonal from Carrer de Còrsega all the way up to Park Güell, Gràcia is bounded by Via Augusta and Carrer Balmes to the west and Carrer de l'Escorial and Passeig de Sant Joan to the east. Today the area is filled with hip bars and trendy restaurants, outdoor cafés, gourmet shops, designer boutiques, and artists' studios. During August's weeklong Festa Major de Gràcia, the barrio fills with people coming to see the elaborately decorated streets and squares, all created by neighborhood residents.

Sights

Casa Comalat

HISTORIC HOME | Located at the bottom of Gràcia, this often overlooked Moderniste house (not open to the public) is worth stopping by to view the exterior—especially from the Carrer Còrsega side of the building, at the corner of Carrer de Pau Claris. Built in 1911, the Salvador Valeri i Pupurull creation is one of Barcelona's most interesting Moderniste houses, with its undulating balconies, Gaudí-onsteroids stone arches, and polychrome ceramic-tiled facade. ⊠ Av. Diagonal 442, Gràcia ⧉ Only viewable from the exterior. Ⓜ Diagonal.

Casa-Museu Gaudí

HISTORIC HOME | Up the steps of Park Güell and to the right is the whimsical Alice-in-Wonderland-esque house where Gaudí lived with his niece from 1906 until 1925. Now a small museum, exhibits include Gaudí-designed furniture and decorations, drawings, and portraits and busts of the architect. Stop by if you are

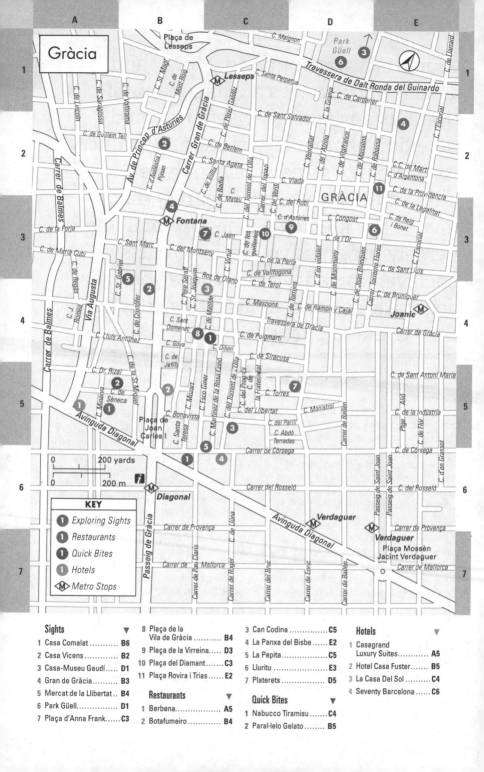

Gràcia

KEY

- ① Exploring Sights
- ① Restaurants
- ① Quick Bites
- ① Hotels
- Ⓜ Metro Stops

Sights ▼
1 Casa Comalat **B6**
2 Casa Vicens **B2**
3 Casa-Museu Gaudí **D1**
4 Gran de Gràcia **B3**
5 Mercat de la Llibertat .. **B4**
6 Park Güell **D1**
7 Plaça d'Anna Frank **C3**

8 Plaça de la
   Vila de Gràcia **B4**
9 Plaça de la Virreina **D3**
10 Plaça del Diamant **C3**
11 Plaça Rovira i Trias **E2**

Restaurants ▼
1 Berbena **A5**
2 Botafumeiro **B4**

3 Can Codina **C5**
4 La Panxa del Bisbe **E2**
5 La Pepita **C5**
6 Lluritu **E3**
7 Platerets **D5**

Quick Bites ▼
1 Nabucco Tiramisu **C4**
2 Paral·lelo Gelato **B5**

Hotels ▼
1 Casagrand
   Luxury Suites **A5**
2 Hotel Casa Fuster **B5**
3 La Casa Del Sol **C4**
4 Seventy Barcelona **C6**

in the park, but the museum is not worth traveling far for. Note that the museum is not included in the admission fee for Park Güell. Additionally, the museum closed during Covid and at the time of writing it was not clear when it will reopen. ✉ *Park Güell, Carretera del Carmel 23A, Gràcia* ☎ *93/208-0414 Ticket information* ⊕ *sagradafamilia.org/casa-museu-gaudi* 🎫 *€5.50* Ⓜ *Lesseps, Vallcarca.*

★ Casa Vicens

HISTORIC HOME | Antoni Gaudí's first important commission as a young architect was built between 1883 and 1885 and it stands out for its colorful facade of green and white checkered tiles, in combination with tiles with floral patterns. The client, Manel Vicens i Montaner, a stock and currency broker, entrusted the young architect with designing his summer residence in the former village of Gràcia. The home is a triumph of early Catalan *modernisme*, borrowing freely from architectural styles around the world including Art Nouveau (with its sinuous nature-inspired motifs) and Orientalist and Mudejar (Moorish-inspired) elements, evident in the ornate tile work.

In 1925 Antonio Jover i Puig, a prominent local doctor, purchased the house and greatly altered the interiors; in 2014, it was sold to the Andorra-based MoraBanc which established a foundation to preserve this remarkable historic property, and opened it to the public in 2017. Recent renovations have restored much of Gaudí's original design. The marvelous interiors feature trompe-l'oeil birds painted on the walls and intricately carved ceilings; the phantasmic Orientalist papier-mâché tiles and cupola in the smoking alcove on the main floor is enough to make you wonder what folks back then were putting in their pipes. In any case, it is a must-visit. ✉ *Carrer de les Carolines 20–26, Gràcia* ☎ *93/271-1064 Tickets* ⊕ *www.casavicens.org* 🎫 *€16* Ⓜ *Fontana, Lesseps.*

Gran de Gràcia

STREET | This highly trafficked central artery and shopping thoroughfare running up through Gràcia is lined with buildings of great artistic and architectural interest, beginning with the hotel Casa Fuster, built between 1908 and 1911 by Palau de la Música Catalana architect Lluís Domènech i Montaner in collaboration with his son Pere Domènech i Roure. As you move up Gran de Gràcia, probable Francesc Berenguer buildings can be identified at No. 15; No. 23, with its scrolled cornice; and Nos. 35, 49, 51, 61, and 77. Officially attributed to a series of architects—Berenguer lacked a formal degree, having left architecture school to become Gaudí's "right hand"—these Moderniste masterworks have long inspired debate over Berenguer's role. ✉ *Gran de Gràcia, Gràcia* Ⓜ *Fontana, Lesseps, Gràcia (FGC).*

Mercat de la Llibertat

MARKET | Far more manageable—both in size and crowds—than Boqueria market, this landmark iron-and-brick structure nonetheless impresses with its high ceilings and ornamental elements. Built between 1888 and 1893 by Catalan architect Miquel Pascual i Tintorer in collaboration with Francesc Berenguer, it features wonderful decorative elements, like the swans swimming along the roof line and the snails surrounding Gràcia's coat of arms. ✉ *Pl. Llibertat 27, Gràcia* ⊕ *www.bcn.es/mercatsmunicipals* 🕐 *Closed Sun.* Ⓜ *Fontana, Gràcia (FGC).*

★ Park Güell

CITY PARK | **FAMILY** | Built between 1900 and 1914, this park is one of Gaudí's, and Barcelona's, most visited attractions. Named for and commissioned by Gaudí's steadfast patron, Count Eusebi Güell, it was originally intended as a gated residential community based on the English Garden City model. The centerpiece of the project was a public square, with a pillared marketplace beneath it. Only two of the houses were ever built, one of which was designed by Gaudí's assistant Francesc Berenguer and became Gaudí's home from 1906 to 1925. It now houses the **Casa-Museu Gaudí** museum of memorabilia.

Ultimately, the Güell family turned the area over to the city as a public park for local residents, and it remains so today. Tickets are required to access most of Park Güell, including the "monumental area," where the main attractions are located. You can purchase timed tickets online and at the park. .

An Art Nouveau extravaganza with gingerbread gatehouses, Park Güell is a perfect place to visit on a sunny morning before the temperature heats up. The gatehouse on the right, topped with a rendition in ceramic tile of the hallucinogenic red-and-white fly amanita wild mushroom (rumored to have been a Gaudí favorite), is now part of the Barcelona History Museum. The exhibition inside has plans, scale models, photos, and suggested routes analyzing the park in detail. Atop the gatehouse on the left sits the *phallus impudicus* (no translation necessary).

Other Gaudí highlights include the Room of a Hundred Columns—a covered market supported by tilted Doric-style columns and mosaic medallions—the double set of stairs, and the iconic lizard guarding the fountain between them. There's also the fabulous serpentine, polychrome bench enclosing the square. The bench is one of Gaudí assistant Josep Maria Jujol's most memorable creations, and one of Barcelona's best examples of the trencadís technique (mosaics of broken tile fragments: recycling as high art).

From the Lesseps metro station, take Bus No. 24 or V19 to the park entrance. From the Bus Turístic stop on Travessera de Dalt, make the steep 10-minute climb up Carrer de Lallard or Avinguda del Santuari de Sant Josep de la Muntanya.

✉ *Carretera del Carmel, 23, Gràcia* ☎ *93/409–1830* ⊕ *parkguell.barcelona/en* 💶 *€10* 🕐 *Tickets have set entry times.* Ⓜ *Lesseps, Vallcarca.*

Plaça d'Anna Frank

PLAZA/SQUARE | Near Plaça del Diamant is a small square honoring Anne Frank, the young woman whose diary was published several years after she perished in the Bergen-Belsen concentration camp in 1945. As you leave Plaça del Diamant on Carrer de l'Or, a left on Torrent de l'Olla and an immediate right on Carrer de Jaén lead down some stairs and into a small space where you will see, lying over the edge of the roof of the CAT (Centre Artesá Tradicionàrius), the bronze figure of a young girl, by Catalan sculptress Sara Pons Arnal, pen and journal in hand, head cocked pensively, her foot raised idly, playfully, behind her. The inscription in the open bronze book on the wall reads "While even the names of her execution-ers are gone, she lives on. But may never return the long shadow and the river of blood and tears and mud and mourning that snuffed out so much beauty, the symbol of which was a young girl in bloom." ✉ *Pl. d'Anna Frank, Gràcia* Ⓜ *L3 Fontana.*

Plaça de la Vila de Gràcia

PLAZA/SQUARE | Originally named (until 2009) for the memorable Gràcia mayor Francesc Rius i Taulet, this is the barrio's most emblematic and historic square, marked by the handsome clock tower in its center. The tower, unveiled in 1864, is just over 110 feet tall. It has water fountains around its base, royal Bourbon crests over the fountains, and an iron balustrade atop the octagonal brick shaft stretching up to the clock and belfry. The symbol of Gràcia, the clock tower was bombarded by federal troops when Gràcia attempted to secede from the Spanish state during the 1870s. The Gràcia Casa de la Vila (town hall) at the lower end of the square is another building by Gaudí's assistant Francesc Berenguer.

Berenguer: Gaudí's Right Hand

Francesc Berenguer's role in Gaudí's work and the Moderniste movement, despite his leaving architecture school prematurely to work for Gaudí, was significant (if not decisive), and has been much debated by architects and Art Nouveau scholars. If Barcelona was Gaudí's grand canvas, Gràcia was Berenguer's. Though he was not legally licensed to sign his projects, Berenguer is known to have designed nearly every major building in Gràcia, including the Mercat de la Llibertat. The house at Carrer de l'Or 44 remains one of his greatest achievements, a vertical tour de force with pinnacles at the stress lines over rich stacks of wrought-iron balconies. The Gràcia Town Hall in Plaça Rius i Taulet and the Centre Moral Instructiu de Gràcia at Carrer Ros de Olano 9 are confirmed as his; the buildings on Carrer Gran de Gràcia at Nos. 15, 23, 35, 49, 51, 61, 77, and 81 are all either confirmed or suspected Berenguer designs. Even Gaudí's first domestic commission, Casa Vicens, owes its palm-leaf iron fence to Berenguer. When Berenguer died young in 1914, at the age of 47, Gaudí said he had "lost his right hand."

✉ *Pl. de la Vila de Gràcia, Gràcia* Ⓜ *Fontana, Gràcia (FGC).*

★ Plaça de la Virreina

PLAZA/SQUARE | The much-damaged and oft-restored church of Sant Joan de Gràcia anchors this lovely square where the Palau de la Virreina once stood; it was the summer residence of the same *virreina* (wife, or in this case, widow of a viceroy) whose 18th-century palace, the Palau de la Virreina, stands on the Rambla. The story of La Virreina, a young noblewoman widowed at an early age by the death of the elderly viceroy of Peru, is symbolized in the bronze sculpture atop the fountain in the center of the square: it portrays Ruth of the Old Testament, represented carrying the sheaves of wheat she was gathering when she learned of the death of her husband, Boaz. Ruth is the Old Testament paradigm of wifely fidelity to her husband's clan, a parallel to La Virreina—who spent her life doing good deeds with her husband's fortune. The rectorial residence at the back of the church is the work of Gaudí's perennial assistant and right-hand man Francesc Berenguer. ✉ *Pl. de la Virreina, Gràcia* Ⓜ *Joanic, Fontana.*

Plaça del Diamant

PLAZA/SQUARE | This little square is of enormous sentimental importance in Barcelona as the site of the opening and closing scenes of 20th-century Catalan writer Mercé Rodoreda's famous 1962 novel *La Plaça del Diamant.* Translated by the late American poet David Rosenthal as *The Time of the Doves,* it is the most widely translated and published Catalan novel of all time: a tender yet brutal story of a young woman devoured by the Spanish Civil War and, in a larger sense, by life itself. An angular and oddly disturbing steel and bronze statue in the square, by Xavier Medina-Campeny, portrays Colometa, the novel's protagonist, caught in the middle of her climactic scream. The bronze birds represent the pigeons that Colometa spent her life obsessively breeding; the male figure on the left pierced by bolts of steel is Quimet, her first love and husband, whom she met at a dance in this square and later lost in the war. Most of the people taking their ease at the cafés in the square will be unaware that some 40 feet below them is one of the largest air-raid shelters in Barcelona, hacked out by the residents of Gràcia during the bombardments of the civil war. ⊠ *Pl. del Diamant, Barcelona* Ⓜ *Fontana.*

★ Plaça Rovira i Trias

PLAZA/SQUARE | This charming little square and the story of Antoni Rovira i Trias shed much light on the true nature of Barcelona's eternal struggle with Madrid and Spanish central authority. Take a careful look at the map of Barcelona positioned at the feet of the bronze statue of the architect, who is seated on the bench, and you'll see a vision of what the city might have looked like if Madrid's (and the Spanish army's) candidate for the design of the Eixample, Ildefons Cerdà, had not been imposed over the plan devised by Rovira i Trias, the legitimate winner of the open competition for the commission. Rovira i Trias's plan shows an astral design radiating out from a central square while Cerdà's design established the emblematic uniformed blocks and wide boulevards that Eixample is known for. ⊠ *Pl. Rovira i Trias, Gràcia* Ⓜ *Joanic.*

🍽 Restaurants

This lively neighborhood is home to many of Barcelona's artists, musicians, and actors, and the bohemian atmosphere is reflected in the eclectic collection of restaurants ranging from street food to traditional tapas joints to thoroughly sophisticated dining.

Berbena

$$ | **CATALAN** | One of the first things you'll notice here is the scent of freshly baked bread, then you'll take in the open kitchen and cozy, ultra-contemporary interior, with oversized windows facing the street. The chef's modern spin on Catalan cuisine features Peruvian and Asian influences, and the dishes are made almost exclusively using locally sourced organic products. **Known for:** excellent selection of cheeses; interesting natural wines; seasonal, organic food. Ⓢ *Average main: €18* ⊠ *Minerva 6, Gràcia* ☎ *93/801–5987*

🌐 *berbenabcn.com* ⊗ *Closed Sun. and Mon.* Ⓜ *Diagonal.*

Botafumeiro

$$$$ | **SEAFOOD** | On Gràcia's main thoroughfare, Barcelona's best-known Galician restaurant has maritime motifs, snowy white tablecloths, wood paneling, and fleets of waiters in spotless white outfits serving über-fresh seafood, from raw platters to whole grilled fish to lobster paella. Prices aren't exactly wallet-friendly, but at the bar an assortment of *media ración* (half-ration) selections is available. **Known for:** seasonal wild fish; pricey but worth it; outstanding seafood. Ⓢ *Average main: €35* ⊠ *Gran de Gràcia 81, Gràcia* ☎ *93/218–4230* 🌐 *www. botafumeiro.es* Ⓜ *Metro: Fontana.*

Can Codina

$ | **CATALAN** | Founded in 1931, this rustic corner restaurant is a local favorite for the array of classic tapas and mains, along with Catalan "pizza"—flatbread topped with traditional ingredients such as caramelized onion and *butifara* (garlicky pork sausage) or *sobrasada* (cured pork sausage) with brie and honey. There's a small but decent wine list featuring several ecological wines. **Known for:** long list of croquetas; affordable prices; artisan cheese board. Ⓢ *Average main: €10* ⊠ *Torrent de l'Olla 20, Gràcia* ☎ *93/516– 1584* 🌐 *www.cancodina-barcelona.com* Ⓜ *Diagonal.*

La Panxa del Bisbe

$$ | **TAPAS** | Literally "The Bishop's Belly," this casual spot achieves a rare feat: putting modern international twists on Mediterranean cuisine without ruining it. La Panxa is a bit off the beaten path and thrives on a steady stream of repeat customers, who come for superb tapas and the restaurant's own craft beer on tap. **Known for:** affordable tasting menu; great tapas; good stop on way back from Park Güell. Ⓢ *Average main: €18* ⊠ *Torrent de les Flors 158, Gràcia* ☎ *93/213–7049* ⊗ *Closed Sun. and Mon.* Ⓜ *Lesseps.*

Park Güell was originally built to be a private garden community. One of the houses built here became Gaudí's residence from 1906 to 1926.

★ La Pepita

$$ | TAPAS | Don't be distracted by the graffitied walls and highly Instagrammable dishes: the innovative tapas at La Pepita lives up to the hipster hype. The room is dominated by long marble-topped bar—there are only a handful of tables in the narrow space—so it's best for couples or small groups. **Known for:** Spanish fried eggs and potatoes with foie gras; popcorn-topped ice cream; shrimp croquetas. $ *Average main: €20* ⊠ *Còrsega 343, Gràcia* ☎ *93/238–4893* ⊕ *www.lapepitabcn.com* Ⓜ *Diagonal.*

★ Lluritu

$$ | SEAFOOD | There's no need for complicated sauces here—the super-fresh grilled fish and seafood here speaks for itself, simply drizzled with olive oil or served with a lemon slice. The diminutive dining space is equally unadorned, with plain white walls and bright, somewhat industrial-style lighting; an illuminated panel above the bar lists what's available that day, which might include razor clams, octopus, sardines, and the restaurant's namesake fish. **Known for:** fresh grilled seafood; a local favorite; daily fish specials. $ *Average main: €22* ⊠ *Torrent de les Flors 71, Gràcia* ☎ *93/855–3866* ⊕ *www.lluritu.com* ⊗ *Closed Mon. and Tues. No lunch Wed.* Ⓜ *Joanic.*

Platerets

$$ | INTERNATIONAL | Seasonal Catalan cuisine with an Asian bent is the theme at this sleek, minimalist dining space, featuring high ceilings and large picture windows. Along with traditional tortillas and croquetas, the menu offers a variety of Asian-inspired bowls and small plates, such as crispy pork with *tonkatsu* sauce. **Known for:** Asian-style bowls; eggplant tempura with honey and lime; good options for vegans and vegetarians. $ *Average main: €22* ⊠ *Milà i Fontanals 29, Gràcia* ☎ *93/463–6585* ⊕ *www.platerets.com* ⊗ *Closed Sun. and Mon.* Ⓜ *Verdaguer.*

Coffee and Quick Bites

★ Nabucco Tiramisu

$ | **ITALIAN** | Top-notch coffee, homemade pastries and cakes, and healthy fare like avocado toasts make this organic café a particularly bustling spot at breakfast. For lunch or a casual dinner, there's a the long list of panini sandwiches, as well as excellent quiches and Italian-inspired salads. **Known for:** terrace seating right on the plaza; healthy menu; great coffee. [$] *Average main: €6* ✉ *Pl. de la Vila de Gràcia 8, Gràcia* ☎ *93/217–6101* 🌐 *nabuccotiramisu.com* [M] *Fontana, Gràcia (FGC).*

Paral·lelo Gelato

$ | **ICE CREAM** | Along with traditional pistachio and chocolate gelato, this artisan gelateria creates some truly out-there flavors, like black licorice and better-than-it sounds dark chocolate with anchovies, as well as seasonal specialties like Panettone. There's also a wide variety of vegan sorbets. **Known for:** great fruit flavors; take-out only; natural ingredients. [$] *Average main: €4* ✉ *Sèneca 18, Gràcia* 🌐 *parallelogelato.com* ☞ *No seating, to-go only* [M] *Diagonal, Gràcia (FGC).*

Hotels

Casagrand Luxury Suites

$$$$ | **HOTEL** | **FAMILY** | Perfect for large families and groups, this apartment-hotel features sprawling four- and five-bedroom luxury apartments, plus a more affordable one-bedroom penthouse, in a stunning 1929 domed building right on Avenue Diagonal. **Pros:** rooftop pool (seasonal); great location; spacious, well-designed apartments. **Cons:** limited services; limited reception hours; only the penthouse has private outdoor space. [$] *Rooms from: €800* ✉ *Av. Diagonal 478, Gràcia* ☎ *93/522–2748* 🌐 *www.casagrand.com* 🛏 *13 apartments* 🍴 *Free Breakfast* [M] *Diagonal.*

Hotel Casa Fuster

$$$$ | **HOTEL** | This luxury hotel offers one of two chances (the other is the Hotel España) to stay in a Modernist masterpiece designed by Lluís Domènech i Montaner, architect of the iconic Palau de la Música Catalana. **Pros:** well situated for exploring both Gràcia and the Eixample; sprawling rooftop terrace with city and mountain views; large rooms with luxury-level amenities. **Cons:** service can be a bit stiff; maybe too much Modernism for some; rooms facing Passeig de Gràcia could use better soundproofing. [$] *Rooms from: €300* ✉ *Passeig de Gràcia 132, Gràcia* ☎ *93/255–3000* 🌐 *www.hotelcasafuster.com* 🛏 *105 rooms* 🍴 *No Meals* [M] *Diagonal.*

La Casa Del Sol

$ | **HOTEL** | In the heart of Gràcia alongside the lively Plaça del Sol, this property is part of the Sonder chain, a hybrid hotel-rental agency that keeps rates low by eschewing a full-time staff for contactless check-in and digital-only concierge service. **Pros:** private seasonal rooftop with plunge pool and bar; good on-site vegetarian restaurant; affordable base in Gràcia. **Cons:** no full-time staff; entry and digital check-in/out requires multiple codes; rooms facing the plaza can be noisy. [$] *Rooms from: €68* ✉ *Pl. del Sol 23, Gràcia* ☎ *608/421–102* 🌐 *www.sonder.com* 🛏 *18 rooms* 🍴 *No Meals* [M] *Fontana.*

★ Seventy Barcelona

$$ | **HOTEL** | On the southern border of Gràcia, a short stroll to the Passeig de Gràcia, this boutique hotel is in an ideal spot for travelers who like to be close to the action, without being in the thick of it. **Pros:** good location; good quality for the price; thoughtful staff. **Cons:** busy street outside; outdoor pool is small; few rooms with patios or balconies. [$] *Rooms from: €160* ✉ *Còrsega 344–352, Barcelona* ☎ *93/012–1270* 🌐 *www.seventybarcelona.com* 🛏 *145 rooms* 🍴 *No Meals* [M] *Diagonal.*

Ⓨ Nightlife

With its bohemian vibe, Gràcia welcomes revelers of all stripes looking for easygoing pleasures. On any given night, people flood the district's plazas to snack on tapas paired with beer or wine, but for the slightly more adventurous, exploring the maze-like back alleyways and side streets provides ample rewards: There are some standout upscale wine bars and speakeasy-inspired *coctelerias* that coexist in perfect harmony with the neighborhood dives.

BARS

★ Elephanta

COCKTAIL LOUNGES | Diminutive in size but huge in personality and warmth, Elephanta is that rare neighborhood spot that offers a little something for everyone. Patrons enjoy an extensive menu of quality gins and seasonal fruity cocktails in a dimly lighted retro space peppered with comfy mismatched furnishings. Music varies though the ambience is always chill. ⊠ *Torrent d'en Vidalet 37, Gràcia* ☎ *93/237–6906* ⊕ *elephanta.cat* Ⓜ *Joanic.*

★ 14 De La Rosa

COCKTAIL LOUNGES | An illuminated red globe marks this speakeasy-style haunt, tucked away on a narrow side street a block from the busy Carrer del Torrent de les Flors. Inside, you can cozy up to the L-shaped marble bar and let the bow-tied British owner, a veteran of London's acclaimed Chiltern Firehouse, mix a classic cocktail that suits your fancy. With its cool jazz soundtrack and tables topped with flickering candles, the space oozes sophistication but the vibe is relaxed thanks to the friendly staff. ⊠ *Martínez de la Rosa 14, Gràcia* ⊕ *14delarosa.com* Ⓜ *Fontana, Diagonal.*

★ La Graciosa

WINE BARS | This unpretentious natural wine bar has a wonderful team of sommeliers who are keen to share their knowledge. There's no formal wine list; just describe what you like and they'll bring you a glass—or you can browse the bottles from small Mediterranean producers that line the red-brick walls. The best seats are out on the back patio: a plant-filled oasis in the heart of this bustling barrio. ⊠ *Milà i Fontanals 88, Gràcia* ☎ *93/663–7997* Ⓜ *Joanic.*

La Rovira

BARS | With a rotating selection of 15 craft beers on tap—including local Catalan brews, international varieties, and its own brand of IPA—as well as a wide selection by the bottle, this lively spot is a beer-lover's dream. There's also a good house vermouth and a nice array of tapas and sandwiches. It has a fantastic setting, on the corner of pretty Plaça de Rovira i Trias. ⊠ *Rabassa 23, Gràcia* ☎ *93/463–8788* Ⓜ *Joanic.*

★ Old Fashioned

COCKTAIL LOUNGES | Reminiscent of a '50s-style gin joint—black and white with red quilted booths and framed prints—this small-but-swanky bar regularly draws in the crowds due in large part to entertaining master mixologists (nattily dressed in suspenders and ties) and their out-of-this-world experimental takes on cocktail classics. ⊠ *Santa Teresa 1, Gràcia* ☎ *93/368–5277* ⊕ *cocktailsbarcelona. oldfashionedbcn.com/wp* Ⓜ *Diagonal.*

⬤ Shopping

Cute and cozy Gràcia has evolved into Barcelona's most eclectic shopping destination, with lots of creatively conceived, owner-run design and fashion shops. Major Spanish brands line Gran de Gràcia, the neighborhood's main drag, while Carrer d'Astúries, Carrer Verdi, Carrer Torrent d'Olla, Carrer Torrijos, and Carrer de Bonavista abound in independent fashion and jewelry boutiques, artsy cafés, and gourmet food stores.

BEAUTY

Herbolari del Cel

OTHER HEALTH & BEAUTY | Gràcia's "Herbolarium from Heaven" is widely considered among the best in Barcelona for herbal remedies, teas, spices, oils, natural cures and treatments, and cosmetics of all kinds. A mere deep breath of air here will probably cure whatever ails you. ✉ *Travessera de Gràcia 120, Gràcia* ☎ *93/218-7331* ⊕ *www.herbolaridelcel. com* Ⓜ *Fontana.*

CLOTHING

★ BeTheStore

DEPARTMENT STORE | This expansive concept store stocks a bit of everything, from men's and women's clothing and accessories to home goods, spices, teas, and soaps, plus a wide range of Spanish-language books and games. ✉ *Bonavista 7, Gràcia* ☎ *93/218-8949* ⊕ *www.bethestore.com* Ⓜ *Diagonal.*

Colmillo de Morsa

WOMEN'S CLOTHING | Local designers Elisabet Vallecillo and Javier Blanco founded this sustainable women's fashion brand, whose casual minimalist pieces are crafted entirely in Barcelona using only natural organic fabrics such as cotton and silk. ✉ *Vic 15, Gràcia* ☎ *6875-28864* ⊕ *www. colmillodemorsa.com.*

FOOD

Planeta Te

OTHER SPECIALTY STORE | With more than 1,000 products on offer, this must be widest variety of teas and infusions available in Barcelona. Planeta Te sell herbs and blends by weight from pretty tin boxes and drawers that line the walls. You will also find organic tea bags, a colorful range of teapots and other tea-making paraphernalia, and a seductive aroma as soon as you enter this old-fashioned shop. ✉ *Asturies 50, Gràcia* ☎ *93/210-3922* ⊕ *planetate.es* Ⓜ *Fontana.*

TOYS

Bateau Lune

TOYS | FAMILY | Crafts, disguises, puzzles, games, and a thousand things to make you want to be a kid again are on display in this creative child-oriented gift shop on one of Gràcia's most emblematic squares. ✉ *Pl. de la Virreina 7, Gràcia* ☎ *93/218-6907* ⊕ *www.bateaulune.com* Ⓜ *Fontana, Joanic.*

Chapter 10

UPPER BARCELONA

SARRIÀ, PEDRALBES, TIBIDABO, AND VALLVIDRERA

Updated by
Jared Lubarsky

⊙ Sights	🍴 Restaurants	🛏 Hotels	🛍 Shopping	🍸 Nightlife
★★★☆☆	★★★★☆	★★★☆☆	★★★☆☆	★★☆☆☆

NEIGHBORHOOD SNAPSHOT

TOP EXPERIENCES

■ **Monestir de Pedralbes:** Meditate in the three-story cloister surrounding a lush garden in this convent founded in 1326 then check out the treasures in the nuns' dormitory.

■ **Torre Bellesguard:** Walk up to one of Gaudí's lesser known and less-trafficked masterpieces, for a fascinating architectural gem and incredible views. A guided tour really enhances the experience so book ahead.

■ **Bar Tomás** Fill up on *patatas bravas* and *patatas bravas y salsa con allioli* (as well as other traditional tapas) widely considered the best in Barcelona.

■ **Tibidabo:** take the funicular up to this mountain overlooking Barcelona and check out the neo-Gothic church and amusement park.

GETTING HERE

Sarrià is best reached on the FGC (Ferrocarril de la Generalitat de Catalunya) line, which is integrated with the city metro system, though a cut above. From Plaça de Catalunya, all the FGC trains (except those bound for Tibidabo) stop at Sarrià; only local trains branch off from there to the terminus at Reina Elisenda. The trip uptown takes about 15 minutes. By bus, you can take the V7, which runs from Plaça d'Espanya to Sarrià, or the No. 64, which takes a somewhat roundabout route from Barceloneta to Pedralbes, with a stop at Plaça Sarrià.

PLANNING YOUR TIME

An exploration of Sarrià and Pedralbes is a three- to four-hour jaunt, including at least an hour in the monastery. Count four or five with lunch included. Plan to visit the monastery in the morning. Bar Tomás serves its famous potatoes with *allioli* (spicy garlic mayonnaise) 1–4 pm and 7–10 pm, another key timing consideration, while the Foix de Sarrià pastry emporium is open until 9 pm.

OFF THE BEATEN PATH

Written records of Vallvidrera, a little village on the heights above Barcelona, date to the 10th century but it wasn't until the 19th century that the city's well-to-do "discovered" its attractions—with its palpably cleaner air it was an ideal location for their summer homes. From Plaça Pep Ventura, in front of the Moderniste funicular station, there are superb views of the city; at the east end of the village is the trailhead for a good forest walk along the Collserola ridge to Tibidabo. Vallvidrera can be reached from the Peu de Funicular train stop and the Vallvidrera funicular (beware: the first cars on the FGC trains do not open at Peu de Funicular), by road, or on foot from Tibidabo or Vil·la Joana. The cozy Can Trampa at the center of town in Plaça de Vallvidrera, nearby El Racó de Collserola, and Can Martí, are good choices for lunch.

To the folks who live here, Upper Barcelona, aka the Zona Alta, is a broad swathe of upscale residential neighborhoods—tree-shaded streets, manicured lawns, blocks of flats with concierges—extending from the Diagonal to the Collserola foothills. There are also a few gems of interest that that should be—time permitting—on any visitor's itinerary.

Sarrià, the centerpiece here, was originally a country village, where Barcelona's 19th-century well-to-do built splendid, Moderniste, family mansions to escape the heat and industrial vapors below. Absorbed by the city in 1921, the village—15 minutes by FGC commuter train from Plaça de Catalunya—now has a unique mix of populations: old-timers who speak mainly Catalan amongst themselves and go "down to Barcelona" to shop; a creative cohort of writers, artists, and designers; and expats, who prize the neighborhood for its multicultural vibe and its proximity to the international schools.

Cross Avinguda Foix (named for J. V. Foix, the famous Catalan poet, who was born in Sarrià), on the west side of the village, and you're in Pedralbes, site of the 14th-century Monestir (Monastery) de Pedralbes, with one of the most beautiful cloisters in Europe. Other points of interest here include Gaudí's Pavellons de la Finca Güell on Avinguda de Pedralbes, and the gardens of the Palau Reial de Pedralbes, a 20-minute walk downhill from the monastery.

To the east of Sarrià lie the subdistricts of Sant Gervasi and Tibidabo, with its CosmoCaixa hands-on science museum, its spectacular lookout over the city, and—for visitors with youngsters in tow—the funicular to the amusement park at the very top.

 Sights

Col·legi de les Teresianes
NOTABLE BUILDING | Built for the Reverend Mothers of St. Theresa in 1889, when Gaudí was still occasionally using straight lines, this former operating school has upper floors that are reminiscent of Berenguer's apartment at Carrer de l'Or 44, with its steep peaks and verticality. Hired to take over for another architect, Gaudí found his freedom of movement somewhat limited in this project. The dominant theme here is the architect's use of steep, narrow catenary arches and Mudejar exposed-brick pillars.

The most striking effects are on the second floor, where two rows of a dozen catenary arches run the width of the building, each of them unique, because, as Gaudí explained, no two things in nature are identical. The brick columns are crowned with T-shaped brick capitals (for St. Theresa). Look down at the marble doorstep for the inscription by mystic writer and poet Santa Teresa de Ávila (1515–82), the much-quoted "todo se pasa" (all things pass). The Col·legi is a private secondary school, and normally not open to visitors, but the sisters sometimes organize guided group visits on request. ✉ *Ganduxer 85, Sant Gervasi* ☎ *93/212–3354* ⊕ *ganduxer.escolateresiana.com* ⊘ *Closed Sat. and Sun.* Ⓜ *La Bonanova, Les Tres Torres (FGC).*

CosmoCaixa–Museu de la Ciència Fundació "La Caixa"

SCIENCE MUSEUM | FAMILY | Young scientific minds work overtime in this interactive science museum, just below Tibidabo. Among the many displays designed for children seven and up are the Geological Wall, a history of rocks and rock formations; the digital Planetarium; and the Underwater Forest, showcasing a slice of the Amazonian rain forest in a large greenhouse. ✉ *Carrer Isaac Newton 26, Sant Gervasi* ☎ *93/212–6050* ⊕ *cosmocaixa.org* 🎟 *€6 (plus €4 per interactive activity inside); accompanied children under 16 free* ⊘ *Closed Mon.* Ⓜ *FGC line L7 to Av. de Tibidabo and Bus #196 or Tramvía Blau.*

Mirador Torre de Collserola

NOTABLE BUILDING | The Collserola communications tower was designed by Norman Foster for the 1992 Olympics. An industrial spike on an otherwise pristine wooded skyline, it was not universally admired. A vertigo-inducing elevator ride takes you to the observation deck on the 10th floor. Take the FGC S1, S2, or S5 line to Peu del Funicular (note that the cars at the front of the train don't open at this station), then the funicular up to Vallvidrera; from the village of Vallvidrera it's a pleasant walk to the tower. Ongoing renovations have led to the tower being

closed, so check the website before you go. ✉ *Ctra. de Vallvidrera al Tibidabo s/n, Tibidabo* ☎ *93/406–9354* ⊕ *www.torredecollserola.com* 🎟 *€5.60* ⊘ *Closed weekdays* ☞ *Guided tours on weekends 10–2* Ⓜ *Peu del Funicular (FGC).*

Museu Verdaguer–Vil·la Joana

HISTORIC HOME | Catalonian priest and poet Jacint Verdaguer died in this house in 1902. Considered the national poet of Catalonia and the most revered and beloved voice of the Catalan "Renaixença" of the 19th century, Verdaguer succumbed to tuberculosis and a general mental collapse. In his most famous work, *La Atlàntida* (1877), which eventually became a Manuel de Falla opera-oratorio, he used the myth of Atlantis to prefigure the prehistoric origins of his native Catalonia.

Verdaguer's death provoked massive mourning. Indeed, his funeral was one of the most heavily attended events in Barcelona history, comparable only to Gaudí's in spontaneity and emotion. On display at Vil·la Joana is the book containing the signatures of the thousands who took part, among them, Pablo Picasso.

The museum, which is part of the MUHBA (Museu d'Història de Barcelona: Barcelona History Museum), is essentially an archival homage to Verdaguer's life and work. Unless you happen to be besotted with 19th-century Catalan poetry, this lovely Moderniste building, originally a *masia* (country house), is best appreciated from the outside, as you pass by. ✉ *Vil·la Joana, Ctra. de l'Església 104, Vallvidrera* ☎ *93/256–2122* ⊕ *www.barcelona.cat/museuhistoria/en/heritages/els-espais-del-muhba/muhba-villa-joana* 🎟 *Free* ⊘ *Closed Mon., Wed., and Fri.* Ⓜ *Baixador de Vallvidrera (FGC) and funicular.*

Pavellons de la Finca Güell–Càtedra Gaudí

NOTABLE BUILDING | Work on the Finca began in 1883 as an extension of Count

Eusebi Güell's family estate. Gaudí, the count's architect of choice, was commissioned to do the gardens and the two entrance pavilions (1884–87); the rest of the project was never finished. The Pavellons (pavilions) now belong to the University of Barcelona, which has handed them over to the Municipal Institute for Urban Landscape (IMPUiQV) for ten years (2015–2024). During this period, IMPUiQV will carry out a comprehensive restoration of Gaudí's work. Depending on the state of the renovation work, the complex may be open for group visits, heritage visits, as well as cultural and educational activities but will largely remain closed. The fierce wrought-iron dragon gate is Gaudí's reference to the Garden of the Hesperides, as described by national poet Jacint Verdaguer's epic poem L'Atlàntida (1877)—the Iliad of Catalonia's historic-mythic origins. ■ TIP→ Entrance is by appointment only. ✉ Av. Pedralbes 7, Pedralbes ☎ 9393/317–7652 guided tours Ⓜ Palau Reial (Metro L3).

★ Real Monestir de Santa Maria de Pedralbes

RELIGIOUS BUILDING | This marvel of a monastery, named for its original white stones (pedres albes, from the Latin petras albas), is really a convent, founded in 1326 for the Franciscan order of Poor Clares by Reina (Queen) Elisenda. The three-story Gothic cloister, one of the finest in Europe, surrounds a lush garden. The day cells, where the nuns spent their mornings praying, sewing, and studying, circle the arcaded courtyard.

The Capella de Sant Miquel, just to the right of the entrance, has murals painted in 1346 by Catalan master Ferrer Bassa. Look for the letters spelling out "No m'oblidi/ digui-li a Joan/ a quatre de setembre de 1415" ("Do not forget me / tell John / September 4, 1415") scratched between the figures of St. Francis and St. Clare (with book and quill). While the true meaning of the

message is unknown, one theory is that it was written by a brokenhearted novice.

The nuns' upstairs dormitory contains the convent's treasures: paintings, liturgical objects, and seven centuries of artistic and cultural patrimony. Temporary exhibits are displayed in this space. The refectory. where the Poor Clares dined in silence, has a pulpit used for readings, while wall inscriptions exhort Silentium ("Silence"), Audi tacens ("Listen carefully"), and Considera morientem ("Consider, we are dying"). Notice the fading mural in the corner, and the broken paving tiles—according to unsubstantiated legend, the result of the heavy cannon positioned here during the 1809 Napoleonic occupation.

The monastery is now a museum, housing permanent exhibitions on its own art and legacy as well as third-party special exhibitions from time to time. ■ TIP→ There are occasional open-air concerts in the cloister, especially of Medieval music; check local event listings and book a seat if you can. ✉ Baixada del Monestir 9, Pedralbes ☎ 93/256–3434 ⊕ monestirpedralbes.bcn.cat/en ☎ €5; free for visitors under 16, and with the Barcelona Card; free Sun. after 3 pm, and 1st Sun. of every month ⊗ Closed Mon. Ⓜ Reina Elisenda (FGC).

Sarrià

NEIGHBORHOOD | Originally a cluster of farms and country houses, Sarrià is now a premier residential neighborhood overlooking Barcelona from the hills. Start an exploration at the main square, Plaça de Sarrià—the site of Tuesday antique and bric-a-brac markets; Sunday morning sardana dances; Christmas pageants; and concerts, book fairs, and artisanal food and wine events at various times during the year. The 10th-century Romanesque Church of Sant Vicenç dominates this square, and its bell tower, illuminated on weekend nights, is truly impressive. Across Passeig de la Reina Elisenda

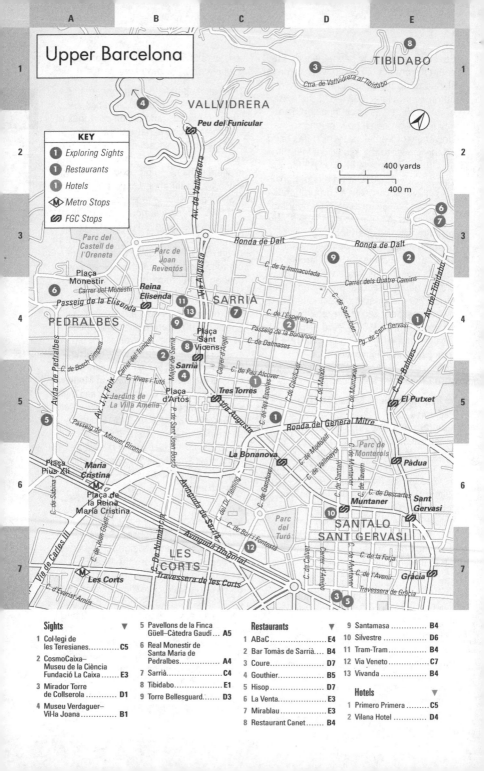

Upper Barcelona

KEY

- **1** Exploring Sights
- **1** Restaurants
- **1** Hotels
- Ⓜ Metro Stops
- Ⓖ FGC Stops

TIBIDABO

Ctra. de Vallvidrera al Tibidabo

VALLVIDRERA

Peu del Funicular

Parc del Castell de l'Oreneta

Parc de Joan Reventós

Ronda de Dalt

Ronda de Dalt

C. de la Immaculada

Carrer dels Quatre Camins

Plaça Monestir

Carrer del Monestir

Reina Elisenda

SARRIÀ

Passeig de la Elisenda

C. de l'Esperança

C. de Sant Joan

PEDRALBES

Plaça Sant Vicens

Passeig de la Bonanova

C. de Dalmases

Pg. de Sant Gervasi

Av. de Pedralbes

C. de Bosch Gimpera

Carrer del Trinquet

Major de Sarrià

Carrer d'Augi

C. de Pau Alcover

C. de les Escoles

C. de Galdàcano

C. de Maroli

C. de Muntaner

Av. del Tibidabo

C. de Balmes

Sarrià

C. Vives i Tutó

Tres Torres

Via Augusta

El Putxet

Jardins de La Vila Amelia

Plaça d'Artós

P. de Sant Joan Bosco

Via Augusta

Ronda del General Mitre

Passeig de Manuel Girona

La Bonanova

C. de Modolell

C. de Vallmajor

Parc de Monterols

Pàdua

Plaça Pius XII

Maria Cristina

C. de Sabina

C. de Joan Güell

Ⓜ Plaça de la Reina Maria Cristina

Avinguda de Sarrià

C. del Dr. Fleming

C. de Ganduxer

C. de Bori i Fontestà

Parc del Turó

C. de Santaló

C. de Muntaner

C. de Descartes

Muntaner

Sant Gervasi

SANTALO SANT GERVASI

Via de Carles III

C. d'Evarist Arnús

Ⓜ Les Corts

LES CORTS

Avinguda Diagonal

Travessera de les Corts

C. de Calvet

C. d'Amigo

C. de Muntaner

C. de la Fatra

C. de l'Avenir

Gràcia

Travessera de Gràcia

0   400 yards
0   400 m

Sights ▼

1 Col·legi de les Teresianes............**C5**

2 CosmoCaixa–Museu de la Ciència Fundació La Caixa.......**E3**

3 Mirador Torre de Collserola **D1**

4 Museu Verdaguer–Vil·la Joana..............**B1**

5 Pavellons de la Finca Güell–Càtedra Gaudí… **A5**

6 Real Monestir de Santa Maria de Pedralbes................**A4**

7 Sarrià....................**C4**

8 Tibidabo.................**E1**

9 Torre Bellesguard.......**D3**

Restaurants ▼

1 ABaC....................**E4**

2 Bar Tomàs de Sarrià.... **B4**

3 Coure....................**D7**

4 Gouthier.................**B5**

5 Hisop....................**D7**

6 La Venta.................**E3**

7 Mirablau.................**E3**

8 Restaurant Canet.......**B4**

9 Santamasa **B4**

10 Silvestre **D6**

11 Tram-Tram..............**B4**

12 Via Veneto **C7**

13 Vivanda................**B4**

Hotels ▼

1 Primero Primera **C5**

2 Vilana Hotel **D4**

An Upper Barcelona Tour

To see more of **Sarrià**, take an L7 train on the FGC line (Ferrocarrils de la Generalitat de Catalunya) from Plaça Catalunya to Avinguda Tibidabo station in Plaça Kennedy, atop Carrer de Balmes. Once there, cross Balmes. The first building on the right, at the foot of Avinguda del Tibidabo, is La Rotonda, or Torre Andreu, built in 1906 and notable for the Art Nouveau ceramic ornamentation on its upper facade.

Stroll around, and then take the Tramvía Blau (Blue Trolley) from just above La Rotonda. After passing the imposing white Casa Roviralta, it drops you at Plaça del Doctor Andreu, where a funicular climbs to the heights of **Tibidabo**. (If the Blue Trolley is out of service, the #196 municipal bus follows the same route.)

Plaça del Doctor Andreu has several restaurants, the best of which is La Venta.

From Tibidabo, you can take a pleasant walk through the Serra de Collserola Natural Park to the Torre de Collserola via the hilltop village of **Vallvidrera**. Ride the cablecar one stop down to the Funicular de Vallvidrera platform (press the button inside the car to request the stop), which is along the **Carretera de les Aigües.** This level, 9-km (5½-mile) path through the park has lovely city views and is popular with dog walkers, runners, and bikers. To return to Barcelona, retrace your steps, take the cablecar down to Peu del Funicular, and transfer to line S1 or S2 on the FGC.

from the church is the Mercat de Sarrià, a Moderniste gem built in 1911, with its intricate brickwork facade, wrought-iron girders and stained-glass windows.

On the cobblestone street behind the Mercat is the Centre i Teatre de Sarrià (✉ *Pare Miquel de Sarrià 8* ☎ *93/03–9772)* a fixture in the village for the past 125 years, with a lovely 340-seat theater (it has red plush seats and gilded fixtures) that hosts a wide range of programs, films, dance performances, and drama—and two or three times a year, professional opera. The Centre also has an indoor café and a pleasant terrace fronting the theater, just right for a short break in your village ramble.

From the square, cut through the Placeta del Roser to the left of the church to the elegant Town Hall (1896) in the Plaça de la Vila. Note the buxom bronze sculpture of Pomona, goddess of fruit, by famed

Sarrià sculptor Josep Clarà (1878–1958). Follow tiny Carrer dels Paletes, to the left of the Town Hall (the saint enshrined in the niche is Sant Antoni, patron saint of *paletes,* or bricklayers). Turn right on Major de Sarrià, the High Street of the village and then left onto Carrer Canet. The two-story row houses on the right—built for workers on the village estates—and the houses opposite at Nos. 15, 21, and 23 are among the few remaining original village structures in Sarrià.

Turn right at the first corner on Carrer Cornet i Mas and walk two blocks down to Carrer Jaume Piquet. On the left is No. 30, Barcelona's most perfect small-format Moderniste house. Thought to be the work of architect Domènech i Montaner, it features faux-medieval upper windows, wrought-iron grillwork, floral and fruited ornamentation, and organically curved and carved wooden doors either by or inspired by Gaudí

A quiet space for reflection; the courtyard of the Monestir de Pedralbes

himself. The next stop down Cornet i Mas is Sarrià's prettiest square, Plaça Sant Vicens, a leafy space ringed by old Sarrià houses and centered on a statue of Sarrià's patron St. Vicenç, portrayed (as always) beside the millstone used to sink him to the bottom of the Mediterranean after he was martyred in Valencia in AD 302. Can Pau, the café on the lower corner with Carrer Mañé i Flaquer, is the local hangout, once a haven for authors Gabriel García Marquez and Mario Vargas Llosa, who lived in Sarrià in the late 1960s and early 1970s.

Other Sarrià landmarks include the two Foix de Sarrià pastry shops, one at Plaça Sarrià 12–13 and the other at Major de Sarrià 57, above Bar Tomás. The late J. V. Foix (1893–1987), son of the shop's founder, was one of the great Catalan poets of the 20th century, a key player in keeping the Catalan language alive during the 40-year Franco regime. The shop on Major de Sarrià has a bronze plaque identifying the house as the poet's birthplace and inscribed with one of his most

memorable verses, translated as, "Every love is latent in the other love / every language is the juice of a common tongue / every country touches the fatherland of all / every faith will be the lifeblood of a higher faith." ✉ *Sarrià*.

Tibidabo

VIEWPOINT | FAMILY | One of Barcelona's two promontories bears a distinctive name, generally translated as "To Thee I Will Give." It refers to the Catalan legend that this was the spot from which Satan tempted Christ with all the riches of the Earth below (namely, Barcelona). On a clear day, the views from this 1,789-foot peak are legendary.

Tibidabo's skyline is marked by a neo-Gothic church, the work of Enric Sagnier in 1902, and—off to one side, near the village of Vallvidrera—the 854-foot communications tower, the Torre de Collserola, designed by Sir Norman Foster. If you're with kids, take the San Francisco–style Tramvía Blau (Blue Trolley) from Plaça Kennedy to the overlook at the top, and transfer to the funicular to the 100-year-old amusement park at the summit. ✉ *Pl. Tibidabo 3–4, Tibidabo* ☎ *93/211–7942 amusement park* ⊕ *www.tibidabo.cat* ✉ *Amusement park €28.50* Ⓜ *Av. Tibidabo (FGC L7), then Tramvía Blau or Bus #196.*

★ Torre Bellesguard

HISTORIC HOME | For an extraordinary Gaudí experience, visit this private residence. It was built between 1900 and 1909 over the ruins of the summer palace of the last of the sovereign count-kings of the Catalan-Aragonese realm, Martí I l'Humà (Martin I the Humane), whose reign ended in 1410. In homage to this medieval history, Gaudí endowed the house with a tower, gargoyles, and crenellated battlements. The rest—the catenary arches, the *trencadís* (pieces of polychromatic ceramic tile) in the facade, the stained-glass windows—is pure Art Nouveau.

Look for the red and gold Catalan *senyera* (banner) on the tower, topped by the four-armed Greek cross Gaudí often used. Over the front door is the inscription *"Sens pecat fou concebuda"* ("Without sin was she conceived"), referring to the Immaculate Conception of the Virgin Mary. On either side of the front door are benches with trencadís of playful fish bearing the crimson *quatre barres* (four bars) of the Catalan flag as well as the Corona d'Aragó (Crown of Aragón).

Guided tours in English available every day at 11 am and 1 pm. The visit includes access to the roof, which Gaudí designed to resemble a dragon, along with the gardens, patio, and stables.

■**TIP**➔ **Reservations are required for the highly recommended guided tour (reserva@ bellesguardgaudi.com).** ✉ *Carrer Bellesguard 16–20, Sant Gervasi* ☎ *93/250–4093* ⊕ *www.bellesguardgaudi.com* ✉ *Guided tour €10 (children under 8 free)* ⊘ *Closed Mon.* Ⓜ *Av. Tibidabo (FGC).*

🍴 Restaurants

Take an excursion to the upper reaches of town for an excellent selection of bars, cafés, and restaurants. You'll also find cool summer evening breezes and a sense of well-heeled village life.

The 1,640-foot mountain Tibidabo has spectacular views and the restaurants here offer some of Barcelona's best cuisine. Prices, however, can be as high as the mountain itself.

ABaC

$$$$ | **CONTEMPORARY** | Chef Jordi Cruz is a celebrity in Spain, and pulls out all the stops with a panoply of artfully-presented dishes that vary from season to season; no expense or effort is ever spared. ABaC is open only for dinner, and serves only a set tasting menu, which you can request with or without paired wines. **Known for:** elegant setting in a boutique hotel; creative in-season dishes; celebrity chef. Ⓢ *Average main: €250* ✉ *Av. del Tibidabo 1–7, Tibidabo* ☎ *93/319–6600* ⊕ *www. abacrestaurant.com/en* Ⓜ *Tibidabo.*

Bar Tomás de Sarrià

$ | **TAPAS** | Famous for its *patatas bravas amb allioli* (potatoes with fiery hot sauce and allioli, an emulsion of crushed garlic and olive oil), accompanied by freezing mugs of San Miguel beer, this old-fashioned Sarrià classic is worth seeking out. You'll have to elbow your way to a tiny table and shout to be heard over the hubbub, but the effort is richly rewarding. **Known for:** sidewalk tables for snacking alfresco; noisy, friendly neighborhood vibe; selection of tapas. Ⓢ *Average main: €8* ✉ *Major de Sarrià 49, Sarrià* ☎ *93/203–1077* ⊕ *www.eltomasdesarria. com* ⊘ *Closed Sun. and part of Aug.* Ⓜ *Sarrià (FGC).*

Coure

$$$ | **MEDITERRANEAN** | *Cuina d'autor* is a Catalan phrase for chef-led original cooking, and that is exactly what you

10

Upper Barcelona

get in this smart subterranean space on restaurant-centric Passatge Marimón, just above the Diagonal thoroughfare. The upstairs bar gets busy with a post-work crowd of food-loving locals, but downstairs is a cool, minimalist restaurant. **Known for:** sushi bar-style counter seating with view of the kitchen; artistic presentation; tasting menu with wine pairing. $ *Average main: €23* ✉ *Passatge Marimón 20, Sant Gervasi* ☎ *93/200–7532* ⊗ *Closed Sun. and Mon., and 3 wks in Aug.* Ⓜ *Diagonal.*

Gouthier
$$ | **SEAFOOD** | Weather permitting, this French-inspired oyster bar puts tables and banquettes out in the Plaça Sant Vicenç, arguably the prettiest square in Sarrià. Make your choice among 12 varieties of oysters—especially the plump sweet ones from Normandy—shucked and served fresh with rye bread and pats of French butter, as well as other more elaborate tapas dishes. **Known for:** pleasant terrace; good wine list; Spanish oysters from the Delta de l'Ebro. $ *Average main: €18* ✉ *Mañé i Flaquer 8, Sarrià* ✛ *Located on Pl. Vicenç de Sarrià* ☎ *93/205–9969* ⊕ *www.gouthier.es* ⊗ *Closed Sun. No lunch Tues.–Thurs.* Ⓜ *Sarrià (FGC).*

Hisop
$$$ | **CATALAN** | The interior design of Oriol Ivern's small restaurant is minimalist, but his cooking is intricate—and wonderful. This is budget-conscious fine dining that avoids exotic ingredients but lifts local dishes to exciting new heights; the menu changes four times a year to take advantage of what's best in season. **Known for:** local, seasonal ingredients; extensive well-chosen wine list; great value tasting menu. $ *Average main: €27* ✉ *Passatge de Marimón 9, Sant Gervasi* ☎ *93/241–3233* ⊕ *www.hisop.com* ⊗ *Closed Sun. and 1st wk of Jan.* Ⓜ *Diagonal.*

La Venta
$$ | **SPANISH** | Come up to Tibidabo for the great views, but budget time at the restaurant La Venta on Plaça Doctor Andrea, across the square from where the vistas unfold, for lunch in a charming *Moderniste* setting. For an unusual appetizer, try the *uni* (sea urchin) *au gratin.* **Known for:** the views; half-portion menu options; Catalan-style seafood. $ *Average main: €15* ✉ *Pl. Doctor Andreu s/n, Tibidabo* ☎ *93/212–6455* ⊕ *www.laventarestaurant.com* ⊗ *Closed Sun. in Aug. No dinner Sun.* Ⓜ *FGC L7 Tibidabo, then Tramvía Blau or Bus #196.*

Mirablau
$ | **SPANISH** | This bar-restaurant on the Mirador de Tibidabo, with its panoramic view of the city, is a popular late-night hangout, especially after 11:30 when it becomes a disco. The menu is strong on sandwiches and tapas, but includes delicacies like grilled sea bass and cod cheeks with roasted red peppers and garlic mousseline. **Known for:** spectacular setting; gin cocktails on the terrace; generous portions. $ *Average main: €13* ✉ *Pl. Doctor Andreu s/n, Tibidabo* ☎ *93/418–5879* ⊕ *www.mirablaubcn.com* Ⓜ *FCG L7 Tibidabo, then Tramvía Blau or Bus #196.*

Restaurant Canet
$$ | **CATALAN** | A fixture in the neighborhood for over 30 years, Canet is a cozy (just 12 tables, seating about 40) little hideaway with a retro decor vibe, much enjoyed by the locals. The *menú del dia* (prix-fixe lunch) is a bit pricy, at €15.75, but the deft touch here, with variations on traditional Catalan cooking, makes it well worthwhile. **Known for:** oxtail stew; warm, friendly atmosphere; pan amb tomaquet (toast rubbed with tomato and garlic). $ *Average main: €15* ✉ *Carrer Canet 38, Sarrià* ☎ *93/205–0768* ⊕ *restaurant-canet-barcelona.makro.rest* ⊗ *Closed Sun.* Ⓜ *Sarrià (FCG).*

Continued on page 234

Vineyard in Rioja.

THE WINES OF SPAIN

After years of being in the shadows of other European wines, Spanish wines are finally gunning for the spotlight—and what has taken place is nothing short of a revolution. The wines of Spain, like its cuisine, are currently experiencing a firecracker explosion of both quality and variety that has brought a new level of interest, awareness, and recognition throughout the world, propelling them to superstar status.

A generation of young, ambitious winemakers has jolted dormant areas awake, and even the most established regions have undergone makeovers in order to compete in the global market.

THE ROAD TO GREAT WINE

Frank Gehry designed the visitor center for the Marqués de Riscal winery in Rioja.

Spain has a long wine history dating from the time when the Phoenicians introduced viticulture, over 3,000 years ago. Some of the country's wines achieved fame in Roman times, and the Visigoths enacted early wine laws. But in the regions under Muslim rule, winemaking slowed down for centuries. Starting in the 16th century, wine trade expanded along with the Spanish Empire, and, by the 18th and 19th centuries, the Sherry region *bodegas* (wineries) were already established.

In the middle of the 19th century, seeds of change blossomed throughout the Spanish wine industry. In 1846, the estate that was to become Vega Sicilia, Spain's most revered winery, was set up in Castile. Three years later the famous Tío Pepe brand was established to produce the excellent dry fino wines. Marqués de Murrieta and the Marqués de Riscal wineries opened in the 1860s creating the modern Rioja region and clearing the way for many centenary wineries. *Cava*—Spain's white or pink sparkling wine—was created the following decade in Catalonia.

After this flurry of activity, Spanish wines languished for almost a century. Vines were hit hard by phylloxera, and the civil war and a long dictatorship left the country stagnant and isolated. Just 30 years ago, Spain's wines were split between the same dominant trio of Sherry, Rioja, and cava, and loads of cheap, watered-down wines were made by local cooperatives with little gumption to improve and even less expertise.

Starting in the 1970s, however, a wave of innovation crashed through Rioja and emergent regions like Ribera del Duero and Penedés. In the 1990s, it turned into a revolution that spread all over the landscape—and is still going strong.

Spain is one of the largest wine producer in the world in terms of land area and volume.

SPANISH WINE CATEGORIES BY AGE

A unique feature of Spanish wines is their indication of aging process on wine labels. DO wines (see "A Vino Primer" on following page) show this on mandatory back panels. Aging requirements are longer for reds, but also apply to white, rosé, and sparkling wines. For reds, the rules are as follows:

Vino Joven
A young wine that may or may not have spent some time aging in oak barrels before it was bottled. Some winemakers have begun to shun traditional regulations to produce cutting-edge wines in this category. An elevated price distinguishes the ambitious new reds from the easy-drinking *jóvenes*.

Crianza
A wine aged for at least 24 months, six of which are in barrels (12 in Rioja, Ribera del Duero, and Navarra). A great bargain in top vintages from the most reliable wineries and regions.

Reserva
A wine aged for a minimum of 36 months, at least 12 of which are in oak.

Gran Reserva
Traditionally the top of the Spanish wine hierarchy, and the pride of the historic Rioja wineries. A red wine aged for at least 24 months in oak, followed by 36 months in the bottle before release.

Joven or Cosecha	Crianza	Reserva	Gran Reserva
Minimum Aging Period in Months	24	36	48	60

READING LABELS LIKE A PRO

Term meaning that the wine was bottled at the property

Name of the wine

For some prestigious wines, each bottle is numbered

Alcohol content

Name of the winery

Aging category

Means the wine was made from vines on a single plot of land

Name of the appellation (look for the expression "Denominación de Origen" displayed in small print just below the appellation's name)

Town where the winery is located

Vintage year

ESTATE BOTTLED — SINGLE VINEYARD — PRODUCE OF SPAIN

CONTINO
RIOJA
DENOMINACION DE ORIGEN CALIFICADA

De esta cosecha se han embotellado
117.139 botellas de Reserva

13,5% Vol.   BOT.   75 cl. ℮
Embotellado en la propiedad
VIÑEDOS DEL CONTINO, S. A.
LAGUARDIA - LASERNA, ESPAÑA

RESERVA 2002

A VINO PRIMER

Spain offers a daunting assortment of wine styles, regions, and varietals. But don't worry: a few pointers will help you understand unfamiliar names and terms. Most of Spain's quality wines come from designated regions called Denominaciones de Origen (Appellations of Origin), often abbreviated as DO. Spain has numerous such areas, which are tightly regulated to protect the integrity and characteristics of the wines produced there.

Beyond international varieties like Cabernet Sauvignon and Chardonnay, the country is home to several high-quality varietals, both indigenous and imported. Reds include Tempranillo, an early-ripening grape that blends and ages well, and Garnacha (the Spanish name for France's Grenache), a spicy, full-bodied red wine. The most popular white wines are the light, aromatic Albariño or Ruedas and the full-bodied Verdejo.

❶ The green and more humid areas of the northwest deliver crisp, floral white albariños in Galicia's Rías Biaxas. In the Bierzo DO, the Mencía grape distills the essence of the schist slopes, where it grows into minerally infused red wines.

❷ Moving east, in the iron-rich riverbanks of the Duero, Tempranillo grapes, here called "Tinto Fino," produce complex and age-worthy Ribera del Duero reds and hefty Toro wines. Close by, the Rueda DO adds aromatic and grassy whites from local Verdejo and adopted Sauvignon Blanc.

❸ The Rioja region is a winemaker's paradise. Here a mild, nearly perfect vine-growing climate marries limestone and clay soils with Tempranillo, Spain's most noble grape, to deliver wines that possess the two main features of every great region: personality and quality. Tempranillo-based Riojas evolve from a young cherry color and aromas of strawberries and red fruits, to a brick hue, infused with scents of tobacco and leather. Whether medium or full-bodied, tannic or velvety, these reds are some of the most versatile and food-friendly wines, and they have set the standard for the country for over a century.

Nearby, Navarra and three small DO's in Aragón deliver great wines made with the local Garnacha, Tempranillo, and international grape varieties.

❹ Southwest of Barcelona is the region of Catalonia, which encompasses the areas of Penedès and Priorat. Catalonia is best known as the heartland of cava, the typically dry, sparkling wine

Vineyard in Navarra

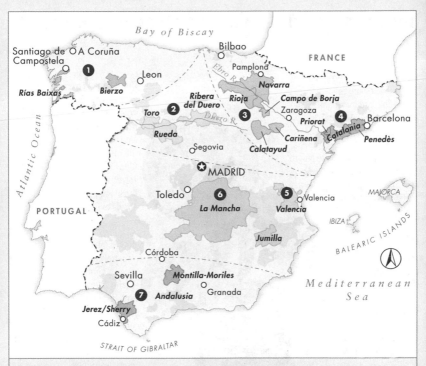

made from three indigenous Spanish varietals: Parellada, Xarel-lo, and Macabeo. The climatically varied Penedès—just an hour south of Barcelona—produces full-bodied reds like Garnacha on coastal plains and cool-climate varietals like Riesling and Sauvignon Blanc in the mountains. Priorat is a region that has emerged into the international spotlight during the past decade, as innovative winemakers have transformed winemaking practices there. Now, traditional grapes like Garnacha and Cariñena are blended with Cabernet Sauvignon and Syrah to produce rich, concentrated reds with powerful tannins.

5 The region of Valencia is south of Catalonia on the Mediterranean coast. The wines of this area have improved markedly in recent years, with red wines from Jumilla and other appellations finding their way onto the international market. Tempranillo and Monastrell (France's Mourvèdre) are the most common reds. An area specialty is Moscatel de Valencia, a highly aromatic sweet white wine.

6 In the central plateau south of Madrid, rapid investment, modernization, and replanting have resulted in medium bodied, easy drinking, and fairly priced wines made with Tempranillo (here called

"Cencíbel"), Cabernet, Syrah, and even Petit Verdot, that are opening the doors to more ambitious endeavors.

7 In sun-drenched Andalusia, where the white albariza limestone soils reflect the powerful sunlight while trapping the scant humidity, the fortified Jerez (Sherry) and Montilla emerge. In all their different incarnations, from dry finos, Manzanillas, amontillados, palo cortados, and olorosos, to sweet creams and Pedro Ximénez, they are the most original wines of Spain.

JUST OFF THE VINE: WINE DEVELOPMENTS

Beyond Tempranillo:
The current wine revolution has recovered many native varieties. Albariño, Godello, and Verdejo among the whites, and Callet, Cariñena, Garnacha, Graciano, Mandó, Manto Negro, Mencía, and Monastrell among the reds, are gaining momentum and will likely become more recognized.

Vinos de Pagos:
Pago, a word meaning plot or vineyard, is the legal term chosen to create Spain's equivalent of a *Grand Cru* hierarchy, by protecting quality oriented wine producers that make wine from their own estates.

Petit Verdot: Winemakers in Spain are discovering that Petit Verdot, the "little green" grape of Bordeaux, ripens much easier in warmer climates than in its birthplace. This is contributing to the rise of Petit Verdot in red blends and even to the production of single varietal wines.

Andalusia's New Wines:
For centuries, scorching southern Andalusia has offered world-class Sherry and Montilla wines. Now trailblazing winemakers are making serious inroads in the production of quality white, red, and new dessert wines, something deemed impossible a few years back.

Cult Wines: For most of the past century, Vega Sicilia Unico was the only true cult wine from Spain. The current explosion has greatly expanded the roster: L'Ermita, Pingus, Clos Erasmus, Artadi, Cirsion, Terreus, and Termanthia are the leading names in a list that grows every year.

V.O.S. and V.O.R.S: Sherry's most dramatic change in over a century is the creation of the "Very Old Sherry" designation for wines over 20 years of age, and the addition of "Rare" for those over 30, to easier distinguish the best, oldest, and most complex wines.

Innovative New Blends:
A few wine regions have strict regulations concerning the varieties used in their wines, but most allow for experimentation. All over the country, *bodegas* are crafting wines with creative blends that involve local varieties, Tempranillo, and famous international grapes.

Island Wines: In both the Balearic and Canary Islands the strong tourist industry helped to revive local winemaking. Although hard to find, the best Callet and Manto Negro based red wines of Majorca, and the sweet *malvasías* of Lanzarote will reward the adventurous drinker.

SPAIN'S SUPERSTAR WINEMAKERS

Mariano García   Peter Sisseck   Alvaro Palacios   Josep Lluís Pérez

The current wine revolution has made superstars out of a group of dynamic, innovative, and visionary winemakers. Here are some of the top names:

Mariano García. His 30 years as winemaker of Vega Sicilia made him a legend. Now García displays his deft touch in the Ribera del Duero and Bierzo through his four wineries: Aalto, Mauro, San Román, and Paixar.

Peter Sisseck. A Dane educated in Bordeaux, Sisseck found his calling in the old Ribera del Duero vineyards, where he crafted Pingus, Spain's most coveted cult wine.

Alvaro Palacios. In Priorat, Palacios created L'Ermita, a Garnacha wine that is one of Spain's most remarkable bottlings. Palacios also is a champion of the Bierzo region, where he produces wines from the ancient Mencía varietal, known for their vibrant berry flavors and stony minerality.

Josep Lluís Pérez. From his base in Priorat and through his work as a winemaker, researcher, teacher, and consultant, Pérez (along with his daughter Sara Pérez) has become the main driving force in shaping the modern Mediterranean wines of Spain.

MATCHMAKING KNOW-HOW

A pairing of wine with jamón and Spanish olives.

Spain has a great array of regional products and cuisines, and its avant-garde chefs are culinary world leaders. As a rule, you should match local food with local wines—but Spanish wines can be matched very well with some of the most unexpected dishes.

Albariños and the white wines of Galicia are ideal partners for seafood and fish. Dry sherries complement Serrano and Iberico hams, *lomo, chorizo,* and *salchichón* (white dry sauggage), as well as olives and nuts. Pale, light, and dry finos and Manzanillas are the perfect aperitif wines, and the ideal companion for fried fish. Fuller bodied amontillados, palo cortados, and olorosos go well with hearty soups. Ribera del Duero reds are the perfect match for the outstanding local lamb. Try Priorat and other Mediterranean reds with strong cheeses and barbecue meats. Traditional Rioja harmonizes well with fowl and game. But also take an adventure off the beaten path: manzanilla and fino are great with sushi and sashimi; Rioja *reserva* fit tuna steaks; and cream sherry will not be out of place with chocolate. ¡*Salud!*

Santamasa

$ | **MEDITERRANEAN** | **FAMILY** | Right on Sarrià's main square, this popular, informal eatery serves an eclectic menu of tapas and main dishes, from *cocas* (Catalan-style focaccia) with Ibérico ham and brie to hummus, quesadillas, and hamburgers piled high with four cheeses, all in generous, affordable portions. Weather permitting, grab a table out on the Plaça, in full view of the village's 10th-century church. **Known for:** wide selection of appetizers; table seating outdoors; bustling, neighborhood vibe. [$] *Average main: €8* ✉ *Major de Sarrià 97, Sarrià* ☎ *93/676–3574* [M] *Sarrià (FGC).*

Silvestre

$$ | **CATALAN** | A graceful and easygoing mainstay in Barcelona's culinary landscape, this restaurant serves modern market cuisine to discerning diners. Pay particular attention to Silvestre's impeccable tuna tartare, the scallops with shiitake mushrooms, or ragout of oxtail in red wine. **Known for:** intimate ambiance; the tuna tartare; well-chosen house wines. [$] *Average main: €16* ✉ *Santaló 101, Sant Gervasi* ☎ *93/241–4031* 🌐 *www.restaurante-silvestre.com* ⏲ *Closed 3 wks in Aug. No lunch weekends* [M] *Muntaner (FGC).*

Tram-Tram

$$$ | **MEDITERRANEAN** | Above Reina Elisenda on Sarrià's main drag, this restaurant is a Barcelona classic, known for using local fresh products and artful presentation. Pride of place on the à la carte menu (alas, there's no prix fixe lunch) goes to dishes like *fondant de cordero lechal* (milk-fed baby lamb) and *bacalao* (cod) with ratatouille. **Known for:** excellent Spanish omelet; pleasant interior garden patio; affordable menú de degustació (tasting menu). [$] *Average main: €26* ✉ *Major de Sarrià 121, Sarrià* ☎ *93/204–8518* 🌐 *tram-tram.com* ⏲ *Closed Mon.–Tues. and 2 wks in Aug. No dinner Sun.* [M] *Sarrià (FGC).*

★ Via Veneto

$$$$ | **MEDITERRANEAN** | Open since 1967, this elegant, family-owned temple of fine Catalan dining was a favorite of Salvador Dalí and now attracts local sports stars and politicians. The menu is a mix of contemporary offerings punctuated by old-school classics, and you can trust the expert sommelier to guide you through the daunting 10,000-bottle-strong wine list. **Known for:** theatrical presentation of roast baby duck; tasting menu; celebrity clientele. [$] *Average main: €38* ✉ *Ganduxer 10, Sant Gervasi* ☎ *93/200–7244* 🌐 *www.viavenetobarcelona.com* ⏲ *Closed Sun. and Aug. No lunch Sat.* [M] *La Bonanova (FGC), Maria Cristina (Metro L3).*

Vivanda

$$ | **CATALAN** | A block or so above Plaça Sarrià, on Major de Sarrià—the village high street—Vivanda is an ideal lunch choice, especially if the weather allows for dining in the tree shaded garden. There's no *menù del dia* (prix-fixe lunch), but à la carte prices are reasonable: standouts include the *arròs caldós de sipia i escamarianets* (black rice in broth with prawns). **Known for:** chic interior; tables in the garden; fish and shellfish. [$] *Average main: €18* ✉ *Major de Sarrià 134, Sarrià* ☎ *93/203–1918* 🌐 *www.vivanda.cat* ⏲ *Closed Mon. No dinner Sun.* [M] *Sarrià (FGC).*

Hotels

Primero Primera

$$ | **HOTEL** | **FAMILY** | The Perez family converted their apartment building on a leafy side street in the quiet, upscale, residential neighborhood of Tres Torres and opened it as an exquisitely designed, homey boutique hotel. **Pros:** retro-modern ambience; private parking; restaurant Planta Baja ($) open to the public. **Cons:** no spa; very small pool; bit of a distance to public transportation. [$] *Rooms from: €180* ✉ *Doctor Carulla 25–29,*

Sant Gervasi ☎ *93/417–5600* ⊕ *www. primeroprimera.com* ↪ *30 rooms* Ⓜ *Tres Torres (FGC).*

Vilana Hotel

$ | HOTEL | In an upscale residential neighborhood above Passeig de la Bonanova, this boutique accommodation can ease some of the budgetary strains of coming to a prime tourist destination. **Pros:** quiet surroundings; pleasant, attentive English-speaking staff; large, sunlit rooms. **Cons:** room service closes at 10:30; small gym, but no pool or spa; €25/day parking fee. Ⓢ *Rooms from: €80* ✉ *Vilana 7, Sant Gervasi* ☎ *93/434–0363* ⊕ *vilanahotel. com* ↪ *22 rooms* Ⓜ *Sarrià (FGC).*

🍸 Nightlife

Upper Barcelona is conspicuous, in a city that so treasures its nightlife, for the scarcity—nay, virtually the absence—of clubs, theaters, and music venues; the one notable exception might be the disco in the **Mirablau**, a restaurant at the vista point on Tibidabo. Sarrià and San Gervasi have no lack of good bars to spend a late-evening hour or two, but for serious nightlife the younger crowd heads down to areas like Poblenou, Barceloneta, or the waterfront.

🛍 Shopping

In the past decade or so, Sarrià has gentrified to the point where every block along Major de Sarrià—the high street—has at least one gourmet emporium, natural foods market, fashion boutique, fabulous bakery, or shop for upscale home furnishings—often more than one.

On Tuesday, there's a lively flea market in the Plaça Sarrià, especially good for silver, ceramics, and antique furniture. Otherwise there's not much of interest in terms of shopping in Upper Barcelona.

BEAUTY

JC Apotecari

SKINCARE | If you're not the sort to flinch at the €100 price tag on a 30 ml bottle of hand lotion, then Sarrià's JC Apotecari, premier purveyors of natural and organic cosmetics and fragrances, is for you. Look for Hierbas de Ibiza bath gel and fragrances, made in Spain exclusively for the shop, as well as global brands like May Lindstrom, Rahua, and Kypris. ✉ *Major de Sarrià 96, Sarrià* ☎ *93/205– 8734* ⊕ *www.jcapotecari.com* Ⓜ *Sarrià (FGC).*

FOOD

★ **Foix de Sarrià**

FOOD | To-die-for pastries, croissants, and chocolates have made Foix de Sarrià, founded in 1886, a Barcelona landmark. J. V. Foix, the son of the patisserie's founder, was an important Catalan poet who managed to survive the Franco regime with his art intact. He was born in the building that houses the branch of the shop at Major de Sarrià 57; one of his best-known poems is engraved in bronze on the outside wall. On Sunday, barcelonins come to Foix de Sarrià from all over town; Sunday just wouldn't be Sunday without a cake from from arguably Barcelona's best *patisserie*, to take to grandma's. ✉ *Pl. Sarrià 12–13, Sarrià* ☎ *93/203–0473* ⊕ *www.foixdesarria.com* Ⓜ *Sarrià (FGC).*

Ískia

WINE/SPIRITS | A fine list, regularly updated, of wines from Spain's top regions, like Priorat, Penedes, Montsant, and Ribera del Duero, make Iskia the *bodega* (cellar) of choice in Sarrià. The English-speaking owners are happy to make recommendations and talk about latest trends and best buys. Save space in your checked luggage for a bottle of fine *tinto* (red) or white. ✉ *Major de Sarrià 132, Sarrià* ☎ *93/205–0070* ⊕ *www.iskiavins. com* Ⓜ *Sarrià (FGC).*

MARKETS
Mercado de San Vicente
MARKET | The Mercado de San Vicente, a *Moderniste* gem built in 1911, with an ornamental brick facade, wrought-iron girders, and stained glass windows, is worth a quick visit, if only to pick up a bit of picnic fare before or after a walk to the Monestir de Pedralbes. ✉ *Passeig de la Reina Elisenda, 8, Sarrià* ☎ *93/413–2326* Ⓜ *Sarrià, Reina Elisenda (FGC line L6)*.

Sarrià Flea Market
MARKET | The small Tuesday flea market/antiques fair in Sarrià's town square is another good reason to explore this charming once-outlying village in the upper part of the city. ✉ *Sarrià* ☎ *93/413–2326* Ⓜ *Sarrià, Reina Elisenda (FGC line L6)*.

 Activities

SOCCER
★ Camp Nou: Futbol Club Barcelona
SOCCER | Founded in 1899, FC Barcelona won its third European Championship in 2009, along with the Liga championship, and its 27th Copa del Rey (King's Cup)—Spain's first-ever *triplete*—and did it again in 2015. Even more impressive was its razzle-dazzle style of soccer, rarely seen in the age of cynical defensive lockdowns and muscular British-style play. Barça, as the club is known, is Real Madrid's nemesis (and vice versa) and a sociological and historical phenomenon of deep significance in Catalonia.

Note that renovations—begun in 2022 and ongoing through 2025 or 2026—to Camp Nou will no doubt disrupt the daily stadium tours and access to the team's very popular museum. Do check on their status, however, as both the tours and the museum are absolute musts for *futbol* fans.

And don't give up on trying to see a Barça match. During the main construction works (the 2023–24 season and possibly beyond), the team will play its home games at the Olympic Stadium in Montjuïc. Check schedules and buy tickets online through the FC Barcelona website. Ticketmaster (⊕ *www.ticketmaster.es*) or Entradas (⊕ *www.entradas.es*) also sell tickets. ✉ *Camp Nou, Aristides Maillol 12, Les Corts* ☎ *902/189900* ⊕ *www.fcbarcelona.com* Ⓜ *Collblanc, Palau Reial (Metro Line 5)*.

Chapter 11

MONTJUÏC AND POBLE SEC

Updated by
Jennifer Ceaser

⊙ **Sights**
★★★★★

🍴 **Restaurants**
★★★☆☆

🛏 **Hotels**
☆☆☆☆☆

🛍 **Shopping**
★★★☆☆

🍸 **Nightlife**
★★★☆☆

NEIGHBORHOOD SNAPSHOT

TOP EXPERIENCES

■ **The Museu Nacional d'Art de Catalunya:** This magnificent domed museum contains what is considered the world's best collection of Romanesque frescoes, removed for restoration from Pyrenean chapels in the 1930s and ingeniously restored with their original contours.

■ **CaixaForum:** A stunning 1911 Art Nouveau factory complex has been reimagined as an art gallery and cultural center.

■ **Poble Espanyol:** Shop for traditional crafts and wander among the boutiques, cafés, workshops, and studios of this recreated Spanish village.

■ **Fundació Miró:** Explore this gleaming white hilltop museum showcasing masterpieces by the Catalan artist Joan Miró.

■ **Tapas crawl on Carrer de Blai:** Hop among dozens of cheap and cheerful tapas bars lining this pedestrian street in the heart of Poble Sec.

GETTING HERE

The most dramatic approach to Montjuïc is the cross-harbor cable car (Telefèric de Montjuïc) from Barceloneta. You can also take Bus No. 150 from Plaça d'Espanya, which makes stops at major sites across the mountain. Yet another option is the funicular from the Paral·lel metro stop (lines L2 and L3). From the funicular stop on the mountain, walk uphill or hop on the cable car to reach the Castell de Montjuïc at the summit

PLANNING YOUR TIME

With visits to the Miró Foundation and the Museu Nacional d'Art de Catalunya, plus a stop at the hilltop castle and unhurried strolls through Montjuïc's many gardens, this is a five-hour excursion, if not a full day. Follow with a casual lunch or dinner in Poble Sec, a lively tapas-filled neighborhood at the base of the mountain.

THE CITY'S BEST VIEWPOINTS

■ With spectacular vistas of Barcelona and its surroundings, Montjuïc provides countless photo-ops. Crowning the southwest part of the mountain is **Castell de Montjuïc**, whose rooftop offers unbeatable panoramic views of the port, the Mediterranean Sea, and the city spread out below, framed by the Collserola mountain range.

■ Scattered across Montjuïc are several *miradores* (viewpoints); one of the most popular is **Mirador Jardins de Miramar**, with its garden terraces overlooking the port and the sea. Here, next to the Telefèric cable car landing, the **Miramar Restaurant Garden & Club** (✉ *Ctra. de Miramar 40*) is a splendid spot for soaking up the views with an alfresco drink.

■ Open in summer, the two **Montjuïc municipal pools** (✉ *Av. Miramar 31*) feature a stunning backdrop of the city below; Kylie Minogue used the location for her 2003 music video "Slow." Another top spot for Instagrammable pics is the Olympic Ring area, featuring a sprawling esplanade dotted with fountains and smokestack-like columns, with Santiago Calatrava's striking needle-shaped communications tower rising above.

Though a bit removed from the hustle and bustle of Barcelona street life, the scenic, hilly area of Montjuïc has a number of high-profile attractions to lure visitors. Down the hill, Poble Sec is a culturally vibrant neighborhood packed with tapas bars and late-night clubs, as well as some of the city's best live music venues.

Montjuïc is home to the Miró Foundation, the Museu Nacional d'Art de Catalunya, the minimalist Mies van der Rohe Pavilion, the lush Jardins de Mossèn Cinto Verdaguer, and the CaixaForum art gallery, just for starters, and public buses within Montjuïc that visitors can take from sight to sight. This hill overlooking the south side of the port is said to have originally been named Mont Juif for the Jewish cemetery once on its slopes, though a 3rd-century Roman document referring to the construction of a road between Mons Taber (around the cathedral) and Mons Jovis (Mount of Jove) suggests that in fact the name may derive from the Roman deity Jupiter.

◉ Sights

★ CaixaForum Barcelona

ARTS CENTER | The 1911 Casaramona textile factory, a neo-Mudejar Art Nouveau masterpiece by Josep Puig i Cadafalch (architect of Casa de les Punxes, Casa Amatller, and Casa Quadras), is now a center for temporary art exhibits, as well as concerts, live performances, and other cultural events. The original brickwork is spectacular, while a 2002 restoration added sleek white modern entryway designed by Japanese architect Arata Isozaki, also responsible for the nearby Palau Sant Jordi. ✉ *Av. Francesc Ferrer i Guàrdia 6–8, Montjuïc* ☎ *93/476–8600* ⊕ *caixaforum.org/es/barcelona* 🎫 *€6* Ⓜ *Pl. Espanya.*

Castell de Montjuïc

CASTLE/PALACE | FAMILY | Built in 1640 by rebels against Felipe IV, the castle has had a dark history as a symbol of Barcelona's military domination by foreign powers, usually the Spanish army. The fortress was stormed several times, most famously in 1705 by Lord Peterborough for Archduke Carlos of Austria. In 1808, during the Peninsular War, it was seized by the French under General Dufresne. During an 1842 civil disturbance, Barcelona was bombed from its heights by a Spanish artillery battery. After the 1936–39 civil war, the castle was used as a dungeon for political prisoners. Lluís Companys, president of the Generalitat de Catalunya during the civil war, was executed by firing squad here on October 14, 1940. In 2007 the fortress was formally ceded back to Barcelona.

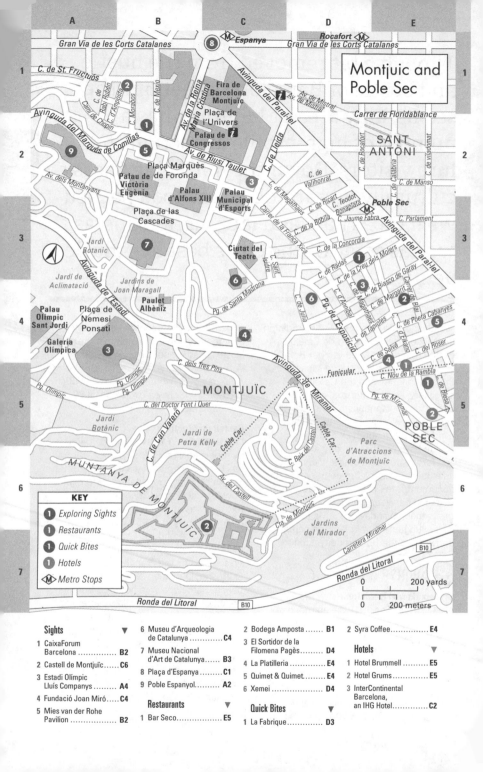

Montjuïc and Poble Sec

KEY

- ① Exploring Sights
- ① Restaurants
- ① Quick Bites
- ① Hotels
- Ⓜ Metro Stops

0 — 200 yards
0 — 200 meters

An excellent visitor center highlights the history of the castle throughout the ages; other spaces are given over to temporary exhibits. The various terraces offer fantastic panoramic views over the city and out to sea. The moat, which contains attractive gardens, is the site of the popular summer Sala Montjuic Open Air Cinema (⊕ *www.salamontjuic. org*), screening original versions of classic films with live music concerts before the showings. ✉ *Ctra. de Montjuïc 66, Montjuïc* ☎ *93/256–4440* ⊕ *ajuntament. barcelona.cat/castelldemontjuic/en* ✉ *€5 (free Sun. from 3 pm)* Ⓜ *Paral·lel and Funicular.*

Estadi Olímpic Lluís Companys (*Olympic Stadium*)

HISTORIC SIGHT | **FAMILY** | The Olympic Stadium was originally built for the International Exhibition of 1929, with the idea that Barcelona would then host the 1936 Olympics (ultimately staged in Hitler's Berlin). After failing twice to win the nomination, the city celebrated the attainment of its long-cherished goal by renovating the semi-derelict stadium—preserving the original facade and shell—in time for 1992, providing seating for 60,000.

Though you can view the stadium for free from the entrance area, the field and indoor areas are not normally open to the public. That said, tickets to a Barcelona Football Club (⊕ *www.fcbarcelona.com*) match will get you in. The beloved team will be playing its home games here while Camp Nou undergoes a multiyear renovation (starting in 2022).

The nearby Museu Olímpic i de l'Esport, a museum about the Olympic movement in Barcelona, shows audiovisual replays from the 1992 Olympics, and provides interactive simulations for visitors to experience the training and competition of Olympic athletes. An information center traces the history of the modern Olympics from Athens in 1896 to the present. Next door and just downhill stands the futuristic Palau Sant Jordi sports and concert arena, designed by the noted Japanese architect Arata Isozaki. ✉ *Passeig Olímpic, 15–17, Montjuïc* ☎ *93/426–2089 Estadi Olímpic, 93/292–5379 Museu Olímpica* ⊕ *www. estadiolimpic.cat (stadium); www.museuolimpicbcn.cat/en (museum)* ✉ *Stadium is free, museum €5.80* ⊙ *Museum closed Mon.* Ⓜ *Pl. Espanya.*

★ **Fundació Joan Miró**

ART MUSEUM | The masterpieces by native Barcelona artist Joan Miró (1893–1983) on display at this museum include paintings, sculpture, and textile works from all periods of his life. They coexist with temporary exhibitions of 20th and 21st century artists, and, in the newer Espai 13 space, cutting-edge contemporary art.

The airy white building, with panoramic views north over Barcelona, was designed by the artist's close friend and collaborator Josep Lluís Sert and opened in 1975. Extensions were added by Sert's pupil Jaume Freixa in 1988 and 2000. Miró's playful and colorful style, filled with Mediterranean light and humor, seems a perfect match for the surroundings. Various patios, as well as the roof terrace, are home to notable Miró sculptures, including the bronze *Sun, Moon and one Star* with a dramatic backdrop of the city. The artist rests in the cemetery on Montjuïc's southern slopes. ✉ *Parc de Montjuïc s/n, Parc de Montjuïc, Montjuïc* ⊹ *Bus stop Fundació Joan Miró* ☎ *93/443–9470* ⊕ *www.fmirobcn. org* ✉ *€13* ⊙ *Closed Mon.–Wed.* Ⓜ *Pl. Espanya, Paral·lel then Funicular.*

Mies van der Rohe Pavilion

NOTABLE BUILDING | One of the masterpieces of the Bauhaus School, the legendary Pavelló Mies van der Rohe—the German contribution to the 1929 International Exhibition, reassembled between 1983 and 1986—remains a stunning "less is more" study in interlocking

In addition to being a social, cultural, and educational centre, CaixaForum is also known for the Moderniste style of its building.

planes of white marble, green onyx, and glass. In effect, it is Barcelona's aesthetic opposite to the flamboyant Art Nouveau/Modernisme of Gaudí and his contemporaries.

Note the mirror play of the black carpet inside the pavilion with the reflecting pool outside, and the iconic Barcelona chair designed by Ludwig Mies van der Rohe (1886–1969) and Lilly Reich (1885–1947). Reproductions have graced modern interiors around the world for decades. ✉ *Av. Francesc Ferrer i Guàrdia 7, Montjuïc* ☎ *93/215–1011* ⊕ *miesbcn. com* ✉ *€8* Ⓜ *Pl. Espanya.*

Museu d'Arqueologia de Catalunya

HISTORY MUSEUM | Just downhill to the right of the Palau Nacional, the Museum of Archaeology holds important finds from the Greek ruins at Empúries, on the Costa Brava. These are shown alongside fascinating objects from, and explanations of, megalithic Spain. ✉ *Passeig Santa Madrona 39–41, Montjuïc*

☎ *93/423–2149* ⊕ *www.mac.cat* ✉ *€6; free first Sun. of month* ⊘ *Closed Sun. afternoon and Mon.* Ⓜ *Pl. Espanya.*

★ Museu Nacional d'Art de Catalunya
(*National Art Museum of Catalonia, MNAC*)

ART MUSEUM | Housed in the imposingly domed, towered, frescoed, and columned Palau Nacional, built in 1929 as the centerpiece of the International Exposition, this superb museum was renovated between 1985 and 1992 by Gae Aulenti, architect of the Musée d'Orsay in Paris. In 2004, the museum's four holdings (Romanesque, Gothic, the photography collection, and the Cambó Collection—an eclectic trove, including a Goya, donated by Francesc Cambó) were joined by the 19th- and 20th-century collection of Catalan Impressionist and Moderniste painters. With this influx of artistic treasure, the Museu Nacional has become Catalonia's grand central museum.

Pride of place goes to the Romanesque exhibition, the world's finest collection of Romanesque frescoes, altarpieces, and wood carvings, most of them rescued from chapels in the Pyrenees during the 1920s to save them from deterioration, theft, and art dealers. Many, such as the famous *Cristo de Taüll* fresco (from the church of Sant Climent de Taüll in Taüll), have been painstakingly removed from crumbling walls of abandoned sites and remounted on ingenious frames that exactly reproduce the contours of their original settings. The stunning central hall of the museum contains an enormous pillared and frescoed cupola. ✉ *Palau Nacional, Parc de Montjuïc s/n, Montjuïc* ☎ *93/622–0360* ⊕ *www.museunacional. cat* ✉ *From €12 (valid for day of purchase and 1 other day in same month); free Sat. after 3 pm and 1st Sun. of month* ⊘ *Closed Mon.* Ⓜ *Pl. Espanya.*

Plaça d'Espanya

PLAZA/SQUARE | This busy circle is a good place to avoid, but you'll probably need to cross it to get to the National Art Museum of Catalonia and other nearby Montjuïc attractions. It's dominated by the so-called Venetian Towers, built as the grand entrance to the 1929 International Exposition. They flank the lower end of the Avinguda Maria Cristina (the buildings on both sides are important venues for the trade fairs and industrial expositions that regularly descend on Barcelona).

At the far end is the Font Màgica (the Magic Fountain), which was created by Josep Maria Jujol, the Gaudí collaborator who designed the curvy and colorful benches in Park Güell, and which has a spectacular nighttime display of lights and music. The sculptures are by Miquel Blay, one of the master artists and craftsmen who put together the Palau de la Música. On the opposite side of the circle from the Towers, the neo-Mudejar bullring, Les Arenes, is now a multilevel shopping mall. ✉ *Pl. Espanya, Sants* Ⓜ *Pl. Espanya.*

Poble Espanyol (*Spanish Village*)

MUSEUM VILLAGE | FAMILY | Created for the 1929 International Exhibition, this faux Spanish village is a sort of open-air architectural museum, with 117 faithful replicas to scale of regional building styles, from an Aragonese Gothic-Mudejar bell tower to the tower walls of Ávila, drawn from all over Spain. The ground-floor spaces are devoted to boutiques, cafés and restaurants, workshops, and artist studios.

The liveliest time to come is at night, and a reservation at one of the half dozen restaurants gets you in for free, as does the purchase of a ticket for either of the two nightclubs or the Tablao del Carmen flamenco show. Its main square also functions as a concert venue, hosting well-known international bands like Bad Religion and Wilco. ✉ *Av. Francesc Ferrer i Guàrdia 13, Montjuïc* ☎ *93/508–6300* ⊕ *www.poble-espanyol.com* ✉ *€14 (€11.20 online); after 8 pm €7* Ⓜ *Pl. Espanya.*

🍴 Restaurants

The dining scene in Poble Sec reflects the humble, largely working-class character of the neighborhood and leans toward traditional Catalan restaurants and homey, affordable tapas spots. That's not to say the food on offer isn't of excellent quality, but menus here typically eschew the gastronomic frills found elsewhere in the city.

This, combined with the barrio's off-the-beaten-path location, means that most places cater to a local crowd. The exceptions are the bustling tapas street of Carrer de Blai and the tourist-packed Quimet i Quimet.

Bar Seco

$ | **TAPAS** | This sun-filled corner lunch spot at the foot of Montjuïc, with coveted terrace seating just across the street, is a cut above the neighborhood's typical

Ground Rules for Coffee 🍴

Coffee culture in Barcelona focuses on simplicity. Of course, this is in defiance of the near-infinite choices offered by certain barista-fronted international chains now scattered around the city. Here's what you can expect.

A normal espresso is *un cafè* or *un café solo*. Add some extra water and it's a *cafè Americá*. Add ice for a *cafè amb gel* (*café con hielo* in Spanish) and a dash of rum or brandy to make a *cigaló* (*carajillo* in Spanish).

A *tallat*, from the Catalan verb *tallar* (to cut), is coffee with just a little milk (*café cortado* in Spanish), while *cafè amb llet* is Catalan for *café con leche*, or coffee mixed more evenly with milk.

Decaf, *descafeinado*, is widely available, as is skim milk, *leche desnatada*. More progressive places offer *l eche de soja* (soy milk) and *l eche de almendra* (almond milk).

tapas joints. Nearly everything is organic, from the simply-prepared Mediterranean-style dishes to the ecological wines; even the sodas are all-natural. **Known for:** healthy menu options; closes early some days; organic ingredients. $ *Average main: €10* ✉ *Passeig de Montjuïc, 74, Poble Sec* ☎ *93/329–6374* 🕒 *No dinner Mon.–Wed.* [M] *Paral·lel.*

Bodega Amposta

$$ | **CATALAN** | A short stroll from the Mies van der Rohe Pavilion and CaixaForum, this bustling brick-walled restaurant serves top-notch seasonal Catalan cuisine prepared on the grill. You order à la carte or go with the four-course prix-fixe menu, which is a good deal. **Known for:** artisanal charcuterie; popular with locals; seasonal ingredients. $ *Average main: €22* ✉ *Carrer d'Amposta 1, Poble Sec* ☎ *93/673–8346* 🌐 *www.bodegaamposta.com* 🕒 *Closed Mon.* [M] *Pl. Espanya.*

El Sortidor de la Filomena Pagès

$ | **CATALAN** | One of the city's oldest restaurants (dating back to 1908), this homey spot that's popular for lunch serves unfussy Catalan cuisine in a lovely rustic dining room, complete with original multicolored-glass windows looking out on the tranquil Plaça del Sortidor. The paellas and *arroz negro* (black rice with squid) are particularly good. **Known for:** historic ambience; affordable prices; paella and rices. $ *Average main: €12* ✉ *Pl. del Sortidor 5, Poble Sec* ☎ *93/6907–65721* 🌐 *www.elsortidor.com* 🕒 *Closed Mon.* ☞ *Dinner Fri. and Sat. only* [M] *Paral·lel, Poble Sec.*

★ La Platilleria

$$ | **TAPAS** | Standards like Ibérico ham and *patatas bravas* are on offer at this snug tapas bar, but it's the rotating selection of seasonal small plates that really make it worth a visit. There's no menu; a chalkboard brought to your table lists the main ingredient—cod, pork rib, sweetbreads, for example—and friendly servers will explain the daily preparation for each. **Known for:** seasonal small plates; friendly service; nice selection of Catalan wines by the glass. $ *Average main: €20* ✉ *Roser 82, Poble Sec* ☎ *93/463–5401* 🕒 *Closed Sun.–Tues.* [M] *Paral·lel.*

Quimet & Quimet

$$ | **TAPAS** | The secret is out about this tiny, century-plus-old tapas bar, which has become so overrun with visitors in recent years that locals have mostly

started steering clear. Nevertheless, it's an atmospheric place, and the innovative tapas—largely made using *conservas* (canned and tinned foods)—are still well worth the visit. **Known for:** arrive early to avoid the crowds; classic foodie haunt; local wines. [$] *Average main: €15* ✉ *Poeta Cabanyes 25, Poble Sec* ☎ *93/442–3142* 🌐 *www.quimetquimet.com* 🕒 *Closed Sun.* [M] *Paral·lel.*

★ Xemei

$$ | ITALIAN | Xemei, meaning "twins" in Venetian dialect, is the brainchild of two Venetian brothers, whose devotion to the cuisine of the Veneto region makes this not a typical Italian dining experience. Exquisitely prepared dishes lean heavily toward seafood, like the fish appetizer (a mix of baked mackerel, marinated anchovies, pickled sardines, and whipped cod) and *spaghetti al nero di sepia* (squid ink spaghetti). **Known for:** Venetian-style liver with polenta; local favorite; daily fish special. [$] *Average main: €20* ✉ *Passeig de l'Exposició 85, Poble Sec* ☎ *93/553–5140* 🌐 *xemei.es* [M] *Poble Sec.*

☕ Coffee and Quick Bites

La Fabrique

$ | BAKERY | Delicious artisanal breads and pastries are baked fresh every day at this patisserie, with different breads available on different days. Their almond croissant is the best in town. **Known for:** organic breads and pastries; croissants; daily bread specials. [$] *Average main: €3* ✉ *Radas 35, Poble Sec* ☎ *93/443–1023* 🌐 *lafabrique.cat* ☞ *Takeaway only* [M] *Poble Sec.*

Syra Coffee

$ | CAFÉ | If you're looking for a shot or two to spur your climb to Montjuïc, stop in for a café latte or a flat white at this specialty coffee shop, which has several locations around the city. The gourmet cookies are excellent, too. **Known for:** locally roasted specialty coffee; takeaway only; gourmet treats. [$] *Average main: €3* ✉ *Margarit 17, Poble Sec* ☎ *7228–73843* 🌐 *syra.coffee* 🕒 *Closed Sun.* [M] *Poble Sec.*

🛏 Hotels

Hotel Brummell

$$ | HOTEL | The rustic-chic lobby with work by local artists sets the tone at this stylish boutique hotel. Along with a small downstairs bar, there's a lovely deck with a narrow plunge pool, sauna, and herb garden. **Pros:** young, friendly international staff; free yoga classes at nearby studio; chic design. **Cons:** no minibar; an uphill walk from closest metro; slightly off the beaten track. [$] *Rooms from: €160* ✉ *Nou de la Rambla 174, Poble Sec* ☎ *93/125–8622* 🌐 *www.hotelbrummell.com* 🛏 *20 rooms* 🍴 *No Meals* [M] *Paral·lel.*

Hotel Grums

$$$ | HOTEL | FAMILY | This pleasant boutique hotel is close to the port—convenient for cruise ship visitors—and has easy access to the museums and gardens of Montjuïc. **Pros:** quiet location; good for families; well-equipped spa with Jacuzzi and sauna. **Cons:** far from Eixample attractions; extra charges for the spa; rooms are on the small side. [$] *Rooms from: €177* ✉ *Carrer Palaudaries 26, Poble Sec* ☎ *93/442066* 🌐 *www.hotelgrumsbarcelona.com* 🛏 *78 rooms* 🍴 *No Meals* [M] *Paral·lel.*

InterContinental Barcelona, an IHG Hotel

$$$$ | HOTEL | At the foot of Montjuïc, just a few minutes' walk to the famous Magic Fountain, this hotel is also near the Fira de Barcelona convention center, which makes it a popular choice for trade show visitors. **Pros:** large rooms; seasonal rooftop terrace with pool and great Montjuïc views; close to many Montjuïc attractions. **Cons:** extra charge to use spa facilities; rates skyrocket during trade shows; somewhat corporate vibe. [$] *Rooms*

Find replicas of buildings from all over Spain and see craftspeople at work in the Spanish village, at the foot of Montjuïc.

from: €295 ⊠ Av. de Rius i Taulet 1–3, Poble Sec ☎ 93/426–2223 ⊕ barcelona. intercontinental.com ✈ 273 rooms ⭐️ No Meals Ⓜ Pl. Espanya, Poble Sec.

Nightlife

If you're looking for swanky cocktail lounges and throbbing nightclubs, you won't find them in Poble Sec. Instead, the steep, narrow streets of this slightly rough-around-the-edges neighborhood are home to low-key local haunts, along with a sprinkling of gay bars and rock-'n'-roll-themed hole-in-the-walls.

The scene heats up along Avinguda del Paral·lel, where the sprawling Sala Apolo concert hall and dance club, and nearby cabaret theater El Molino, draw evening crowds.

BARS

Celler Cal Marino
WINE BARS | Rustic and charming with an arched, brick-wall, barrel tables, and rows of multicolor *sifón* fizzy-water bottles, this homey venue serves wine by the glass or liter (for takeaway) from the wine cellar, artisanal beers, and vermouth paired with homemade tapas. ⊠ Margarit 54, Poble Sec ⊕ calmarino.tumblr.com Ⓜ Poble Sec, Paral·lel.

★ Cerveceria Jazz
BARS | As the name implies, there's a jazz soundtrack and a wide selection of local and international craft beers available here, on tap and by the bottle. The stone walls adorned with antique paintings and clocks give the space a warm ambiance. ⊠ Margarit 43, Poble Sec ☎ 93/443–3259 ⊕ www.cerveceriajazz.com Ⓜ Poble Sec.

La Federica
BARS | One of the city's liveliest gay bars features a funky retro-style interior. It's a colorful backdrop for drag shows, including the venue's Queer Flamenco events. ⊠ Salvà 3, Poble Sec ☎ 93/600–5901 Ⓜ Paral·lel.

Lilith & Sons

COCKTAIL LOUNGES | Come to this corner bar for inventive, beautifully executed, seasonal craft cocktails like the Blood Muse, an umami twist on the classic Negroni, with soy sauce, balsamic vinegar, and a garnish of nori seaweed. ⊠ *Fontrodona 23, Poble Sec* ☎ *6054–29647* ⊕ *www.lilithandsons.com* Ⓜ *Paral·lel.*

★ Malevo

WINE BARS | A mish-mash of retro furniture and black-and-white vintage photos decorate this cozy wood-paneled bar, a great spot to chill with a glass of wine or vermouth and nibble on tapas before or after dinner. ⊠ *Margarit 52, bajos 1, Poble Sec* ☎ *93/137–5770* Ⓜ *Paral·lel, Poble Sec.*

Psycho Rock & Roll Club

BARS | Plastered with photos and posters of legendary musicians and bands, this bar pays homage to all styles of rock-n'-roll, with DJs spinning everything from old-school rock to punk to heavy metal. There are also occasional live concerts. ⊠ *Piquer 27, Poble Sec* Ⓜ *Paral·lel.*

🎭 Performing Arts

CONCERTS

Barts (Arts on Stage)

THEATER | This state-of-the-art theater on Paral·lel—remodeled from the old Artèria Music Hall—has wildly diverse programming, with everything from performance art to the latest indie bands. There are also musicals, magic shows, and theater, though all mostly in Catalan. ⊠ *Av. Paral·lel 62, Poble Sec* ☎ *93/324–8492* ⊕ *www.barts.cat* Ⓜ *Paral·lel.*

Palau Sant Jordi

CONCERTS | Arata Isozaki's immense domed venue, built for the 1992 Olympic Games, has hosted superstar performers such as Bruce Springsteen and Beyoncé. Also presented are Disney specials, Cirque de Soleil, and other musical

Tapas Crawl on Carrer de Blai

Evenings and weekends, Poble Sec's Carrer de Blai buzzes with hungry diners. Dozens of cheap and cheerful tapas spots line this seven-block-long pedestrian street, stretching from Carrer de la Creu del Molers to Carrer d'En Fontrodona. The best thing to do is hop from bar to bar, sampling tapas and pintxos (miniature tapas affixed to a slice of bread with a toothpick), which can be had for as little as one euro. Good bets include La Tasqueta De Blai (⊠ *Blai 15*), Bota Bar (⊠ *Blai 29*), and Koska Taverna (⊠ *Blai 8*).

events. ⊠ *Palau Sant Jordi, Passeig Olímpic 5–7, Montjuïc* ☎ *93/426–2089* ⊕ *www.palausantjordi.cat/en* Ⓜ *Pl. Espanya.*

DANCE

El Mercat de les Flors

MODERN DANCE | An old flower market converted into a modern performance space, theater, and dance school, the Mercat de Les Flors forms part of the Institut de Teatre and is set on lovely, expansive grounds at the foot of Montjuïc. Modern dance is the Mercat's raison d'être, and it remains one of the few theaters in Spain that is exclusively dedicated to contemporary dance. The on-site bar-restaurant, La Soleá, is ideal or pre- or post-performance drinks and tapas or pintxos, as well as other dishes. ⊠ *Lleida 59, Poble Sec* ☎ *93/256–2600* ⊕ *mercatflors.cat/en* Ⓜ *Poble Sec, Pl. Espanya.*

FLAMENCO

El Tablao de Carmen

FOLK/TRADITIONAL DANCE | Large tour groups come to this venerable flamenco dinner-theater venue in the Poble

Espanyol named after, and dedicated to, the legendary dancer Carmen Amaya. Die-hard flamenco aficionados might dismiss the ensembles that perform here as a tad touristy, but the dancers, singers, and guitarists are pros. Visitors can enjoy one of the two nightly performances over a drink or over their choice of a prix-fixe meal, with prices ranging from €45 to €154. Reservations are recommended. Dinner shows are held daily at 6 pm and 8:30 pm. ⊠ *Poble Espanyol, Av. Francesc Ferrer i Guàrdia 13, Montjuïc* ☎ *93/325–6895* ⊕ *www.tablaodecarmen. com* ✉ *Starting from €45 for a flamenco show and a drink* Ⓜ *Pl. Espanya.*

THEATER
El Molino
CABARET | For most of the 20th century, this venue was the most legendary of all the cabaret theaters on Paral·lel. Modeled after Paris's Moulin Rouge, it closed in the late 1990s as the building was becoming dangerously run-down. After an ambitious refurbishment in 2010, El Molino reopened as one of the most stunning state-of-the-art cabaret theaters in Europe. The building now has five—instead of the original two—stories, with a bar and terrace on the third. What has remained the same, however, is its essence—a contemporary version of burlesque, but bump-and-grind all the same. You can purchase tickets online or before performances (which usually start at 9:30 pm). Note that shows are performed in Spanish, but you can still enjoy the spectacle. ⊠ *Vilà i Vilà 99, Poble Sec* ☎ *93/205–5111* ⊕ *www.elmolinobcn. com* Ⓜ *Paral·lel.*

Chapter 12

CATALONIA, VALENCIA, AND THE COSTA BLANCA

Updated by
Jennifer Ceaser

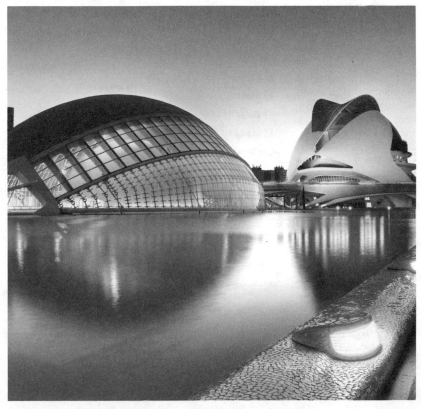

👁 Sights	🍴 Restaurants	🛏 Hotels	🛍 Shopping	🍸 Nightlife
★★★★☆	★★★★★	★★★☆☆	★★☆☆☆	★★★☆☆

WELCOME TO CATALONIA, VALENCIA, AND THE COSTA BLANCA

TOP REASONS TO GO

★ **Girona:** Explore a town where monuments of Christian, Jewish, and Islamic cultures have coexisted for centuries and are just steps apart.

★ **Valencia:** Discover a treasure trove of museums, concert halls, riverfront parks, and architecture old and new in Spain's third-largest city.

★ **Great restaurants:** Foodies argue that the fountainhead of creative gastronomy has moved from France to Spain— and in particular to the great restaurants of the Empordà and Costa Brava.

★ **Dalí's home and museum:** "Surreal" doesn't begin to describe the Teatre-Museu Dalí in Figueres or the artist's eccentric home in Portlligat.

★ **Beaches:** From the Costa Brava, with its secluded beaches framed by dramatic rocky cliffs, down to the wide, golden strands of the Costa Daurada, some of the country's most spectacular beaches dot the Catalan coast.

Year-round, Catalonia is the most visited of Spain's autonomous communities. In summer, the rugged Costa Brava and the Costa Daurada's sandy beaches are havens for sun-worshippers, while its mountainous interior hides medieval wonders. Excellent rail, air, and highway connections link Catalonia to Valencia, its neighbor to the south.

1 Girona

2 Figueres

3 Besalú

4 Tossa de Mar

5 Sant Feliu de Guixols

6 S'Agaró

7 Calella de Palafrugell and Around

8 Begur and Around

9 Cadaqués and Around

10 Montserrat

11 Sitges

12 Santes Creus

13 Santa Maria de Poblet

14 Tarragona

15 Valencia

16 Albufera Nature Park

17 Dénia

18 Calpe

19 Altea

20 Alicante

12

Catalonia, Valencia, and the Costa Blanca WELCOME TO CATALONIA, VALENCIA, AND THE COSTA BLANCA

EATING AND DRINKING WELL IN CATALONIA AND VALENCIA

Paella valenciana in a classic paella pan.

Cuisine in both Catalonia and Valencia runs the gamut of classic Mediterranean fare, with paella being one of the most renowned and popular dishes. Fish preparations are similar along the coast, though inland favorites vary from place to place.

The grassy meadows of Catalonia's northern Alt Empordà region put quality beef on local tables; from the Costa Brava comes fine seafood, such as anchovies from L'Escala and *gambas* (prawns) from Palamós, both deservedly famous. *Romesco*—a blend of almonds, peppers, garlic, and olive oil—is used as a vegetable, fish, and seafood sauce in Tarragona, especially during the *calçotadas* (spring onion feasts). *Allioli*, garlicky mayonnaise, is another popular topping. The Ebro Delta is renowned for fresh fish, oysters, and eels, as well as *rossejat* (fried rice in a fish broth). Valencia and the Mediterranean coast are the homeland of *paella valenciana*. *Arròs a banda* is a variant in which the fish and rice are cooked separately.

CALÇOTS

The *calçot* is a sweet spring onion developed by a 19th-century farmer who discovered how to extend the edible portion by packing soil around the base. It is grilled on a barbecue, then peeled and dipped into romesco sauce. In January, the town of Valls holds a *calçotada* where upward of 30,000 people gather for meals of onions, sausage, lamb chops, and red wine.

RICE

Paella valenciana is one of Spain's most famous gastronomic contributions. A simple country dish dating to the early 18th century, "paella" refers to the wide frying pan with short, sturdy handles that's used to cook the rice. Anything fresh from the fields that day, along with rice and olive oil, traditionally went into the pan, but paella valenciana has particular ingredients: short-grain rice, chicken, rabbit, *garrofó* (a local legume), tomatoes, green beans, sweet peppers, olive oil, and saffron. *Paella marinera* (seafood paella) is a different story: rice, cuttlefish, squid, mussels, shrimp, prawns, lobster, clams, garlic, olive oil, sweet paprika, and saffron, all stewed in fish broth. Other paella variations include *paella negra* or *arròs negre*, a black rice dish made with squid ink, and *fideuà*, made with short noodles instead of rice.

SEAFOOD STEWS

Sèpia amb pèsols is a vegetable and seafood *mar i muntanya* ("surf and turf") beloved on the Costa Brava: cuttlefish and peas are stewed with potatoes, garlic, onions, tomatoes, and a splash of wine. The *picadillo*—the finishing touches of flavors and textures—includes parsley, black pepper, fried bread, pine nuts, olive oil, and salt. *Es niu* ("the nest") of game fowl,

Fresh calçots

cod, tripe, cuttlefish, pork, and rabbit is another Costa Brava favorite. Stewed for a good five hours, this is a much-celebrated wintertime classic. You'll also find *suquet de peix,* a potato-based fish stew, at restaurants along the Costa Brava.

FRUITS AND VEGETABLES

Valencia and the eastern Levante region have long been famous as Spain's *huerta,* or garden. The alluvial soil of the littoral produces an abundance of everything from tomatoes to asparagus, peppers, chard, spinach, onions, artichokes, cucumbers, and the whole range of Mediterranean bounty. Valencia is also the country's largest producer of oranges. Catalonia's Maresme and Empordà regions are also fruit and vegetable centers, making this coastline a cornucopia of fresh produce.

WINES

The Penedès wine region west of Barcelona has been joined by new wine Denominations of Origin from all over Catalonia. Alt Camp, Tarragona, Priorat, Montsant, Costers del Segre, Pla de Bages, Alella, and Empordà all produce excellent reds and whites to join Catalonia's sparkling cava on local wine lists. The rich, full-bodied reds of Montsant and Priorat, especially, are among the best in Spain.

Suquet of fish, potatoes, onions, and tomatoes

The long curve of the Mediterranean from the French border to Cabo Cervera below Alicante encompasses the two autonomous communities of Catalonia and Valencia, with the country's second- and third-largest cities (Barcelona and Valencia, respectively). Rivals in many respects, the two communities share a language, history, and culture that set them apart from the rest of Spain.

Girona is the gateway to Northern Catalonia's attractions—the Pyrenees, the volcanic region of La Garrotxa, and the beaches of rugged Costa Brava. The region is memorable for the soft, green hills of the Empordà farm country and the Alberes mountain range at the eastern end of the Pyrenees. Across the landscape are *masías* (farmhouses) with staggered-stone roofs and square towers that make them look like fortresses. Even the tiniest village has its church, arcaded square, and *rambla,* where villagers take their evening *paseo* (stroll).

Over the years these Mediterranean shores entertained Phoenician, Greek, Carthaginian, and Roman visitors; the Romans stayed several centuries and left archaeological remains all the way down the coast, particularly in Tarragona, the capital of Rome's Spanish empire by 218 BC.

The province of Valencia was incorporated into the Kingdom of Aragón, Catalonia's medieval Mediterranean empire, when it was conquered by Jaume I in the 13th century. Along with

Catalonia, Valencia became part of the united Spanish state in the 15th century, but defenders of its separate cultural and linguistic identity still resent the centuries of Catalan domination. The Catalan language prevails in Catalonia, but Valenciano—a dialect of Catalan—is spoken and used on street signs in the Valencian provinces.

The coastal farmland and beaches that attracted the ancients now call to mod- ern-day tourists, and in parts, a number of "mass-tourism" resorts have marred the shore. Inland, however, local culture survives intact. The rugged and beautiful territory is dotted with small fortified towns, several of which bear the name of Spain's 11th-century national hero, El Cid, commemorating the battles he fought here against the Moors some 900 years ago.

MAJOR REGIONS
For many, **Northern Catalonia** is one of the top reasons to visit Spain. The historic center of Girona, its principal city, is a labyrinth of climbing cobblestone streets and staircases, with remarkable Gothic

and Romanesque buildings at every turn. El Call, the Jewish Quarter, is one of the best-preserved areas of its kind in Europe, and the Gothic cathedral is an architectural masterpiece. Streets in the modern part of the city are lined with smart shops and boutiques, and the overall quality of life in Girona is considered among the best in Spain.

Nearby is Figueres, an unremarkable town made exceptional by the Dalí Museum. Lesser known are the medieval towns in and around the volcanic (now extinct) area of La Garrotxa: the most charming is Besalú, a picture-perfect Romanesque village on a bluff overlooking the Riu Fluvià.

The **Costa Brava** (Wild Coast) is a nearly unbroken series of sheer rock cliffs dropping down to clear blue-green waters, punctuated by innumerable coves and tiny beaches on narrow inlets, called *calas*. It basically begins at Blanes and continues north along 135 km (84 miles) of coastline to the French border at Portbou.

Although the area does have spots of real-estate excess, the rocky terrain of many pockets (Tossa de Mar, Begur, and Cadaqués) has discouraged overbuilding. On a good day here, the luminous blue of the sea contrasts with red-brown headlands and cliffs, and the distant lights of fishing boats reflect on wine-colored waters at dusk. Stands of pine trees veil the footpaths to the many secluded coves and little patches of sand—often, the only access is by boat.

Southern Catalonia is home to the long, wide sand beaches of the Costa Daurada (Golden Coast) and the lively seaside town of Sitges. The region's principal city, Tarragona, brims with magnificent Roman-era sites. Inland, the Cistercian monasteries of Santes Creus and Santa Maria de Poblet impress, while Montserrat, home to the shrine of La Moreneta

(the Black Virgin of Montserrat), is one of most popular day trips from Barcelona.

Farther south lies **Valencia**, Spain's third-largest city and the capital of its region and province, equidistant from Barcelona and Madrid. For a day trip there's the Albufera, a scenic coastal wetland teeming with native wildlife, especially migratory birds.

The **Costa Blanca** (White Coast) begins at Dénia, south of Valencia, and stretches down roughly to Torrevieja, below Alicante. It's best known for its magical vacation combo of sand, sea, and sun, with popular beaches and more secluded coves and stretches of sand. Alicante itself has two long beaches, a charming old quarter, and mild weather most of the year.

Planning

When to Go

Come for the beaches in the hot summer months, but expect crowds and serious heat—in some places up to 40°C (104°F). The Mediterranean coast is more comfortable in May and September.

Winter travel in the region has its advantages: Valencia still has plenty of sunshine, and if you're visiting villages and wineries in the countryside, you might have the place all to yourself. Note that many restaurants and hotels outside the major towns may close on weekdays or longer in winter, so call ahead. Many museums and sites also close early in winter.

The Costa Brava, Costa Daurada, and Costa Blanca beach areas get hot and crowded in summer, and accommodations are at a premium. In contrast, spring is mild and an excellent time to tour the region, particularly the rural areas.

Planning Your Time

Northeast of Barcelona, the beautiful town of Girona is easily reachable from the city by train in under an hour. Nearby Figueres is a must if you want to see the Teatre-Museu Dalí. Girona makes an excellent base from which to explore La Garrotxa and the Costa Brava—for that, you'll need to rent a car.

Trains and buses from Barcelona service the beaches and seaside towns of the Costa Daurada, including Castelldefels, Altafulla, and Sitges, which can be reached in as little as a half-hour. Tarragona, less than one hour from Barcelona by train or a 1½-hour drive, is worth allotting a couple of days to explore its Roman wonders on foot.

Valencia is less than three hours by express train from Barcelona. Historic Valencia and the Santiago Calatrava–designed City of Arts and Sciences complex can be covered in two days, but stay longer and indulge in the city's food and explore the nightlife in the Barrio del Carmen.

Travel agencies in Alicante can arrange tours of the city and bus and train tours to Guadalest, the Algar waterfalls, the Peñón de Ifach (Calpe) on the Costa Blanca, and inland to Elche.

FESTIVALS

In Valencia, **Las Fallas** fiestas begin March 1 and reach a climax between March 15 and El Día de San José (St. Joseph's Day) on March 19, Father's Day in Spain. Las Fallas originated from St. Joseph's role as patron saint of carpenters; in medieval times, carpenters' guilds celebrated the arrival of spring by cleaning out their shops and making bonfires with scraps of wood.

These days, it's a 19-day celebration ending with fireworks, floats, carnival processions, and bullfights. On March 19, huge wood and papier-mâché effigies of political figures and other personalities (the result of a year's work by local community groups) are torched to end the fiestas.

Getting Here and Around

AIR

El Prat de Llobregat in Barcelona is the main international airport for the Costa Brava. Girona is the closest airport to the region, with bus connections directly into the city and to Barcelona. Valencia has an international airport with direct flights to London, Paris, Brussels, Lisbon, Zurich, and Milan as well as regional flights from Barcelona, Madrid, Málaga, and other cities in Spain. There is a regional airport in Alicante serving the Valencian region and Murcia.

BOAT

Short-cruise lines along the coast offer the chance to view the Costa Brava from the sea. Plan to spend around €25, depending on the length of the cruise. Many longer cruises include a stop en route for a swim. Nautilus is one such outfit, offering a variety of excursions, including ones to the Medes Islands underwater park in a glass-keel boat. The cost is around €22. Boats run daily April–October and weekends November–March.

BOAT AND FERRY INFORMATION Nautilus. ⊠ *Passeig Marítim 23,* ☎ *972/751–489* ⊕ *www.nautilus.es.*

BUS

Private companies run buses down the coast and from Madrid to Valencia, and to Alicante. ALSA is the main bus line in this region; check local tourist offices for schedules. Sarfa operates limited bus service from the Barcelona airport to many towns along the Costa Brava including Sant Feliu de Guixols, Platja d'Aro, Palamos, Palafrugell, and Begur. Sagalés mainly services Girona, Lleida, and the Costa Brava, and runs buses between the Girona and Barcelona airports.

CONTACTS ALSA. ☏ *902/422–242* ⊕ *www.alsa.es.* **Moventis Sarfa.** ☏ *902/302–025* ⊕ *compras.moventis. es/online.* **Sagalés.** ☏ *902/130014 tickets* ⊕ *www.sagales.com.* **Sagalés AirportLine.** ☏ *902/130014* ⊕ *www.sagalesairportline. com.*

CAR

A car is necessary for explorations inland and is far more convenient for reaching locations on the Costa Brava, where drives are scenic, though coastal roads can have a lot of twists and turns. Catalonia and Valencia have excellent roads; the only drawbacks are the high cost of fuel and the high tolls on the *autopistas* (highways, usually designated by the letters "AP"). The national roads (starting with the letter N) can get clogged, however, so you're often better off on toll roads if your time is limited.

TRAIN

Most of the Costa Brava is not served directly by railroad. A local line runs up the coast from Barcelona to Blanes, then turns inland and connects at Maçanet-Massanes with the main line up to France. Direct trains stop only at major connections, such as Girona, Llançà, and Figueres.

By contrast, a train line runs from Barcelona south along the coast, making it easy to reach many of the Costa Daurada's main seaside towns.

Keep in mind that some cities—including Tarragona and Valencia—have two train stations; one serving high-speed trains and located outside the city center, and one in the city center serving slower (and usually less expensive) regional trains.

From Barcelona to Tarragona, there are trains running approximately every 15 minutes. Regional trains take just over an hour and stop at the Tarragona station in the city center; direct high-speed trains

cut that time in half, arriving at Camp de Tarragona station, a 10-minute taxi ride to the center.

Express trains reach Valencia from all over Spain, arriving at the Joaquin Sorolla station; from there, a shuttle bus takes you to the Estación del Norte, the terminus in the center of town, for local connections. From Barcelona there are 15 trains a day, including the fast train Euromed, which takes 2 hours 40 minutes. There are 22 daily trains to Valencia from Madrid; the high-speed train takes about 1 hour 40 minutes.

For the Costa Blanca, the rail hub is Alicante.

CONTACTS RENFE. ☏ *912/320–320* ⊕ *www.renfe.com.*

Farmhouse Stays in Catalonia

Dotted throughout Catalonia are farmhouses (*casas rurales* in Spanish, and *cases de pagès* or *masies* in Catalan), where you can spend a weekend or longer. Accommodations vary from small rustic homes to spacious luxurious farmhouses with fireplaces and pools. Stay in a guest room at a bed-and-breakfast, or rent an entire house and do your own cooking. Most tourist offices, including the main Catalonia Tourist Office, have information and listings. Several organizations in Spain have detailed listings and descriptions of Catalonia's farmhouses.

CONTACTS Agroturisme. ☏ *932/680–900* ⊕ *www.agroturisme.cat.* **Cases Rurals.** ☏ *660/576–834* ⊕ *www.casesrurals.com.*

Restaurants

The region has several internationally acclaimed restaurants, but they aren't the only options when it comes to dining well. From traditional paella in a family-run restaurant to tapas at a *chiringuito* (beach shack) with tables on the sand, there are many ways to enjoy the gourmet delights.

Catalonia's eateries are deservedly famous. Girona's El Celler de Can Roca was voted Best Restaurant in the World multiple times in recent years in the annual critics' poll conducted by British magazine *Restaurant,* and a host of other first-rate establishments continue to offer inspiring fine dining in Catalonia.

Valencia is fast becoming one of Spain's culinary hot spots, counting eight Michelin-starred restaurants in 2022, including the two-starred El Poblet from chef Quique Dacosta, whose three-starred eponymous establishment in Dénia is a Costa Blanca must.

Restaurant reviews have been shortened. For full information, visit Fodors. com. Restaurant prices are the average cost of a main course at dinner or, if dinner is not served, at lunch.

Hotels

Lodgings on the Costa Brava, Costa Daurada, and Costa Blanca range from the finest hotels to spartan pensions. If you plan to visit during the high season (July and August), be sure to book reservations well in advance at almost any hotel in these areas; Costa Brava, in particular, is one of the most popular summer resort areas in Spain. Note that many hotels in resort towns are closed for all or part of the winter season (November–March).

Hotel reviews have been shortened. For full information, visit Fodors.com. Hotel prices are the lowest cost of a standard double room in high season.

What It Costs in Euros			
$	$$	$$$	$$$$
RESTAURANTS			
under €12	€12–€17	€18–€22	over €22
HOTELS			
under €90	€90–€125	€126–€180	over €180

Girona

97 km (60 miles) northeast of Barcelona.

At the confluence of four rivers, Northern Catalonia's Girona (population: 104,000) keeps intact the magic of its historic past. With its ancient city walls and soaring Gothic cathedral (which made an appearance in *Game of Thrones*), it resembles a vision from the Middle Ages.

Today, as a university center, Girona combines past and vibrant present: art galleries, chic cafés, and trendy boutiques have set up shop in many of the restored buildings of the old quarter, known as the Força Vella (Old Fortress), which is on the east side of the Riu Onyar (Onyar River). Built on the side of the mountain, it presents a tightly packed labyrinth of medieval buildings and monuments on narrow cobblestone streets with connecting stairways. You can still see vestiges of the Iberian and Roman walls in the cathedral square and in the patio of the old university. In the central quarter is El Call, one of Europe's best-preserved medieval (12th- to 15th-century) Jewish communities and an important center of Kabbalistic studies.

The main street of the Força Vella is Carrer de la Força, which follows the old Via Augusta, the Roman road that connected Rome with its provinces.

Costa Brava, Costa Blanca and Costa Daurada Beaches

Costa Brava Beaches

The beaches on the Costa Brava range from stretches of fine white sand to rocky coves and inlets; summer vacationers flock to **Tossa de Mar, Roses, Begur** and **Calella de Palafrugell**; in all but the busiest weeks of July and August, the tucked-away coves of **Cap de Creus National Park** are oases of peace and privacy.

Costa Blanca Beaches

The southeastern coastline of the Costa Blanca varies from the long stretches of sand dunes north of **Dénia** and south of **Alicante** to the coves and crescents in between. The benign climate permits lounging on the beach at least eight months of the year. **Altea**, popular with families, is busy and pebbly, but the old town has retained a traditional pueblo feel with narrow cobbled streets and attractive squares. **Calpe's** beaches have the scenic advantage of the sheer outcrop Peñón de Ifach (Cliff of Ifach), which stands guard over stretches of sand to either side. Dénia has family-friendly beaches to the north, where children paddle in relatively shallow waters, and rocky inlets to the south.

Costa Daurada Beaches

The Costa Daurada (Costa Dorada in Spanish) begins southwest of Barcelona and continues through the Tarragona province and down to L'Ampolla. It's characterized by wide, long, golden-sand beaches—those of **Castelldefels** (technically in neighboring Costa Garraf) and **Altafulla** are popular with day-trippers from Barcelona—interspersed with rocky coves that can be reached only on foot. **Sitges** is one of this coast's brightest stars, with its mix of great beaches, historical architecture, and a heady party scene. Southwest of Tarragona lies the mega-resort town of **Salou** and the quainter beaches of **Cambrils**.

Explore Girona on foot to discover many of its delights. One of Girona's treasures is its setting, high above where the Onyar merges with the Ter; the latter flows from a mountain waterfall that can be glimpsed in a gorge above the town. Walk first along the west bank of the Onyar, between the train trestle and the Plaça de la Independència, to admire the classic view of the old town, with its multicolored riverfront facades. Note how many of the windows and balconies are adorned with fretwork grilles of embossed wood or delicate iron tracery.

Cross Pont de Sant Agustí over to the old quarter from under the arcades in the corner of Plaça de la Independència and find your way to the Punt de Benvinguda tourist office, to the right at Rambla Llibertat 1. Work your way up through the labyrinth of steep streets, using the cathedral's huge baroque facade as a guide. Try to be in Girona during the second week of May, when the streets of the old quarter are festooned with the flowers of spring during the Girona Flower Festival.

GETTING HERE AND AROUND

More than 20 trains run daily from Barcelona to Girona (continuing on to the French border). Regional trains, which take between one and two hours, can be picked up from a number of stations in Barcelona, while the high-speed AVE train service is a convenient option, running from Barcelona Sants station to

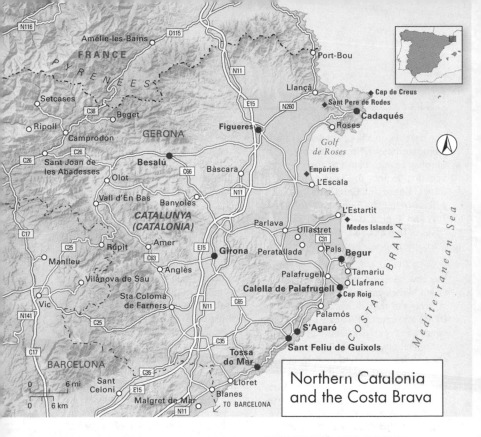

Northern Catalonia
and the Costa Brava

Girona in under 40 minutes (it's advisable to prebook the AVE). Tickets are around €35 round-trip. The train station is about a 20-minute walk from the old quarter; alternatively, taxis can be picked up in front of the train station on arrival.

Far less efficient Sagalés buses run from Barcelona's El Prat de Llobregat airport and Estació del Nord, in the center of Barcelona, to Girona city bus station, with a stop at the Girona Airport. They take an average of 75 minutes and cost €15 one-way, €24 round-trip.

Getting around the city is easiest on foot or by taxi. Several bridges connect the historic old quarter with the more modern town across the river.

CONTACTS Sagalés. ☎ *902/130014* ⊕ *www.sagales.com.*

DISCOUNTS AND DEALS

GironaMuseus (⊕ *museus.girona.cat*) offers discounted admission to six city museums after paying full price for the first museum. ■ **TIP→ Some museums are free on the first Sunday of every month.** Check the tourist office or at the Punt de Benvinguda welcome center, which can also arrange guided tours.

VISITOR INFORMATION

VISITOR INFORMATION Girona Office of Tourism. ⊠ *Rambla de la Llibertat 1,* ☎ *972/010–001* ⊕ *www.girona.cat/ turisme.* **Punt de Benvinguda.** ⊠ *Berenguer Carnicer 3,* ☎ *972/011–669* ⊕ *www. girona.cat/turisme.*

◉ Sights

Banys Arabs (*Arab Baths*)
HISTORIC SIGHT | A misnomer, the Banys Arabs were actually built by Morisco craftsmen (workers of Moorish descent) in the late 12th century, long after Girona's Islamic occupation (714–797) had ended. Following the old Roman model that had disappeared in the West, the custom of bathing publicly may have been brought back from the Holy Land with the Crusaders. These baths are sectioned off into three rooms in descending order: a *frigidarium*, or cold bath, a square room with a central octagonal pool and a skylight with cupola held up by two stories of eight fine columns; a *tepidarium*, or warm bath; and a *caldarium*, or steam room, beneath which is a chamber where a fire was kept burning. Here the inhabitants of old Girona came to relax, exchange gossip, or do business. ⊠ *Carrer Ferran el Catòlic s/n, Girona* ☎ *972/190–969* ⊕ *www. banysarabs.cat* ⊠ *€3.*

Basílica de Sant Feliu
CHURCH | One of Girona's most beloved churches and its first cathedral until the 10th century, Sant Feliu was repeatedly rebuilt and altered over four centuries and stands today as an amalgam of Romanesque columns, a Gothic nave, and a baroque facade. The vast bulk of this structure is landmarked by one of Girona's most distinctive belfries, topped by eight pinnacles. The basilica was founded over the tomb of St. Felix of Africa, a martyr under the Roman emperor Diocletian. ⊠ *Pujada de Sant Feliu 29, Girona* ☎ *972/201–407* ⊕ *www. catedraldegirona.cat* ⊠ *€7 (includes Girona Cathedral).*

★ Catedral de Girona (*Girona Cathedral*)
CHURCH | At the heart of the Força Vella, the cathedral looms above 90 steps and is famous for its nave—at 75 feet, the widest in the world and the epitome of the spatial ideal of Catalan Gothic

architects. Since Charlemagne founded the original church in the 8th century, it has been through many fires and renovations.

Take in the rococo-era facade, "eloquent as organ music" and impressive flight of 17th-century stairs, which rises from its own *plaça*. Inside, three smaller naves were compressed into one gigantic hall by the famed architect Guillermo Bofill in 1416. The change was typical of Catalan Gothic "hall" churches, and it was done to facilitate preaching to crowds. Note the famous silver canopy, or *baldaquí* (baldachin). The oldest part of the cathedral is the 11th-century Romanesque Torre de Carlemany (Charlemagne Tower).

The cathedral's exquisite 12th-century cloister has an obvious affinity with the cloisters in the Roussillon area of France. Inside the Treasury there's a variety of precious objects. They include a 10th-century copy of Beatus's manuscript *Commentary on the Apocalypse* (illuminated in the dramatically primitive Mozarabic style), the Bible of Emperor Charles V, and the celebrated *Tapís de la Creació* (*Tapestry of the Creation*), considered by most experts to be the finest tapestry surviving from the Romanesque era. ⊠ *Pl. de la Catedral s/n, Girona* ☎ *972/427–189* ⊕ *www.catedraldegirona. cat* ⊠ *€7 (includes Basílica de Sant Feliu).*

★ El Call (*Jewish Quarter*)
HISTORIC DISTRICT | Girona is especially noted for its 12th-century Jewish Quarter, El Call, which branches off Carrer de la Força, south of the Plaça Catedral. The quarter is a network of lanes that crisscross above one another, and houses built atop each other in disorderly fashion along narrow stone medieval streets. The earliest presence of Jews in Girona is uncertain, but the first historical mention dates from 982. This once-prosperous community—one of the most flourishing in Europe during the Middle Ages—was, at its height, a leading center of Kabbalistic learning. ⊠ *Girona.*

12

Catalonia, Valencia, and the Costa Blanca GIRONA

There's more to Girona's cathedral than the 90 steps to get to it; inside there's much to see, including the Treasury.

Monestir de Sant Pere de Galligants

RELIGIOUS BUILDING | The church of St. Peter, across the Galligants River, was finished in 1131, and is notable for its octagonal Romanesque belfry and the finely detailed capitals atop the columns in the cloister. It now houses the **Museu Arqueològic** (Museum of Archaeology), which documents the region's history since Paleolithic times and includes some artifacts from Roman times. ⊠ *Santa Llúcia 8, Girona* ☎ *972/202–632* ⊕ *www. macgirona.cat* ⊟ *€6* ⊘ *Closed Mon.*

Museu d'Art

ART MUSEUM | The Episcopal Palace near the cathedral contains the wide-ranging collections of Girona's main art museum. On display is everything from superb Romanesque *majestats* (carved wood figures of Christ) to reliquaries from Sant Pere de Rodes, illuminated 12th-century manuscripts, and works of the 20th-century Olot school of landscape painting. ⊠ *Pujada de la Catedral 12, Girona* ☎ *972/203–834* ⊕ *museuart.cat* ⊟ *€6* ⊘ *Closed Mon.*

Museu d'Història de Girona (*Girona History Museum*)

HISTORY MUSEUM | From pre-Roman objects to paintings and drawings from the notorious siege at the hands of Napoleonic troops, to the early municipal lighting system and the medieval printing press, artifacts from Girona's long and embattled past are exhibited in this fascinating museum. Rooms organized chronologically and by theme educate visitors on the ways the city has developed. ⊠ *Carrer de la Força 27, Girona* ☎ *972/222–229* ⊕ *www.girona. cat/museuhistoria* ⊟ *€4; free 1st Sun. of month* ⊘ *Closed Mon.*

★ Museu d'Història dels Jueus (*Museum of Jewish History*)

HISTORY MUSEUM | Housed in a former synagogue, this museum examines the history, daily life, and artistic and cultural traditions of Catalonia's Jewish communities in medieval times, with a focus on Girona. A highlight is the 21 stone tablets, one of the finest collections in the world of medieval Jewish funerary slabs. These came from the old Jewish cemetery of Montjuïc, revealed when the railroad between Barcelona and France was laid out in the 19th century.

The museum organizes conferences, exhibitions, and seminars. It also contains the Institut d'Estudis Nahmànides, with an extensive library of Judaica. ✉ *Carrer de la Força 8, Girona* ☎ *972/216–761* 🌐 *www.girona.cat/call/eng/museu.php* 🎟 *€4.*

Passeig Arqueològic

HISTORIC SIGHT | The landscaped gardens of this stepped archaeological walk are below the Força Vella's restored Carolingian walls (which you can walk, in parts) and enjoy superlative views of the city from belvederes and watchtowers. From there, climb through the Jardins de la Francesa to the highest ramparts for a view of the cathedral's 11th-century Torre de Carlemany. ✉ *Girona.*

🍴 Restaurants

Café le Bistrot

$ | **CATALAN** | This bistro's menu includes a 20-strong list of Catalan-style pizzas, served on peasant bread and incorporating regional ingredients like *botifarra* (sausage) and seasonal mushrooms. The delightful terrace is situated below a flight of stone stairs leading to the 17th-century Sant Martí church. **Known for:** affordable pizzas; lovely terrace; regional cheese plate. [$] *Average main: €10* ✉ *Pujada de Sant Domènec 4, Girona* ☎ *972/218–803* 🌐 *lebistrot.cat.*

Cal Ros

$$$$ | **CATALAN** | Tucked under the arcades just behind the north end of Plaça de la Llibertat, this restaurant combines ancient stone arches with crisp, contemporary furnishings and cheerful lighting. The menu changes regularly, featuring organically raised local produce in season, and fresh fish in updated versions of traditional Catalan cuisine. **Known for:** traditional cuisine with a modern spin; atmospheric setting; rice dishes. [$] *Average main: €24* ✉ *Carrer Cort Reial 9, Girona* ☎ *972/219176* 🕒 *Closed Mon. and Tues. No dinner Sun.*

★ **El Celler de Can Roca**

$$$$ | **CONTEMPORARY** | Holder of three Michelin stars since 2009, El Celler de Can Roca, helmed by the Roca brothers—Joan, Josep, and Jordi—is a life-changing culinary experience. Its two tasting menus, ranging from 14 to 22 courses and priced in the €200 range, feature wildly inventive dishes and daring presentations. **Known for:** reservations required many months or even a year ahead; expansive wine list; considered one of the best restaurants in the world. [$] *Average main: €200* ✉ *Can Sunyer 48, Girona* ☎ *972/222–157* 🌐 *cellercanroca.com* 🕒 *Closed Sun. and Mon., Easter and Christmas holidays, and most of Aug. No lunch Tues.*

La Fabrica

$ | **CAFÉ** | Owned by a professional cyclist and decorated with an abundance of bike memorabilia, this inviting cafe serves healthy, organic breakfasts and lunches—avocado toast, egg dishes, quinoa bowls—along with superb locally roasted coffee. It's a popular fuel-up stop for local cyclists. **Known for:** vegan options; excellent coffee; healthy breakfast and lunch bowls. [$] *Average main: €9* ✉ *Carrer de la Llebre 3, Girona* ☎ *872/000–273* 🌐 *www.lafabricagirona.com* 🕒 *No dinner.*

Mimolet

$$ | **CATALAN** | Contemporary architecture and cuisine in the old part of Girona make for interesting dining at this sleek, streamlined restaurant. Grilled eel and pepper rice and *fideuà* with shrimp in a seafood emulsion are typical dishes, and there's a frequently changing five- and 10-course tasting menu. **Known for:** tasting menu of seasonal dishes; local oysters on the half-shell; good wine list. [$] *Average main: €21* ✉ *Pou Rodó 12, Girona* ☎ *972/297973* 🌐 *www.mimolet.cat* 🕒 *Closed Mon.*

With its picturesque rivers, Girona is often called the Spanish Venice.

Rocambolesc

$ | ICE CREAM | FAMILY | Not your average ice-cream parlor, this to-go spot is the brainchild of master confectioner Jordi Roca, of El Celler de Can Roca fame. Exquisite *helados*, fanciful toppings, and popsicles in the shape of Girona's famous climbing bear are just some of the treats you'll find here. **Known for:** molded popsicles; fun toppings; excellent ice cream. [$] *Average main: €5* ✉ *Carrer Santa Clara 50, Girona* ☎ *972/416–667* 🌐 *www.rocambolesc.com.*

Hotels

Casa Cacao

$$$$ | HOTEL | The first hotel from the three-Michelin-starred Roca Brothers occupies a historic building in the medieval center. **Pros:** large rooms; gourmet breakfast included; excellent location in the medieval center. **Cons:** rooms are pricey; smaller rooms lack views; parking is extra. [$] *Rooms from: €250* ✉ *Carrer Ginesta 2, Girona* ☎ *972/282–828* 🌐 *hotelcasacacao.com* 🛏 *15 suites* 🍴 *Free Breakfast.*

Hotel Peninsular

$ | HOTEL | In a handsomely restored 19th-century building across the Onyar River, with views into Girona's historic Força Vella, this modest hotel occupies a strategic spot at the end of the Pont de Pedra (Stone Bridge), a Girona landmark in the center of the shopping district. **Pros:** good location at the hub of Girona life; friendly staff; near the stop for the bus from Girona airport. **Cons:** no frills; basic decor; smallish rooms. [$] *Rooms from: €90* ✉ *Carrer Nou 3, Av. Sant Francesc 6, Girona* ☎ *972/203800* 🌐 *www.hotelpeninsulargirona.com* 🛏 *48 rooms* 🍴 *No Meals.*

Nightlife

Girona is a university town, so the night scene is especially lively during the school year. In the labyrinth of small streets throughout the pedestrianized Barri Vell (Old Town), several *vermuterias*

(vermouth-focused bars), wine bars, and affable taverns provide entertainment as night falls.

Sunset Jazz Club
LIVE MUSIC | As the evening develops, drop into the Sunset Jazz Club to catch some live jazz by national and international artists in a softly lit, buzzing venue with exposed brick walls and dark furnishings. ⊠ *Calle Jaume Pons i Martí 12, Girona* ☎ *872/080145* ⊕ *www.sunsetjazz-club.com.*

🛍 Shopping

CRAFTS
Recorda-te'n
SOUVENIRS | Local crafts, from wood puzzles of the Girona Cathedral to ceramic versions of the city's famous colorful houses along the Onyar River, are for sale at this small shop on Carrer de la Força, in the heart of the old quarter. ⊠ *Carrer de la Força 2, Girona* ☎ *972/227–890* ⊕ *recordaten.cat.*

FOOD, CANDY, AND WINE
Gluki
CHOCOLATE | This Olot-based chocolatier and confectioner has been in business since 1870. ⊠ *Carrer Nou 9, Girona* ☎ *972/201–989* ⊕ *www.gluki.cat.*

La Simfonia
WINE/SPIRITS | At this relaxed wine shop that has a small restaurant, you can get a tour through a stellar range of regional wines (and cheeses)—and sample before you buy. ⊠ *Pl. de l'Oli 6, Girona* ☎ *972/411253* ⊕ *www.lasimfonia.com.*

JEWELRY
Baobab
JEWELRY & WATCHES | A lot of designer Anna Casal's original jewelry seems at first sight to be rough-hewn; it takes a second careful look to realize how sophisticated it really is. This shop doubles as her studio. ⊠ *Carrer de les Hortes 18, Girona* ☎ *972/410–227* ⊕ *baobabjoieriagirona.blogspot.com.*

Figueres

37 km (23 miles) north of Girona.

Figueres is the capital of the *comarca* (county) of the Alt Empordà, the bustling county seat of this predominantly agricultural region. People come from the surrounding area to shop at its many stores and stock up on farm equipment and supplies. Thursday is market day, and farmers gather at the top of La Rambla to do business and gossip while taking refreshments at cafés.

What brings the tourists to Figueres in droves, however, has little to do with agriculture and everything to do with Salvador Dalí's jaw-droppingly surreal "theater-museum"—one of the most visited museums in Spain.

GETTING HERE AND AROUND
There's regular regional train service from Barcelona to Figueres and the trip takes about two hours. (The high-speed train is half that, but you'll have to take a shuttle from the Figueres Vilafant station, which is outside the city.)

Local buses are also frequent, especially from Cadaqués, which is about an hour away, with more than eight scheduled daily. If you're driving, take the AP7 north from Girona. The town is small enough to explore on foot.

VISITOR INFORMATION
CONTACTS Figueres. ⊠ *Pl. de l'Escorxador 2,* ☎ *972/503155* ⊕ *en.visitfigueres.cat.*

👁 Sights

Castell de Sant Ferran (*Sant Ferran Castle*)
CASTLE/PALACE | Just a minute's drive northwest of Figueres is this imposing 18th-century fortified castle, one of the largest in Europe—only when you start exploring can you appreciate how immense it is. The parade grounds extend for acres, and the arcaded stables

Figueres's Famous Son

With a painterly technique that rivaled that of Jan van Eyck, a flair for publicity so aggressive it would have put P. T. Barnum to shame, and a penchant for the shocking (he loved telling people Barcelona's historic Barri Gòtic should be knocked down), artist Salvador Dalí, whose most lasting image may be the melting watches in his iconic 1931 painting *The Persistence of Memory*, enters art history as one of the foremost proponents of surrealism, the movement launched in the 1920s by André Breton. The artist, who was born in Figueres and died there in 1989, decided to create a museum-monument to himself during the last two decades of his life. Dalí often frequented the Cafeteria Astòria at the top of La Rambla (still the center of social life in Figueres), signing autographs for tourists or just being Dalí: he once walked down the street with a French omelet in his breast pocket instead of a handkerchief.

can hold more than 500 horses; the perimeter is roughly 4 km (2½ miles around). This castle was the site of the last official meeting of the Republican parliament (on February 1, 1939) before it surrendered to Franco's forces. Ironically, it was here that Lieutenant Colonel Antonio Tejero was imprisoned after his failed 1981 coup d'état in Madrid.

■ TIP→ Call ahead and arrange for the two-hour Catedral de l'Aiguas guided tour in English (€15), which includes a trip through the castle's subterranean water system by Zodiac pontoon boat. ⊠ *Pujada del Castell s/n, Figueres* ☎ *972/506–094* ⊕ *castell-santferran.com* 🖘 *€4* ⊘ *Closed Mon.*

Museu del Joguet de Catalunya (*Toy Museum*)

OTHER MUSEUM | FAMILY | Hundreds of antique dolls and toys are on display here—including collections owned by, among others, Salvador Dalí, Federico García Lorca, and Joan Miró. The museum also hosts Catalonia's only *caganer* exhibit. These playful little figures answering nature's call have long had a special spot in the Catalan *pessebre* (Nativity scene). Farmers are the most traditional figures, squatting discreetly behind the animals, but these days you'll find Barça soccer players and politicians, too. ⊠ *Carrer de Sant Pere 1, Figueres* ☎ *972/504585* ⊕ *www.mjc.cat* 🖘 *€7* ⊘ *Closed Sun. and Mon.*

★ Teatre-Museu Dalí (*Dalí Theater Museum*)

ART MUSEUM | "Museum" was not a big enough word for Dalí, so he christened his monument a theater. In fact, the building was once the Força Vella theater, reduced to a ruin in the Spanish Civil War. Now topped with a glass geodesic dome and studded with Dalí's iconic egg shapes, the multilevel structure pays homage to his fertile imagination and artistic creativity. It includes gardens, ramps, and a spectacular drop cloth Dalí painted for Les Ballets de Monte Carlo. Don't look for his greatest paintings here, although there are some memorable images, including *Gala at the Mediterranean,* which takes the body of Gala (Dalí's wife) and morphs it into the image of Abraham Lincoln once you look through coin-operated viewfinders.

The Dalí Museum in Figueres is itself a work of art. Note the eggs on the exterior: they're a common image in the artist's work.

The sideshow theme continues with other coin-operated pieces, including *Taxi Plujós* (*Rainy Taxi*), in which water gushes over the snail-covered occupants sitting in a Cadillac once owned by Al Capone, or *Sala de Mae West*, a trompe-l'oeil vision in which a pink sofa, two fireplaces, and two paintings morph into the face of the onetime Hollywood sex symbol. Fittingly, another "exhibit" on view is Dalí's own crypt. ✉ *Pl. Gala-Salvador Dalí 5, Figueres* ☎ *972/677–500* 🌐 *www.salvador-dali.org* 🎫 *€15* 🕒 *Closed Mon. except July and Aug. and public holidays.*

🍴 Restaurants

Bocam

$$ | **SPANISH** | This stylish restaurant, just around the corner from the Dalí Theatre-Museum, focuses on seasonal Empordà ingredients from the Pyrenees and the Mediterranean. Look for classic Catalan fare like prawn and cuttlefish fideuá alongside more modern dishes such as tuna tataki with black garlic. **Known for:** seasonal ingredients; pleasant terrace; local Empordà wines. [$] *Average main: €17* ✉ *Carrer de la Jonquera 18, Figueres* ☎ *972/539–494* 🌐 *bocam.cat/ca/inici/* 🕒 *Closed Mon. No dinner Sun.*

★ El Motel

$$$$ | **CATALAN** | Just 1½ km (1 mile) north of town, this restaurant—housed within a rather nondescript hotel—has been hailed as the birthplace of modern Catalan cuisine and is a beacon for gourmands. The hyper-local menu changes with the seasons and features such dishes as eggplant with anchovies from Cadaqués, black truffle risotto, and a vanilla tart topped with strawberries from nearby Vilafant. **Known for:** impeccable service; marvelous cheese selection; historic culinary destination. [$] *Average main: €29* ✉ *inside Hotel Empordà, Av. Salvador Dalí i Domènech 170, Figueres* ☎ *972/500562* 🌐 *www.elmotelrestaurant.com.*

Dali's Castle [👁]

Castell Gala Dalí - Púbol. The third point of the Dalí triangle (along with the Teatre-Museu Dalí and Casa Salvador Dalí - Portlligat, his summer house) is the medieval castle of Púbol, where the artist's wife and perennial model, Gala, is buried in the crypt. During the 1970s this was Gala's residence, though Dalí also lived here in the early 1980s. It contains paintings and drawings, Gala's haute-couture dresses, and other objects chosen by the couple. It's also a chance to wander through another Daliesque landscape, with lush gardens, fountains decorated with masks of Richard Wagner (the couple's favorite composer), and distinctive elephants with giraffe's legs and claw feet. Púbol, a small village roughly between Girona and Figueres, is near the C66. If you are traveling by train, get off at the Flaçà station on the Barcelona–Portbou line; take a taxi 4 km (2½ miles) to Púbol. ✉ *Púbol-la Pera, Púbol* ☎ *972/488–655* 🌐 *www.salvador-dali.org* 🎫 *€8* 🕒 *Hours and opening days vary month to month* ✍ *Booking tickets in advance (online) is essential.*

Hotels

Hotel Duràn

$ | **HOTEL** | Dalí had his own private dining room in this former stagecoach relay station, though the guest rooms, refurbished in bland pale-wood tones and standard contemporary furnishings, offset the hotel's historic 19th-century exterior. **Pros:** good central location; family-friendly; dining room has pictures of Dalí. **Cons:** somewhat erratic service; parking inconvenient and an extra charge; rooms lack character. [$] *Rooms from: €85* ✉ *Carrer Lasauca 5, Figueres* ☎ *972/501–250* 🌐 *www.hotelduran.com* 🛏 *65 rooms* 🍴 *No Meals.*

Besalú

34 km (21 miles) northwest of Girona, 25 km (15 miles) west of Figueres.

Besalú is one of the best-preserved medieval towns in Catalonia. Among its main sights are the 12th-century Romanesque fortified bridge over the Riu Fluvià; two churches—Sant Vicenç (set on an attractive, café-lined plaza) and Sant Pere; and the ruins of the convent of Santa Maria on the hill above town.

GETTING HERE AND AROUND

With a population of less than 2,500, the village is easily small enough to stroll through—restaurants and sights are within walking distance of each other. There is bus service to Besalú from Figueres and Girona.

VISITOR INFORMATION

CONTACTS Besalú Tourist Office. ✉ *Carrer del Pont Vell 1,* ☎ *972/591240* 🌐 *www.besalu.cat.*

Sights

Església de Sant Pere

CHURCH | This 12th-century Romanesque church is part of a 10th-century monastery, still in an excellent state of preservation. It's set on the town's main plaza, Sant Pere, with many cafes and terraces. ✉ *Pl. de Sant Pere s/n, Besalú.*

Església de Sant Vicenç

CHURCH | Founded in 977, this pre-Romanesque gem contains the relics of St. Vincent as well as the tomb of its benefactor, Pere de Rovira. La Capella de la Veracreu (Chapel of the True Cross)

Besalú contains astonishingly well-preserved medieval buildings.

displays a reproduction of an alleged fragment of the True Cross brought from Rome by Bernat Tallafer in 977 and stolen in 1899. ✉ *Pl. Sant Vicenç s/n, Besalú.*

Jewish Ritual Bath

RUINS | The remains of this 13th-century *mikvah,* or Jewish ritual bath, were discovered in the 1960s; it's one of the few surviving in Spain. A stone stairway leads down into the chamber where the water was drawn from the river, but little else indicates the role that the baths played in the medieval Jewish community. Access is by guided tour only (organized through the tourist office). ✉ *Calle de Pont Vell 1, Besalú* ☎ *972/591–240 tourist office* 🎟 *€2.50* 🕒 *Admission by guided tour only, Jul.–Sept., Tues. 11 am (in English)* ✍ *Reservations essential.*

Pont Fortificat

BRIDGE | The town's most emblematic feature is this Romanesque 11th-century fortified bridge with crenellated battlements spanning the Riu Fluvià. ✉ *Carrer del Pont, Besalú.*

Santa Maria de Besalú

RUINS | The ruins of the 13th-century Santa Maria Convent, on a hill just outside of town, make a good walk and offer a panoramic view over Besalú. ✉ *Besalú.*

🍴 Restaurants

★ Restaurant Pont Vell

$$$$ | **CATALAN** | Book in advance for a table on the romantic riverfront terrace and you'll be rewarded with exceptional views of Besalu's iconic medieval bridge. The prix-fixe menu changes monthly and offers a wide array of traditional Catalan dishes of superb quality, with seasonal ingredients sourced from the nearby Banyols market. **Known for:** warm, friendly service; seasonal menu; terrace with views. [$] *Average main: €38* ✉ *Pont Vell 24, Besalú* ☎ *972/591–027* 🌐 *www.restaurantpontvell.com* 🕒 *Closed Mon. and Tues. No dinner Sun. Dinner Fri. and Sat. only in winter.*

Did You Know?

In the 1950s, Tossa de Mar was famous for the arrival of Ava Gardner to film "The Flying Dutchman" with James Mason. In 1998 a bronze statue was erected within the castle walls to honor her.

Tossa de Mar

80 km (50 miles) northeast of Barcelona, 41 km (25 miles) south of Girona.

Christened "Blue Paradise" by painter Marc Chagall, who summered here for four decades, Tossa's pristine beaches are among Catalonia's best. Set around a gorgeous bay, it's comprised of the the Vila Vella (Old Town) and the Vila Nova (New Town). The Vila Vella is a lovely district open to the sea and threaded by steep cobblestone streets with many restored buildings.

Ava Gardner filmed the 1951 British drama *Pandora and the Flying Dutchman* here (a statue dedicated to her stands on a terrace on the medieval walls). Things may have changed since those days, but this beautiful village retains much of the unspoiled magic of its past. The primary beach at Tossa de Mar is the Platja Gran (Big Beach) in front of the town beneath the walls, and just next to it is Mar Menuda (Little Sea), where the small, colorfully painted fishing boats—maybe the same ones that caught your dinner—pull up onto the beach.

The beaches and town are a magnet for vacationers in July and August. Out of season, it's far more sedate, but the mild temperatures make it an ideal stop for coastal strolls.

GETTING HERE AND AROUND

By car, the fastest way to Costa Brava's Tossa de Mar from Barcelona is to drive up the inland C-33 tollway toward Girona, then take Sortida 10 (Exit 9A). The C-32 can also get you there in a similar length of time. Direct buses from Barcelona's Estació del Nord run regularly and take about 1 1/4 hours. The main bus station (as well as the local tourist office inside the station) is on Plaça de les Nacions Sense Estat.

Sights

Museu Municipal

ART MUSEUM | In a lovingly restored 14th-century house, this museum is said to be Catalonia's first dedicated to modern art. It is home to one of the only three Chagall paintings in Spain, *Celestial Violinist.* ⊠ *Pl. Pintor Roig i Soler 1, Tossa de Mar* ☎ *972/340–709* 🖼 *€3* ⊙ *Closed Mon.*

Vila Vella and Castillo de Tossa de Mar

HISTORIC DISTRICT | Listed as a national artistic-historic monument in 1931, Tossa de Mar's Vila Vella (Old Town) is the only remaining example of a fortified medieval town in Catalonia. Set high above the town on a promontory, the Old Town is presided over by the ramparts and towers of the 13th-century Castillo de Tossa de Mar, and is a steep yet worthy climb up from the main town, accessed from the western side of Platja Gran Tossa de Mar (Playa Grande).

The cliff-top views, particularly at sunset, are remarkable, and the labyrinth of narrow, cobblestone lanes lined with ancient houses (some dating back to the 14th century) is a delight to explore at a leisurely pace. ■TIP→ **Bar del Far de Tossa, near the lighthouse, has some of the best views in town, plus drinks, snacks, and light meals.** ⊠ *Tossa de Mar.*

Beaches

Mar Menuda (*Little Sea*)

BEACH | FAMILY | Just north of the town center, this small sandy crescent is a pleasant Blue Flag beach that's popular with local families. The sand is coarse, but the calm, shallow waters make it ideal for children. Fishing boats bob peacefully in the water nearby after completing their morning's work. At the top of the beach there is a second cove called La Banyera de Ses Dones (the women's bathtub), which provides ideal conditions for diving, though if the sea is not calm, it is dangerous for swimmers. By day there is little natural shade, so bring adequate sunblock and an umbrella if you plan a long beach session. It gets extremely busy in high season. **Amenities:** none. **Best for:** snorkeling; sunset; swimming. ✉ *Av. Mar Menuda, Tossa de Mar.*

Platja Gran (*Big Beach*)
BEACH | FAMILY | Sweeping past the Vila Vella, this well-maintained, soft-sand Blue Flag beach runs along the front of town to meet the base of the Cap de Tossa. One of the most photographed coastlines in this area of Spain, it is also, at the height of summer, one of the busiest. Conditions are normally fine for swimming (any warnings are announced via loudspeaker). Running behind the beach, there is no shortage of cafés and kiosks selling ice cream and snacks. There is no natural shade, but you can rent deck chairs and umbrellas. **Amenities:** food and drink; lifeguards; showers; toilets; water sports. **Best for:** snorkeling; sunset; swimming. ✉ *Av. de sa Palma, Tossa de Mar.*

🍴 Restaurants

La Cuina de Can Simon
$$$$ | CATALAN | Elegantly rustic, this restaurant beside Tossa de Mar's medieval walls serves classical Catalan cuisine from the sea, including lobster rice, and the mountains, such as a traditional mixed-meat stew. A tapas tasting menu (€98) lets you sample a bit of everything. **Known for:** welcoming tapa and cava upon entrance; seasonal menu; top-notch service. [$] *Average main: €32* ✉ *Carrer del Portal 24, Tossa de Mar* ☎ *972/341–269* 🌐 *cuinacansimon.com* 🕒 *Closed Mon. No dinner Sun.*

Restaurant Minerva
$$$ | SEAFOOD | Dine on fresh seafood and paella on the terrace with fabulous views of the sea and the castle beyond. **Known for:** fresh fish; great views from the terrace; seafood paella. [$] *Average main: €22* ✉ *Carrer Sant Ramon de Penyafort 7, Tossa de Mar* ☎ *972/340–939* 🌐 *restaurantminerva.es* 🕒 *Closed Wed.*

🛏 Hotels

Hotel Capri
$$ | HOTEL | FAMILY | Located on the beach, this hotel is in hailing distance of the old quarter in the medieval fortress; rooms are simple, and those with sea views have private terraces. **Pros:** family-friendly option; good value; great location. **Cons:** no private parking; minimal amenities; rooms are small. [$] *Rooms from: €110* ✉ *Passeig del Mar 17, Tossa de Mar* ☎ *972/340358* 🌐 *www.hotelcapritossa.com* 🕒 *Closed Nov.–Feb.* 🔑 *24 rooms* 🍽 *Free Breakfast.*

★ Hotel Diana
$$$ | HOTEL | Built in 1906 by architect Antoni de Falguera i Sivilla, disciple of Antoni Gaudí, this Moderniste gem sits on the square in the heart of the Vila Vella, steps from the beach. **Pros:** attentive service; Moderniste touches; ideal location, with sea views. **Cons:** some rooms are small; room rates unpredictable; minimal amenities. [$] *Rooms from: €176* ✉ *Pl. de Espanya 6, Tossa de Mar* ☎ *972/341886* 🌐 *www.hotelesdante.com* 🕒 *Closed Nov.–Apr.* 🔑 *21 rooms* 🍽 *Free Breakfast.*

Sant Feliu de Guixols

23 km (14 miles) northeast of Tossa de Mar.

Sant Feliu de Guixols is set on a small bay with Moderniste mansions lining the seafront promenade, recalling a time when the cork industry made this one of the wealthier towns on the coast. In front of them, a long crescent beach of fine white sand leads around to the fishing harbor at its north end. Behind the promenade, a well-preserved old quarter of narrow streets and squares leads to a 10th-century gateway with horseshoe arches (all that remains of a pre-Romanesque monastery); also here is a church that combines Romanesque, Gothic, and baroque styles. Nearby, the iron-structured indoor market, which dates back to the 1930s, sells fresh local produce, with colorful stalls often overflowing onto the Plaça del Mercat in front.

GETTING HERE AND AROUND

To get here, take the C65 from Tossa de Mar—though adventurous souls might prefer the harrowing hairpin curves of the G1-682 coastal road.

Sights

Museu d'Història de Sant Feliu de Guíxols
HISTORY MUSEUM | Inside the Romanesque Benedictine monastery is this museum, which contains interesting exhibits about the town's cork and fishing trades, and displays local archaeological finds. ✉ *Pl. del Monestir s/n, Sant Feliu de Guixols* ☎ *972/821575* 🌐 *www.museu.guixols.cat* 🎫 *€2* 🕒 *Closed Mon.*

Restaurants

Can Segura
$$ | **CATALAN** | Half a block in from the beach at Sant Feliu de Guixols, this restaurant serves house-cooked seafood and upland specialties. The *pimientos de piquillos rellenos de brandada* (sweet red peppers stuffed with codfish mousse) are first-rate, as are the rice dishes. **Known for:** excellent rice dishes; daily menu specials; first-rate seafood. [$] *Average main: €15* ✉ *Carrer de Sant Pere 11, Sant Feliu de Guixols* ☎ *972/321–009* 🌐 *cansegurahotel.com/en/restaurant.*

Hotel Restaurant Sant Pol
$$$ | **SPANISH** | This casual restaurant with a beachfront terrace serves fresh seafood and rice dishes, plus an affordable three-course lunch menu (€16.50). **Known for:** paella and fideuà; sea views; local fish. [$] *Average main: €22* ✉ *Passeig de Sant Pol 125, Sant Feliu de Guixols* ☎ *972/321070* 🌐 *www.hotelsantpol.com* 🕒 *Closed Thurs.*

Hotels

Hostal del Sol
$$ | **HOTEL** | **FAMILY** | Once the summer home of a wealthy family, this Moderniste hotel has a grand stone stairway and medieval-style tower, as well as a garden and a lawn where you can relax by the pool. **Pros:** family-friendly option; good breakfast; good value. **Cons:** on a busy road; far from the beach; bathrooms a bit claustrophobic. [$] *Rooms from: €120* ✉ *Ctra. a Palamós 194, Sant Feliu de Guixols* ☎ *972/320193* 🌐 *www.hostaldelsol.cat/en* 🕒 *Closed mid-Oct.–Easter* 🔑 *41 rooms* 🍴 *Free Breakfast.*

S'Agaró

3 km (2 miles) north of Sant Feliu de Guixols.

S'Agaró is an elegant gated community on a rocky point at the north end of the cove. The 30-minute walk along the sea wall from Hostal de La Gavina to Sa Conca Beach is a delight, and the one-hour hike from Sant Pol Beach over to Sant Feliu de Guixols offers views of the Costa Brava at its best.

Restaurants

Villa Mas
$$$$ | **CATALAN** | Set in a Moderniste villa with a lovely turn-of-the-20th-century zinc bar, this restaurant serves typical Catalan and seasonal Mediterranean dishes like *arròs a la cassola* (deep-dish rice) with shrimp brought fresh off the boats in Palamos, just up the coast. The terrace is a popular spot just across the road from the beach. **Known for:** fresh seafood catches; across from beach; terrace dining. [$] *Average main: €28* ✉ *Passeig de Sant Pol 95, S'Agaro* ☎ *972/822526*

⊕ *www.restaurantvillamas.com* ⊗ *Closed Mon. and Tues. No dinner Sun.*

 Hotels

★ Hostal de la Gavina

$$$$ | **HOTEL** | Opened in 1932 by farmer-turned-entrepreneur Josep Ensesa, the original hotel grew from a cluster of country villas into a sprawling complex of buildings of extraordinary splendor that have attracted celebrity guests from Orson Welles and Ava Gardner to Sean Connery. **Pros:** museum-quality furnishings; sea views, including from pool and terrace; impeccable service and amenities. **Cons:** expensive restaurant; walls are thin; hard on the budget. $ *Rooms from: €490* ✉ *Pl. Roserar s/n, S'Agaró* ☎ *972/321–100* ⊕ *www.lagavina. com* ⊗ *Closed Nov.–Easter* ⇄ *74 rooms* ⦿ *Free Breakfast.*

S'Agaró Hotel Wellness & Spa

$$ | **HOTEL** | **FAMILY** | Surrounded by gardens with the Sant Pol Beach just below, this elegant, family-friendly property features a modern spa with an indoor pool and an outdoor pool with views of the sea. **Pros:** kid-friendly accommodations; beautiful gardens; all rooms have terraces. **Cons:** popular hotel for weddings and conventions; rooms could be better soundproofed; charge to use spa. $ *Rooms from: €120* ✉ *Platja de Sant Pol s/n, S'Agaró* ☎ *972/325200* ⊕ *www. sagarohotel.com* ⇄ *95 rooms* ⦿ *Free Breakfast.*

Calella de Palafrugell and Around

25 km (15½ miles) north of S'Agaró.

Up the coast from S'Agaró, the C31 brings you to Palafrugell; to the east are some of the prettiest, least developed inlets of the Costa Brava. One road leads to **Llafranc,** a small port with waterfront hotels and restaurants, and forks right to the fishing village of **Calella de Palafrugell,** known for its July habaneras festival. (The *habanera* is a form of Cuban dance music brought to Europe by Catalan sailors in the late 19th century; it still enjoys a nostalgic cachet here.) Just south is the panoramic promontory of **Cap Roig,** with views of the barren Formigues Isles.

North along the coast lies **Tamariu,** a largely unspoiled former fishing village backed by simple whitewashed houses and a small strip of seafood restaurants that hug the shoreline, is reached by descending a vertiginous road set between mountains and pine forests.

 Restaurants

★ Pa i Raïm

$$$ | **CATALAN** | "Bread and Grapes" in Catalan, Pa i Raïm is an excellent restaurant set in writer Josep Pla's ancestral family home in Palafrugell. It has one rustic dining room as well as another in a glassed-in winter garden, plus a leafy terrace, which is the place to be in summer. **Known for:** garden terrace; traditional and contemporary menu; grilled whole fish. $ *Average main: €20* ✉ *Torres i Jonama 56, Palafrugell* ☎ *972/447278* ⊕ *www. pairaim.com* ⊗ *Closed Mon. No dinner Sun.–Thurs.*

 Hotels

Hotel Llevant

$$$ | **HOTEL** | This charming family-run boutique hotel in the village of Llafranc sits just across from the main beach. **Pros:** friendly service; heated outdoor pool; seaside location. **Cons:** rooms facing the street can be noisy; petite rooms; rates soar in summer. $ *Rooms from: €170* ✉ *Pere Pascuet 3, Llafranc* ☎ *972/300–366* ⊕ *www.hotel-llevant.com* ⇄ *24 rooms* ⦿ *No Meals.*

Hotel-Restaurant El Far

$$$$ | **B&B/INN** | **FAMILY** | Rooms in this 17th-century hermitage attached to a 15th-century watchtower have original vaulted ceilings, hardwood floors, and interiors accented with floral prints; the larger doubles and the suite can accommodate extra beds for children. **Pros:** friendly service; spectacular views of bay; graceful architecture. **Cons:** need car; pricey for what you get; a bit of a distance from the beach. ⓢ *Rooms from: €330* ✉ *Muntanya de Sant Sebastia, Carrer Uruguai s/n, Llafranc* ☎ *972/301639* ⊕ *www.hotelelfar.com/en* ⤳ *9 rooms* ⓘⓄⓘ *Free Breakfast.*

Begur and Around

11 km (7 miles) north of Calella de Palafrugell.

Carved into a hillside above the Costa Brava, Begur is an enchanting maze of steep, narrow streets lined with lavish 19th-century Spanish Colonial mansions, now housing smart restaurants, shops, and boutique hotels. The crumbling ruins of the 11th-century hilltop fortress lord over the town below, and offer magnificent panoramic views of the Mediterranean sea.

From Begur, go east through the calas or take the inland route past the rose-color stone houses and ramparts of the restored medieval town of **Pals.** Nearby **Peratallada** is another medieval fortified town with an 11th-century castle, tower, and palace. The name is derived from *pedra tallada,* meaning "carved stone," and behind its well-preserved walls is a maze of narrow streets and ivy-covered houses built from stone that was carved from the moat, which still encircles the town. In the center, the arcaded Plaça de les Voltes is alive with restaurants, shops, and cafés.

North of Pals there are signs for **Ullastret,** an Iberian village dating to the 5th century BC. **L'Estartit** is the jumping-off point for the spectacular natural park surrounding the **Medes Islands,** famous for its protected marine life and consequently for diving and underwater photography.

◉ Sights

Beaches

BEACH | The Begur coast is dotted with idyllic swimming coves and sandy beaches, from the northernmost Platja del Racó south to Aiguablava, its loveliest strand, framed by rugged cliffs and pine trees. Parking can be limited, so it's best to take advantage of the shuttle bus that leaves from Begur's Plaça Forgas, near the main tourist office, and drops you at the three main beaches: Sa Tuna, Sa Riera, and Aiguablava. A coastal footpath, the Camí de Ronda, links many of the beaches and coves. ✉ *Sa Tuna, Begur.*

Empúries

RUINS | The Greco-Roman ruins here are Catalonia's most important archaeological site, and this port is one of the most monumental ancient engineering feats on the Iberian Peninsula. As the Greeks' original point of arrival in Spain, Empúries was also where the Olympic Flame entered Spain for Barcelona's 1992 Olympic Games. ✉ *Puig i Cadafalch s/n* ☎ *972/770–208* ⊕ *www.macempuries. cat* 🎫 *€6.*

ⓘⓘ Restaurants

★ Hostal Restaurant Sa Rascassa

$$$ | **SPANISH** | Dine on fresh seafood, grilled meats, and pasta on the tranquil, tree-shaded patio or inside the rustic-chic dining room. From here, it's a short stroll to the secluded Aiguafreda swimming cove. **Known for:** variety of seafood tapas; attractive patio; grilled specialties. ⓢ *Average main: €20* ✉ *Cala Aiguafreda 3,*

Begur ☎ *972/622–845* 🌐 *hostalsarascassa.com* 🕓 *Closed Tues. and Nov.–Mar.*

Restaurant Ibèric

$$$ | **CATALAN** | This excellent pocket of authentic Costa Brava cuisine serves everything from snails to wild boar in season. Wild mushrooms scrambled with eggs or stewed with hare are specialties. **Known for:** excellent local wine list; lovely terrace; eclectic cuisine. [$] *Average main: €20* ✉ *Carrer Valls 11, Ullastret* ☎ *972/757108* 🌐 *www.restaurantiberic.com* 🕓 *Closed Mon. No dinner Sun.–Thurs.*

Hotels

★ Hotel Aigua Blava

$$$$ | **HOTEL** | **FAMILY** | What began as a small hostel in the 1920s is now a sprawling luxury hotel, run by the fourth generation of the same family. **Pros:** impeccable service; private playground; gardens and pleasant patios at every turn. **Cons:** expensive restaurant; no beach in the inlet; no elevator. [$] *Rooms from: €200* ✉ *Platja de Fornells s/n, Begur* ☎ *972/622–058* 🌐 *www.aiguablava.com* 🕓 *Closed Nov.–mid-Apr.* 🛏 *85 rooms* 🍴 *Free Breakfast.*

La Bionda

$$$ | **HOTEL** | Located in Begur's medieval old town, this eco-friendly boutique hotel embraces the building's 17th-century architecture while introducing modern elements, like a greenhouse-style breakfast room. **Pros:** beautifully designed interiors; rooftop hot tub; medieval center location. **Cons:** rooms are on the smaller side; far from the beaches; parking is off-site. [$] *Rooms from: €175* ✉ *Carrer Francesc Forgas 1, Begur* ☎ *621/315–283* 🌐 *labiondabegur.com* 🛏 *8 rooms* 🍴 *Free Breakfast.*

Cadaqués and Around

70 km (43 miles) north of Begur.

Spain's easternmost town, Cadaqués, still has the whitewashed charm that transformed this fishing village into an international artists' haunt in the early 20th century. Salvador Dalí's house, now a museum, is at Portlligat, a 15-minute walk north of town.

Sights

★ Cap de Creus

NATURE SIGHT | North of Cadaqués, Spain's easternmost point is a fundamental pilgrimage, if only for the symbolic geographical rush. The hike out to the lighthouse—through rosemary, thyme, and the salt air of the Mediterranean—is unforgettable. The Pyrenees officially end (or rise) here. New Year's Day finds mobs of revelers awaiting the first emergence of the "new" sun from the Mediterranean.

Gaze down at heart-pounding views of the craggy coast and crashing waves with a warm mug of coffee in hand or fine fare on the table at Bar Restaurant Cap de Creus, which sits on a rocky crag above the Cap de Creus. On a summer evening, you may be lucky and stumble upon some live music on the terrace. ✉ *Carrer de Cadaqués al Cap de Creus.*

★ Casa Salvador Dalí - Portlligat

HISTORIC HOME | This was Dalí's summerhouse and a site long associated with the artist's notorious frolics with everyone from poets Federico García Lorca and Paul Eluard to filmmaker Luis Buñuel. Filled with bits of the surrealist's daily life, it's an important point in the "Dalí triangle," completed by the castle at Púbol and the Teatre-Museu Dalí in Figueres.

You can get here by a 3-km (2-mile) walk north along the beach from Cadaqués. Only small groups of visitors are

The popular harbor of Cadaqués

admitted at any given time, and advance reservations are required. ✉ *Portlligat s/n, Cadaqués* ☎ *972/251–015* 🌐 *www.salvador-dali.org* 🎟 *€14; advance reservations required* 🕓 *Closed Mon. Nov.–Mar.* ✍ *Reservations essential.*

★ Sant Pere de Rodes

HISTORIC SIGHT | The monastery of Sant Pere de Rodes, 7 km (4½ miles) by car (plus a 20-minute walk) above the pretty fishing village of El Port de la Selva, is a spectacular site. Built in the 10th and 11th centuries by Benedictine monks—and sacked and plundered repeatedly since—this restored Romanesque monolith commands a breathtaking panorama of the Pyrenees, the Empordà plain, the sweeping curve of the Bay of Roses, and Cap de Creus. (Topping off the grand trek across the Pyrenees, Cap de Creus is a spectacular six-hour walk from here on the well-marked GR11 trail.)

■ TIP→ In July and August, the monastery is the setting for the annual Festival Sant Pere (🌐 *www.festivalsantpere.com*), drawing top-tier classical musicians from all over the world. Find event listings online (in Catalan); phone for reservations or to book a post-concert dinner in the monastery's refectory-style restaurant (☎ *972/194–233*).

✉ *Camí del Monestir s/n, El Porte de la Selva* ☎ *972/387–559* 🌐 *patrimoni.gencat.cat/en/monuments* 🎟 *€6* 🕓 *Closed Mon.*

🍴 Restaurants

★ Casa Anita

$$$$ | **SEAFOOD** | Simple, fresh, and generous dishes are the draw at this informal little eatery, an institution in Cadaqués. Tables are shared, and there is no menu; the staff recite the offerings of the day, which might include local prawns and sardines *a la plancha* (grilled), mussels, and sea bass. **Known for:** convivial atmosphere; regional wines; no menu. [$] *Average main: €30* ✉ *Carrer Miquel Rosset 16, Cadaqués* ☎ *972/258471* 🌐 *www.facebook.com/vipcasaanita* 🕓 *Closed Mon.*

Compartir

$$$$ | CATALAN | The word "compartir" means "to share" and this excellent restaurant bases its menu on a small-plate sharing approach that has been taken to another level by the culinary team of Mateu Casañas, Oriol Castro, and Eduard Xatruch (who also run Barcelona's two-Michelin-starred Disfrutar). Each dish is served by attentive staff within an 18th-century courtyard. **Known for:** beautiful courtyard setting; creative gastronomy; sharing plates. $ *Average main: €24* ✉ *Riera Sant Vicenç s/n, Cadaqués* ☎ *972/258482* ⊕ *www.compartir-cadaques.com* ⊗ *Closed Sun. and Mon.*

Restaurant Can Rafa

$$$$ | SEAFOOD | With picture-perfect views of the Cadaqués seafront, this restaurant's terrace is always packed. Check the chalkboard for the day's offerings, which overwhelmingly focus on local seafood and seafood-based rice dishes. **Known for:** seaside location; excellent wine list; local seafood. $ *Average main: €24* ✉ *Plaça del Passeig 7, Cadaqués* ☎ *972/159–401* ⊕ *martinfaixo.com/en/can-rafa.html* ⊗ *No dinner Sun. Winter openings times vary.*

Hotels

Hotel Llané Petit

$$$ | HOTEL | This small, typically Mediterranean bay-side hotel has a quiet location, a 10-minute seafront amble from Cadaqués center. **Pros:** semiprivate beach next to hotel; outdoor pool; free Wi-Fi. **Cons:** some soundproofing issues; somewhat lightweight beds and furnishings; small rooms. $ *Rooms from: €176* ✉ *Doctor Bartolmeus 37, Cadaqués* ☎ *972/251–020* ⊕ *www.llanepetit.com* ⊗ *Closed Nov.–Mar.* ⇆ *37 rooms* ¶ *Free Breakfast.*

Hotel Playa Sol

$$$$ | HOTEL | FAMILY | In business for more than 50 years, this hotel on the cove of Es Pianc is just a five-minute walk from Cadaqués's center and is a good option for families, with its dedicated family rooms, pool, and bike rental. **Pros:** attentive, friendly service; great views; family-friendly. **Cons:** small rooms; rooms with balcony and sea views are harder to book; pricey rates in summer. $ *Rooms from: €250* ✉ *Platja Pianc 3, Cadaqués* ☎ *972/258100* ⊕ *www.playasol.com* ⊗ *Closed Nov.–mid-Feb.* ⇆ *48 rooms* ¶ *No Meals.*

Montserrat

50 km (31 miles) west of Barcelona.

An easy side trip from Barcelona is a visit to the dramatic, sawtooth peaks of Montserrat, where the shrine of La Moreneta (the Black Virgin of Montserrat) sits. Montserrat is as memorable for its strange topography as it is for its religious treasures. The views over the mountains that stretch all the way to the Mediterranean and, on a clear day, to the Pyrenees, are breathtaking, and the rugged, boulder-strewn terrain makes for exhilarating walks and hikes.

GETTING HERE AND AROUND

The easiest way to get to Montserrat from Barcelona is by train. Take the FGC (Ferrocarriles) from the Plaça d'Espanya metro station, connecting with either the cable car at Aeri Montserrat or with the rack railway (Cremallera) at Monistrol Montserrat. There are combination tickets sold at the station. Both the cable car and rack railway take 15 minutes and depart every about every 20 minutes. Once you arrive at the monastery, several funiculars can take you farther up the mountain. By car from Barcelona, follow the A2/A7 autopista on the upper ring road (Ronda de Dalt), or from the western end of the Diagonal as far as Salida 25 to Martorell. Bypass this industrial center and follow signs to Montserrat.

👁 Sights

★ La Moreneta

RELIGIOUS BUILDING | The shrine of La Moreneta, one of Catalonia's patron saints, resides in a Benedictine monastery high in the Serra de Montserrat, surrounded by—and dwarfed by the grandeur of—sheer, jagged peaks. The crests above the monastic complex bristle with chapels and hermitages. The shrine and its setting have given rise to countless legends about what happened here: St. Peter left a statue of the Virgin Mary carved by St. Luke, Parsifal found the Holy Grail, and Wagner (who wrote the opera *Parsifal*) sought musical inspiration.

The shrine is world famous and one of Catalonia's spiritual sanctuaries, and not just for the monks who reside here—honeymooning couples flock here by the thousands seeking La Moreneta's blessing on their marriages, and twice a year, on April 27 and September 8, the diminutive statue of Montserrat's Black Virgin becomes the object of one of Spain's greatest pilgrimages. Only the basilica and museum are regularly open to the public. ■**TIP→ The famous Escolania de Montserrat boys' choir sings the Salve and Virulai from the liturgy weekdays at 1 pm and Sunday at noon.** ✉ *Montserrat* ☎ *93/877–7777* ⊕ *www.montserratvisita.com* 🎫 *€16 sanctuary, audio guide, museum, and audiovisual presentation.*

Sitges

43 km (27 miles) southwest of Barcelona.

Sitges is the prettiest and most popular resort in Barcelona's immediate environs, with excellent beaches and a whitewashed and flowery old quarter. It's also one of Europe's premier gay resorts. From April through September, and on sunny, warm weekends year-round, its wide, sandy beaches swell with tourists and local day-trippers.

On the eastern end of the strand is an alabaster statue of the 16th-century painter El Greco, usually associated with Toledo, where he spent most of his professional career. The artist Santiago Rusiñol is responsible for this surprise; he was such a Greco fan that he not only installed two of his paintings in his Museu del Cau Ferrat but also had this sculpture planted on the beach.

Two nearby Cistercian monasteries to the west of Sitges, Santes Creus and Santa Maria de Poblet, can be seen in a day—provided you have a car.

GETTING HERE AND AROUND

There's regular train service from all three Barcelona stations to Sitges. The journey takes about 40 minutes (€4.10 each way). It's about a 10-minute walk to the nearest beach from the station.

Buses, roughly the same price, run at least hourly from Plaza Espanya and take about 45 minutes, depending how many stops they make. If you're driving, head south on the C32; for more dramatic vistas, take the C31 coastal road.

👁 Sights

Beaches

BEACH | FAMILY | Sitges's coastline counts around 18 beaches, with many being easily accessible by foot from the old town. The most central, and hence the busiest, are Ribera and Fragata. Neighboring Bassa Rodona is a popular gay beach. Quieter, more family-friendly beaches are Sant Sebastià, to the east, which also has a large playground, and at the far western edge, Terramar, with a swimming cove that allows for calm, protected swimming. ✉ *Sitges.*

Museu de Maricel

ART MUSEUM | American industrialist Charles Deering's magnificent early 20th-century palace, perched on a cliff

Whitewashed buildings dominate the landscape in Sitges.

overlooking the Mediterranean, is home to this eclectic collection that spans 10 centuries. It includes Romanesque and Gothic altarpieces, paintings from the Neoclassic period, and Modernisme works by artists linked to Sitges. It's worth a visit if only to see the dedicated sculpture room, with *noucentista* sculptures by Joan Rebull framed by enormous windows offering jaw-dropping views of crashing waves below. ✉ *Carrer Fonollar s/n, Sitges* ☎ *938/940–364* ⊕ *museusdesitges.cat/en* ✆ *€10, includes Museu del Cau Ferrat* ☾ *Closed Mon.*

★ Museu del Cau Ferrat
ART MUSEUM | This is the most interesting museum in Sitges, established by the bohemian artist and cofounder of the Quatre Gats café in Barcelona, Santiago Rusiñol (1861–1931), and containing some of his own paintings together with works by El Greco and Picasso. Connoisseurs of wrought iron will love the beautiful collection of *cruces terminales*, crosses that once marked town

boundaries. ✉ *Carrer Fonollar 6, Sitges* ☎ *938/940–364* ⊕ *www.museusdesitges. com* ✆ *€10, includes Museu del Maricel* ☾ *Closed Mon.*

Passeig Marítim
PROMENADE | A focal point of Sitges life, this 1½-mile-long esplanade is an iconic pedestrianized promenade that sweeps along the bay of Sitges. It's backed by upmarket villas, boutique hotels, restaurants, and bars. ✉ *Passeig Marítim, Sitges.*

🍴 Restaurants

Chiringuito
$$$ | TAPAS | Spelled with a capital C, this legendary seaside spot opened in 1913 and spawned the term that's given to similar bars dotting the Spanish coast. There's nothing particularly outstanding about the food—typical seafood tapas, much of it fried—but the waterfront terrace is ideal for soaking up the sun and more than a century of history. **Known for:** sea views; so-so food; historical eatery.

$ Average main: €18 ⊠ Passeig de la Ribera 31, Sitges ☎ 938/947–596 ⊕ www.facebook.com/chiringuitositges.

★ El Cable

$$ | TAPAS | There's almost always a line outside this old-school, family-owned tapas bar, a local favorite since its founding in 1940. If you can't get a table, sidle up to the long wood bar, choose from the display of bite-sized, toothpick-speared *pintxos*, and eat them standing, just like a local. **Known for:** patatas bravas; inexpensive food and drink; variety of pintxos. $ *Average main: €12* ⊠ *Carrer Barcelona 1, Sitges* ☎ *938/948–761* ⊕ *www.elcable. cat.*

Vivero

$$$ | SEAFOOD | Carved into a rocky point above Playa San Sebastiá, the multi-level Vivero is actually three distinct spaces: a casual, alfresco tapas spot up top; a swankier "beach club" at the bottom; and sandwiched between is a bi-level indoor/outdoor restaurant, with a wide variety of seafood dishes and paellas. Whichever you choose, the real reason to come is for the magnificent views, especially at sunset. **Known for:** outdoor dining; several spaces with different vibes; wonderful sea views. $ *Average main: €22* ⊠ *Passeig Balmins s/n, Playa San Sebastián, Sitges* ☎ *938/942–149* ⊕ *www.elviverositges.com* ☾ *No dinner.*

Hotels

★ ME Sitges Terramar

$$$$ | HOTEL | From the buzzy rooftop with cocktails and street food to the superb seaside restaurant to the beach club where you can lounge in a hammock with your toes in the sand, this beachfront hotel is one of Sitges' top stays. **Pros:** excellent dining and drinking options; organic spa with vegan products; seaside location. **Cons:** a half-hour walk to town center; some amenities are only open seasonally; no restaurants nearby. $ *Rooms from: €200* ⊠ *Passeig*

Marítim 80, Sitges ☎ 938/940–050 ⊕ www.mebymelia.com ⇨ 213 rooms ¶⊙¶ No Meals.

Meliá Sitges

$$$ | HOTEL | FAMILY | Set on a hilltop in a peaceful residential area, this hotel offers bright, spacious, contemporary rooms with furnished balconies—many of which have sea views. **Pros:** all rooms have balconies; wide variety of room/bed configurations; family-friendly with kids' amenities. **Cons:** somewhat corporate in feel; a 15-minute walk to town; common areas could use a refresh. $ *Rooms from: €150* ⊠ *Carrer de Joan Salvat Papasseit 38, Sitges* ☎ *9938/110–811* ⊕ *www.melia.com* ⇨ *307 rooms* ¶⊙¶ *No Meals.*

 Nightlife

Much of Sitges' nightlife revolves around gay bars and dance clubs, with a high concentration along Carrer Sant Bonaventura, Carrer de Joan Tarrida, Carrer Bonaire, and Carrer Primer de Maig (aka the Street of Sin). Some are hard-core leather and biker bars, while others have a more straight-friendly vibe. Keep in mind that most don't open until 11 pm.

El Gin Tub

COCKTAIL LOUNGES | Head down a flight of stairs to this underground speakeasy, decorated in a Victorian style and featuring a menu of classic cocktails—many made with house-infused gin. There's live music and burlesque nearly every night. ⊠ *Calle Parellades 43, Sitges* ☎ *65/600–693* ⊕ *elgintub.com.*

Pub Voramar

BARS | Nautical knick-knacks line every square inch of this cozy tavern, which dates back to 1956. A small terrace overlooks Sant Sebastià beach. ⊠ *Port Alegre 55, Sitges* ☎ *938/944–403.*

Santes Creus

95 km (59 miles) west of Barcelona.

Head inland and you discover how much the art and architecture—the very tone of Catalan culture—owes to its medieval religious heritage. Monolithic Romanesque architecture and beautiful cloisters characterize the Cistercian monastery of Santes Creus.

GETTING HERE AND AROUND

It's a 1¼-hour drive to Santes Creus from Barcelona via the AP-7, followed by the AP-2 (Lleida), C51 and TP2002. From Sitges, it's 45 minutes; take the C32 west to the AP-7 and follow the above directions.

Sights

Santes Creus

RELIGIOUS BUILDING | Founded in 1158 on the banks of the Gaià River, Santes Creus is one of Catalonia's largest and best-preserved Cistercian monasteries. Its otherwise austere church features glorious Cistercian and Gothic stained-glass windows and the royal tombs of King Peter III and James II and his wife Blanche of Anjou of the Kingdom of Aragón. Other highlights include the ornate 14th-century Gothic cloisters. ⊠ *Pl. Jaume el Just s/n, Santes Creus* ☎ *977/638329* ⊕ *patrimoni. gencat.cat/en/monuments/monuments/ royal-monastery-of-santes-creus* ☜ *€6* ☺ *Closed Mon.*

Santa Maria de Poblet

8 km (5 miles) west of Santes Creus.

This splendid Cistercian monastery, located at the foot of the Prades Mountains, is one of the great masterpieces of Spanish monastic architecture. Declared a UNESCO World Heritage site, the cloister is a stunning combination of lightness and size, and on sunny days the

shadows on the yellow sandstone are extraordinary.

GETTING HERE AND AROUND

From Barcelona to Poblet, it's a 1½-hour drive via the AP7 and AP2, or about one hour from Sitges, via the C32 and AP-2 (Exit 9 when coming from Sitges).

Sights

★ Monasterio de Santa María de Poblet

RELIGIOUS BUILDING | Founded in 1150 by Ramón Berenguer IV in gratitude for the Christian Reconquest, the monastery first housed a dozen Cistercians from Narbonne. Later, the Crown of Aragón used Santa Maria de Poblet for religious retreats and burials. The building was damaged in an 1836 anticlerical revolt, and monks of the reformed Cistercian Order have managed the difficult task of restoration since 1940. Today, a community of 25 monks and novices still pray before the splendid retable over the tombs of Aragonese rulers, restored to their former glory by sculptor Frederic Marès. ⊠ *Off AP-2 (Exit 9 from Barcelona, Exit 8 from Lleida), Pl. Corona de Aragón 11* ☎ *977/870–089* ⊕ *www. poblet.cat* ☜ *€8.50.*

Tarragona

98 km (61 miles) southwest of Barcelona, 251 km (156 miles) northeast of Valencia.

Tarragona, the principal town of southern Catalonia, today is a vibrant center of culture and art, a busy fishing and shipping port, and a natural jumping-off point for the towns and pristine beaches of Sitges and the Costa Daurada, 216 km (134 miles) of coastline. However, in Roman times, Tarragona was one of the finest and most important outposts of the Empire, and was famous for its wine even before that. The town's population was the first *gens togata* (literally, the toga-clad people) in Spain, which conferred on them equality with the citizens of Rome. Its vast Roman remains, chief among them the Circus Maximus, bear witness to Tarragona's grandeur, and to this the Middle Ages added wonderful city walls and citadels. Due to its Roman remains and medieval Christian monuments, Tarragona has been designated a UNESCO World Heritage site.

Though modern, Tarragona has preserved its heritage superbly. Stroll along the town's cliff-side perimeter and you'll see why the Romans set up shop here: Tarragona is strategically positioned at the center of a broad, open bay, with an unobstructed view of the sea. As capital of the Roman province of Hispania Tarraconensis (from 218 BC), Tarraco (as it was then called) formed the empire's principal stronghold in Spain. St. Paul preached here in AD 58, and Tarragona became the seat of the Christian church in Spain until it was superseded by Toledo in the 11th century.

If you're entering the city en route from Barcelona, you'll pass the **Triumphal Arch of Berà**, dating from the 3rd century BC, 19 km (12 miles) north of Tarragona; and from the Lleida (Lérida) autopista, you can see the 1st-century **Roman aqueduct** that helped carry fresh water 32 km (20 miles) from the Gaià River. Tarragona is divided clearly into old and new by Rambla Vella; the old town and most of the Roman remains are to the north, while modern Tarragona spreads out to the south. Start your visit at acacia-lined Rambla Nova, at the end of which is a balcony overlooking the sea, the **Balcó del Mediterrani.** Then walk uphill along Passeig de les Palmeres and look below to view the ancient amphitheater in all its glory.

GETTING HERE AND AROUND

Tarragona is well connected by train. From Barcelona, direct high-speed trains take about 35 minutes, arriving at Camp de Tarragona station, a 10-minute taxi ride to the center. Slower regional trains take about 1 hour 15 minutes but do stop in the city center. Tickets start at €8.05. There is also regular train service from other major cities, including Madrid.

Buses are frequent between Barcelona and Tarragona—7 to 10 leave Barcelona's Estació del Nord for Tarragona every day. Connections between Tarragona and Valencia are frequent, too. There are also bus connections with the main Andalusian cities, plus Alicante and Madrid.

Tours of the cathedral and archaeological sites are organized by the tourist office, located just below the cathedral.

VISITOR INFORMATION
CONTACTS Visitor Information Tarragona. ✉ *Carrer Major 37, Tarragona* ☎ *977/250795* ⊕ *www.tarragonaturisme.cat/en.*

Sights

Amphitheater
RUINS | Tarragona, the Emperor Augustus's favorite winter resort, had arguably the finest amphitheater in Roman Iberia, built in the 2nd century AD for gladiatorial and other contests. The remains have a spectacular view of the sea. You're free

to wander through the access tunnels and along the tiers of seats. In the center of the theater are the remains of two superimposed churches, the earlier of which was a Visigothic basilica built to mark the bloody martyrdom of St. Fructuós and his deacons in AD 259. ⊠ *Parc de l'Amphiteatre Roma s/n, Tarragona* ☎ *977/242–579* ⊕ *www.tarragona.cat/ patrimoni/museu-historia* ⌨ *€3.30 (joint entry with 4 monuments, €7.40; all monuments €11.05)* ☉ *Closed Mon.*

Casa Castellarnau

HISTORY MUSEUM | The headquarters of the city's Museu d'Història (History Museum), with plans showing the evolution of the city, this Gothic *palauet* (town house) built by Tarragona nobility in the 18th century includes stunning furnishings from the 18th and 19th centuries. The last member of the Castellarnau family vacated the house in 1954. The museum's highlight is the Hippolytus Sarcophagus, which bears a bas-relief depicting the legend of Hippolytus and Fraeda. ⊠ *Carrer dels Cavallers 14, Tarragona* ☎ *977/242–220* ⊕ *www.tarragona. cat/patrimoni/museu-historia* ⌨ *€3.30 (joint entry with 4 monuments, €7.40; all monuments €11.05)* ☉ *Closed Mon.*

Catedral

RELIGIOUS BUILDING | Built between the 12th and 14th centuries on the site of a Roman temple and a mosque, this cathedral shows the transition from Romanesque to Gothic style. The initial rounded placidity of the Romanesque apse gave way to the spiky restlessness of the Gothic—the result is somewhat confusing.

The main attraction here is the 15th-century Gothic alabaster altarpiece of Sant Tecla by Pere Joan, a richly detailed depiction of the life of Tarragona's patron saint. Converted by Sant Paul and subsequently persecuted by local pagans, Sant Tecla was repeatedly saved from demise through divine intervention. ⊠ *Pl. de la Seu s/n, Tarragona* ☎ *977/226935*

⊕ *www.catedraldetarragona.com* ⌨ *€5 (cathedral and museum)* ☉ *Closed Sun. mid-Sept.–mid-Jun.*

Circ Romà (*Roman Circus*)

RUINS | Students have excavated the vaults of the 1st-century AD Roman arena, near the amphitheater. The plans just inside the gate show that the vaults now visible formed only a small corner of a vast space (350 yards long), where 23,000 spectators gathered to watch chariot races. As medieval Tarragona grew, the city gradually engulfed the circus. ⊠ *Rambla Vella 2, Tarragona* ☎ *977/221736* ⊕ *www.tarragona.cat/ patrimoni/museu-historia* ⌨ *€3.30 (joint entry with 4 monuments, €7.40; all monuments €11.05)* ☉ *Closed Mon.*

El Serrallo

NEIGHBORHOOD | The always-entertaining fishing quarter and harbor are below the city near the bus station and the mouth of the Francolí River. Restaurants in the port, such as the popular El Pòsit del Serrallo (Moll des Pescadors 25), offer fresh fish in a rollicking environment. ⊠ *Tarragona.*

Museu Paleocristià i Necròpolis (*Early-Christian Museum and Necropolis*)

RUINS | Just uphill from the fish market are this early Christian necropolis and museum. In 1923, the remains of a burial ground were discovered during the construction of a tobacco factory. The excavations on display—more than 2,000 tombs, sarcophagi, and funeral objects—allow visitors a fascinating insight into Roman funeral practices and rituals. ⊠ *Av. Ramon y Cajal 84, Tarragona* ☎ *977/251–515* ⊕ *www.mnat.cat/ museu-i-necropolis-paleocristians* ⌨ *€4* ☉ *Closed Mon.*

Passeig Arqueològic

PROMENADE | A 1½-km (1-mile) circular path skirting the surviving section of the 3rd-century-BC Ibero-Roman ramparts, this walkway was built on even earlier walls of giant rocks. On the other side of

Tarragona's cathedral is a mix of Romanesque and Gothic styles.

the path is a glacis, a fortification added by English military engineers in 1707 during the War of the Spanish Succession. Look for the rusted bronze of Romulus and Remus. ✉ *Access from Via de l'Imperi Romà, Tarragona.*

Praetorium

RUINS | This towering building was Augustus's town house, and is reputed to be the birthplace of Pontius Pilate. Its Gothic appearance is the result of extensive alterations in the Middle Ages, when it housed the kings of Catalonia and Aragón during their visits to Tarragona. ✉ *Pl. del Rei, Tarragona* ☎ *977/221–736,* 🌐 *www.tarragona.cat/patrimoni/museu-historia* 🎫 *€3.30 (joint entry with 4 monuments, €7.40; all monuments €11.05)* 🕒 *Closed Mon.*

🍴 Restaurants

Arcs

$$$ | **CATALAN** | Stone arches dating from the 14th century frame the tables at this atmospheric restaurant in the historical Part Alta. The cooking is smart and modern, with a focus on seasonal, local ingredients, like the crispy veal canneloni topped with a reduction of Priorat, an intense red wine from the Tarragona province. **Known for:** innovative cooking; great service; dramatic setting. [$] *Average main: €20* ✉ *Carrer Misser Sitges 13, Tarragona* ☎ *977/218–040* 🌐 *restaurantarcs.com* 🕒 *Closed Mon. No dinner Sun.–Wed.*

Les Coques

$$$ | **CATALAN** | If you have time for only one meal in the city, take it at this elegant little restaurant in the heart of historic Tarragona. The menu is bursting with both mountain and Mediterranean fare, and the prix fixe lunch is a bargain at €19. **Known for:** good wine list; good-value prix fixe lunch; mountain fare. [$] *Average main: €22* ✉ *Carrer Sant Llorenç 15, Tarragona* ☎ *977/228300* 🌐 *www.les-coques.com* 🕒 *Closed Mon. No dinner Sun.–Thurs.*

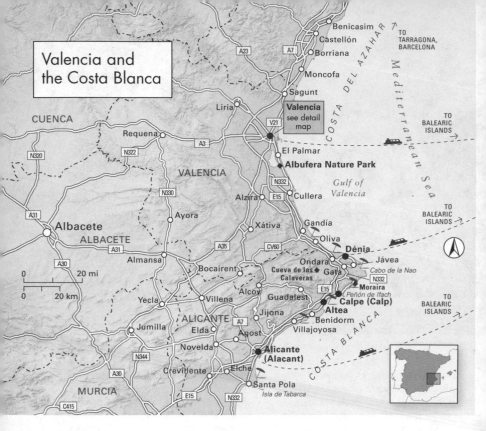

Valencia and the Costa Blanca

 Hotels

Hotel Plaça de la Font

$ | HOTEL | The central location and the cute rooms at this budget choice just off the Rambla Vella in the Plaça de la Font make for a practical base for exploring downtown Tarragona. **Pros:** easy on the budget; nearby public parking lot; comfortable, charming rooms. **Cons:** basic facilities; rooms with balconies can be noisy on weekends; rooms are on the small side. $ *Rooms from: €78* ✉ *Pl. de la Font 26, Tarragona* ☎ *977/240–882* ⊕ *www.hotelpdelafont.com* ⤴ *20 rooms* ⊙ *No Meals.*

 Nightlife

Nightlife in Tarragona takes two forms: older and quieter in the upper city, younger and more raucous down below. There are some lovely rustic bars and wine bars in the *casco antiguo*, the upper section of Old Tarragona, around Plaça del Forum and Carrer de Santa Anna. Port Esportiu, a pleasure-boat harbor separate from the working port, has another row of dining and dancing establishments; young people flock here on weekends and summer nights.

El Korxo

WINE BARS | This popular, cozy wine bar, with chunky wooden tables, subdued lighting, and quirky creative details, offers its clientele a taste of different wines from around Spain, as well as craft beers, charcuterie and cheeses, and other light snacks. ✉ *Santa Anna 6, Tarragona* ☎ *692/460018* ⊕ *www.facebook.com/korxo.vinsitapes/.*

🛍 Shopping

Carrer Major

ANTIQUES & COLLECTIBLES | You have to bargain hard but Carrer Major has some exciting antiques stores. They're worth a thorough rummage, as the gems tend to be hidden. ⊠ *Carrer Major, Tarragona.*

Valencia

351 km (218 miles) southwest of Barcelona, 357 km (222 miles) southeast of Madrid.

Valencia, Spain's third-largest municipality, is a proud city with a thriving nightlife and restaurant scene, quality museums, and spectacular contemporary architecture, juxtaposed with a thoroughly charming historic quarter. During the civil war, it was the last seat of the Republican Loyalist government (1935–36), holding out against Franco's National forces until the country fell to 40 years of dictatorship. Today it represents the essence of contemporary Spain—daring design and architecture along with experimental cuisine—but remains deeply conservative and proud of its traditions. Although it faces the Mediterranean, Valencia's history and geography have been defined most significantly by the Turia River and the fertile huerta that surrounds it.

The city has been fiercely contested ever since it was founded by the Greeks. El Cid captured Valencia from the Moors in 1094 and won his strangest victory here in 1099: he died in the battle, but his corpse was strapped into his saddle and so frightened the besieging Moors that it caused their complete defeat. In 1102 El Cid's widow, Jimena, was forced to return the city to Moorish rule; Jaume I finally drove them out in 1238. Modern Valencia was best known for its frequent disastrous floods until the Turia River was diverted to the south in the late 1950s. Since then the city has been on a steady course of urban beautification. The lovely bridges that once spanned the Turia look equally graceful spanning a wandering municipal park, and the spectacularly futuristic Ciutat de les Arts i les Ciències (City of Arts and Sciences), most of it designed by Valencia-born architect Santiago Calatrava, has at last created an exciting architectural link between this river town and the Mediterranean. If you're in Valencia, an excursion to Albufera Nature Park (which is said to be the birthplace of paella) is a worthwhile day trip.

GETTING HERE AND AROUND

By car, Valencia is about 3½ hours from Madrid via the A3 motorway, and about the same from Barcelona on the AP-7 toll road. Valencia is well connected by bus and train, with regular service to and from cities throughout the country, including 10 daily AVE high-speed express trains from Madrid, making the trip in 1 hour 40 minutes, and six express trains (Euromed and ALVIA) daily from Barcelona, taking 2 hours 40 minutes. Valencia's bus station is across the river from the old town; frequent buses make the four-hour trip from Madrid and the five-hour trip from Barcelona. Dozens of airlines, large and small, serve Valencia airport, connecting the city with cities throughout Spain and the rest of Europe.

Once you're here, the city has an efficient network of bus, tram, and metro service. For timetables and more information, stop by a local tourist office. There are six of them throughout the city, including at the airport, the Joaquín Sorolla train station, and city hall.

BUS CONTACT Valencia Bus Station. ⊠ *Carrer de Menendez Pidal 11,* ☎ *963/466266.*

FESTIVALS

Gran Fira de València (Great Valencia Fair)

ARTS FESTIVALS | Valencia's monthlong festival, in July, celebrates theater, film, dance, and music. Check the website for the latest updates. ⊠ *Valencia* ⊕ *granfiravalencia.com.*

★ Las Fallas

FESTIVALS | If you want nonstop nightlife at its frenzied best, come during the climactic days of Las Fallas, March 15–19 (the festival begins March 1), when revelers throng the streets to see the gargantuan *ninots,* effigies made of wood, paper, and plaster depicting satirical scenes and famous people. Last call at many bars and clubs isn't until the wee hours, if at all. On the last night, all the effigies but one (the winner is spared) are burned to the ground during La Crema, and it seems as though the entire city is ablaze. ⊠ *Valencia* ⊕ *www. visitvalencia.com.*

TOURS

Valencia Bus Turístic

BUS TOURS | **FAMILY** | Valencia's double-decker tourist bus allows you to hop on and hop off as you please, while audio commentary introduces the city's history and highlights. It runs daily, from approximately 10–9 (hours vary depending on the season), and departs every 20–30 minutes from 17 boarding points. The cost of the 24- and 48-hour tickets are €19 and €20, respectively. The same company also offers a two-hour guided trip (€19) to Albufera Nature Park, including an excursion by boat through the wetlands, departing from the Plaza de la Reina. ⊠ *Valencia* ☎ *699/982514* ⊕ *www. valenciabusturistic.com* ⌸ *From €17.*

VISITOR INFORMATION

CONTACTS Valencia Tourist Office. ⊠ *Pl. del Ayuntamiento 1,* ☎ *963/524908* ⊕ *www.visitvalencia.com.*

 Sights

Casa Museo José Benlliure

ART MUSEUM | The modern Valencian painter and sculptor José Benlliure (1858–1937) is known for his intimate portraits and massive historical and religious

paintings, many of which hang in Valencia's Museo de Bellas Artes (Museum of Fine Arts). Here in his elegant house and studio are 50 of his works, including paintings, ceramics, sculptures, and drawings. Also on display are works by his son, Pepino, who painted in the small, flower-filled garden in the back of the house, and iconographic sculptures by Benlliure's brother, the well-known sculptor Mariano Benlliure. ⊠ *Calle Blanquerías 23, Valencia* ☎ *963/911662* ⌸ *€2; free Sun.* ☾ *Closed Mon.*

★ Catedral de Valencia

CHURCH | Valencia's 13th- to 15th-century cathedral is the heart of the city. The building has three portals—Romanesque, Gothic, and rococo. Inside, Renaissance and baroque marble were removed to restore the original Gothic style, as is now the trend in Spanish churches. The Capilla del Santo Cáliz (Chapel of the Holy Chalice) displays a purple agate vessel purported to be the Holy Grail (Christ's cup at the Last Supper) and thought to have been brought to Spain in the 4th century. Behind the altar is the left arm of St. Vincent, martyred in Valencia in 304.

Stars of the cathedral museum are Goya's two famous paintings of St. Francis de Borja, Duke of Gandia. Left of the entrance is the octagonal tower El Miguelete, which you can climb (207 steps) to the top (entry, €2): the roofs of the old town create a kaleidoscope of orange and brown terra-cotta, with the sea in the background. ⊠ *Pl. de l'Almoina, s/n, Ciutat Vella* ☎ *963/918127* ⊕ *www. catedraldevalencia.es* ⌸ *€8, includes audio guide.*

★ Centre del Carme Cultura Contemporánia (CCCC)

ARTS CENTER | Occupying a 13th-century Cistercian monastery in the old city's bohemian Carmen quarter, this arts center showcases contemporary art juxtaposed against a historical setting. Rotating exhibitions featuring paintings,

Valencia's L'Oceanogràfic (Ciutat de les Arts i les Ciències) has amazing exhibits, as well as an underwater restaurant.

sculpture, and video installations take place in marvelously dramatic spaces, including a 13th-century monks' dormitory and an ancient Gothic cloister. ⊠ *Carrer del Museu 2, El Carmen* ☎ *961/922640* ⊕ *www.consorcimuseus.gva.es* ✉ *Free* ☾ *Closed Mon.*

★ **Ciutat de les Arts i les Ciències** (*City of Arts and Sciences*)
SCIENCE MUSEUM | FAMILY | Designed mainly by native son Santiago Calatrava, this sprawling futuristic complex is the home of Valencia's Museu de les Ciències (Science Museum), Hemisfèric (Hemispheric Planetarium), Oceanogràfic (Oceanographic Park), and Palau de les Arts (Palace of the Arts, an opera house and cultural center). With resplendent buildings resembling crustaceans, the Ciutat is a favorite of architecture buffs and curious kids.

The Science Museum has soaring platforms filled with lasers, holograms, simulators, hands-on experiments, and a swell "zero gravity" exhibition on space exploration. The eye-shaped planetarium projects 3-D virtual voyages on its huge IMAX screen. At Oceanogràfic (the work of architect Felix Candela), home to the largest aquarium in Europe, you can take a submarine ride through a coastal marine habitat. ⊠ *Av. del Profesor López Piñero 7, Valencia* ☎ *961/974686* ⊕ *www.cac.es* ✉ *Science Museum €8, Oceanogràfic €32, Hemisfèric €8. Combined ticket €39.*

Institut Valencià d'Art Modern (IVAM)
ART MUSEUM | Dedicated to modern and contemporary art, this blocky building on the edge of the old city—where the riverbed makes a loop—houses a permanent collection of 20th-century avant-garde painting, European Informalism (including the Spanish artists Antonio Saura, Antoni Tàpies, and Eduardo Chillida), pop art, and photography. Note that, during recent renovations (slated to end in early 2023), the permanent collection was being temporarily housed in Alicante, so only a small portion of the museum was open and entrance was free. Check on the status of the renovations and

Valencia

KEY

- 1 Exploring Sights
- 1 Restaurants
- 1 Hotels

1/8 mi

200 meters

Sights ▼

1 Casa Museo José
   Benlliure B1
2 Catedral de Valencia C3
3 Centre del Carme
   Cultura Contemporánia
   (CCCC).................... B1
4 Ciutat de les Arts i les
   Ciències.................. E7
5 Institut Valencià d'Art
   Modern (IVAM) A1
6 Lonja de la Seda B3
7 Mercado Central........ B4
8 Museo de Bellas
   Artes D1
9 Palacio del Marqués
   de Dos Aguas C4
10 Palau de la
   Generalitat............... C2
11 Real Colegio de
   Corpus Christi D4
12 San Nicolás B3

Restaurants ▼

1 La Pepica E6
2 La Riuà D3
3 Tinto Fino Ultramarino... C3

Hotels ▼

1 Ad Hoc Monumental ... D2
2 Caro Hotel D2
3 Palau de la Mar.......... E6
4 SH Inglés D4
5 Westin Valencia E6

admission fees before visiting. ⊠ *Carrer de Guillem de Castro 118, Ciutat Vella* ☎ *963/176600* ⊕ *www.ivam.es* ⊙ *Closed Mon.* Ⓜ *Line 1.*

Lonja de la Seda (*Silk Exchange*)
NOTABLE BUILDING | On the Plaza del Mercado, this 15th-century building is a product of Valencia's golden age, when the city's prosperity as one of the capitals of the Corona de Aragón made it a leading European commercial and artistic center. The Lonja, a UNESCO World Heritage Site, was constructed as an expression of this splendor and is widely regarded as one of Spain's finest civil Gothic buildings. Its facade is decorated with ghoulish gargoyles, complemented inside by the high vaulting and slender helicoidal (twisted) columns of the cavernous Contract Hall, one of the building's three separate sections. The upper level of the Pavilion of the Consulate of the Sea is particularly impressive, with its ornate 15th-century wood ceiling. ⊠ *Lonja 2, Ciutat Vella* ☎ *962/084153* ⊠ *€2; free Sun.* ⊙ *Closed Mon.*

★ **Mercado Central** (*Central Market*)
MARKET | This bustling food market (at nearly 88,000 square feet, one of the largest in Europe) is open from 7:30 am to 3 pm, Monday through Saturday. Locals and visitors alike line up at its more than 1,200 colorful stalls to shop for fruit, vegetables, meat, fish, and confectionery. Hop on a stool at The Central Bar, located in the heart of the throng, and taste award-winning chef Ricard Camarena's casual yet no less tasty take on tapas and *bocadillos* (sandwiches), while enjoying front-row-seat viewing of the action. ⊠ *Pl. Ciudad de Brujas s/n, Valencia* ☎ *963/829100* ⊕ *www.mercadocentralvalencia.es* ⊙ *Closed Sun.*

★ **Museo de Bellas Artes** (*Museum of Fine Arts*)
ART MUSEUM | Valencia was a thriving center of artistic activity in the 15th century—one reason that the city's Museum of Fine Arts, with its lovely palm-shaded cloister, is among the best in Spain. Its permanent collection includes many of the finest paintings by Jacomart and Juan Reixach, members of the group known as the Valencian Primitives, as well as work by Hieronymus Bosch—or El Bosco, as they call him here. The ground floor has a number of brooding, 17th-century Tenebrist masterpieces by Francisco Ribalta and his pupil José Ribera, a Diego Velázquez self-portrait, and a room devoted to Goya.

The museum is at the edge of the Jardines del Real (Royal Gardens; open daily 8–dusk), with its fountains, rose gardens, tree-lined avenues, and small zoo. To get here, cross the old riverbed by the Puente de la Trinidad (Trinity Bridge) to the north bank. ⊠ *Calle Sant Pius V 9, Trinitat* ☎ *963/870300* ⊕ *www.museobellasartesvalencia.gva.es* ⊠ *Free* ⊙ *Closed Mon.*

Palacio del Marqués de Dos Aguas (*Ceramics Museum*)
HISTORY MUSEUM | Since 1954, this palace has housed the Museo Nacional de Cerámica, with a magnificent collection of local and artisanal ceramics from ancient Greek, Iberian, and Roman times through the 20th century. The selection of traditional Valencian ceramics is especially noteworthy (look for the Valencian kitchen on the second floor).

The building itself, near Plaza Patriarca, has gone through many changes over the years and now has elements of several architectural styles, including a fascinating baroque alabaster facade. Embellished with carvings of fruits and vegetables, the facade was designed in 1740 by Ignacio Vergara. It centers on the two voluptuous male figures representing the Dos Aguas (Two Waters), a reference to Valencia's two main rivers and the origin of the noble title of the Marqués de Dos Aguas. ⊠ *Rinconada Federico García Sanchiz 6, Valencia* ☎ *963/516392* ⊠ *€3; free Sat. 4–8 and Sun.* ⊙ *Closed Mon.*

Palau de la Generalitat

NOTABLE BUILDING | On the left side of
the Plaza de la Virgen, fronted by orange
trees and box hedges, is this elegant
facade. The Gothic building was once the
home of the Cortes Valencianas (Valencian Parliament), until it was suppressed
by Felipe V for supporting the losing side
during the 1700–14 War of the Spanish
Succession. The two *salones* (reception
rooms) in the older of the two towers
have superb woodwork on the ceilings.
Don't miss the Salon de los Reyes, a long
corridor lined with portraits of Valencia's kings through the ages; 30-minute
weekday guided tours (required) are
available by calling or emailing (*protocolo.
visitaspalau@gva.es*) in advance. ⊠ *Calle
Caballeros 2, Valencia* ☎ *963/424636*
🕑 *Closed weekends.*

Real Colegio Seminario de Corpus Christi

RELIGIOUS BUILDING | This seminary, with
its church, cloister, and library, is the
crown jewel of Valencia's Renaissance
architecture. Founded by San Juan
de Ribera in the 16th century, it has a
lovely Renaissance patio and an ornate
church, and its museum—Museum of
the Patriarch—holds artworks by Juan de
Juanes, Francisco Ribalta, and El Greco.
⊠ *Calle de la Nave 1, Casco Antiguo*
☎ *963/514176* ⊕ *www.seminariocorpus-
christi.org* 🎫 *€5.*

San Nicolás

CHURCH | A small plaza contains Valencia's
oldest church (dating to the 13th century), once the parish of the Borgia Pope
Calixtus III. The first portal you come to,
with a tacked-on, rococo bas-relief of
the Virgin Mary with cherubs, hints at
what's inside: every inch of the originally
Gothic church is covered with exuberant
ornamentation. ⊠ *Calle Caballeros 35,
Casco Antiguo* ☎ *963/913317* ⊕ *www.
sannicolasvalencia.com* 🎫 *€7* 🕑 *Closed
Mon.*

Beaches

Playa de las Arenas

BEACH | This wide (nearly 450 feet) and
popular grand municipal beach stretches
north from the port and the America's
Cup marina more than a kilometer (½
mile) before it gives way to the even
busier and livelier Platja de Malvarossa.
The Paseo Marítimo promenade runs
the length of the beach and is lined with
restaurants and hotels. There's no shade
anywhere, but the fine golden sand
is kept pristine and the water is calm
and shallow. **Amenities:** food and drink;
lifeguards; showers; toilets; water sports.
Best for: sunset; swimming; walking;
windsurfing. ⊠ *Valencia* ⊕ *www.playad-
elasarenas.com/en.*

Restaurants

La Pepica

$$$ | SPANISH | Locals regard this bustling,
informal restaurant, on the promenade at
El Cabanyal beach, as the best in town
for seafood paella. Founded in 1898, the
walls of the establishment are covered
with signed pictures of appreciative
visitors, from Ernest Hemingway to
King Juan Carlos and the royal family.
Known for: historic locale; sea views;
locally revered seafood paella. 💲 *Average
main: €20* ⊠ *Av. Neptuno 6, Valencia*
☎ *963/710366* ⊕ *www.lapepica.com*
🕑 *Closed Mon. Closed evenings except
Fri. and Sat. in Dec. and Jan.*

La Riuà

$$ | SPANISH | A favorite of Valencia's well
connected and well-to-do since 1982,
this family-run restaurant a few steps
from the Plaza de la Reina specializes in
seafood dishes like *anguilas* (eels) prepared with *all i pebre* (garlic and pepper),
parrillada de pescado (selection of freshly
grilled fish), and traditional paellas. Lunch
begins at 2 and not a moment before.
Known for: longtime family-run establishment; award-winning dining; specialty
eel dish. 💲 *Average main: €16* ⊠ *Calle del*

Mar 27, Valencia ☎ 963/914571 ⊕ www.lariua.com ⊙ Closed Mon. and Wed. No dinner Tues. and Sun.

Tinto Fino Ultramarino

$$$ | **ITALIAN** | A few steps from the Plaza de la Reina, this cozy spots blends the concept of a tapas bar with that of an Italian wine bar, with dishes like oxtail cannelloni, eggplant "meatballs," and classic lasagna served small plates-style. There's a fantastic list of Valencian, Spanish, and Italian wines, with many available by the glass. **Known for:** tapas-style Italian dishes; friendly service; Valencian wines by the glass. $ *Average main: €20* ⊠ *Carrer de la Corretgeria 38,, Ciutat Vella* ☎ *963 154–599* ⊕ *www.facebook.com/TintoFinoUltramarino* ⊙ *No lunch weekdays.*

Hotels

Ad Hoc Monumental

$$ | **HOTEL** | This nicely designed 19th-century town house sits on a quiet street at the edge of the old city, a minute's walk from the Plaza Almoina and the cathedral in one direction, and steps from the Turia gardens in the other. **Pros:** close to sights but quiet; great value; courteous, helpful staff. **Cons:** small rooms; not especially family-oriented; parking can be a nightmare. $ *Rooms from: €90* ⊠ *Carrer Boix 4, Ciutat Vella* ☎ *963/919140* ⊕ *www.adhochoteles.com* ⤳ *28 rooms* ⏍ *No Meals.*

★ Caro Hotel

$$$$ | **HOTEL** | Set in a former palace and fusing ancient remnants—including sections of the city's original medieval walls—with sophisticated, contemporary design, this boutique hotel offers a quiet yet central location to explore the old town. **Pros:** close to central attractions; excellent breakfast (€22); unique, stylish design. **Cons:** some rooms are on the smaller side; minimalist design may not appeal to all; tall guests should avoid upper-floor rooms with sloped ceilings. $ *Rooms from: €200* ⊠ *Carrer de*

l'Almirall 14, Ciutat Vella ☎ *963/059–000* ⊕ *www.carohotel.com* ⤳ *26 rooms* ⏍ *No Meals.*

Palau de la Mar

$$$$ | **HOTEL** | In a restored 19th-century palace, this boutique hotel looks out at the Porta de La Mar, which marked the entry to the old walled quarter of Valencia. **Pros:** big bathrooms with double sinks; courtyard and garden; great location near the sights and shops. **Cons:** small gym; rooms overlooking road can be noisy; top-floor rooms have low, slanted ceilings. $ *Rooms from: €240* ⊠ *Av. Navarro Reverter 14, Ciutat Vella* ☎ *963/162884* ⊕ *www.hospes.com/en/palau-mar* ⤳ *66 rooms* ⏍ *Free Breakfast.*

SH Inglés

$$ | **HOTEL** | This nicely designed boutique hotel, located in a renovated 18th-century building, features a wide variety of layouts in its 63 rooms. **Pros:** attractive design; friendly service; central location. **Cons:** rooms at the front have street noise; little soundproofing between rooms; beds are small. $ *Rooms from: €110* ⊠ *Carrer del Marquès de Dos Aigües 6, Ciutat Vella* ☎ *963/516–426* ⊕ *www.sh-hoteles.com* ⤳ *63 rooms* ⏍ *No Meals.*

Westin Valencia

$$$$ | **HOTEL** | Set in 1917 building in a quiet area of the city, this stately hotel features an enormous, lushly planted interior garden surrounded by dining terraces of its three restaurants. **Pros:** professional multilingual staff; large rooms; beautiful courtyard garden. **Cons:** surrounding area not particularly interesting; 20-minute walk to the old town; rooms could use a refresh. $ *Rooms from: €250* ⊠ *Av. Amadeo de Saboya 16, Pl. del Reial* ☎ *963/625–900* ⊕ *www.marriott.com* ⤳ *135 rooms* ⏍ *No Meals.*

Did You Know?

Valencia's March festival, Las Fallas, is a fabulous 19-day celebration. means "bonfires," and a highlight of the party is when the larger-than-life papier-mâché effigies of various celebrities and political figures are torched to end the festival.

Nightlife

Valencianos have perfected the art of doing without sleep. Nightlife in the old town centers on Barrio del Carmen, a lively web of streets that unfolds north of Plaza del Mercado. Popular bars and pubs dot Calle Caballeros, starting at Plaza de la Virgen; the Plaza del Tossal also has some buzzy cafés, as does Calle Alta, off Plaza San Jaime.

The newest, hippest district is Russafa (Ruzafa in Spanish), where on any given night, a trendy, mostly younger crowd hops among its many bars, restaurants, and café terraces. Most can be found along the main thoroughfare, Calle de Ruzafa, and the surrounding streets of Cadiz, Sueca, and Literat Azorín.

Check out the English-language nightlife and culture website *24/7 Valencia* (⊕ www.247valencia.com) to see the latest on what's happening in the city.

BARS AND CAFÉS
Café de las Horas
BARS | This surreal bordello-style bar is an institution for Valencia's signature cocktail, Agua de Valencia (a syrupy blend of cava or champagne, orange juice, vodka, and gin). The bar's warm atmosphere and convivial vibe are perfect for whiling away the hours at the start (or end) of the night. ⊠ *Calle Conde de Almodóvar 1, Valencia* ☎ *963/917–336* ⊕ *cafedelashoras.com.*

★ La Fabrica de Hielo
BARS | A former ice factory on Cabanyal Beach has been transformed into this industrial-chic drinking spot, complete with soaring ceilings, exposed brick walls, and vintage furnishings. Inexpensive drinks and bar food and a seaside terrace attract a trendy crowd, as does the free live music most nights. ⊠ *C. de Pavia 37, Trinitat* ☎ *963/682–619* ⊕ *www.lafabricadehielo.net.*

Mes Amours
WINE BARS | A more sedate entry in the Russafa district's buzzy nightlife scene, this wine bar specializes in natural wines from small producers, mainly from Spain and France. Inside is charmingly retro, while a nice-sized corner terrace lets you soak in the lively street life. ⊠ *Carrer de la Reina Doña Maria 1, Eixample* ☎ *611/349–008* ⊕ *www.mesamours.es.*

MUSIC CLUBS
Jimmy Glass Jazz Bar
LIVE MUSIC | Aficionados of modern jazz gather at this bar, which books an impressive range of local and international combos and soloists. Opening times vary according to the performance schedule, with up to four shows on different nights each week. ⊠ *Carrer Baja 28, El Carmen* ⊕ *www.jimmyglassjazz.net.*

Performing Arts

MUSIC
Palau de la Música
PERFORMANCE VENUE | On one of the nicest stretches of the Turia riverbed is this huge glass vault, Valencia's main concert venue. Home of the Orquesta de Valencia, the main hall also hosts touring performers from around the world, including chamber and youth orchestras, opera, and an excellent concert series featuring early, baroque, and classical music. ⊠ *Passeig de l'Albereda 30, Valencia* ☎ *963/375020* ⊕ *www.palauvalencia.com.*

⬤ Shopping

Plaza Redonda
MARKET | A few steps from the cathedral, off the upper end of Calle San Vicente Mártir, the restored Plaza Redonda ("Round Square") is lined with stalls selling all sorts of souvenirs and traditional crafts. ⊠ *Pl. Redonda, El Carmen.*

Underwood

MIXED CLOTHING | An ever-changing selection of cool designs emblazon the t-shirts and hoodies of this independently-owned shop, which produces all of its eco-friendly fashions locally. ⊠ *C. del Trench 16, Ciutat Vella* ☎ *644/612–146* ⊕ *underwoodpeople.com.*

Albufera Nature Park

11 km (7 miles) south of Valencia.

South of Valencia, Albufera Nature Park is one of Spain's most spectacular wetland areas. Home to the largest freshwater lagoon on the peninsula, this protected area and bird-watcher's paradise is bursting with unusual flora and fauna, such as rare species of wading birds. Encircled by a tranquil backdrop of rice fields, it's no surprise that the villages that dot this picturesque place have some of the best options in the region for trying classic Valencian paella or *arròs a banda* (rice cooked in fish stock).

GETTING HERE AND AROUND

From Valencia, buses 24 and 25 depart for El Palmar; get off at the Pinars-Carretera del Palmar stop, about a 45-minute ride. From there, it's a short walk to the Centre d'Interpretació Raco de l'Olla, the park's information center, which provides maps, guides, and tour arrangements. It's open daily from 9 am–2 pm.

Sights

★ **Albufera Nature Park**

NATURE PRESERVE | This beautiful freshwater lagoon was named by Moorish poets—*albufera* means "the sun's mirror." The park is a nesting site for more than 300 bird species, including herons, terns, egrets, ducks, and flamingos. Bird-watching companies offer boat rides all along the Albufera. You can also explore the park on foot or by bike. ⊠ *Ctra. de El Palmar s/n, El Palmar* ✛ *Carrer de Vicente Baldoví s/n* ☎ *963/868050* ⊕ *parquesnaturales.gva. es* ✉ *Free.*

El Palmar

TOWN | This is the major village in the area, with streets lined with restaurants specializing in various types of paella. The most traditional kind is made with rabbit or game birds, though seafood is also popular. ⊠ *El Palmar.*

Restaurants

Maribel Arroceria

$$ | SPANISH | So tasty is the paella here that even Valencianos regularly travel out of the city to Maribel Arroceria, off the main drag in El Palmar. Sit surrounded by the rice fields of Albufera Nature Park, either in the contemporary, air-conditioned dining room or outside at pavement tables overlooking the canal. **Known for:** canal seating; fresh whole fish; paella and fideuà. $ *Average main: €17* ⊠ *Carrer de Francisco Monleón 5, El Palmar* ☎ *961/620060* ⊕ *www.arroceria-maribel.com* ⊙ *Closed Wed. No dinner.*

Dénia

The stretch of coastline known as the Costa Blanca (White Coast) begins at Dénia, south of Valencia. Dénia is the port of departure on the Costa Blanca for the ferries to Ibiza, Formentera, and Mallorca—but if you're on your way to or from the islands, stay a night in the lovely little town in the shadow of a dramatic cliff-top fortress. Or, spend a few hours wandering in the Baix la Mar, the old fishermen's quarter with its brightly painted houses, and exploring the historic town center. The town has become something of a culinary hot spot and is home to award-winning restaurants, which for its compact size is something of an achievement.

Dénia's massive fort overlooks the harbor and provides a dramatic element to the skyline, with the Montgü mountains in the background.

GETTING HERE AND AROUND

Dénia is linked to other Costa Blanca destinations via Line 1 of the Alicante–Benidorm narrow-gauge TRAM train. There's also regular bus service from major towns and cities, including Madrid (7¼–9 hours) and Valencia (1¾–2½ hours). Local buses can get you around all of the Costa Blanca communities.

The Playa del Arenal, a tiny bay cut into the larger one, is worth a visit in summer. You can reach it via the coastal road (CV736) between Dénia and Jávea.

VISITOR INFORMATION

CONTACTS Visitor Information Dénia.
✉ Pl. Oculista Buigues 9, ☎ 966/422367 ⊕ www.denia.net.

Sights

Castillo de Dénia

CASTLE/PALACE | The most interesting architectural attraction here is the castle overlooking the town, and the Palau del Governador (Governor's Palace) inside.

On the site of an 11th-century Moorish fortress, the Renaissance-era palace was built in the 17th century and was later demolished. The fortress has an interesting archaeological museum as well as the remains of a Renaissance bastion and a Moorish portal with a lovely horseshoe arch. ✉ Av. del Cid–Calle San Francisco s/n, Dénia ☎ 966/422367 ⊠ €3 (includes entrance to archaeological museum).

Cueva de las Calaveras (Cave of the Skulls)

CAVE | FAMILY | About 15 km (9 miles) inland from Dénia, this 400-yard-long cave was named for the 12 Moorish skulls found here when it was discovered in 1768. The cave of stalactites and stalagmites has a dome rising to more than 60 feet and leads to an underground lake. ✉ Ctra. Benidoleig–Pedreguera, Km 1.5, Benidoleig ☎ 966/404235 ⊕ www.cuevadelascalaveras.com ⊠ €4.

🍴 Restaurants

El Raset

$$$ | **SEAFOOD** | Across the harbor, this Valencian favorite has been serving traditional cuisine with a modern twist for more than 30 years. From a terrace with views of the water you can choose from an array of excellent seafood dishes, including house specialties such as *arroz en caldero* (rice with monkfish, lobster, or prawns) and *gambas rojas* (local red prawns). À la carte dining can be expensive, while set menus are easier on your wallet. **Known for:** tasty paella; reasonably priced set menus; excellent seafood dishes. [$] *Average main: €20* ✉ *Calle Bellavista 7, Dénia* ☎ *965/785040* 🌐 *www.grupoelraset.com.*

🛏 Hotels

★ Art Boutique Hotel Chamarel

$$$ | **B&B/INN** | Ask the staff and they'll tell you that *chamarel* means a "mixture of colors," and this hotel brimming with charm, built as a grand family home in 1840, is certainly an eccentric blend of styles, cultures, periods, and personalities. **Pros:** friendly, helpful staff; interior courtyard; individual attention. **Cons:** rooms over the street are noisy; not on the beach; minimum stay required. [$] *Rooms from: €150* ✉ *Calle Cavallers 3, Dénia* ☎ *966/435007* 🌐 *www.hotelchamarel.com* 🛏 *15 rooms* 🍴 *Free Breakfast.*

★ Hostal Loreto

$ | **HOTEL** | Travelers on tight budgets will appreciate this basic yet impeccable lodging, set in a former nunnery and located on a central pedestrian street in the historic quarter just steps from the Town Hall. **Pros:** great central location; roof terrace; good value. **Cons:** rooms can be dark; dated room decor; no elevator. [$] *Rooms from: €82* ✉ *Calle Loreto 12, Dénia* ☎ *966/435419* 🌐 *www.hostalloreto.com* 🛏 *43 rooms* 🍴 *Free Breakfast.*

Calpe (Calp)

35 km (22 miles) south of Dénia.

Calpe has an ancient history, as it was chosen by the Phoenicians, Greeks, Romans, and Moors as a strategic point from which to plant their Iberian settlements. The real-estate developers were the latest to descend upon it: much of Calpe today is overbuilt with high-rise resorts and *urbanizaciónes*. But the old town is a delightful maze of narrow streets and small squares, archways and cul-de-sacs, with houses painted in Mediterranean blue, red, ocher, and sandstone; wherever there's a broad expanse of building wall, you'll likely discover a mural. Calpe is a delightful place to wander.

GETTING HERE AND AROUND

The narrow-gauge TRAM railway from Dénia to Alicante also serves Calpe, as do local buses.

VISITOR INFORMATION

CONTACTS Visitor Information Calpe. ✉ *Av. Ejércitos Españoles 44,* ☎ *965/836920* 🌐 *www.calpe.es.*

👁 Sights

Fish Market

MARKET | The fishing industry is still very important in Calpe, and every evening the fishing boats return to port with their catch. The subsequent auction at the fish market can be watched from the walkway of La Lonja de Calpe. ✉ *Port, Calp* 🕒 *Closed weekends.*

Peñón d'Ifach Natural Park

NATURE SIGHT | The landscape of Calpe is dominated by this huge calcareous rock more than 1,100 yards long, 1,090 feet high, and joined to the mainland by a narrow isthmus. The area is rich in flora and fauna, with more than 300 species of plants and 80 species of land and marine birds. A visit to the top is not for the fainthearted; wear shoes with traction for the hike, which includes a trip through a tunnel to the summit. The views are spectacular, reaching to the island of Ibiza on a clear day. ✉ *Calp* 🌐 *parquesnaturales.gva.es.*

🍴 Restaurants

Patio de la Fuente

$$$ | MEDITERRANEAN | In an intimate little space with wicker chairs and pale mauve walls, this restaurant in the old town serves a bargain Mediterranean three-course prix fixe dinner, wine included; you can also order à la carte. In summer, dine on the comfortable patio out back. **Known for:** house-made Scotch eggs; good-value three-course dinner; outdoor dining. [$] *Average main: €18* ✉ *Carrer Dos de Mayo 16, Calp* ☎ *965/831695* 🌐 *www.patiodelafuente.com* 🕒 *Closed Sun. and Mon.*

🛏 Hotels

Pensión el Hidalgo

$ | B&B/INN | This family-run pension near the beach has small but cozy rooms with a friendly, easygoing feel, and several have private balconies overlooking the Mediterranean. **Pros:** beachfront location; breakfast terrace with sea views; reasonable prices. **Cons:** snug rooms; you must book far ahead in summer; basic design. [$] *Rooms from: €70* ✉ *Av. Rosa de los Vientos 19, Calp* ☎ *965/839862* 🌐 *pensionelhidalgo.es* 🔑 *9 rooms* 🍽 *No Meals.*

🏃 Activities

Mundo Marino

BOATING | FAMILY | Choose from a wide range of sailing trips, including cruises up and down the coast, and sunset trips with a glass of cava. Glass-bottom boats make it easy to observe the abundant marine life. ✉ *Puerto Pesquero, Calp* ☎ *966/423066* 🌐 *www.mundomarino.es.*

Altea

11 km (7 miles) southwest of Calpe.

Perched on a hill overlooking a bustling beachfront, Altea (unlike some of its neighboring towns) has retained much of its original charm, with an atmospheric old quarter laced with narrow cobblestone streets and stairways, and gleaming white houses. At the center is the striking church of Nuestra Señora del Consuelo, with its blue ceramic-tile dome, and the Plaza de la Iglesia in front.

GETTING HERE AND AROUND

Also on the Dénia–Alicante narrow-gauge TRAM train route, Altea is served by local buses, with connections to major towns and cities. The old quarter is mainly pedestrianized.

VISITOR INFORMATION

CONTACTS Visitor Information Altea. ✉ *Calle Sant Pere 14,* ☎ *965/844114* 🌐 *www.visitaltea.es.*

🍴 Restaurants

La Costera

$$$ | FRENCH | This popular restaurant focuses on fine French fare, with such specialties as house-made foie gras, fillet of turbot, and beef entrecôte. There's also a variety of game in season, including venison and partridge. **Known for:** French specialties; in-season game; bucolic outdoor terrace. [$] *Average main: €22* ✉ *Costera Mestre de Música 8, Altea* ☎ *965/840230* 🌐 *www.altealacostera.com* 🕒 *Closed Mon. and Tues. No lunch weekdays. No dinner Sun.*

Oustau de Altea

$$ | EUROPEAN | In one of the prettiest corners of Altea's old town, this eatery was formerly a cloister and a school. Today the dining room and terrace combine contemporary design gracefully juxtaposed with a rustic setting, and the restaurant is known for serving polished international cuisine with French flair.

Did You Know?

The town of Altea
(from the Moorish
name Althaya, which
means "health to all")
has a popular seafront
promenade. The church
is easily recognized by its
blue-tile domes.

Known for: prix-fixe menu (€45) includes bottle of wine; dishes named after classic films; French-style cuisine. $ *Average main: €16* ✉ *Calle Mayor 5, Casco Antiguo* ☎ *965/842078* ⊕ *www.oustau.com* ⊙ *Closed Mon. and Feb.–mid-Mar.*

Hotels

Hostal Fornet

$ | HOTEL | The pièce de résistance at this simple, pleasant hotel, at the highest point of Altea's historic center, is the roof terrace with its stunning view; from here, you look out over the church's distinctive blue-tiled cupola and the surrounding tangle of streets, with a Mediterranean backdrop. **Pros:** lovely views; multilingual owners; top value. **Cons:** door is locked when reception is not staffed, and you have to call to be let in; small rooms; no pool or beach. $ *Rooms from: €55* ✉ *Calle Beniardá 1, Casco Antiguo* ☎ *965/843005* ⊕ *web.hostalfornetaltea. com* ➯ *23 rooms* ‖❚ *No Meals.*

Alicante (Alacant)

183 km (114 miles) south of Valencia, 52 km (32 miles) south of Altea.

The Greeks called it Akra Leuka (White Summit) and the Romans named it Lucentum (City of Light). A crossroads for inland and coastal routes since ancient times, Alicante has always been known for its luminous skies. The city is dominated by the 16th-century grande dame castle, **Castillo de Santa Bárbara,** a top attraction. The best approach is via the elevator cut deep into the mountainside.

Also memorable is Alicante's grand **Esplanada,** lined with date palms. Directly under the castle is the city beach, the Playa del Postiguet, but the city's pride is the long, curved Playa de San Juan, which runs north from the Cap de l'Horta to El Campello.

GETTING HERE AND AROUND

Alicante has two train stations: the main Estación de Madrid and the local Estación de la Marina, from which the local FGV line runs along the Costa Blanca from Alicante to Dénia. Playa Postiguet can be reached by several buses from downtown, including 21 and 22.

The slower narrow-gauge TRAM train goes from the city center on the beach to El Campello. From the same open-air station in Alicante, the Line 1 train departs to Benidorm, with connections on to Altea, Calpe, and Dénia.

VISITOR INFORMATION

CONTACTS Tourist Information Alicante. ✉ *Muelle Levante 6,* ☎ *965/177201* ⊕ *www.alicanteturismo.com.* **TRAM.** ✉ *Alicante-Luceros,* ☎ *900/720472* ⊕ *www. tramalicante.es.*

Sights

Ayuntamiento

NOTABLE BUILDING | Constructed between 1696 and 1780, the town hall is a beautiful example of baroque civic architecture. Inside, a gold sculpture by Salvador Dalí of San Juan Bautista holding the famous cross and shell rises to the second floor in the stairwell. Ask gate officials for permission to explore the ornate halls and rococo chapel on the first floor. Look for the plaque on the first step of the staircase that indicates the exact sea level, used to define the rest of Spain's altitudes "above sea level." ✉ *Pl. de Ayuntamiento, Alicante* ☎ *966/900886* ➯ *Free* ⊙ *Closed weekends.*

Basílica de Santa María

CHURCH | Constructed in a Gothic style over the city's main mosque between the 14th and 16th century, this is Alicante's oldest house of worship. The main door is flanked by beautiful baroque stonework by Juan Bautista Borja, and the interior highlights are the golden rococo high altar, a Gothic image in stone of St. Mary, and a sculpture of Sts. Juanes by

Alicante's Esplanada de España, lined with date palms, is the perfect place for a stroll. The municipal brass band offers concerts on the bandstand of the Esplanada on Sunday evenings In July and August.

Rodrigo de Osona. ⊠ *Pl. de Santa María 1, Alicante* ☎ *965/177201 tourist office (for information)* ⊙ *Closing times can vary due to religious services.*

★ Castillo de Santa Bárbara (*Santa Barbara Castle*)

CASTLE/PALACE | One of the largest existing medieval fortresses in Europe, Castillo de Santa Bárbara sits atop 545-foot-tall Monte Benacantil. From this strategic position you can gaze out over the city, the sea, and the whole Alicante plain for many miles. Remains from civilizations dating from the Bronze Age onward have been found here; the oldest parts of the castle, at the highest level, are from the 9th through 13th centuries.

The castle also houses the Museo de la Ciudad de Alicante (MUSA), which uses audiovisual presentations and archaeological finds to tell the story of Alicante, its people, and the city's enduring relationship with the sea. ⊠ *Monte Benacantil s/n, Alicante* ☎ *965/152969* ⊕ *www.*

castillodesantabarbara.com ✉ *Castle and museum free.*

Concatedral de San Nicolás de Bari

CHURCH | Built between 1616 and 1662 on the site of a former mosque, this church (called a *con*catedral because it shares the seat of the bishopric with the Concatedral de Orihuela) has an austere facade designed by Agustín Bernardino, a disciple of the great Spanish architect Juan de Herrera. Inside, it's dominated by a dome nearly 150 feet high, a pretty cloister, and a lavish baroque side chapel, the Santísima Sacramento, with an elaborate sculptured stone dome of its own. Its name comes from the day that Alicante was reconquered (December 6, 1248) from the Moors, the feast day of San Nicolás. ⊠ *Pl. Abad Penalva 2, Alicante* ☎ *965/212662* ⊕ *concatedralalicante.com* ✉ *Free.*

Museo Arqueológico de Alicante

HISTORY MUSEUM | Inside the old hospital of San Juan de Dios, the MARQ has a collection of artifacts from the Alicante region dating from the Paleolithic era to modern times, with a particular emphasis on Iberian art. ⊠ *Pl. Dr. Gómez Ulla s/n, Alicante ☎ 965/149000 ⊕ www.marqalicante.com ☜€3 ⊙ Closed Mon.*

🍴 Restaurants

El Buen Comer
$$ | **SPANISH** | On the edge of the old town, this relaxed bi-level restaurant serves enticing dishes in plentiful portions. Downstairs, indulge in tapas and simpler dishes, or head to the fancier dining space upstairs for specialties like roast suckling pig, lamb chops, and sea bass baked in rock salt. **Known for:** specialty meat and seafood dishes; well-priced prix-fixe menus; rice dishes. Ⓢ *Average main: €15 ⊠ Calle Mayor 8, Alicante ☎ 965/213103 ⊕ www.elbuencomer.es ⊙ Closed Tues.*

La Taberna del Gourmet
$$$ | **TAPAS** | This wine bar and restaurant in the heart of the *casco antiguo* (old town) earns high marks from locals and international visitors alike. There's a wide selection of montaditos (sandwiches), paella, and fresh seafood tapas—oysters, mussels, razor clams—complemented by a well-chosen list of Spanish wines. **Known for:** reservations essential; tapas tasting menu (€30); excellent wine list. Ⓢ *Average main: €20 ⊠ Calle San Fernando 10, Alicante ☎ 965/204233 ⊕ www.latabernadelgourmet.com.*

Nou Manolín
$$$$ | **SPANISH** | An Alicante institution, this inviting exposed-brick and wood-lined restaurant is very popular with locals, who come for the excellent-value tapas, market produce, and freshly caught fish, a tribute to the city's enduring relationship with the sea. **Known for:** buzzy atmsophere; authentic local vibe; market-fresh produce and fish. Ⓢ *Average main: €25 ⊠ Calle Villegas 3, Alicante ☎ 965/616425 ⊕ www.grupogastronou.com ⊙ No dinner Sun.*

Hotels

Hotel Les Monges Palace Boutique
$ | **HOTEL** | In a restored 1912 building, this family-run hotel in central *casco antiguo* features lovingly preserved exposed stone walls, ceramic tile floors, and rooms furnished with eccentric artwork and quirky charm. **Pros:** personalized service; lots of character; rooftop terrace with castle views. **Cons:** bathrooms in standard rooms are small; must book well in advance; the newer, modern part is not as atmospheric. Ⓢ *Rooms from: €75 ⊠ Calle San Agustín 4, Alicante ☎ 965/215046 ☜ 24 rooms ⍦ Free Breakfast.*

Nightlife

El Barrio, the old quarter west of Rambla de Méndez Núñez, is the prime nightlife area of Alicante, with music bars and discos every couple of steps. In summer, or after 3 am, the liveliest places are along the water, on Ruta del Puerto and Ruta de la Madera.

Shopping

Mercado Central
MARKET | Bulging with fish, vegetables, and other local items, this is the place to stop by and discover Alicante's fresh produce, traded from this Moderniste-inspired building since 1921. ⊠ *Av. Alfonso el Sabio 10, Alicante.*

Index

Mies van der Rohe Pavilion, 241–242

Mimolet ✕, 263

Mirablau ✕, 226

Mirador de Colom, 75–76

Mirador Torre de Collserola, 220

Miró, Joan, 241

Moments ✕, 189

Monasteries and convents

Catalonia, Valencia, and the Costa Blanca, 262, 277, 279, 282

Upper Barcelona, 221

Monasterio de Santa Maria de Poblet, 282

Monestir de Sant Pere de Galligants, 262

Mont Bar ✕, 189

Montjuïc and Poble Sec, 21, 238–248

dining, 243–245, 247

exploring, 239–243

lodging, 245–246

Montjuïc Magic Fountain, 30

Montserrat, 29, 278–279

Monument Hotel ⊡, 194

Mordisco ✕, 189

Motel One Barcelona-Ciutadella ⊡, 155

Museo Arqueològica de Alicante, 302–303

Museu Arqueològic, 262

Museu d'Arquelogia de Catalunya, 242

Museu d'Art (Girona), 262

Museu d'Art Contemporani de Barcelona (MACBA), 111–112

Museo de Bellas Artes, 291

Museu de la Xocolata, 128

Museu de Maricel, 279–280

Museu del Cau Ferrat, 280

Museu del Disseny de Barcelona, 148

Museu del Joguet de Catalunya, 266

Museu del Modernisme de Barcelona, 170

Museu d'Història de Barcelona, 94–95

Museu d'Història de Catalunya, 148

Museu d'Història de Girona, 262

Museu d'Història de Sant Feliu de Guixols, 273

Museu d'Història dels Jueus, 262–263

Museu Egipci de Barcelona, 170

Museu Marítim, 76–77

Museu Municipal, 271

Museu Nacional d'Art de Catalunya, 242–243

Museu Paleocristià i Necròpolis, 284

Museu Picasso, 128

Museu Verdaguer-Vil-la Joana, 220

Museum of Jewish History (Girona), 262–263

Museums and art galleries, 26–27, 29

Barri Gòtic, 91, 94–95, 96, 98, 103

Catalonia, Valencia, and the Costa Blanca, 262–263, 266–267, 271, 273, 279–280, 284, 288–289, 291

El Raval, 111–112, 119

Eixample, 169–171, 173

free hours, 30

Gràcia, 207, 209

La Ciutadella, Barceloneta, Port Olímpic, and Poblenou, 148, 157

La Rambla, 76–77, 83

Montjuïc and Poble Sec, 239, 241, 242–243

Sant Pere and La Ribera, 128

Upper Barcelona, 220

Music, 31, 63–64, 102, 118–119, 120, 157, 157, 198, 246, 247, 265, 295, 303

N

Nabucco Tiramisu ✕, 214

Nightlife and the arts, 57, 59

Barri Gòtic, 102–103

Catalonia, Valencia, and the Costa Blanca, 264–265, 281, 286, 295, 303

Eixample, 196–198

El Raval, 117–119

Gràcia, 215

La Ciutadella, Barceloneta, Port Olímpic, and Poblenou, 155–157

La Rambla, 82–83

Montjuïc and Poble Sec, 246–248

Sant Pere and La Ribera, 137–138

Upper Barcelona, 235

Norman Vilalta (shop), 204

Northern Catalonia, 254–255

Nou Manolín ✕, 303

N2 (gallery), 170–171

O

OFFSónar (festival), 64

Ohla Barcelona ⊡, 101

Ohla Eixample ⊡, 194

Old Fashioned (bar), 215

Oustau de Altea ✕, 299, 301

Outpost, The (shop), 204

P

Pa i Raïm ✕, 274

Packing, 62

Paco Meralgo ✕, 189

Palaces and castles

Barri Gòtic, 91, 95

Catalonia, Valencia, and the Costa Blanca, 265–266, 268, 271, 291, 292, 297, 301, 302

La Rambla, 77–78

Sant Pere and La Ribera, 128, 130

Palacio del Marqués de Dos Aguas, 291

Palau Baró de Quadras, 171

Palau Dalmases, 128, 130

Palau de la Generalitat, 292

Palau de la Mar ⊡, 293

Palau de la Música Catalana, 130

Palau de la Virreina, 77

Palau del Lloctinent, 95

Palau Güell, 77–78

Palau Reial Major, 95

Palo Alto Market, 158

Pals, 275

Paral-lelo Gelato ✕, 214

Parc de la Ciutadella, 30, 146–147

Parc Natural de la Zona Volcànica de la Garrotxa, 29

Park Güell, 30, 209–210

Parlament de Catalunya, 148–149

Passatge Permanyer, 171

Passeig Arqueològic (Girona), 263

Passeig Arqueològic (Tarragona), 284–285

Passeig del Born, 130–131

Passig Maritim, 280

Passports, 57

Pastelería Hofmann ✕, 136

Patio de la Fuente ✕, 299

Pavellones de la Finca Güell-Càtedra Gaudí, 220–221

Peñón d'Ifach Natural Park, 298–299

Pensión el Hidalgo ⊡, 299

Pepa Bar a Vins, 196

Peratallada, 275

Picasso, Pablo, 128, 133

Picnic ✕, 135

Pla B ✕, 100

Plaça d'Anna Frank, 210

Plaça de Garriga i Bachs, 95

Plaça de la Vila de Gràcia, 210–211

Plaça de la Virreina, 211

Plaça de les Olles, 131

Plaça del Diamant, 211–212

Plaça del Pedró, 112

Plaça del Rei, 95–96

Plaça d'Espanya, 243

Plaça Reial, 78

Plaça Rovira i Trias, 212

Plaça Sant Felip Neri, 96

Plaça Sant Jaume, 96

Plaça Sant Just, 96

Platerets ✕, 213

Platja Gran, 272

Playa de las Arenas, 292

Poble Espanyol, 243

Poble Sec. ⇨ See Montjuïc and Poble Sec

Poblenou, 31. ⇨ See also La Ciutadella, Barceloneta, Port Olímpic, and Poblenou

Pont Fortificat, 269

Port de Barcelona, 78

Port Olímpic, 58, 149. ⇨ See also La Ciutadella, Barceloneta, Port Olímpic, and Poblenou

Port Vell, 149

Portaferrissa Fountain, 78

Praetorium, 285

Pride Barcelona (festival), 64

Primavera Sound (festival), 63–64

Primero Primera ⊡, 234–235

Projecte SD (gallery), 171

Proper ✕, 135

Q

Quimet i Quimet ✕, 244–245

Photo Credits

Front Cover: Art Kowalsky/ Alamy Stock Photo [Description: Casa Batllo by Gaudi in Barcelona]. **Back cover, from left to right:** Boule/ Shutterstock, Ismel Leal Pichs/Shutterstock, Catarina Belova/Shutterstock. **Spine:** Jacekkadaj/Dreamstime. **Interior, from left to right:** Valeri Potapova/Shutterstock (1). Cezary Wojtkowski/is (2-3). Tigerpike/Dreamstime (5). **Chapter 1: Experience Barcelona:** Krasnevsky/ istockphoto (6-7). Mihai-Bogdan Lazar/ Shutterstock (8-9). Shootdiem/istockphoto (9). Kert/shutterstock (9). Pere Sanz/dreamstime (10). Rafael Vargas/MACBA (10). Turisme de Barcelona (10). Danny Fernandez (10). Pere Pratdesaba/Fundació Joan Miró, Barcelona (11). Pep Daude/Junta Constructora del Temple de la Sagrada Família (11). La Manual Alpargatera (12). La Vinya del Senyor (12). Nelgphotography/ FC Barcelona (12). Stvcr,[CC BY-SA 2.0]/Flickr (12). Christian Bertrand/ Shutterstock (13). Pe3k/shutterstock (14). Ingrid Prats/shutterstock (14). Turisme de Barcelona (14). Roger Colom/Ajuntament de Girona (14). Catalunya La Pedrera Foundation (15). Museu Nacional d'Art de Cataluyna (15). Museu Picasso, Barcelona (16). VitalyEdush/ istockphoto (16). Nito/shutterstock (16). Catedral de Barcelona, Guillem F. Gel (17). Hemis / Alamy Stock Photo (17). Isolda Delgado Mora (22). Cinco Jotas (23). Sergio G. Canizares/Espardenyes Torres (24). Art Escudellers (25). Pere de Prada i Arana (26). Poble Espanyol de Barcelona (26). Pit Stock/Shutterstock (26). CastecoDesign/shutterstock (27). Marcorubino/dreamstime (27). KavalenkavaVolha/istockphoto (28). KavalenkavaVolha (29). Pit Stock/Shutterstock (30). Peresanz/ shutterstock (30). Boule/shutterstock (30). Georgios Tsichlis/shutterstock (31). Iakov Filimonov/shutterstock (31). Magi_Turmo (36). Nickos (37). Public Domain (38). Zina Seletskaya/Shutterstock (38). Some pictures here/ Shutterstock (38). 22tomtom/Dreamstime (38). Luis M. Seco/ Shutterstock (38). Pol.Alharran/Shutterstock (39). Public Domain (39). Public Domain (39). NadyaEugene/ Shutterstock (39). ValeryEgorov (39). Solodovnikova Elena/Shutterstock (40). Kylie Ellway/ Shutterstock (40). Nickos (40). Tigerpike/Dreamstime (41). Diegomartincoppola/ Dreamstime (41). Kalman89/Dreamstime (42). **Chapter 3: La Rambla:** Lals Stock/shutterstock (69). Luciano Mortula - LGM/shutterstock (72). BearFotos/Shutterstock (76). Steve Allen/dreamstimes (79). **Chapter 4: The Barri Gòtic:** ToniFlap/istockphoto (85) Xavier Caballé,[CC BY-SA 2.0]/ Wikimedia Commons (94). Kemaltaner/Dreamstime (97). **Chapter 5: El Raval:** Dyniun/shutterstock (107). Tumklang/Dreamstime (111). Heracles Kritikos/Shutterstock (113). **Chapter 6: Sant Pere and La Ribera:** Marcorubino/dreamstime (121). Marco Rubino/ Shutterstock (129). Agefotostock/Ken Walsh/Alamy (132). **Chapter 7: La Ciutadella, Barceloneta, Port Olímpic, and Poblenou:** Eye35.pix / Alamy Stock Photo (141). S-F/shutterstock (146). **Chapter 8: The Eixample:** PumpizoldA/istockphoto (159). Vvoe/Shutterstock (163). Astroid/Dreamstime (178). Sedmak/Dreamstime (179). Marcorubino/Dreamstime (180). Sylvain Grandadam / agefotostock (180). Irina Girich/ iStockphoto (180). Almotional/Shutterstock (180). Evgeniy Pavlenko/ iStockphoto (181). Rumata7/Dreamstime (181). Kayihan Bolukbasi/ iStockphoto (182). Pep Daudé/Temple de la Sagrada Família (182). Salvador_Badiella (183). Achimhb/Dreamstime (183). Jose Antonio Sanchez/Shutterstock (184). William Krumpelman/ iStockphoto (184). Polhansen/ iStockphoto (184). Temple de la Sagrada Família (184). Temple de la Sagrada Família (185). Public Domain (185). Achim Prill/iStockphoto (185). Sylvain Grandadam / agefotostock (185). **Chapter 9: Gràcia:** Olga Visavi/dreamstime (205). Dimbar76/shutterstock (213). **Chapter 10: Upper Barcelona: Sarrià, Pedralbes, Tibidabo, and Vallvidrera:** Silviacrisman/istockphoto (217). Solodovnikova Elena/Shutterstock (224). AlbertoLoyo (227). JJFarq/Shutterstock (228). Ralf Liebhold/Shutterstock (230). Pedro salaverria (230). AlbertoLoyo (232). KikoStock/Shutterstock (232). Fernandogarcia (232). Fdevalera/ Dreamstime.com (232). JBencievennga/iStockphoto (232). Barmalini/ Dreamstime (232). Mmg | Dreamstime.com (232). Public Domain (233). Cephas Picture Library / Alamy (233). Álvaro Palacios (233). Public Domain (233). Alicja neumiler/Shutterstock (233). **Chapter 11: Montjuïc and Poble Sec:** Mistervlad/Shutterstock (237). Toniflap/Dreamstime.com (242). Catarina Belova/shutterstock (246). **Chapter 12: Catalonia, Valencia, and the Costa Blanca:** Nito/Shutterstock (249). Patty Orly/Shutterstock (252). Mauricio Pellegrinetti, [CC BY 2.0]/Flickr (253). Patty Orly/ Shutterstock (253). Nito/Shutterstock (262). Irina Papoyan/ Dreamstime (264). Taras Verkhovynets/Shutterstock (267). Jorge Fuentes Quero/Shutterstock (269). Kavalenkava/Shutterstock (270). Helio San Miguel (277). Gitanna/Dreamstime (280). Lianem/ Dreamstime (285). AndreiRybachuk/iStockphoto (289). Jorgefontestad/iStockphoto (294). Aleksandrs Tihonovs/Alamy (297). Dennis Maecker /Shutterstock (300). Allard One/Shutterstock (302). **About Our Writers:** All photos are courtesy of the writers.

*Every effort has been made to trace the copyright holders, and we apologize in advance for any accidental errors. We would be happy to apply the corrections in the following edition of this publication.

Notes

Notes

Notes

Notes

Notes

Notes

Notes

Notes

Fodor's BARCELONA

Publisher: Stephen Horowitz, *General Manager*

Editorial: Douglas Stallings, *Editorial Director;* Jill Fergus, Amanda Sadlowski, *Senior Editors;* Kayla Becker, Brian Eschrich, Alexis Kelly, *Editors;* Angelique Kennedy-Chavannes, *Assistant Editor*

Design: Tina Malaney, *Director of Design and Production;* Jessica Gonzalez, *Graphic Designer;* Erin Caceres, *Graphic Design Associate*

Production: Jennifer DePrima, *Editorial Production Manager;* Elyse Rozelle, *Senior Production Editor;* Monica White, *Production Editor*

Maps: Rebecca Baer, *Senior Map Editor;* David Lindroth, Mark Stroud (Moon Street Cartography), *Cartographers*

Photography: Viviane Teles, *Senior Photo Editor;* Namrata Aggarwal, Payal Gupta, Ashok Kumar, *Photo Editors;* Eddie Aldrete, *Photo Production Intern;* Kadeem McPherson, *Photo Production Associate Intern*

Business and Operations: Chuck Hoover, *Chief Marketing Officer;* Robert Ames, *Group General Manager;* Devin Duckworth, *Director of Print Publishing*

Public Relations and Marketing: Joe Ewaskiw, *Senior Director of Communications and Public Relations*

Fodors.com: Jeremy Tarr, *Editorial Director;* Rachael Levitt, *Managing Editor*

Technology: Jon Atkinson, *Director of Technology;* Rudresh Teotia, *Lead Developer*

Writers: Jennifer Ceaser, Isabelle Kligor, Jared Lubarsky, Megan Eileen McDonough

Editors: Laura M. Kidder, Amanda Sadlowski, Douglas Stallings, Caroline Trefler

Production Editor: Elyse Rozelle

8th Edition

ISBN 978-1-64097-529-3

ISSN 1554-5865

SPECIAL SALES

This book is available at special discounts for bulk purchases for sales promotions or premiums. For more information, e-mail SpecialMarkets@fodors.com.

PRINTED IN CANADA

10 9 8 7 6 5 4 3 2 1

MIX
Paper from responsible sources
FSC® C016245

About Our Writers

 Jennifer Ceaser has been a freelance writer and editor for 20 years. A former New Yorker and editor at the *New York Post*, Jennifer now splits her time between Germany and Spain. She regularly contributes to *Condé Nast Traveler*, *Condé Nast Traveller UK*, *AFAR*, *Business Insider*, *Time Out*, and a number of other U.S. and U.K. publications. In this edition of Barcelona, Jennifer updated the following chapters: La Ciutadella, Barceloneta, Port Olímpic, and Poblenou; Gràcia; Montjuïc and Poble Sec; and Catalonia, Valencia, and the Costa Brava.

 Raised in Sweden, educated in the U.K., and currently based in Barcelona, **Isabelle Kliger**—who covered Sant Pere and La Ribera, as well as The Eixample for this edition—is a freelance writer specializing in travel, food, and pop culture. Her work has appeared in *Condé Nast Traveler*, *Forbes*, *The Guardian*, *The Times*, and other publications. Isabelle can usually be found in a local restaurant, eating all the food and drinking all the wine—preferably somewhere in Spain, Italy, Tel Aviv, or Southeast Asia. Follow her on Instagram at @ikliger.

 Jared Lubarsky is a teacher and freelance travel writer who has been writing for Fodor's since 1997, first on Japan, where he lived for 30 years, and more recently on Spain—having relocated to Barcelona in 2005. He still wonders how it took him so long to discover that eminently livable city. He has written for *Travel & Leisure*, *National Geographic Traveler*, the *New York Times Magazine*, and a variety of inflight publications. For this edition, Jared updated the Experience, Travel Smart, and Upper Barcelona chapters.

 Megan Eileen McDonough, an award-winning writer and photojournalist who splits her time between Barcelona and the Washington, D.C. area, updated the chapters on La Rambla, Barri Gòtic, and El Raval. In addition to running the top-ranked blog, Bohemian Trails, Megan's writing has appeared in publications such as *US Airways*, *Teen Vogue*, *Budget Travel* and *Bustle*. She's been featured in *Travel + Leisure*, *AFAR*, *Refinery29*, and *Forbes* as a leader in the travel space. Megan also works as a brand strategist, helping to define content direction, curation, and compelling storytelling. Follow her on Instagram @itsmeganeileen.

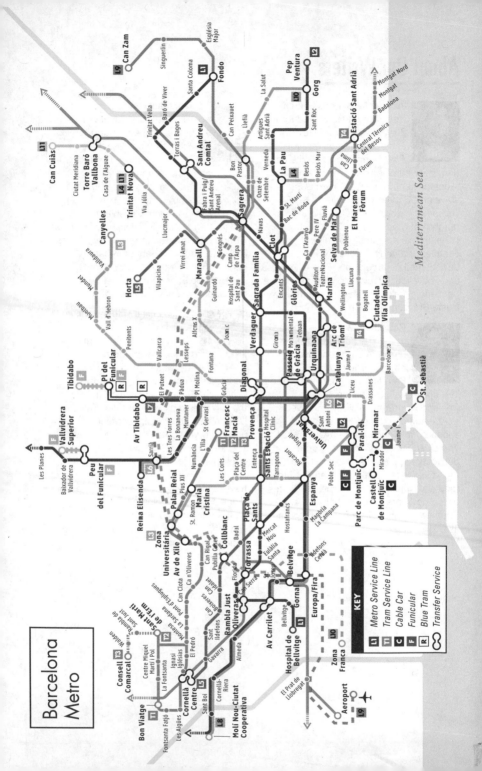

Barcelona Metro